STORY & ART BY MOTORO MASE

IKIGAMI

THE ULTIMATE LIMIT

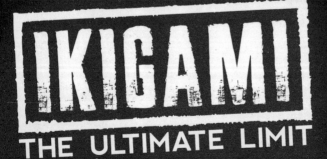

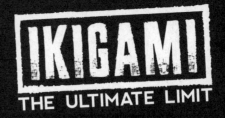

THE ULTIMATE LIMIT

VIZ Signature Edition

STORY AND ART BY Motoro Mase

Translation/John Werry
English Adaptation/Kristina Blachere
Touch-up Art & Lettering/Freeman Wong
Design/Amy Martin
Editor/Rich Amtower

VP, Production/Alvin Lu
VP, Publishing Licensing/Rika Inouye
VP, Sales & Product Marketing/Gonzalo Ferreyra
VP, Creative/Linda Espinosa
Publisher/Hyoe Narita

IKIGAMI 3 by Motoro MASE
© 2007 Motoro MASE
All rights reserved. Original Japanese edition
published in 2007 by Shogakukan, Inc., Tokyo.

Printed in the U.S.A.

Published by VIZ Media, LLC
P.O. Box 77010
San Francisco, CA 94107

10 9 8 7 6 5 4 3 2 1
First printing, November 2009

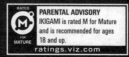

www.viz.com

www.vizsignature.com

IKIGAMI

THE ULTIMATE LIMIT

VOL. 3 STORY & ART BY MOTORO MASE

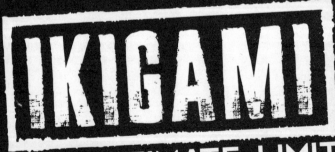

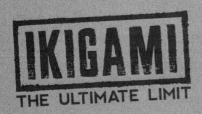

THE ULTIMATE LIMIT

CONTENTS

Episode 5 Life Out of Control
   Act 1.. 5
   Act 2 43
   Act 3 81

Episode 6 The Loveliest Lie
   Act 1..111
   Act 2 145
   Act 3 179

Episode 5 Life Out of Control Act1

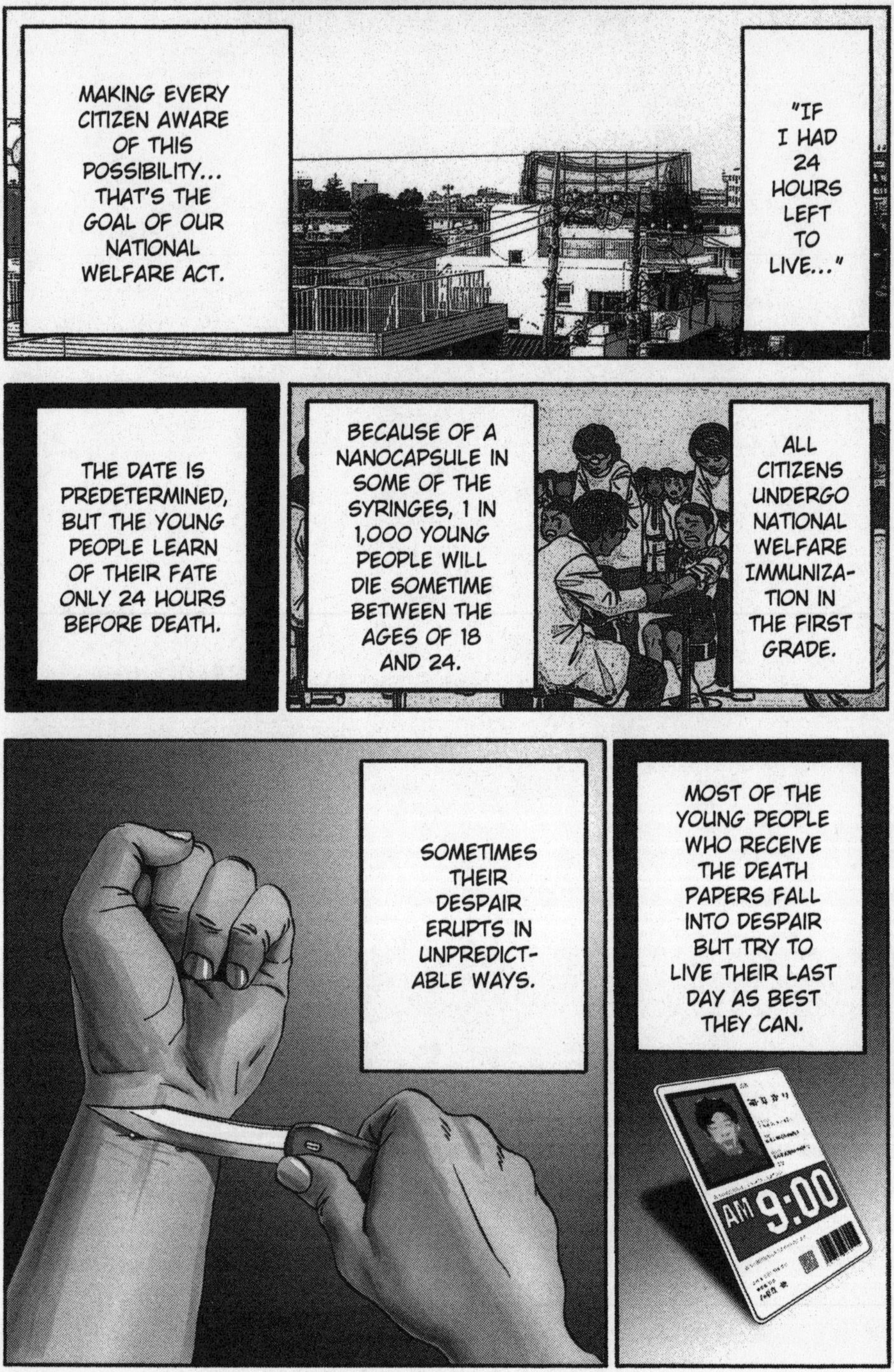
"IF I HAD 24 HOURS LEFT TO LIVE..."
MAKING EVERY CITIZEN AWARE OF THIS POSSIBILITY... THAT'S THE GOAL OF OUR NATIONAL WELFARE ACT.
ALL CITIZENS UNDERGO NATIONAL WELFARE IMMUNIZATION IN THE FIRST GRADE.
BECAUSE OF A NANOCAPSULE IN SOME OF THE SYRINGES, 1 IN 1,000 YOUNG PEOPLE WILL DIE SOMETIME BETWEEN THE AGES OF 18 AND 24.
THE DATE IS PREDETERMINED, BUT THE YOUNG PEOPLE LEARN OF THEIR FATE ONLY 24 HOURS BEFORE DEATH.
MOST OF THE YOUNG PEOPLE WHO RECEIVE THE DEATH PAPERS FALL INTO DESPAIR BUT TRY TO LIVE THEIR LAST DAY AS BEST THEY CAN.
AM 9:00
SOMETIMES THEIR DESPAIR ERUPTS IN UNPREDICTABLE WAYS.

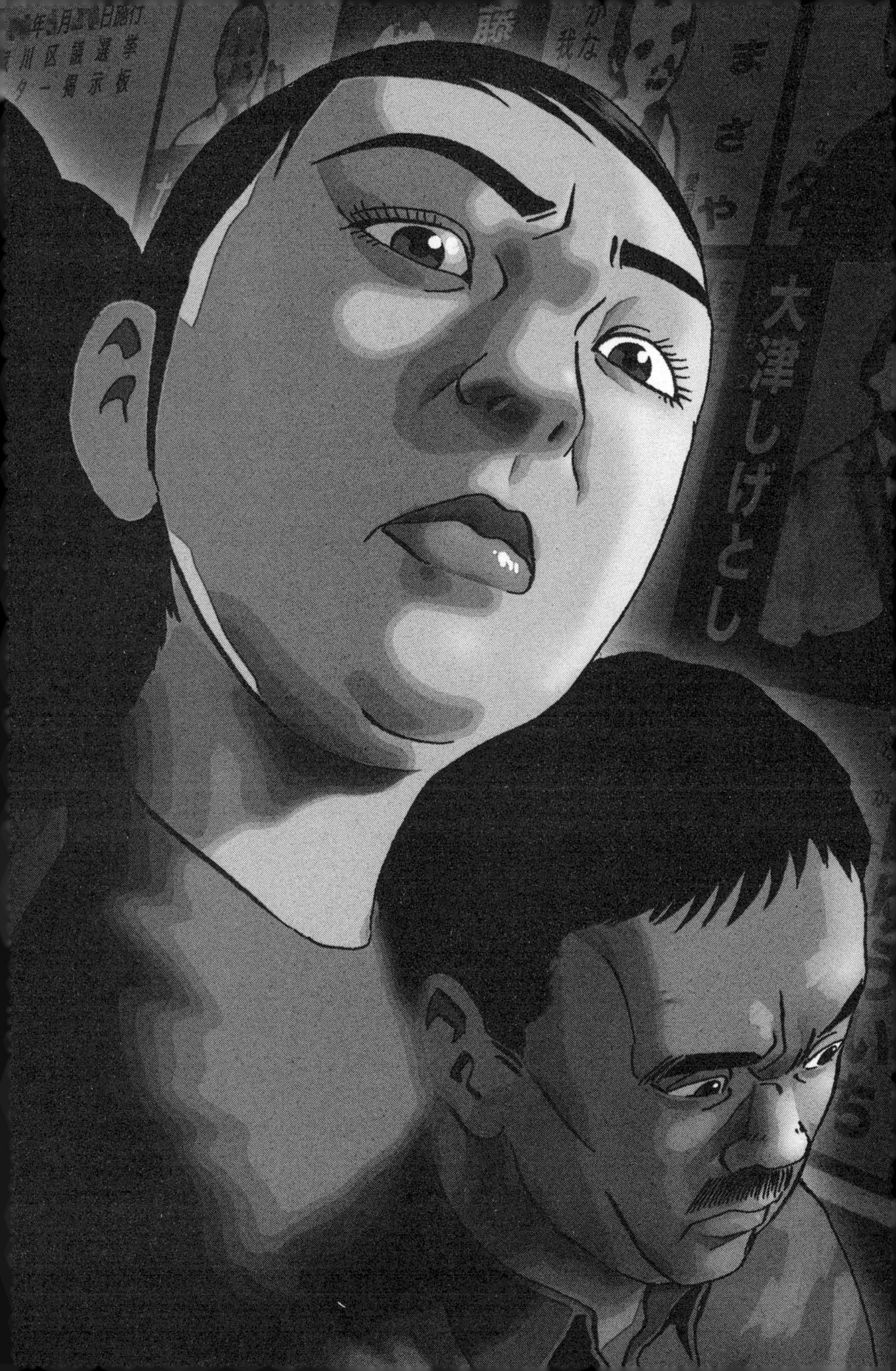
大澤しげとし

Episode 5 Life Out of Control Act 1

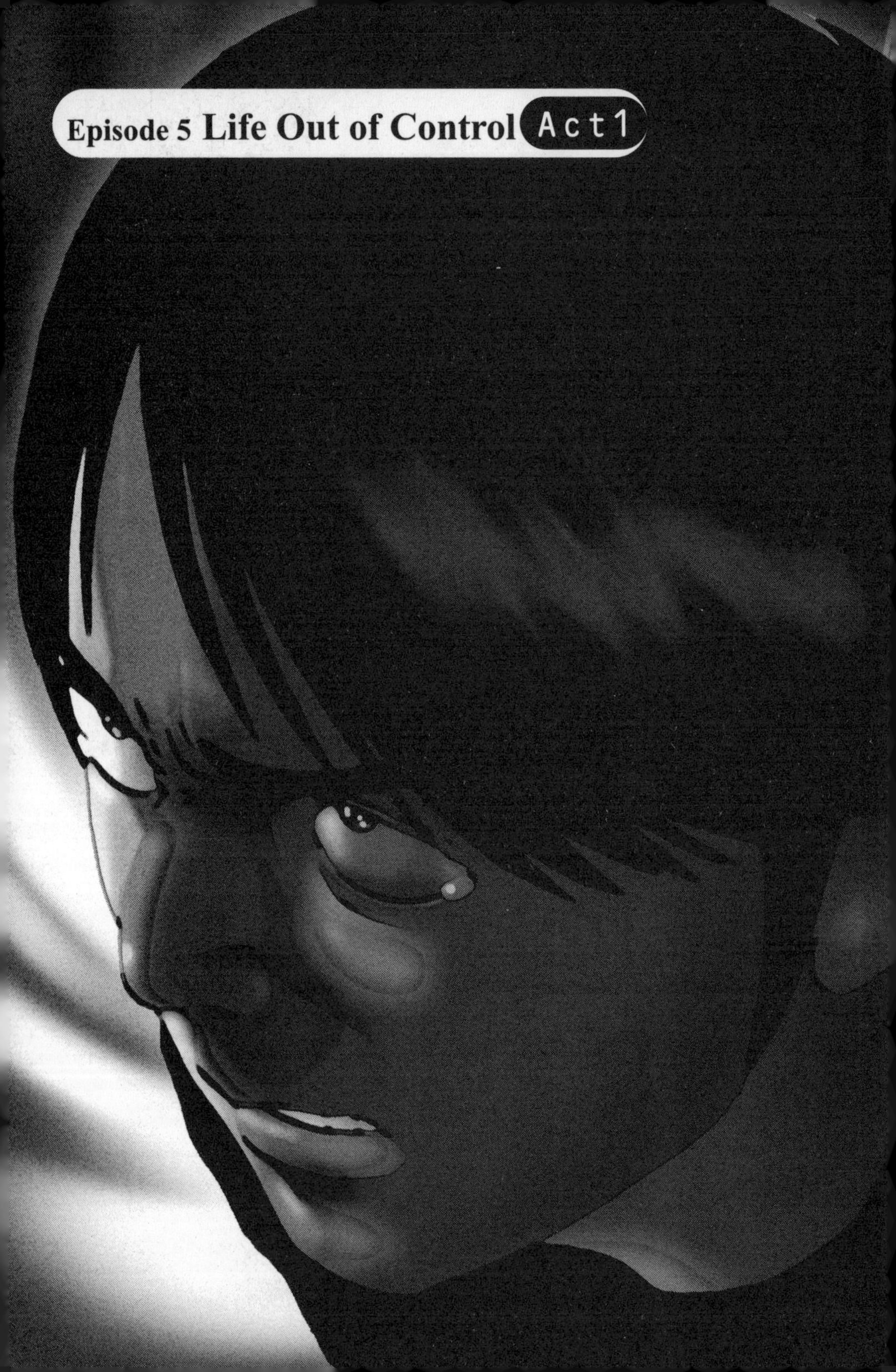

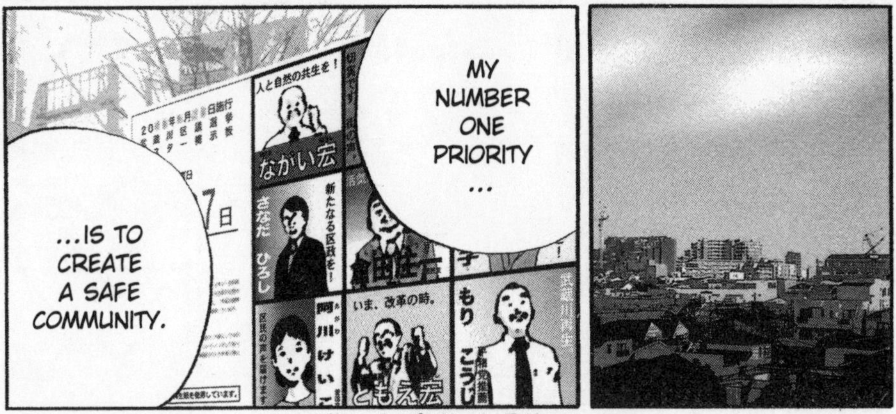
MY NUMBER ONE PRIORITY...
...IS TO CREATE A SAFE COMMUNITY.

Signs: Vote for Kazuko Takimoto

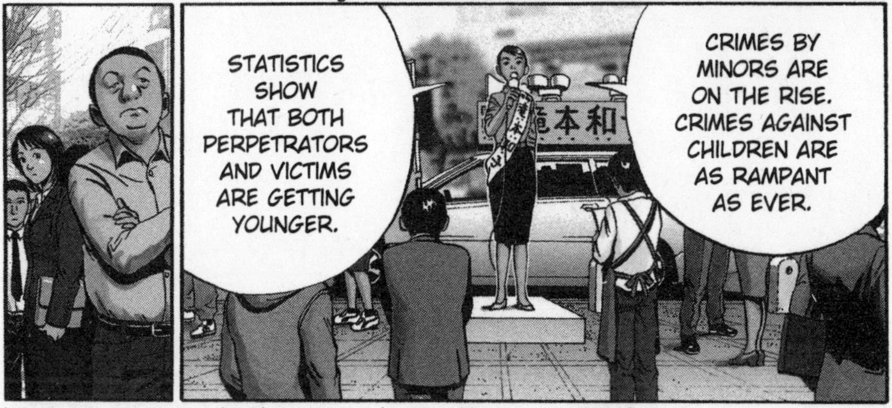
CRIMES BY MINORS ARE ON THE RISE. CRIMES AGAINST CHILDREN ARE AS RAMPANT AS EVER.
STATISTICS SHOW THAT BOTH PERPETRATORS AND VICTIMS ARE GETTING YOUNGER.

*The stories, characters, and incidents mentioned in this publication are entirely fictional.

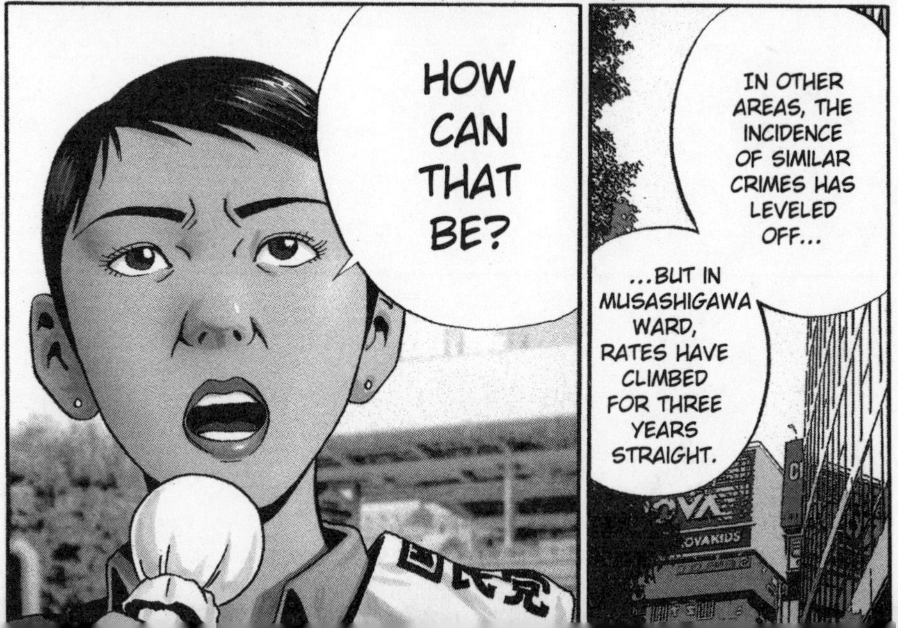
IN OTHER AREAS, THE INCIDENCE OF SIMILAR CRIMES HAS LEVELED OFF...
...BUT IN MUSASHIGAWA WARD, RATES HAVE CLIMBED FOR THREE YEARS STRAIGHT.
HOW CAN THAT BE?

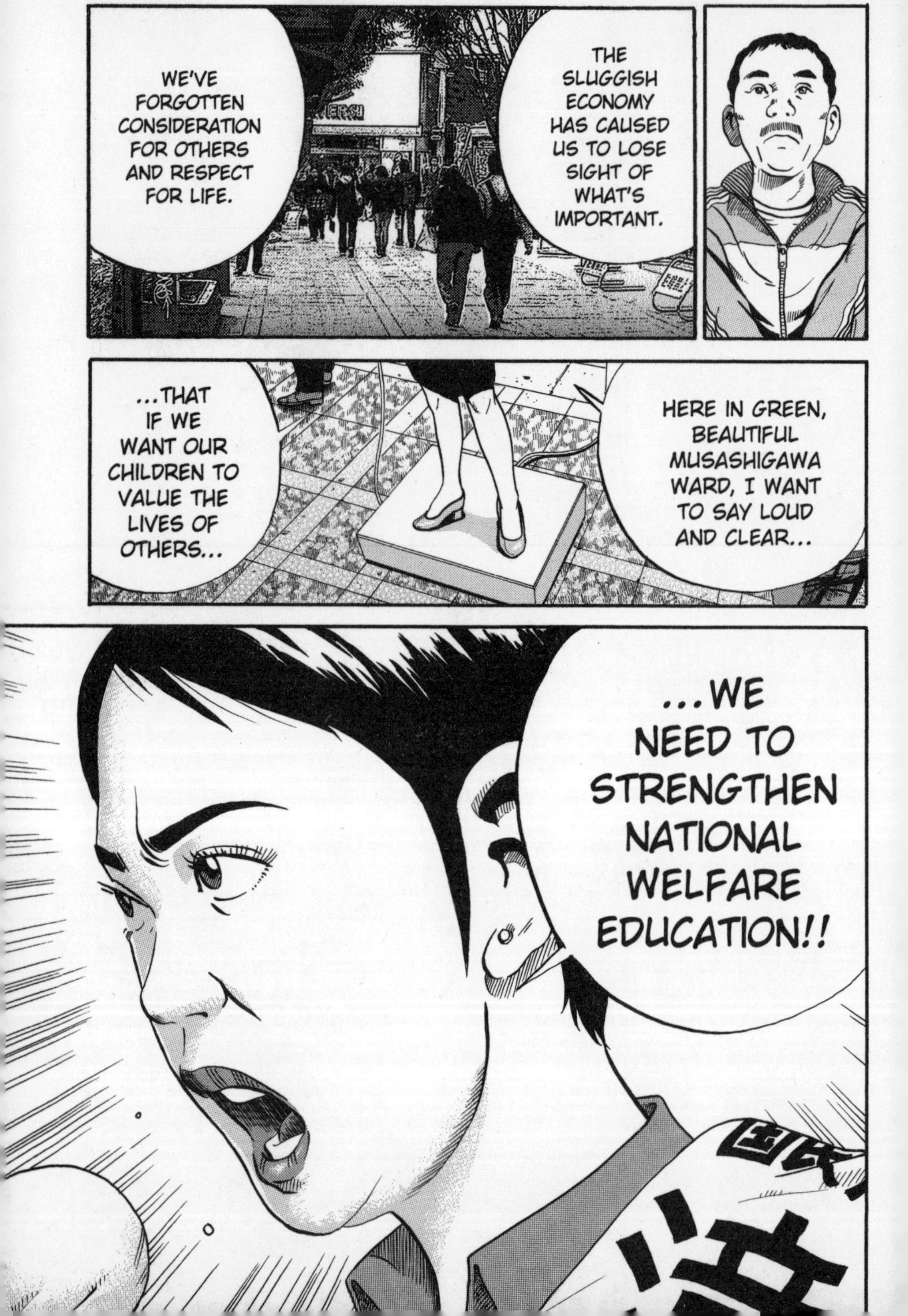
THE SLUGGISH ECONOMY HAS CAUSED US TO LOSE SIGHT OF WHAT'S IMPORTANT.
WE'VE FORGOTTEN CONSIDERATION FOR OTHERS AND RESPECT FOR LIFE.
HERE IN GREEN, BEAUTIFUL MUSASHIGAWA WARD, I WANT TO SAY LOUD AND CLEAR...
...THAT IF WE WANT OUR CHILDREN TO VALUE THE LIVES OF OTHERS...
...WE NEED TO STRENGTHEN NATIONAL WELFARE EDUCATION!!

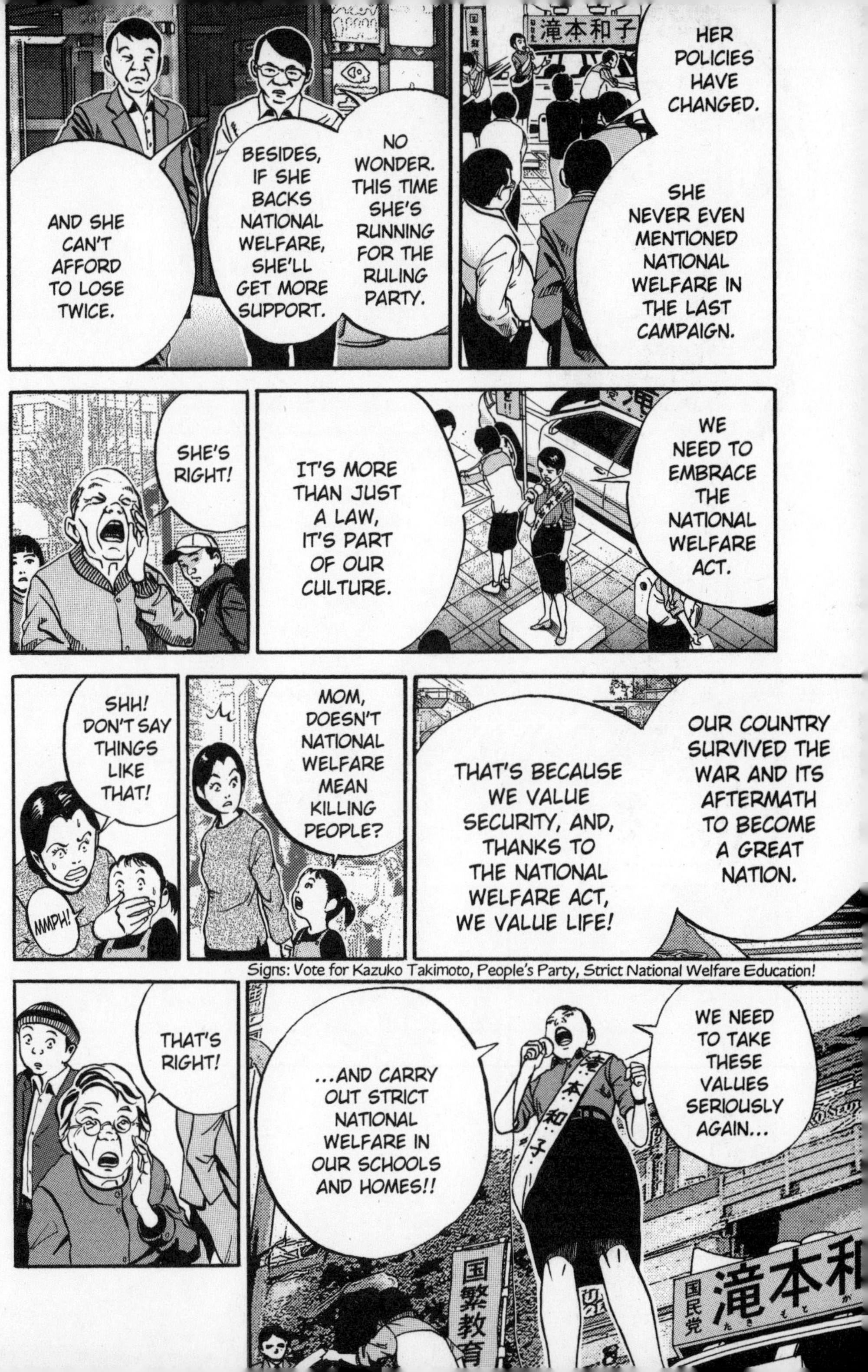
HER POLICIES HAVE CHANGED.
SHE NEVER EVEN MENTIONED NATIONAL WELFARE IN THE LAST CAMPAIGN.
NO WONDER. THIS TIME SHE'S RUNNING FOR THE RULING PARTY.
BESIDES, IF SHE BACKS NATIONAL WELFARE, SHE'LL GET MORE SUPPORT.
AND SHE CAN'T AFFORD TO LOSE TWICE.
WE NEED TO EMBRACE THE NATIONAL WELFARE ACT.
IT'S MORE THAN JUST A LAW, IT'S PART OF OUR CULTURE.
SHE'S RIGHT!
OUR COUNTRY SURVIVED THE WAR AND ITS AFTERMATH TO BECOME A GREAT NATION.
THAT'S BECAUSE WE VALUE SECURITY, AND, THANKS TO THE NATIONAL WELFARE ACT, WE VALUE LIFE!
MOM, DOESN'T NATIONAL WELFARE MEAN KILLING PEOPLE?
SHH! DON'T SAY THINGS LIKE THAT!
MMPH!
Signs: Vote for Kazuko Takimoto, People's Party, Strict National Welfare Education!
WE NEED TO TAKE THESE VALUES SERIOUSLY AGAIN...
...AND CARRY OUT STRICT NATIONAL WELFARE IN OUR SCHOOLS AND HOMES!!
THAT'S RIGHT!

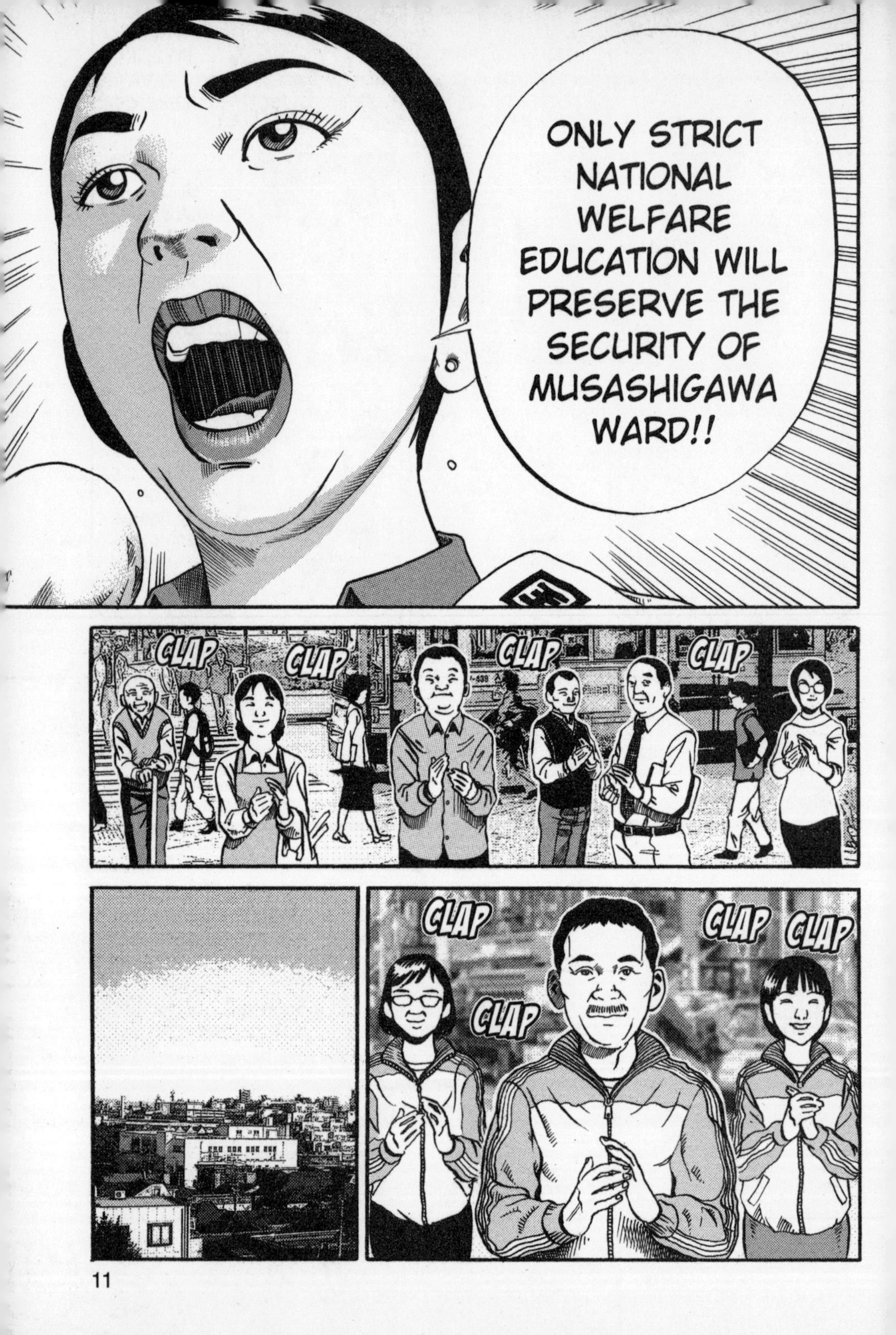
ONLY STRICT NATIONAL WELFARE EDUCATION WILL PRESERVE THE SECURITY OF MUSASHIGAWA WARD!!
CLAP
CLAP
CLAP
CLAP
CLAP
CLAP
CLAP
CLAP

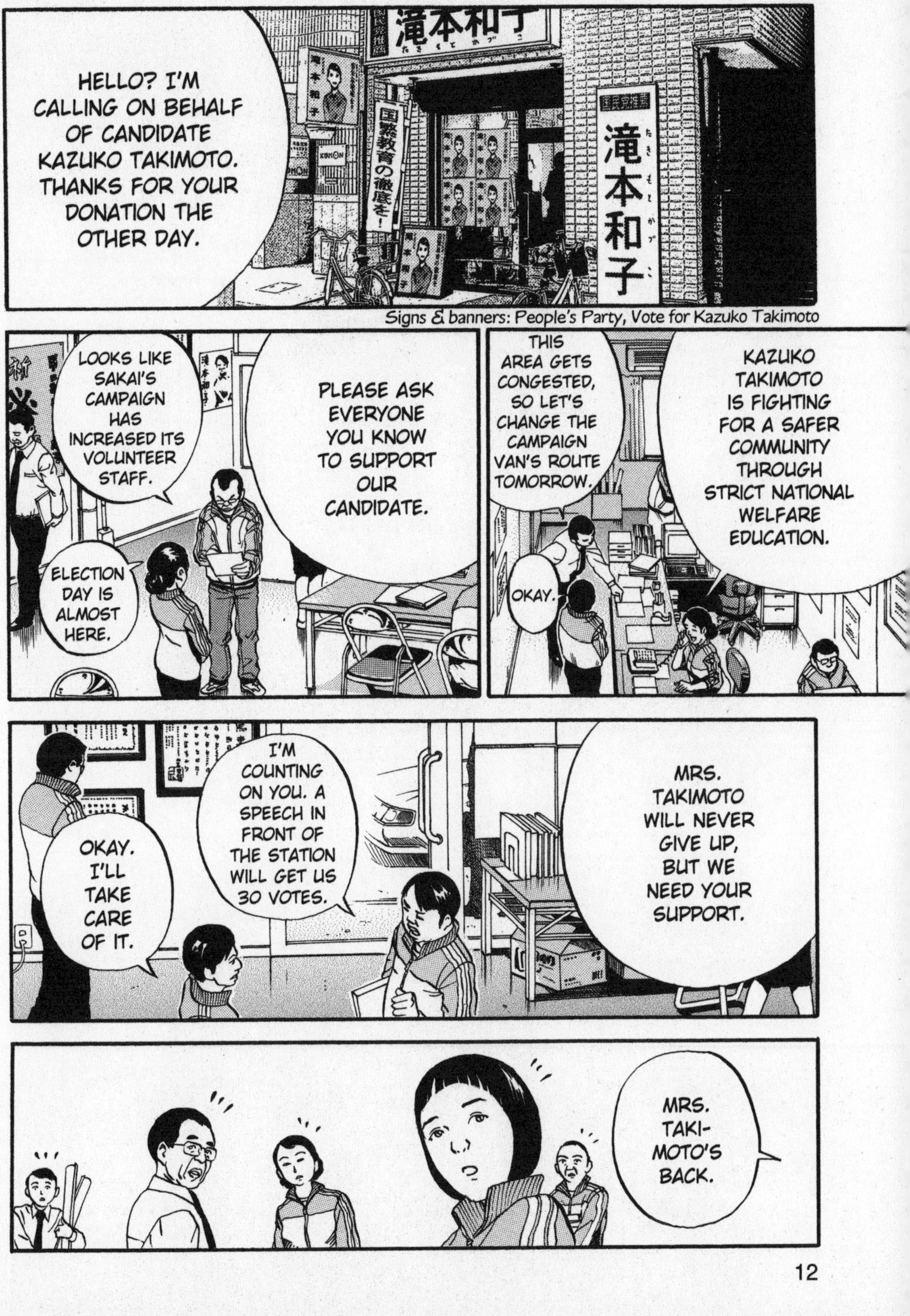

HELLO? I'M CALLING ON BEHALF OF CANDIDATE KAZUKO TAKIMOTO. THANKS FOR YOUR DONATION THE OTHER DAY.
滝本和子
国家教育の徹底を!
Signs & banners: People's Party, Vote for Kazuko Takimoto
KAZUKO TAKIMOTO IS FIGHTING FOR A SAFER COMMUNITY THROUGH STRICT NATIONAL WELFARE EDUCATION.
THIS AREA GETS CONGESTED, SO LET'S CHANGE THE CAMPAIGN VAN'S ROUTE TOMORROW.
OKAY.
PLEASE ASK EVERYONE YOU KNOW TO SUPPORT OUR CANDIDATE.
LOOKS LIKE SAKAI'S CAMPAIGN HAS INCREASED ITS VOLUNTEER STAFF.
ELECTION DAY IS ALMOST HERE.
MRS. TAKIMOTO WILL NEVER GIVE UP, BUT WE NEED YOUR SUPPORT.
I'M COUNTING ON YOU. A SPEECH IN FRONT OF THE STATION WILL GET US 30 VOTES.
OKAY. I'LL TAKE CARE OF IT.
MRS. TAKI-MOTO'S BACK.

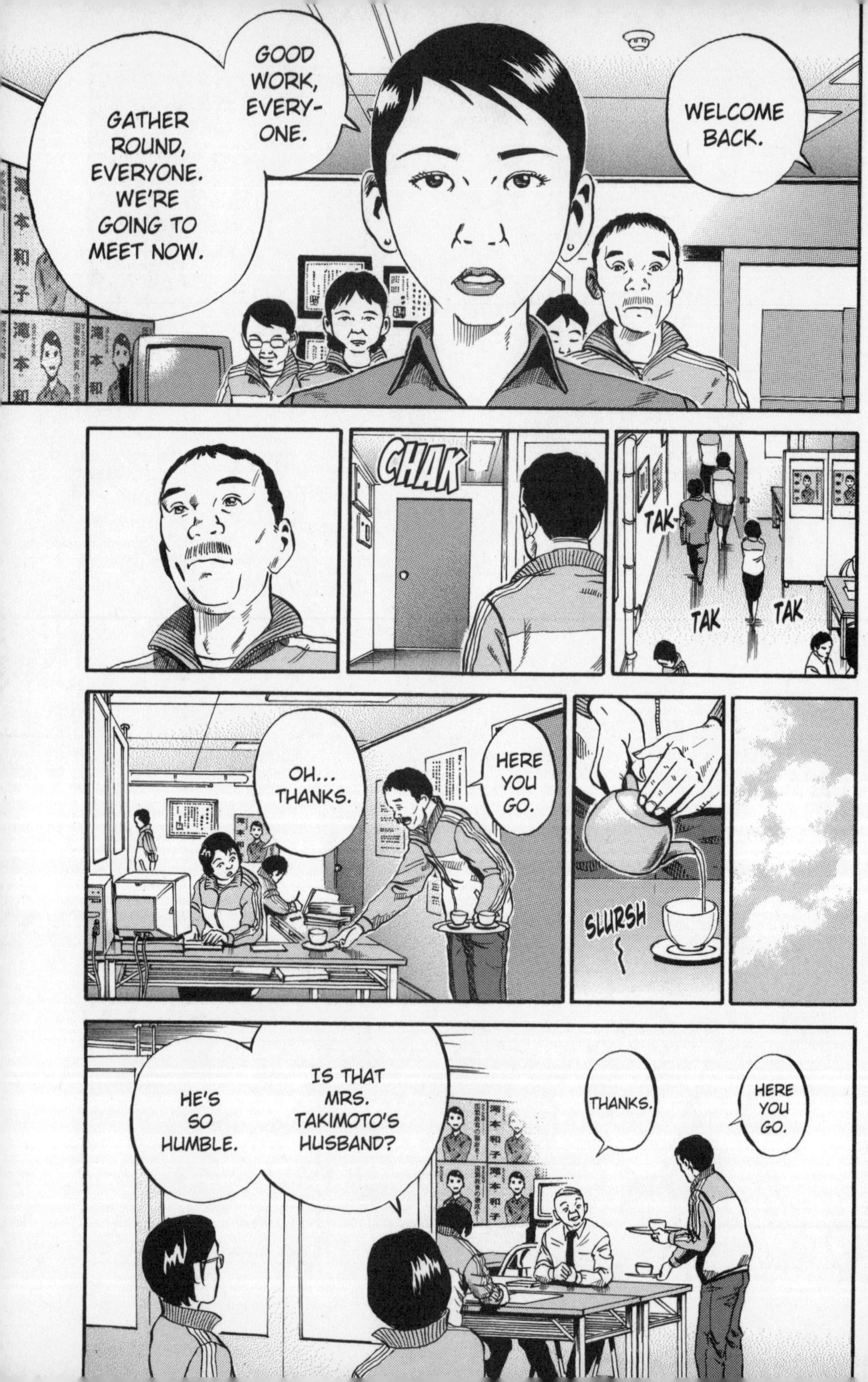
WELCOME BACK.
GOOD WORK, EVERYONE.
GATHER ROUND, EVERYONE. WE'RE GOING TO MEET NOW.
TAK
TAK
TAK
CHAK
SLURSH
HERE YOU GO.
OH... THANKS.
HERE YOU GO.
THANKS.
IS THAT MRS. TAKIMOTO'S HUSBAND?
HE'S SO HUMBLE.

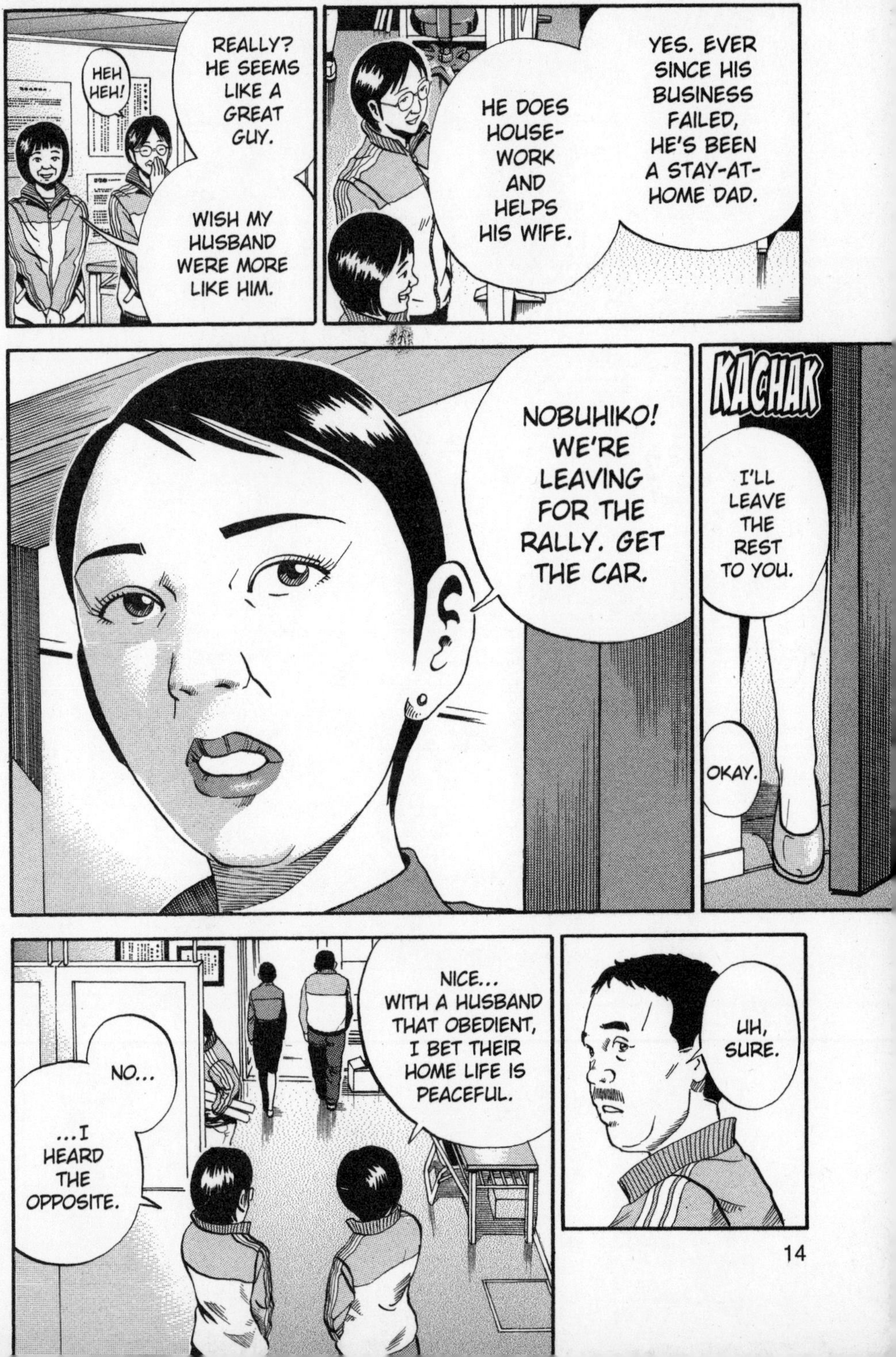
YES. EVER SINCE HIS BUSINESS FAILED, HE'S BEEN A STAY-AT-HOME DAD.
HE DOES HOUSE-WORK AND HELPS HIS WIFE.
REALLY? HE SEEMS LIKE A GREAT GUY.
HEH HEH!
WISH MY HUSBAND WERE MORE LIKE HIM.
KACHAK
I'LL LEAVE THE REST TO YOU.
OKAY.
NOBUHIKO! WE'RE LEAVING FOR THE RALLY. GET THE CAR.
UH, SURE.
NICE... WITH A HUSBAND THAT OBEDIENT, I BET THEIR HOME LIFE IS PEACEFUL.
NO...
...I HEARD THE OPPOSITE.

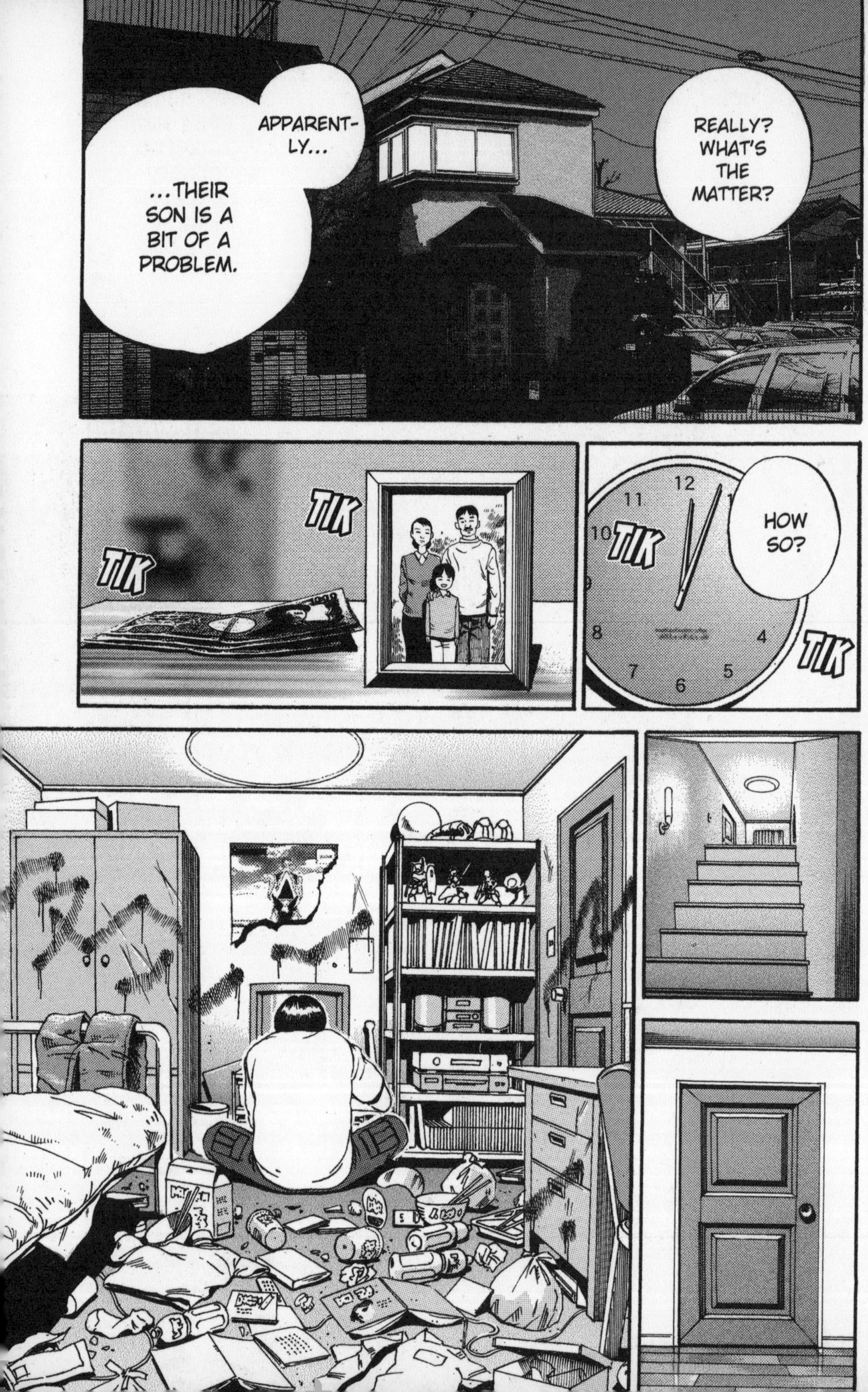
REALLY? WHAT'S THE MATTER?
APPARENT-LY...
...THEIR SON IS A BIT OF A PROBLEM.
HOW SO?
TIK
TIK
TIK
TIK

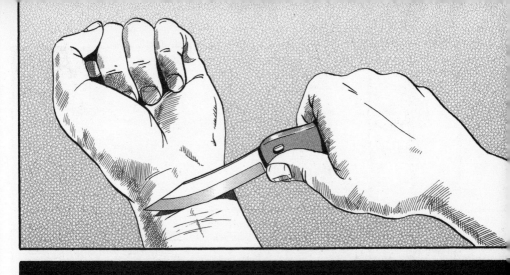

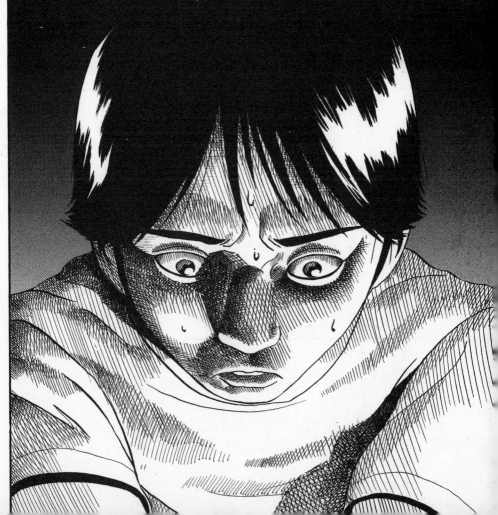

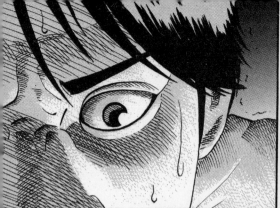
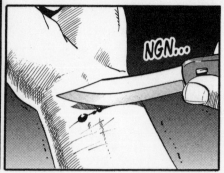

NGN...

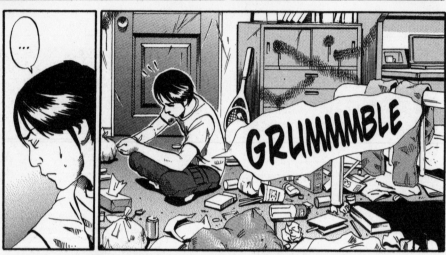

...

GRUMMMBLE

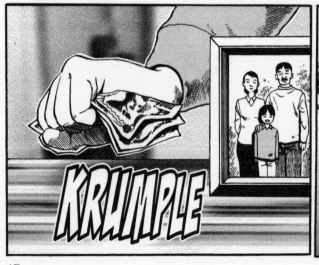

KRUMPLE

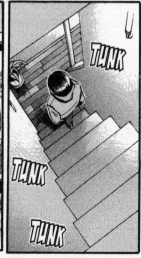

TUNK

TUNK

TUNK

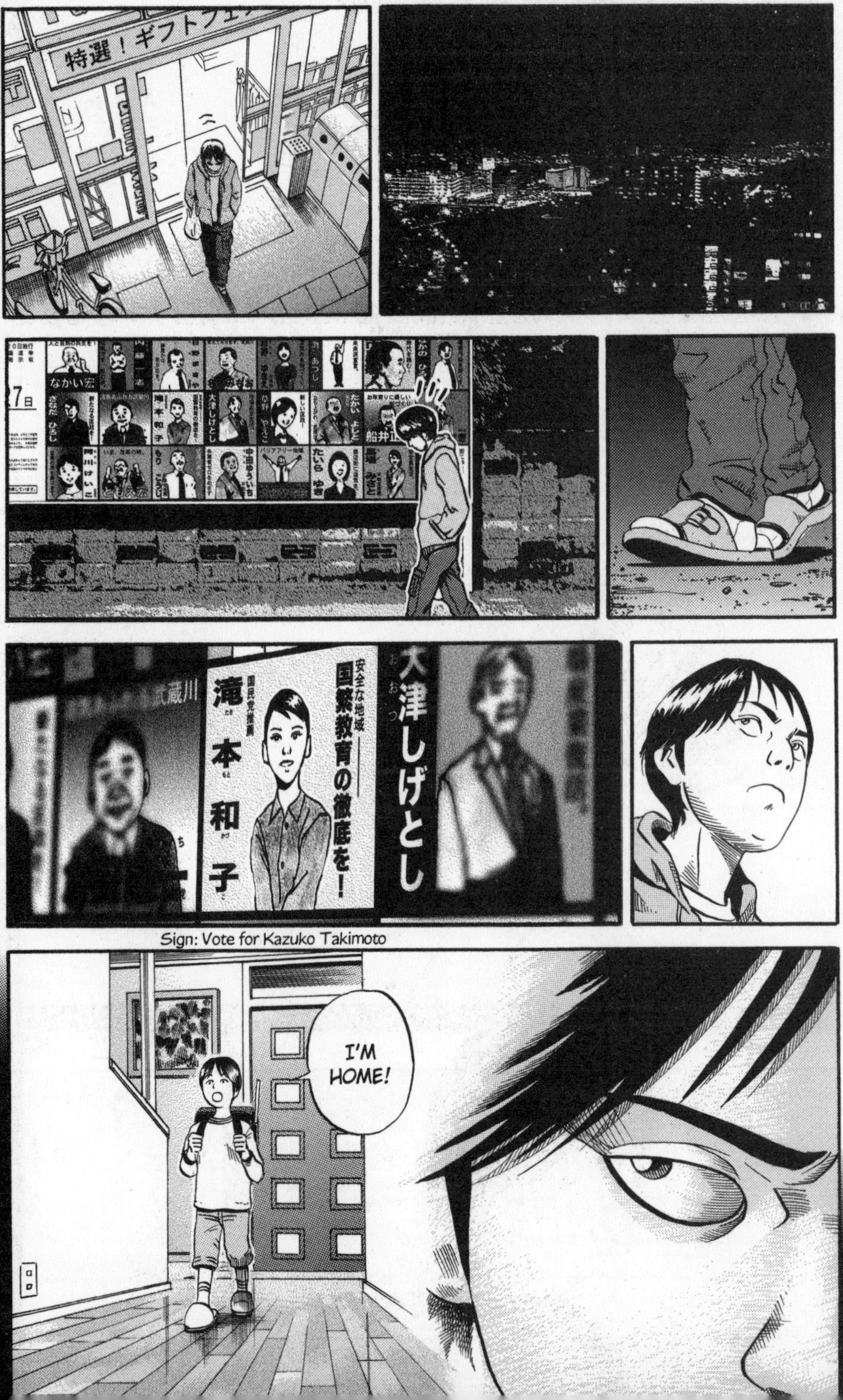

なかい宏
大津しげとし
船井正
大津しげとし
安全な地域
国際教育の徹底を！
国民党推薦
滝本和子
Sign: Vote for Kazuko Takimoto
I'M HOME!

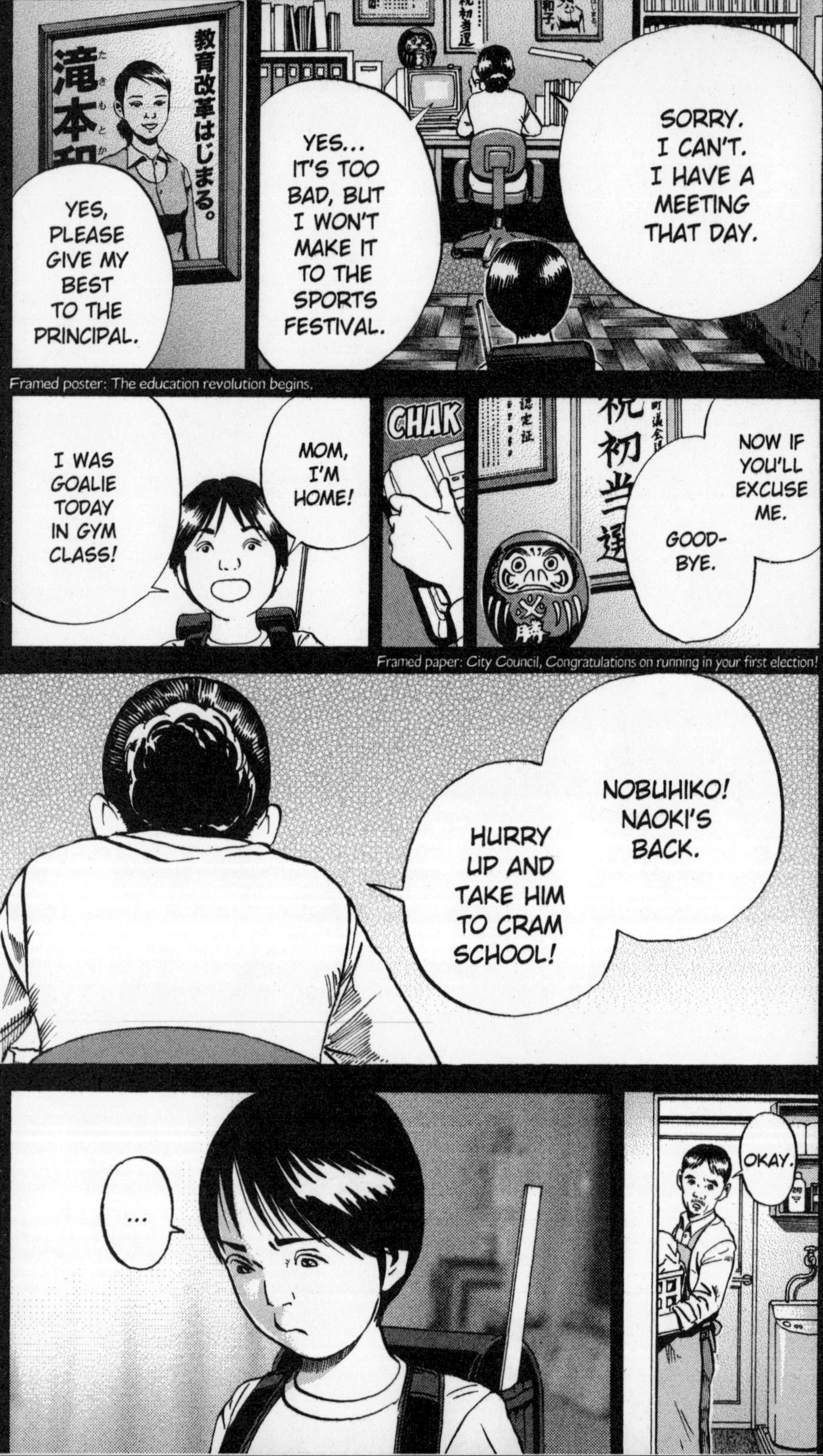

SORRY. I CAN'T. I HAVE A MEETING THAT DAY.
YES... IT'S TOO BAD, BUT I WON'T MAKE IT TO THE SPORTS FESTIVAL.
YES, PLEASE GIVE MY BEST TO THE PRINCIPAL.
教育改革はじまる。
滝本和
Framed poster: The education revolution begins.
NOW IF YOU'LL EXCUSE ME.
GOOD-BYE.
CHAK
MOM, I'M HOME!
I WAS GOALIE TODAY IN GYM CLASS!
Framed paper: City Council, Congratulations on running in your first election!
NOBUHIKO! NAOKI'S BACK.
HURRY UP AND TAKE HIM TO CRAM SCHOOL!
OKAY.
...

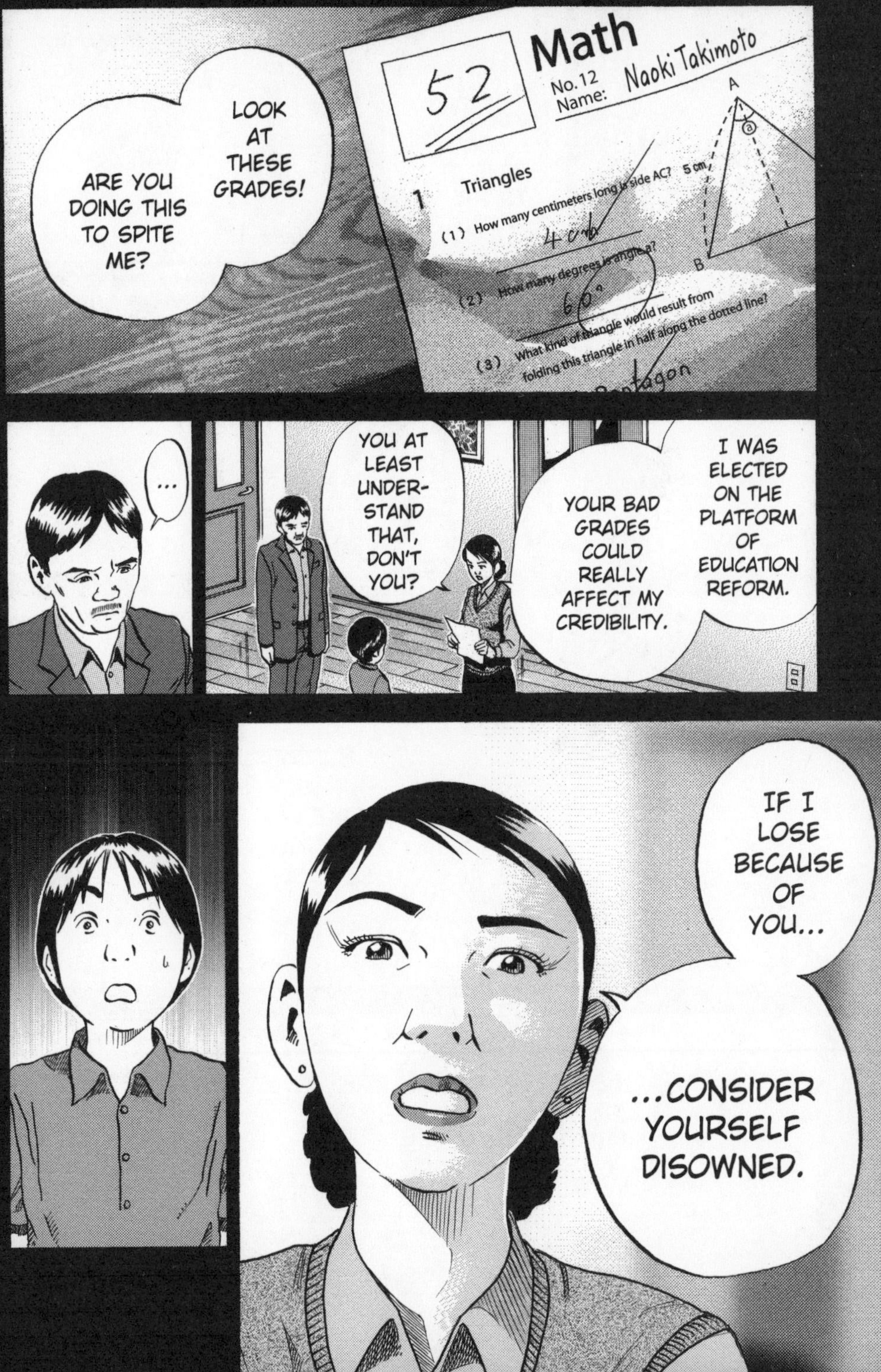
Math
52
No.12
Name: Naoki Takimoto
A
1 Triangles
(1) How many centimeters long is side AC? 5 cm
4 cm
B
(2) How many degrees is angle a?
60°
(3) What kind of triangle would result from folding this triangle in half along the dotted line?
LOOK AT THESE GRADES!
ARE YOU DOING THIS TO SPITE ME?
I WAS ELECTED ON THE PLATFORM OF EDUCATION REFORM.
YOUR BAD GRADES COULD REALLY AFFECT MY CREDIBILITY.
YOU AT LEAST UNDER-STAND THAT, DON'T YOU?
...
IF I LOSE BECAUSE OF YOU...
...CONSIDER YOURSELF DISOWNED.

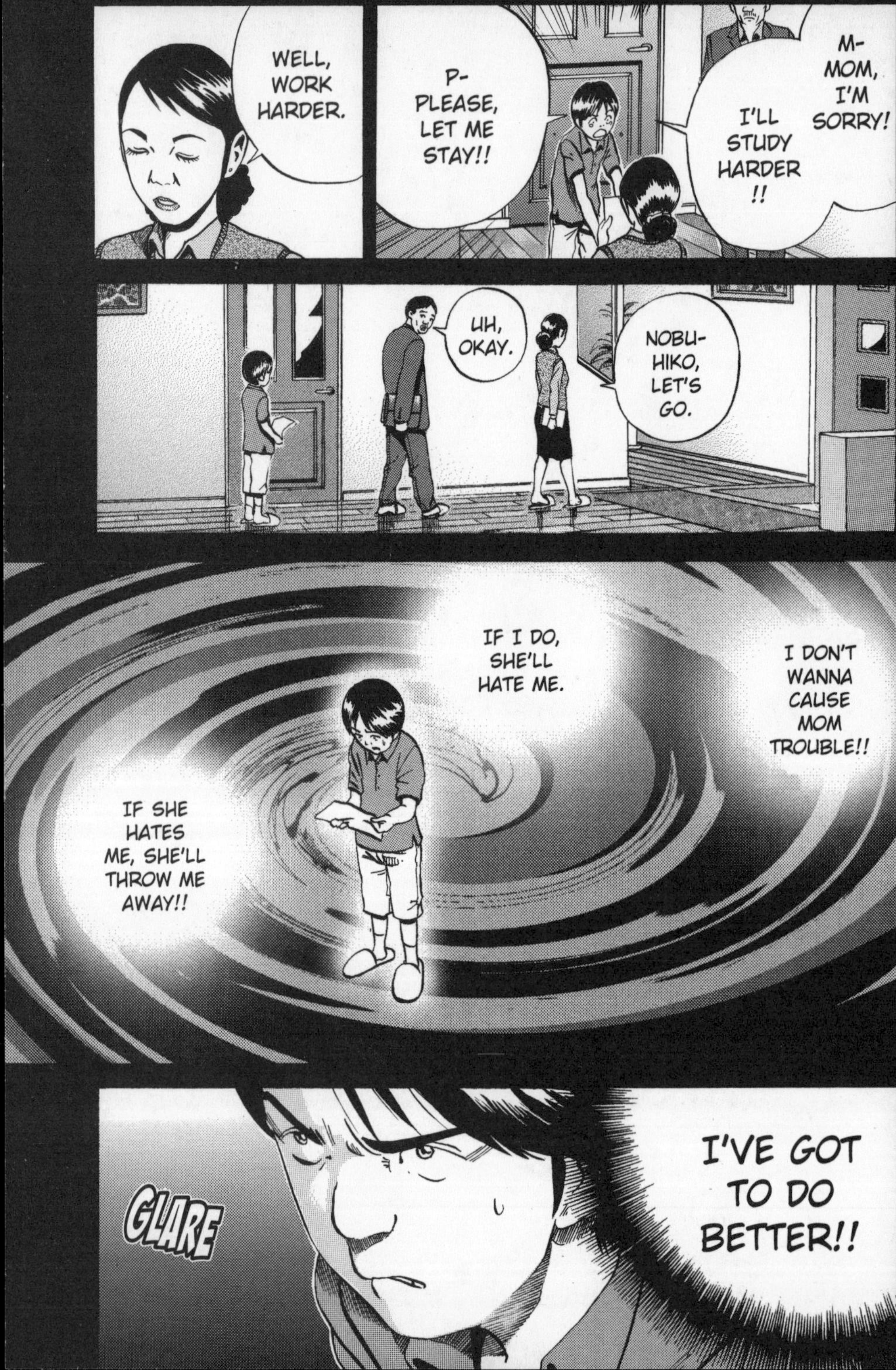
M-MOM, I'M SORRY!
I'LL STUDY HARDER!!
P-PLEASE, LET ME STAY!!
WELL, WORK HARDER.
NOBUHIKO, LET'S GO.
UH, OKAY.
I DON'T WANNA CAUSE MOM TROUBLE!!
IF I DO, SHE'LL HATE ME.
IF SHE HATES ME, SHE'LL THROW ME AWAY!!
I'VE GOT TO DO BETTER!!
GLARE

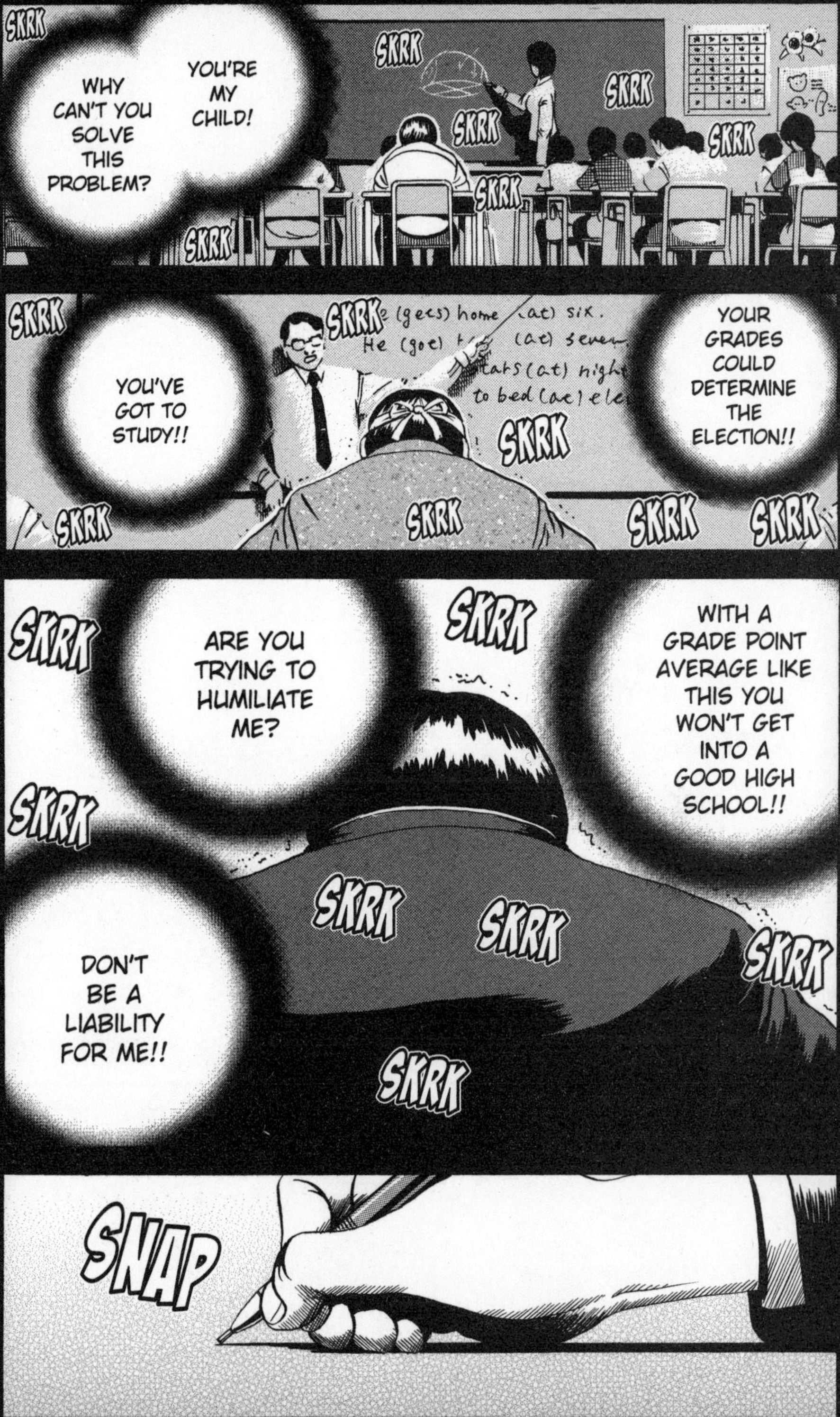
SKRK
SKRK
YOU'RE MY CHILD!
WHY CAN'T YOU SOLVE THIS PROBLEM?
SKRK
SKRK
SKRK
SKRK
SKRK
YOUR GRADES COULD DETERMINE THE ELECTION!!
SKRK
YOU'VE GOT TO STUDY!!
SKRK
SKRK
SKRK
SKRK
SKRK
WITH A GRADE POINT AVERAGE LIKE THIS YOU WON'T GET INTO A GOOD HIGH SCHOOL!!
SKRK
ARE YOU TRYING TO HUMILIATE ME?
SKRK
SKRK
SKRK
SKRK
SKRK
DON'T BE A LIABILITY FOR ME!!
SKRK
SNAP

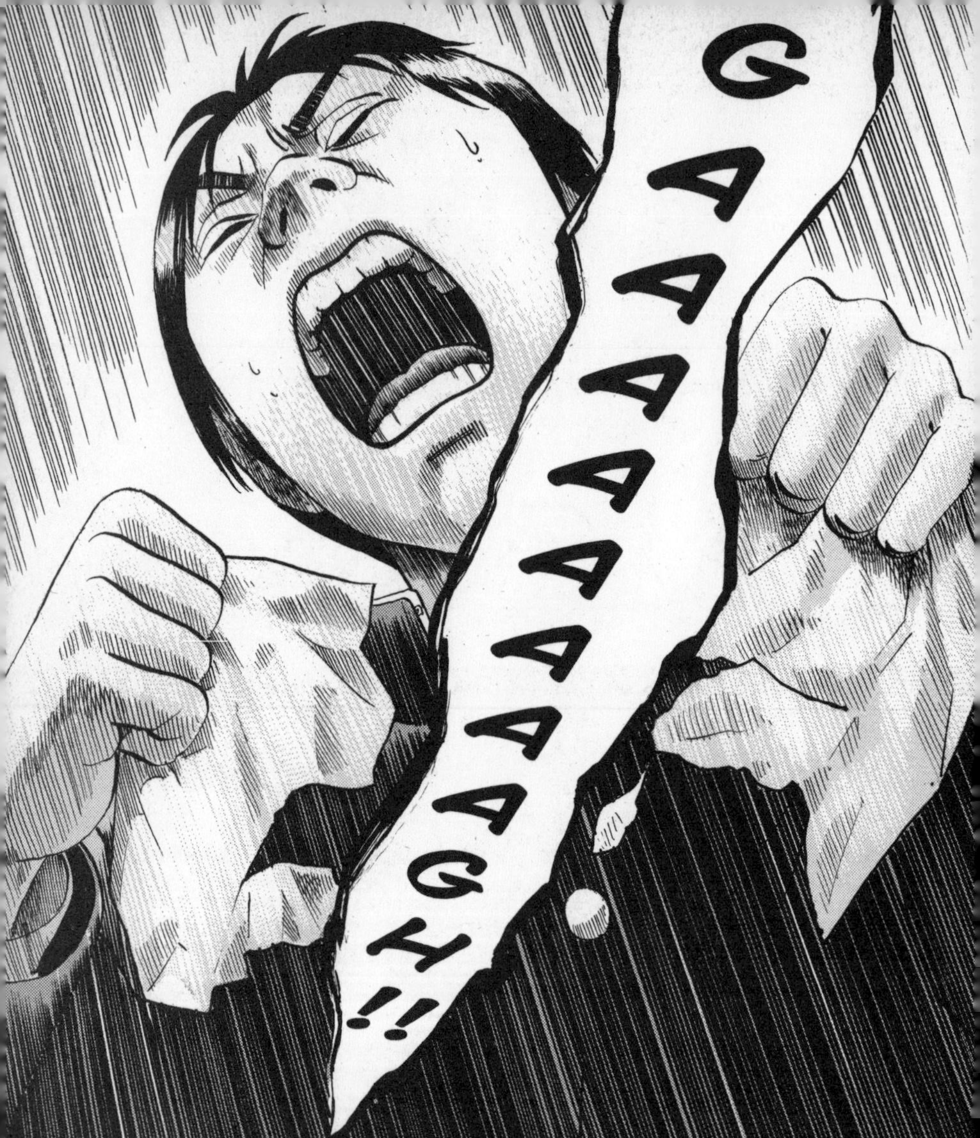
GAAAAAAAAGH!!

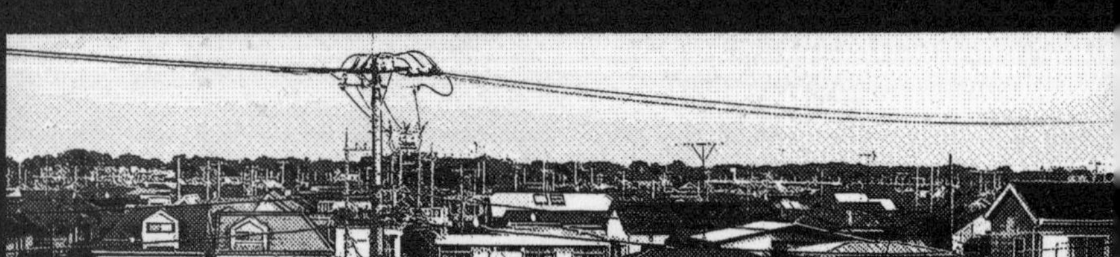

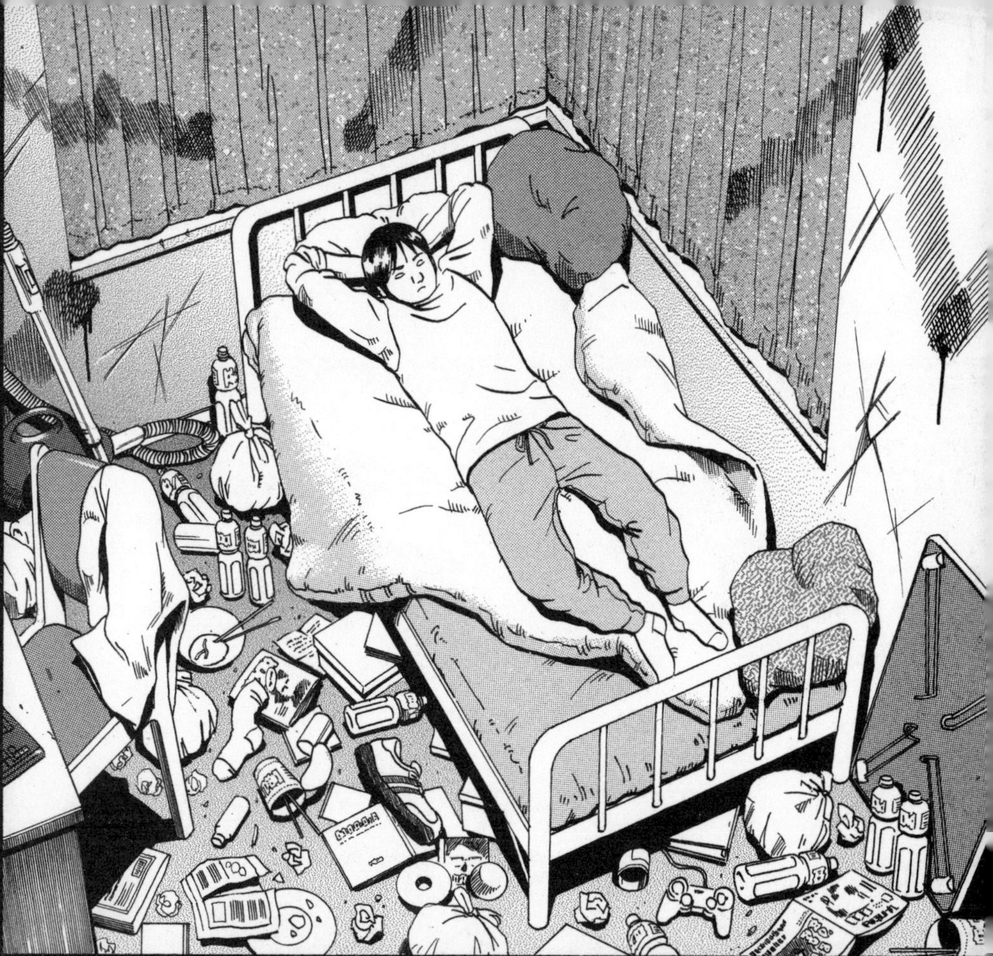

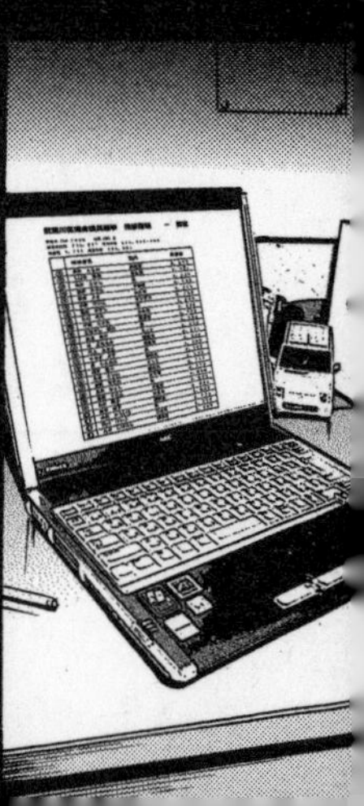

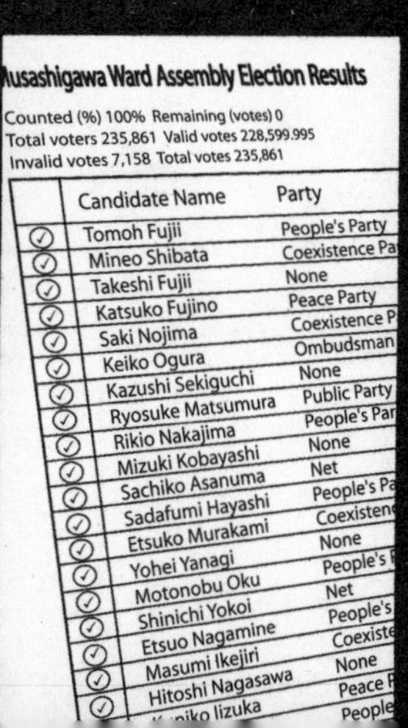
usashigawa Ward Assembly Election Results
Counted (%) 100% Remaining (votes) 0
Total voters 235,861 Valid votes 228,599.995
Invalid votes 7,158 Total votes 235,861
Candidate Name
Party
Tomoh Fujii
People's Party
Mineo Shibata
Coexistence Pa
Takeshi Fujii
None
Katsuko Fujino
Peace Party
Saki Nojima
Coexistence P
Keiko Ogura
Ombudsman
Kazushi Sekiguchi
None
Ryosuke Matsumura
Public Party
Rikio Nakajima
People's Par
Mizuki Kobayashi
None
Sachiko Asanuma
Net
Sadafumi Hayashi
People's Pa
Etsuko Murakami
Coexistenc
Yohei Yanagi
None
Motonobu Oku
People's
Shinichi Yokoi
Net
Etsuo Nagamine
People's
Masumi Ikejiri
Coexiste
Hitoshi Nagasawa
None
Peace
People

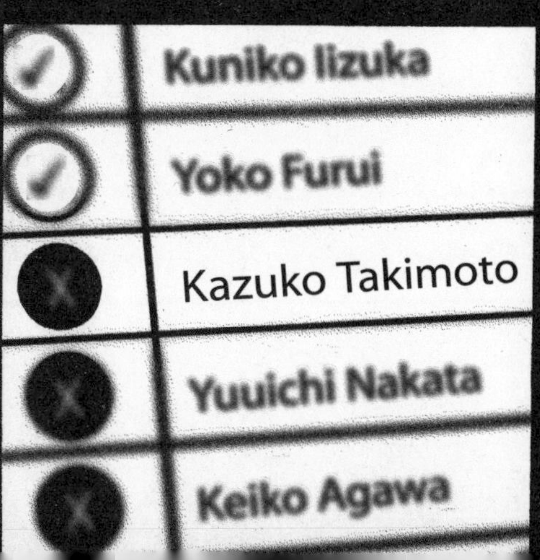
Kuniko Iizuka
Yoko Furui
Kazuko Takimoto
Yuuichi Nakata
Keiko Agawa

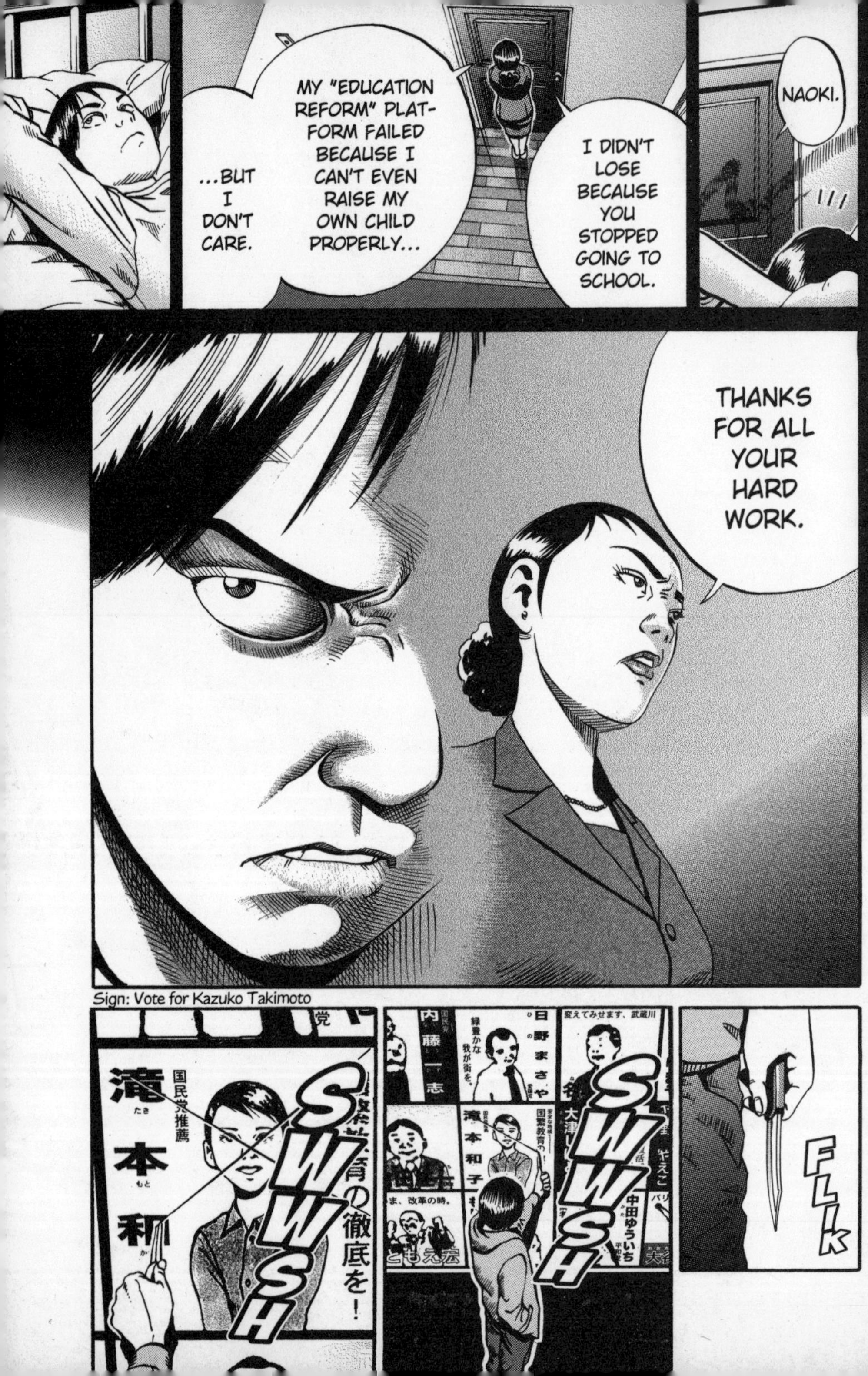
NAOKI.
I DIDN'T LOSE BECAUSE YOU STOPPED GOING TO SCHOOL.
MY "EDUCATION REFORM" PLATFORM FAILED BECAUSE I CAN'T EVEN RAISE MY OWN CHILD PROPERLY...
...BUT I DON'T CARE.
THANKS FOR ALL YOUR HARD WORK.
Sign: Vote for Kazuko Takimoto
FLIK
SWWSH
変えてみせます、武蔵川
日野まさや
緑豊かな我が街を。
内藤一志
滝本和子
中田ゆういち
いま、改革の時。
SWWSH
国民党推薦
滝本和
の徹底を！

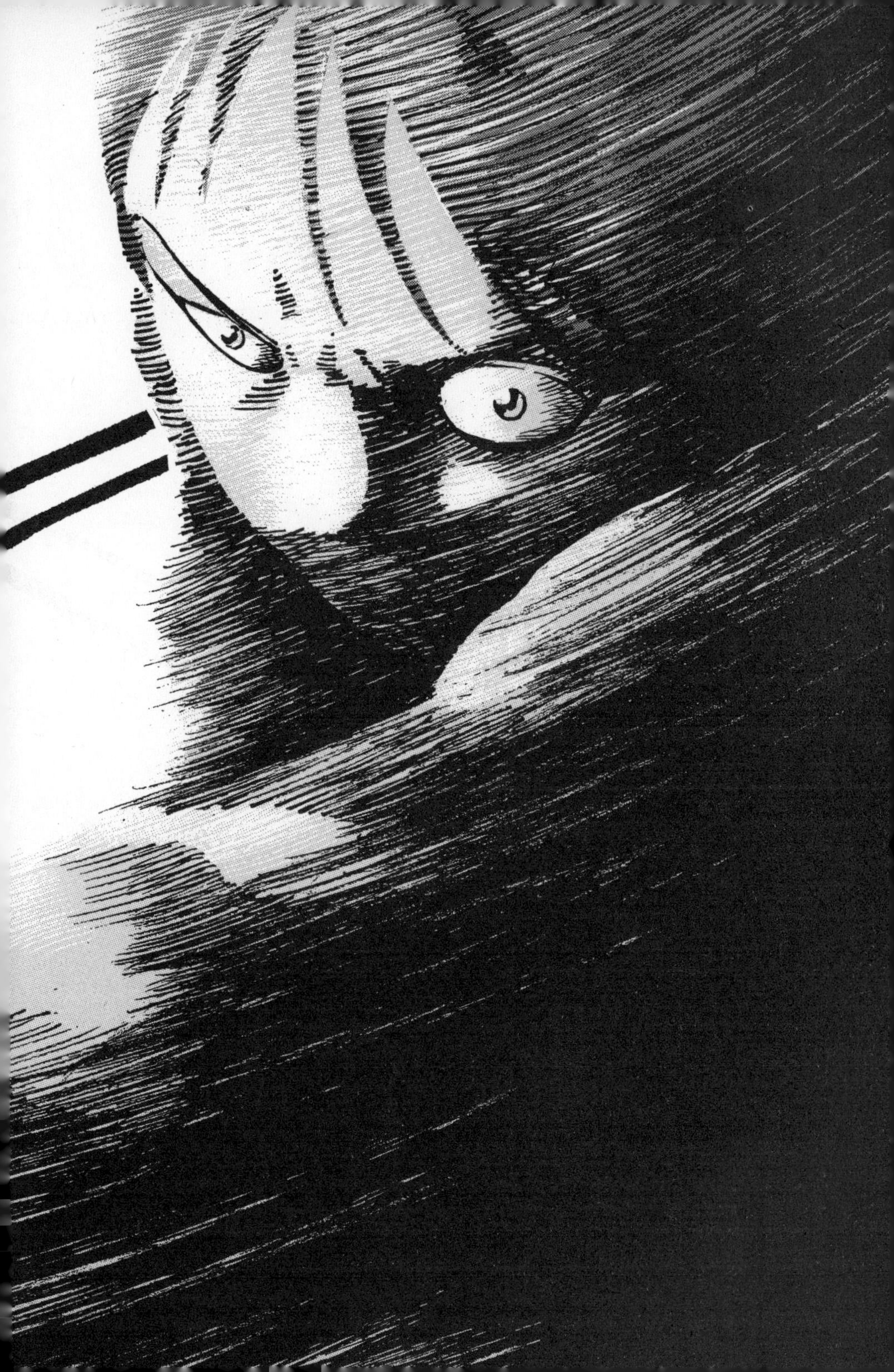

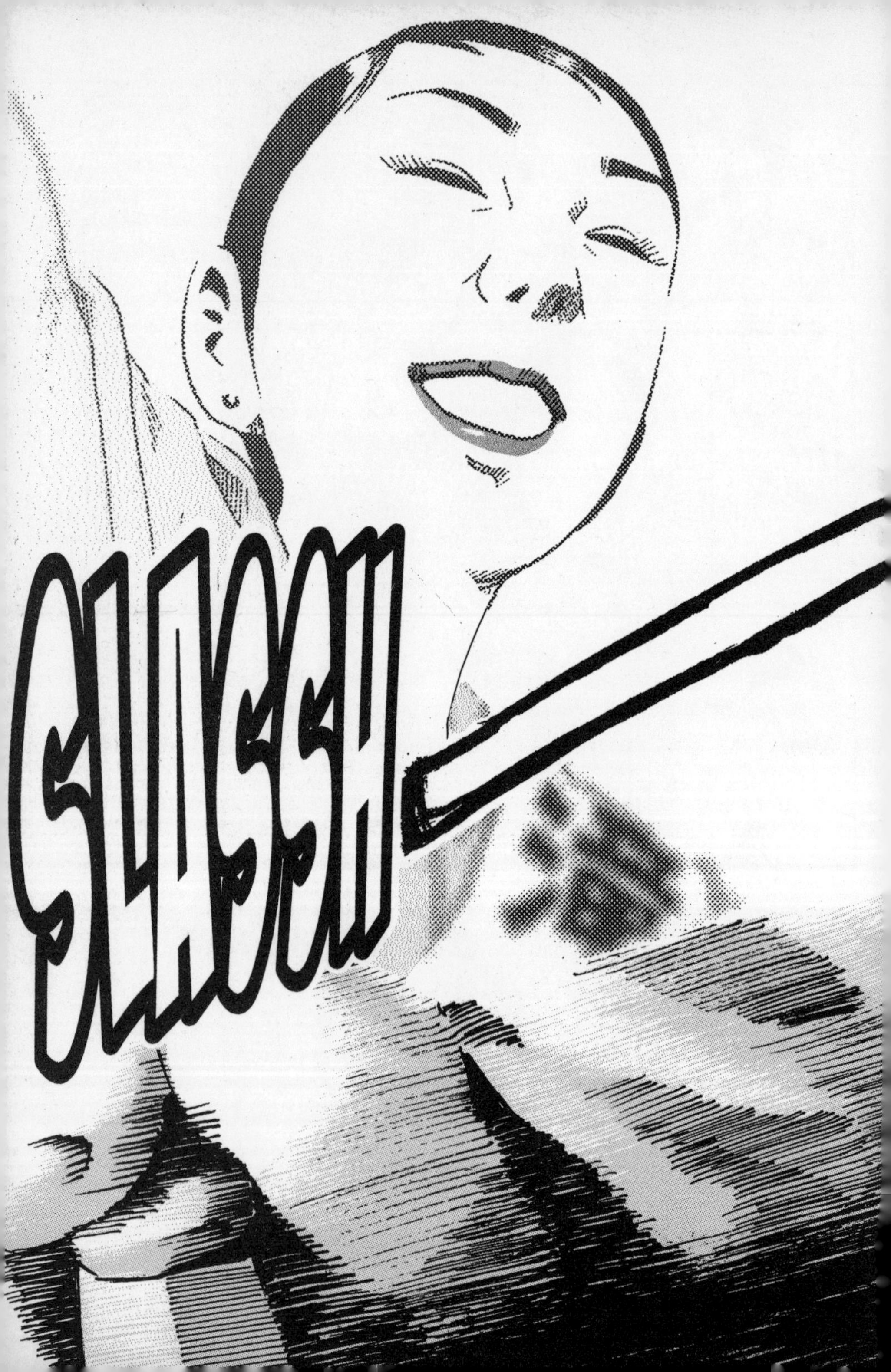
SLASH

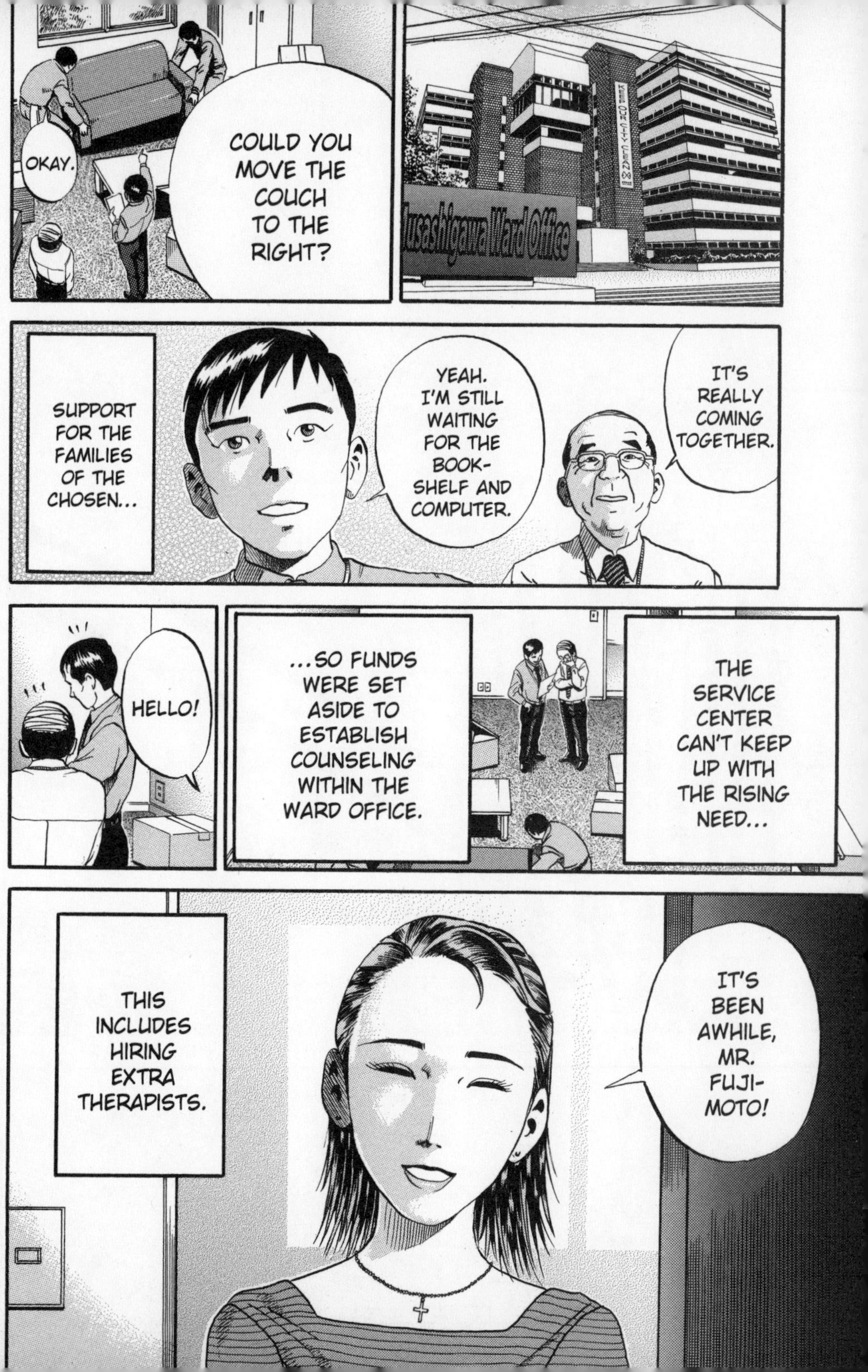
KEEP OUR CITY CLEAN
usashigawa Ward Office
COULD YOU MOVE THE COUCH TO THE RIGHT?
OKAY.
IT'S REALLY COMING TOGETHER.
YEAH. I'M STILL WAITING FOR THE BOOK-SHELF AND COMPUTER.
SUPPORT FOR THE FAMILIES OF THE CHOSEN...
THE SERVICE CENTER CAN'T KEEP UP WITH THE RISING NEED...
...SO FUNDS WERE SET ASIDE TO ESTABLISH COUNSELING WITHIN THE WARD OFFICE.
HELLO!
IT'S BEEN AWHILE, MR. FUJI-MOTO!
THIS INCLUDES HIRING EXTRA THERAPISTS.

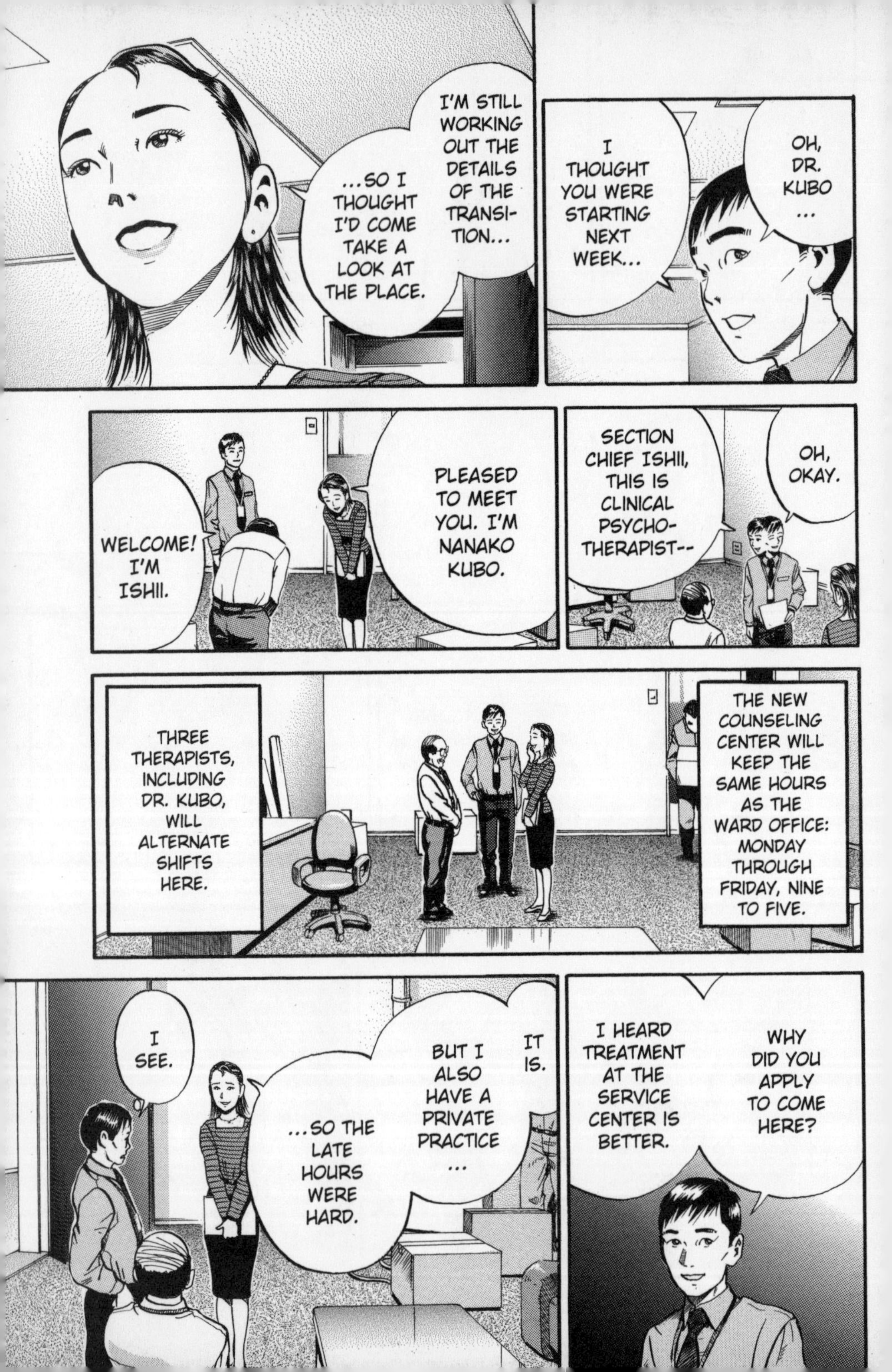
OH, DR. KUBO ...
I THOUGHT YOU WERE STARTING NEXT WEEK...
I'M STILL WORKING OUT THE DETAILS OF THE TRANSITION...
...SO I THOUGHT I'D COME TAKE A LOOK AT THE PLACE.
OH, OKAY.
SECTION CHIEF ISHII, THIS IS CLINICAL PSYCHOTHERAPIST--
PLEASED TO MEET YOU. I'M NANAKO KUBO.
WELCOME! I'M ISHII.
THE NEW COUNSELING CENTER WILL KEEP THE SAME HOURS AS THE WARD OFFICE: MONDAY THROUGH FRIDAY, NINE TO FIVE.
THREE THERAPISTS, INCLUDING DR. KUBO, WILL ALTERNATE SHIFTS HERE.
WHY DID YOU APPLY TO COME HERE?
I HEARD TREATMENT AT THE SERVICE CENTER IS BETTER.
IT IS.
BUT I ALSO HAVE A PRIVATE PRACTICE ...
...SO THE LATE HOURS WERE HARD.
I SEE.

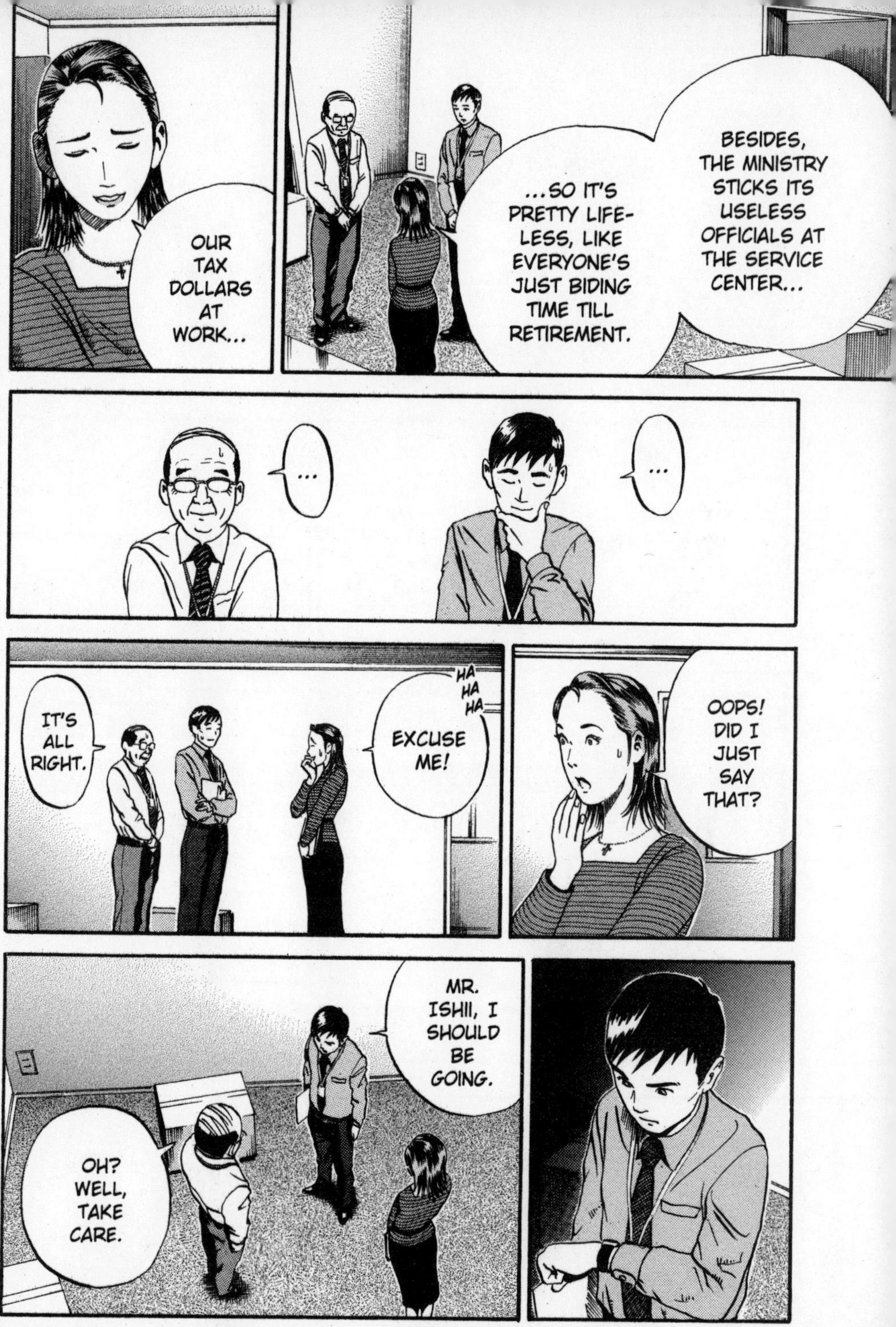
BESIDES, THE MINISTRY STICKS ITS USELESS OFFICIALS AT THE SERVICE CENTER...
...SO IT'S PRETTY LIFE-LESS, LIKE EVERYONE'S JUST BIDING TIME TILL RETIREMENT.
OUR TAX DOLLARS AT WORK...
...
...
OOPS! DID I JUST SAY THAT?
HA HA HA
EXCUSE ME!
IT'S ALL RIGHT.
MR. ISHII, I SHOULD BE GOING.
OH? WELL, TAKE CARE.

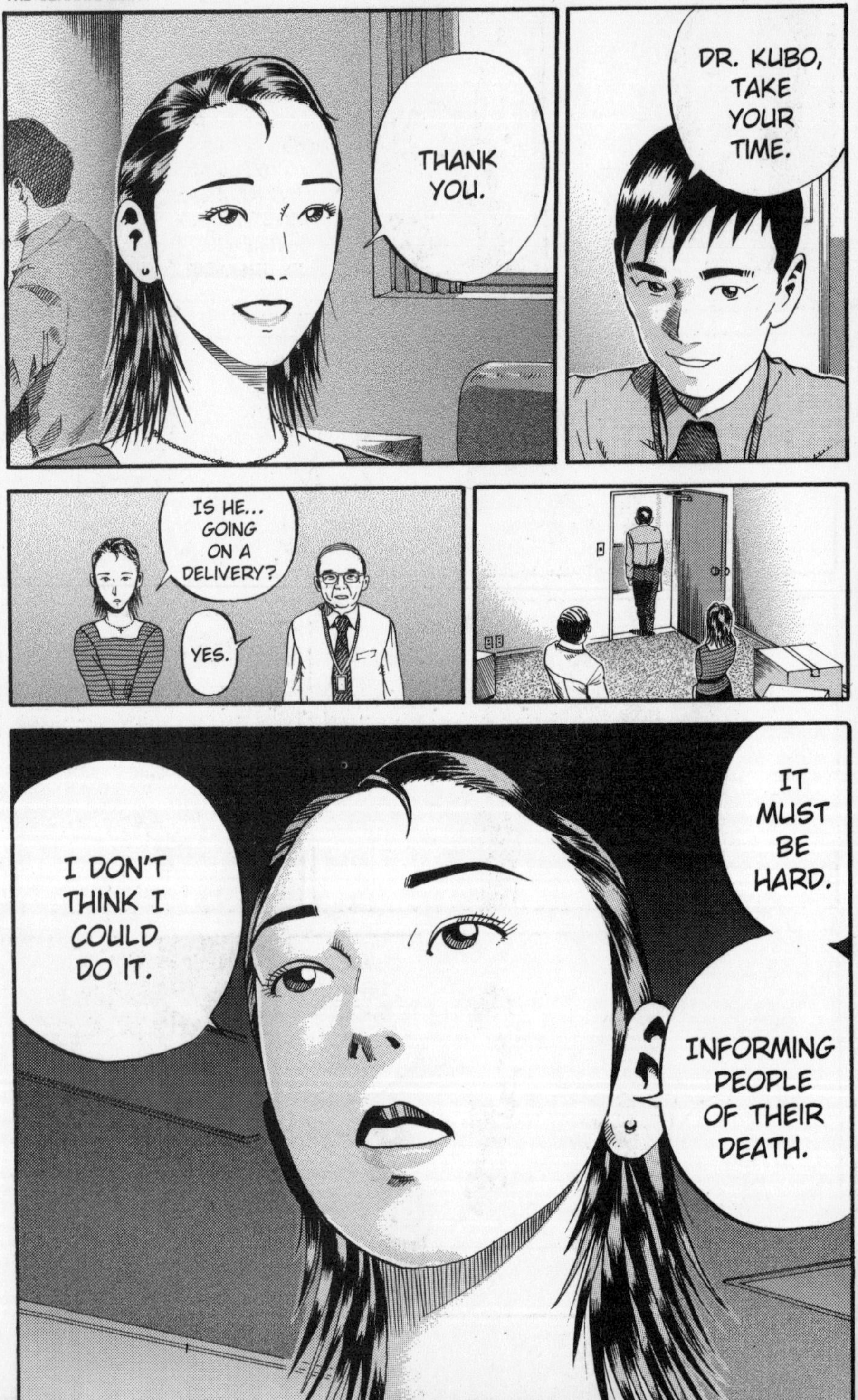
DR. KUBO, TAKE YOUR TIME.
THANK YOU.
IS HE... GOING ON A DELIVERY?
YES.
IT MUST BE HARD.
INFORMING PEOPLE OF THEIR DEATH.
I DON'T THINK I COULD DO IT.

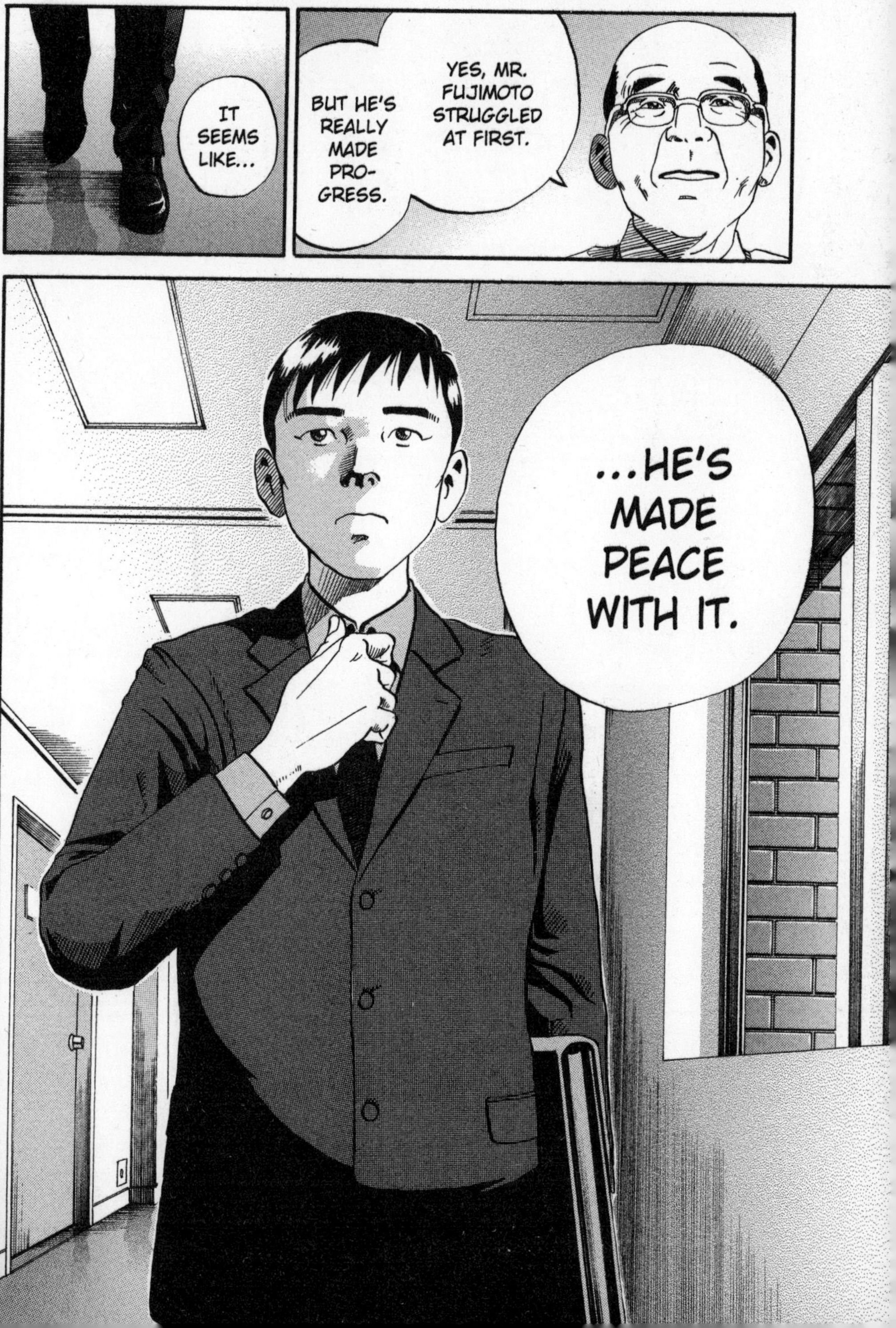
YES, MR. FUJIMOTO STRUGGLED AT FIRST.
BUT HE'S REALLY MADE PRO-GRESS.
IT SEEMS LIKE...
...HE'S MADE PEACE WITH IT.

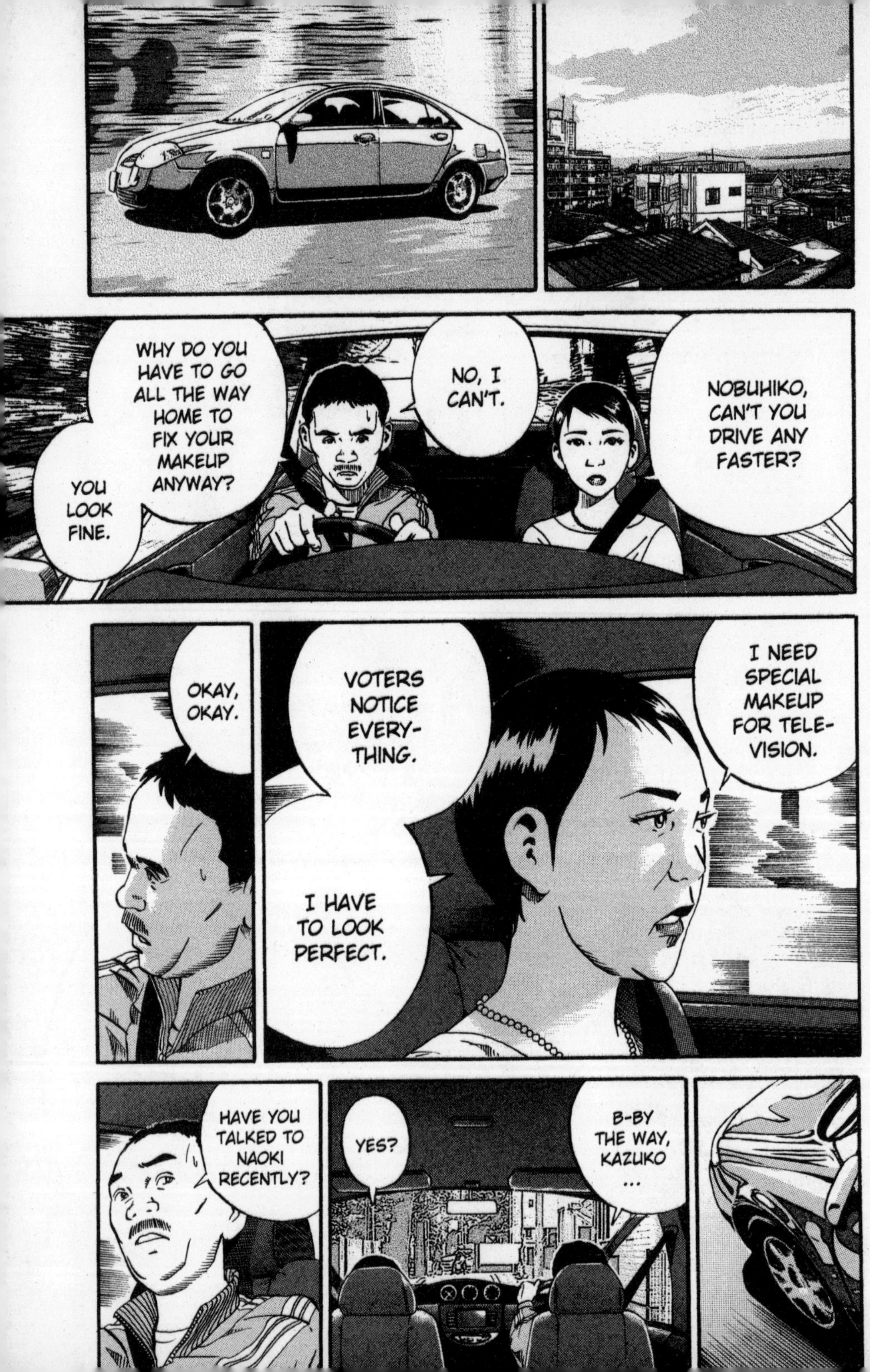
NOBUHIKO, CAN'T YOU DRIVE ANY FASTER?
NO, I CAN'T.
WHY DO YOU HAVE TO GO ALL THE WAY HOME TO FIX YOUR MAKEUP ANYWAY?
YOU LOOK FINE.
I NEED SPECIAL MAKEUP FOR TELE-VISION.
VOTERS NOTICE EVERY-THING.
I HAVE TO LOOK PERFECT.
OKAY, OKAY.
B-BY THE WAY, KAZUKO ...
YES?
HAVE YOU TALKED TO NAOKI RECENTLY?

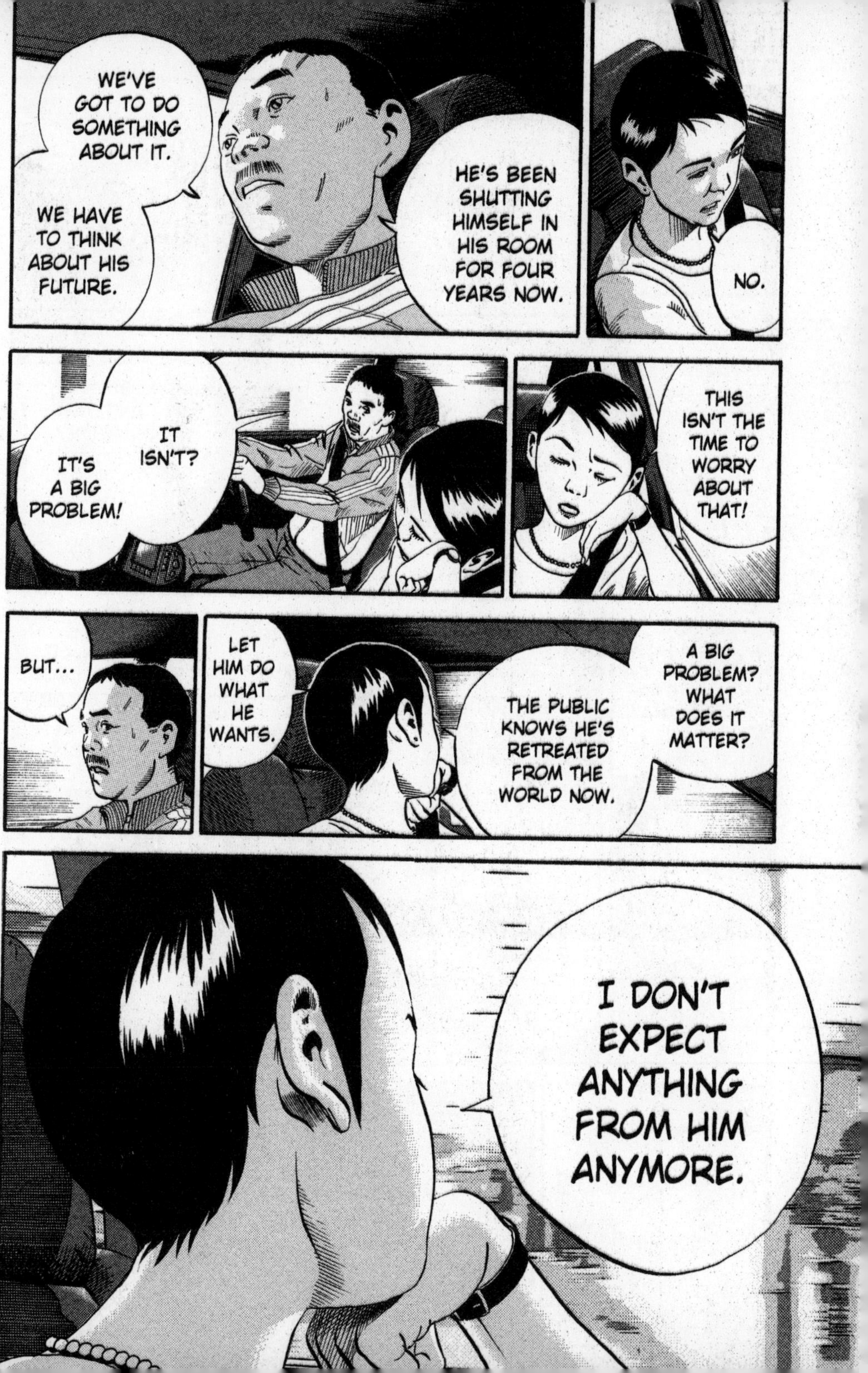
NO.
HE'S BEEN SHUTTING HIMSELF IN HIS ROOM FOR FOUR YEARS NOW.
WE'VE GOT TO DO SOMETHING ABOUT IT.
WE HAVE TO THINK ABOUT HIS FUTURE.
THIS ISN'T THE TIME TO WORRY ABOUT THAT!
IT ISN'T?
IT'S A BIG PROBLEM!
A BIG PROBLEM? WHAT DOES IT MATTER?
THE PUBLIC KNOWS HE'S RETREATED FROM THE WORLD NOW.
LET HIM DO WHAT HE WANTS.
BUT...
I DON'T EXPECT ANYTHING FROM HIM ANYMORE.

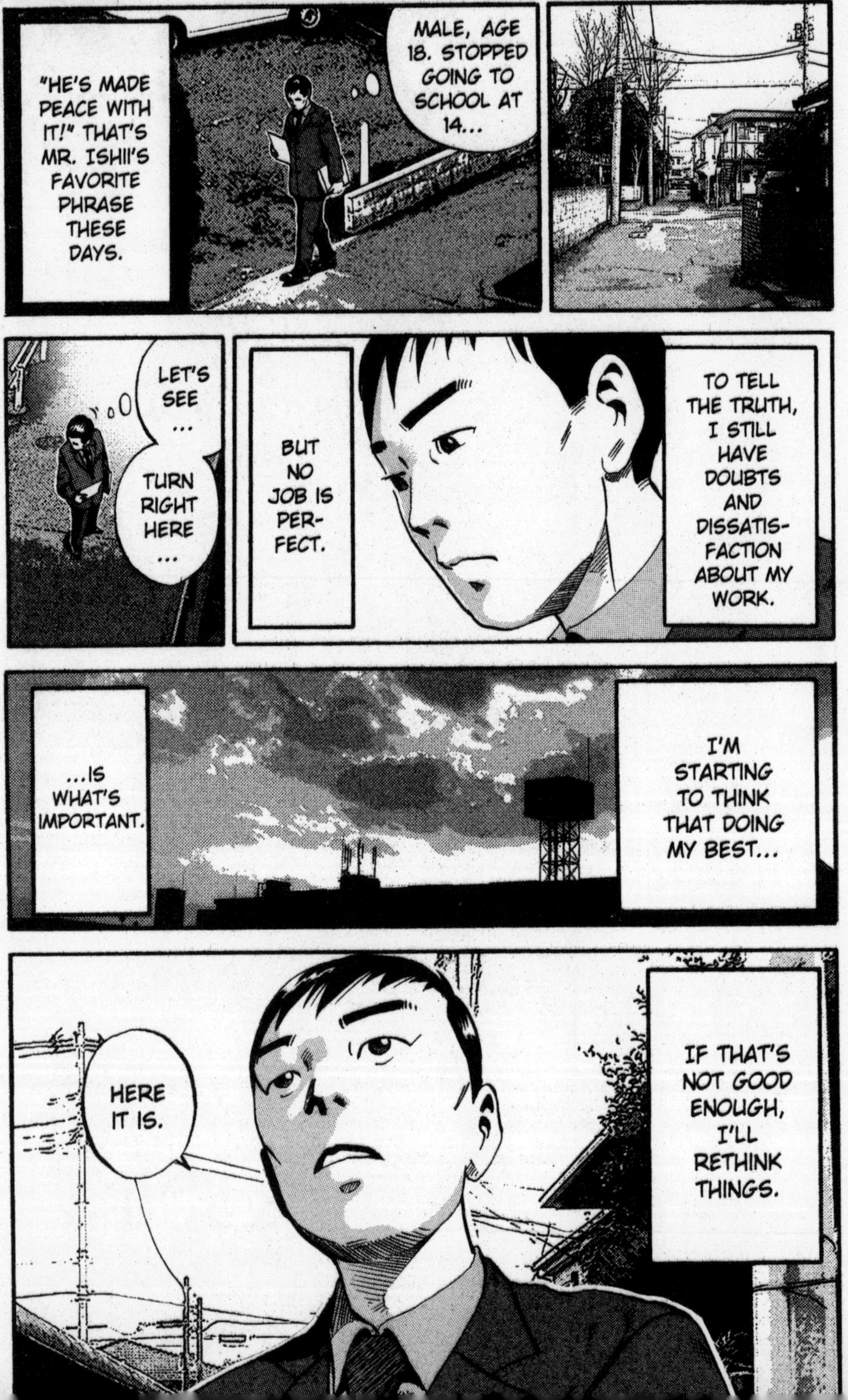
MALE, AGE 18. STOPPED GOING TO SCHOOL AT 14...
"HE'S MADE PEACE WITH IT!" THAT'S MR. ISHII'S FAVORITE PHRASE THESE DAYS.
TO TELL THE TRUTH, I STILL HAVE DOUBTS AND DISSATIS-FACTION ABOUT MY WORK.
BUT NO JOB IS PER-FECT.
LET'S SEE ...
TURN RIGHT HERE ...
I'M STARTING TO THINK THAT DOING MY BEST...
...IS WHAT'S IMPORTANT.
IF THAT'S NOT GOOD ENOUGH, I'LL RETHINK THINGS.
HERE IT IS.

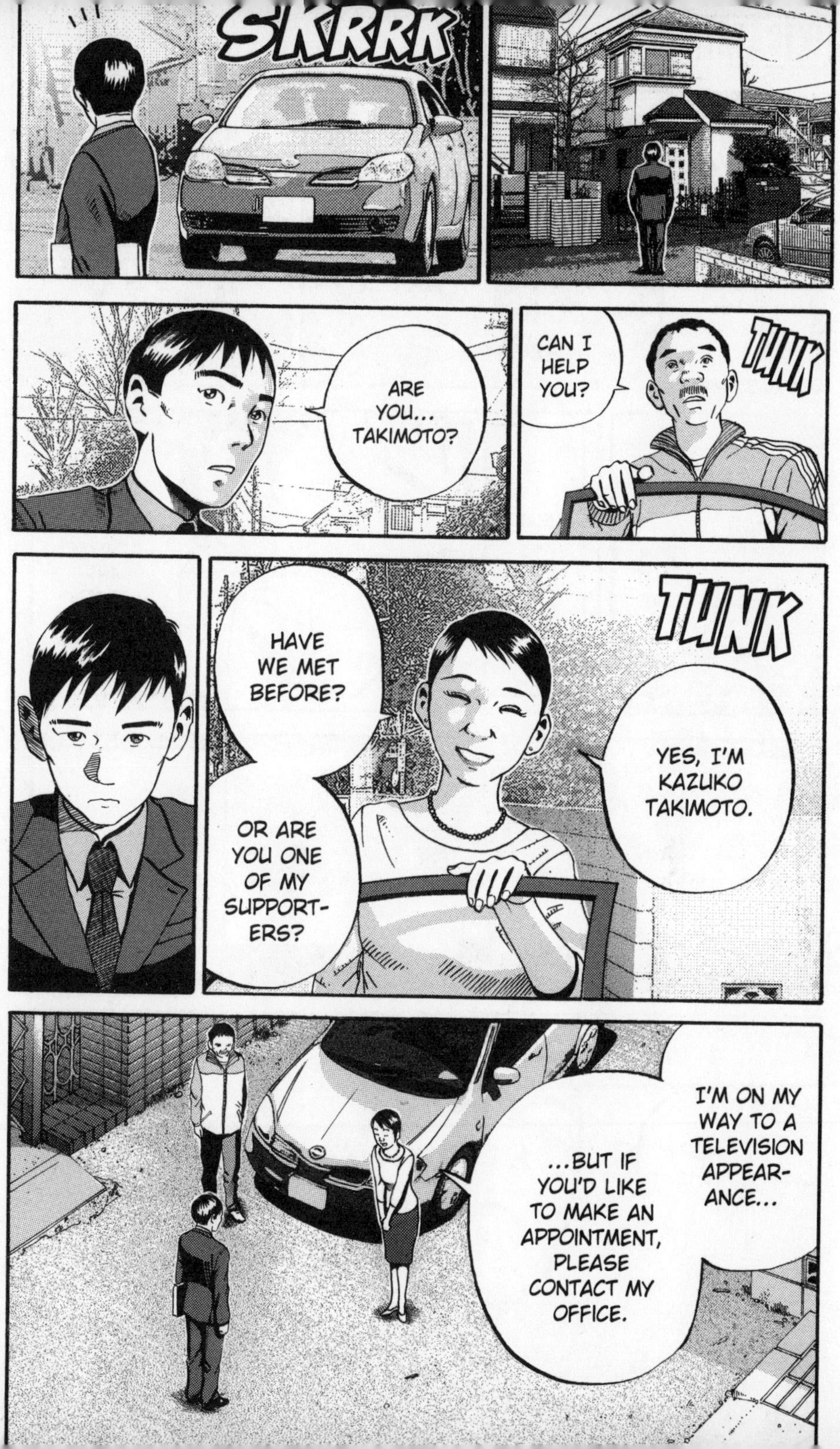
SKRRK
CAN I HELP YOU?
TUNK
ARE YOU... TAKIMOTO?
TUNK
YES, I'M KAZUKO TAKIMOTO.
HAVE WE MET BEFORE?
OR ARE YOU ONE OF MY SUPPORT-ERS?
I'M ON MY WAY TO A TELEVISION APPEAR-ANCE...
...BUT IF YOU'D LIKE TO MAKE AN APPOINTMENT, PLEASE CONTACT MY OFFICE.

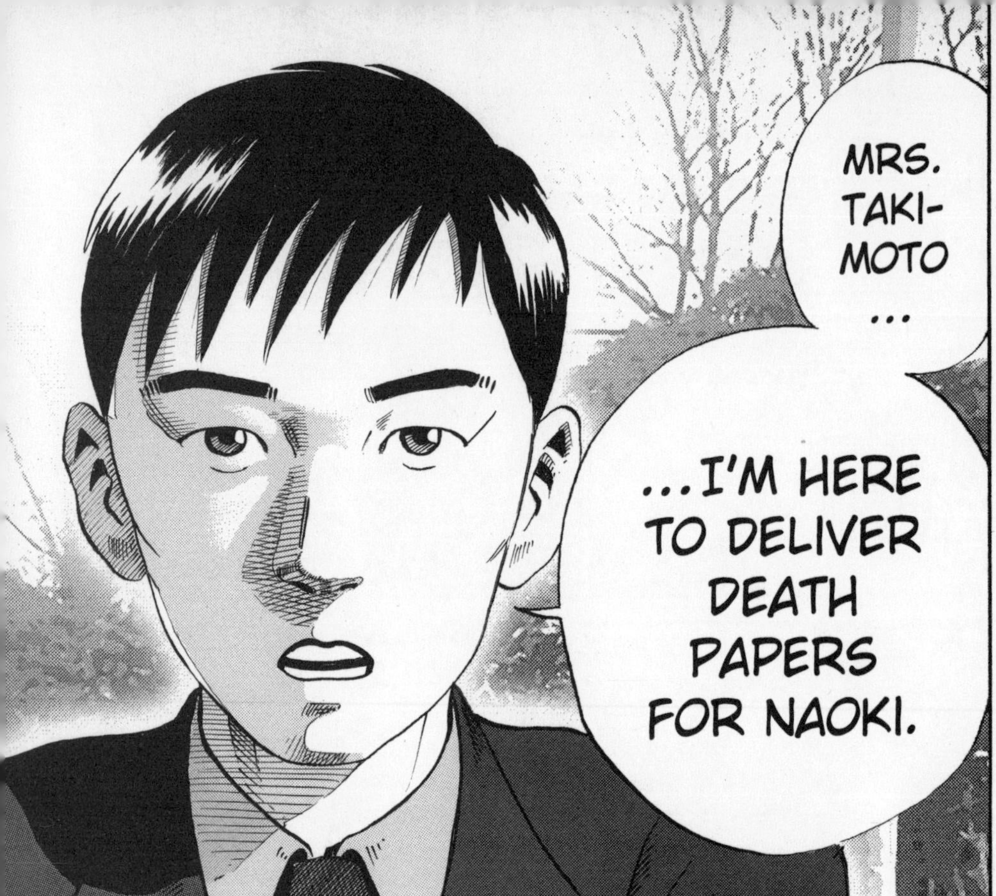
MRS. TAKI-MOTO ...
...I'M HERE TO DELIVER DEATH PAPERS FOR NAOKI.
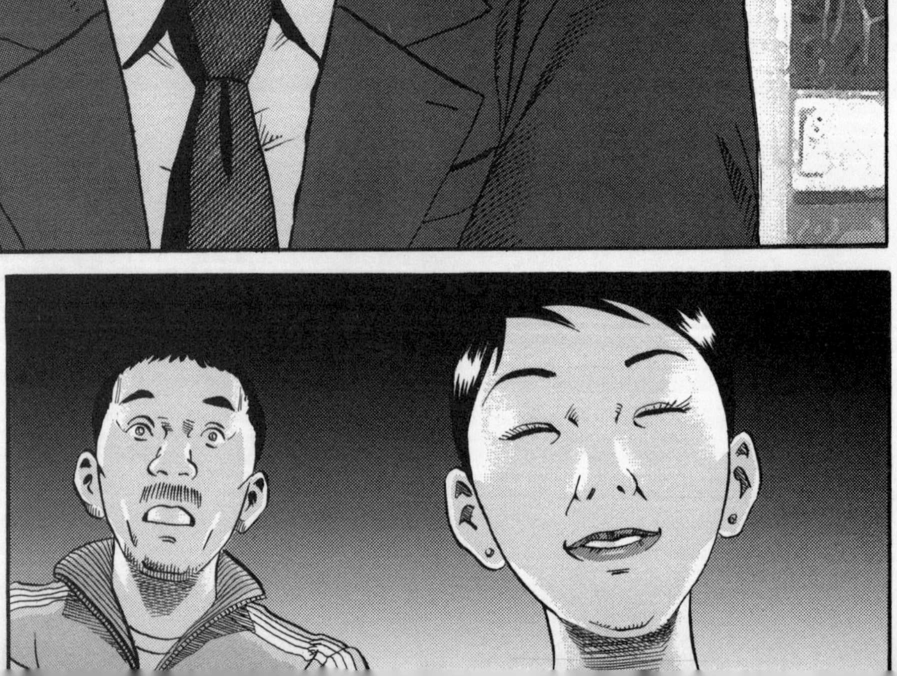

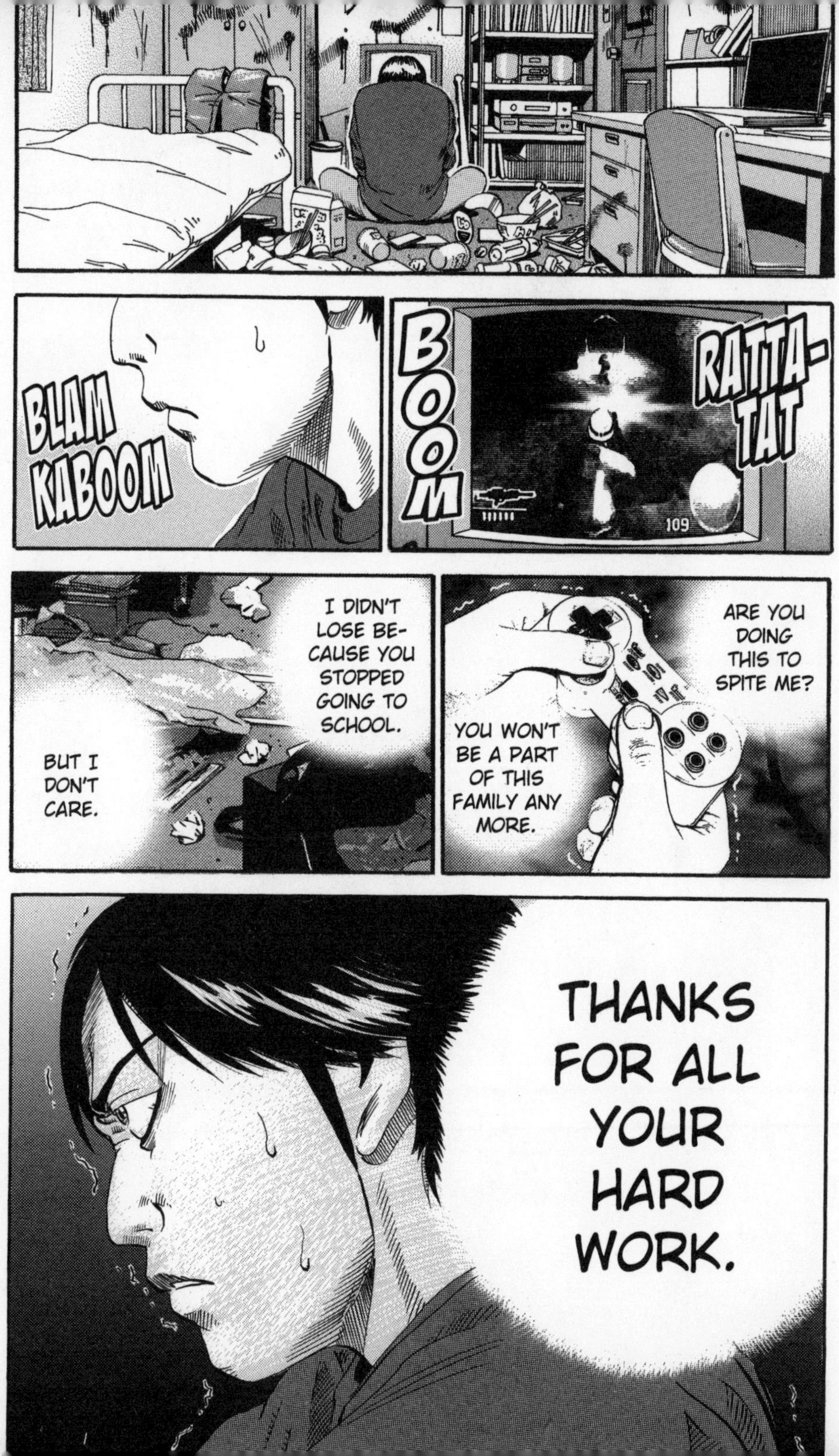
RATTA-TAT
BOOM
BLAM KABOOM
ARE YOU DOING THIS TO SPITE ME?
YOU WON'T BE A PART OF THIS FAMILY ANY MORE.
I DIDN'T LOSE BE-CAUSE YOU STOPPED GOING TO SCHOOL.
BUT I DON'T CARE.
THANKS FOR ALL YOUR HARD WORK.

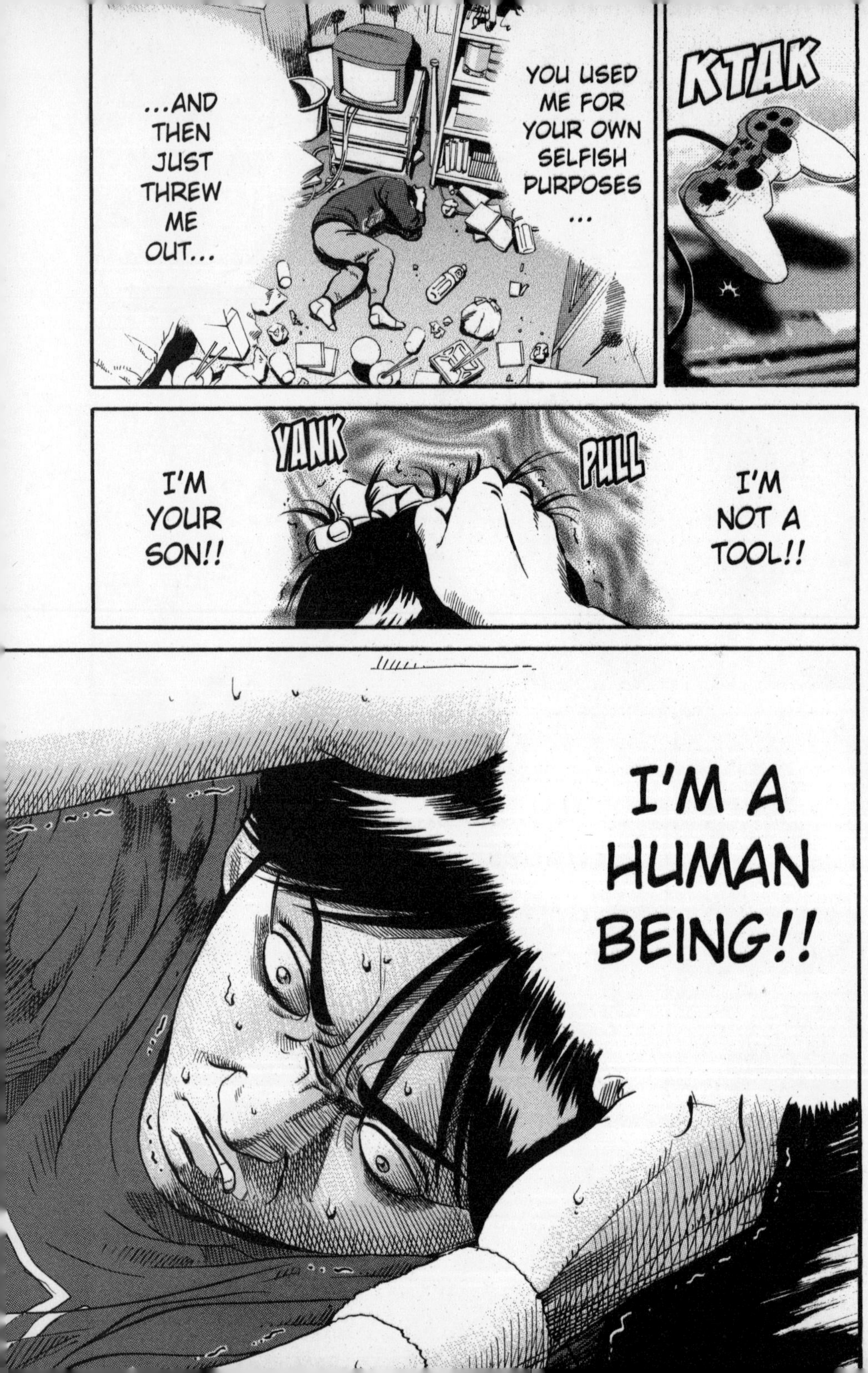
KTAK
YOU USED ME FOR YOUR OWN SELFISH PURPOSES...
...AND THEN JUST THREW ME OUT...
I'M NOT A TOOL!!
PULL
YANK
I'M YOUR SON!!
I'M A HUMAN BEING!!

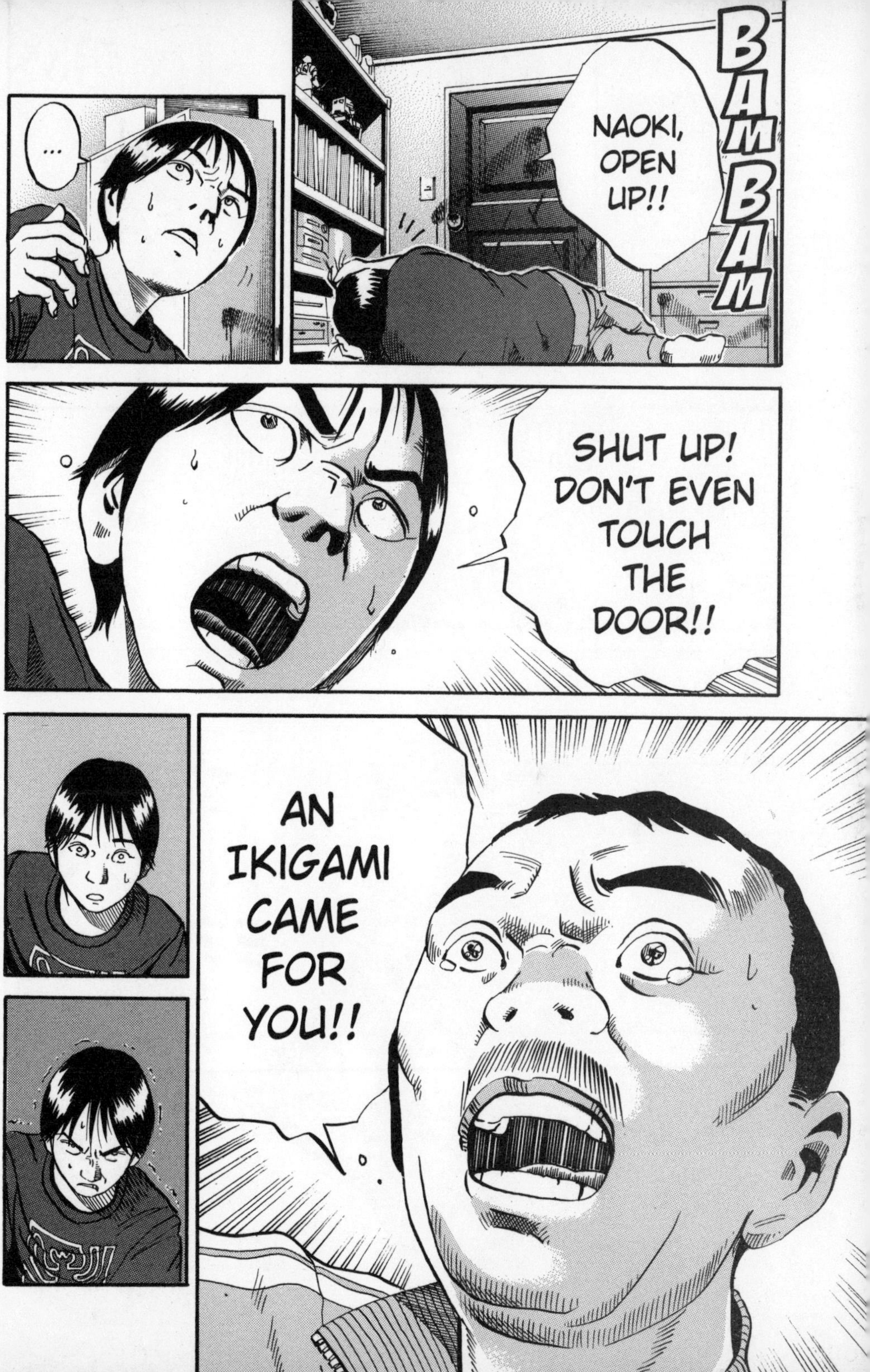
BAM BAM
NAOKI, OPEN UP!!
...
SHUT UP! DON'T EVEN TOUCH THE DOOR!!
AN IKIGAMI CAME FOR YOU!!

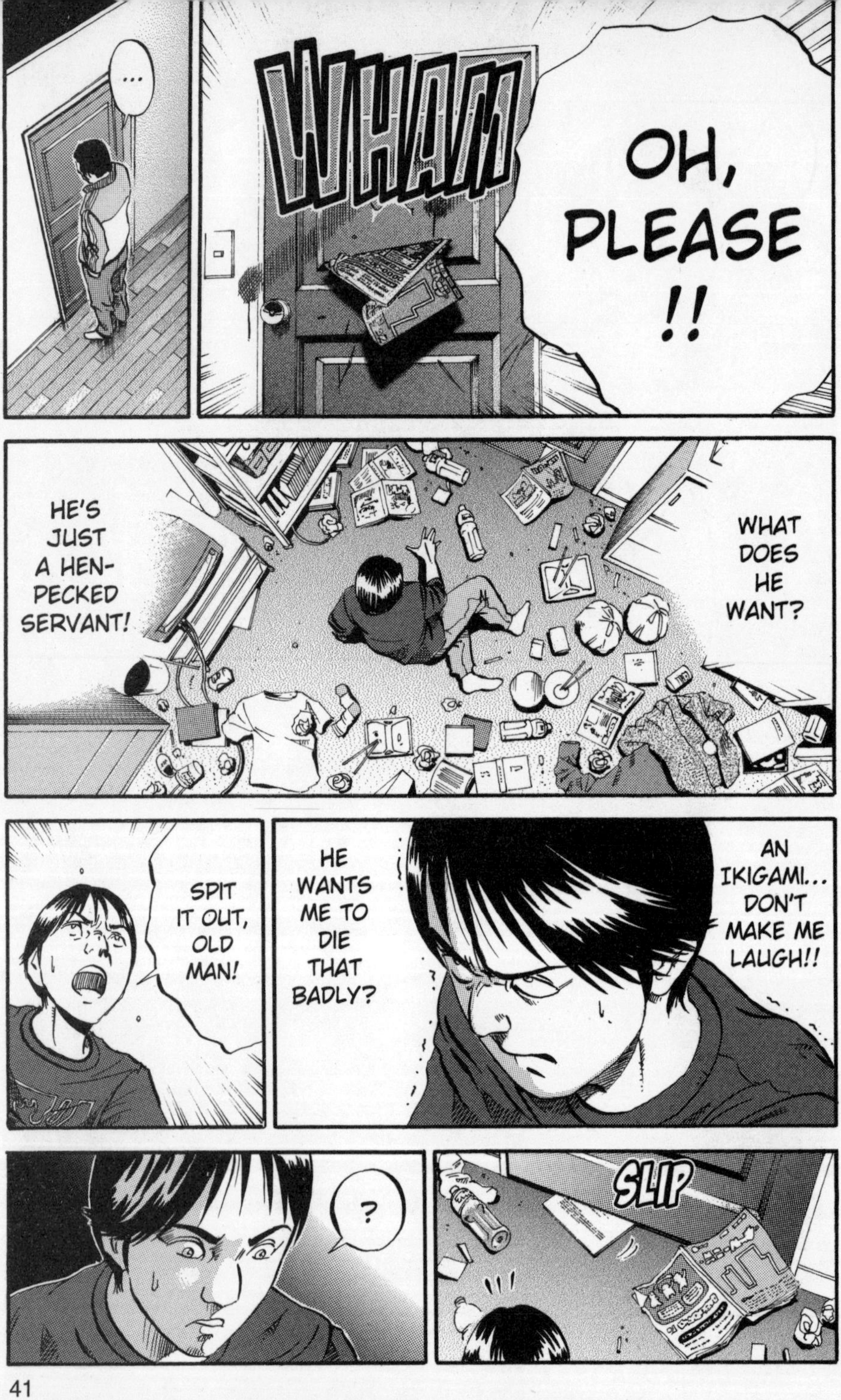
WHAM
OH, PLEASE!!
...
WHAT DOES HE WANT?
HE'S JUST A HEN-PECKED SERVANT!
AN IKIGAMI... DON'T MAKE ME LAUGH!!
HE WANTS ME TO DIE THAT BADLY?
SPIT IT OUT, OLD MAN!
SLIP
?

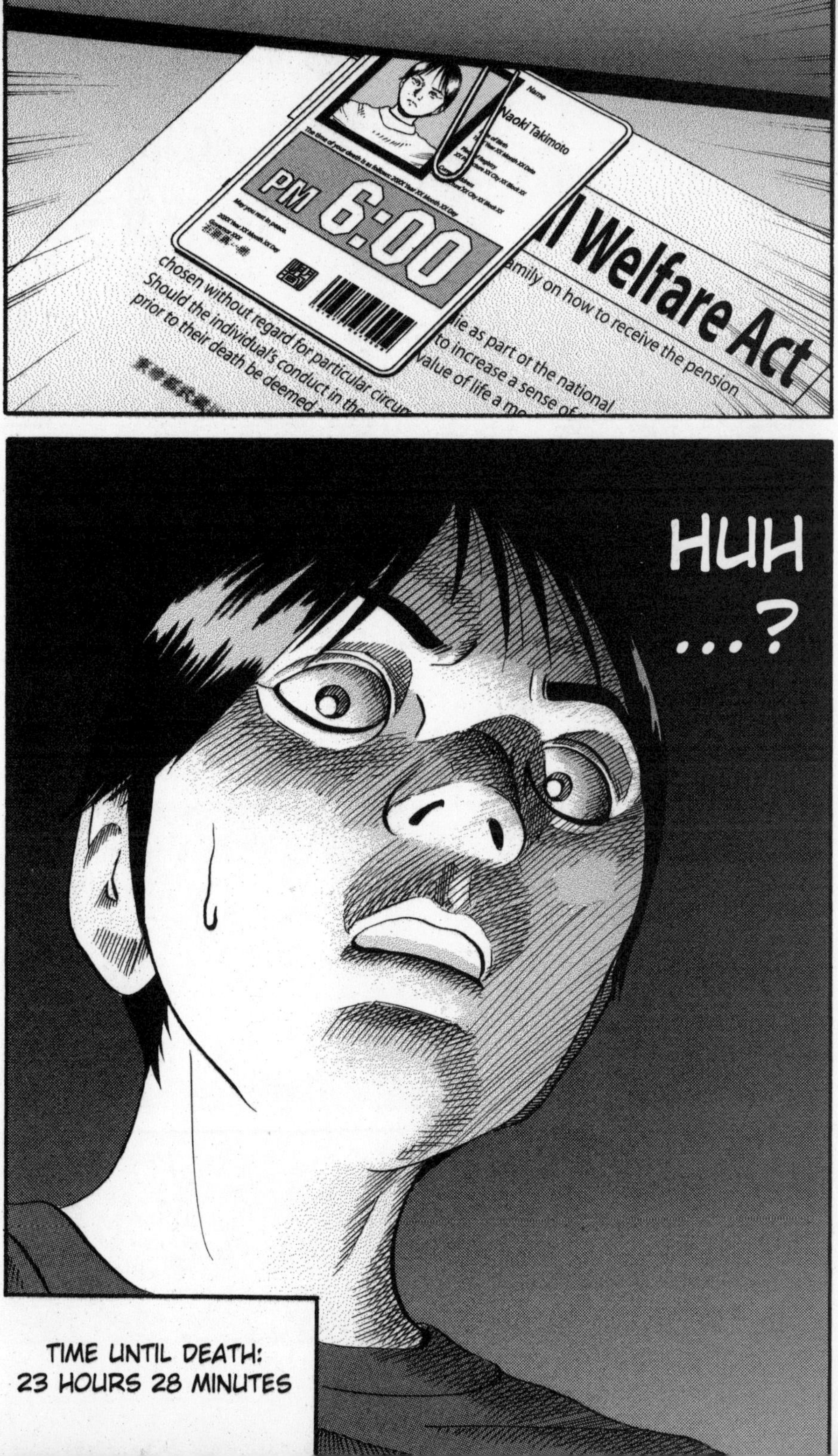

Name
Naoki Takimoto
PM 6:00
Welfare Act
HUH ...?
TIME UNTIL DEATH:
23 HOURS 28 MINUTES

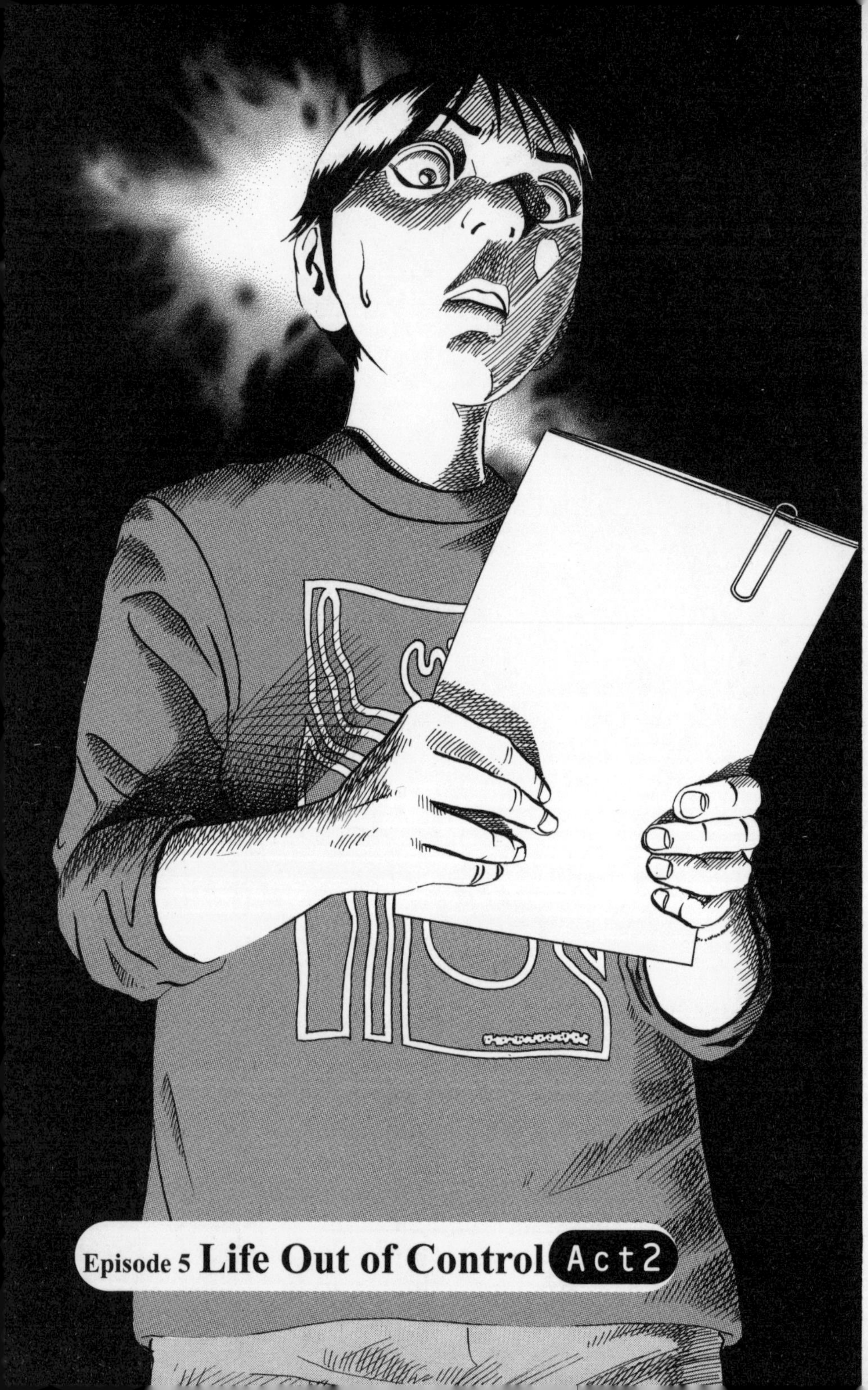
Episode 5 Life Out of Control Act 2

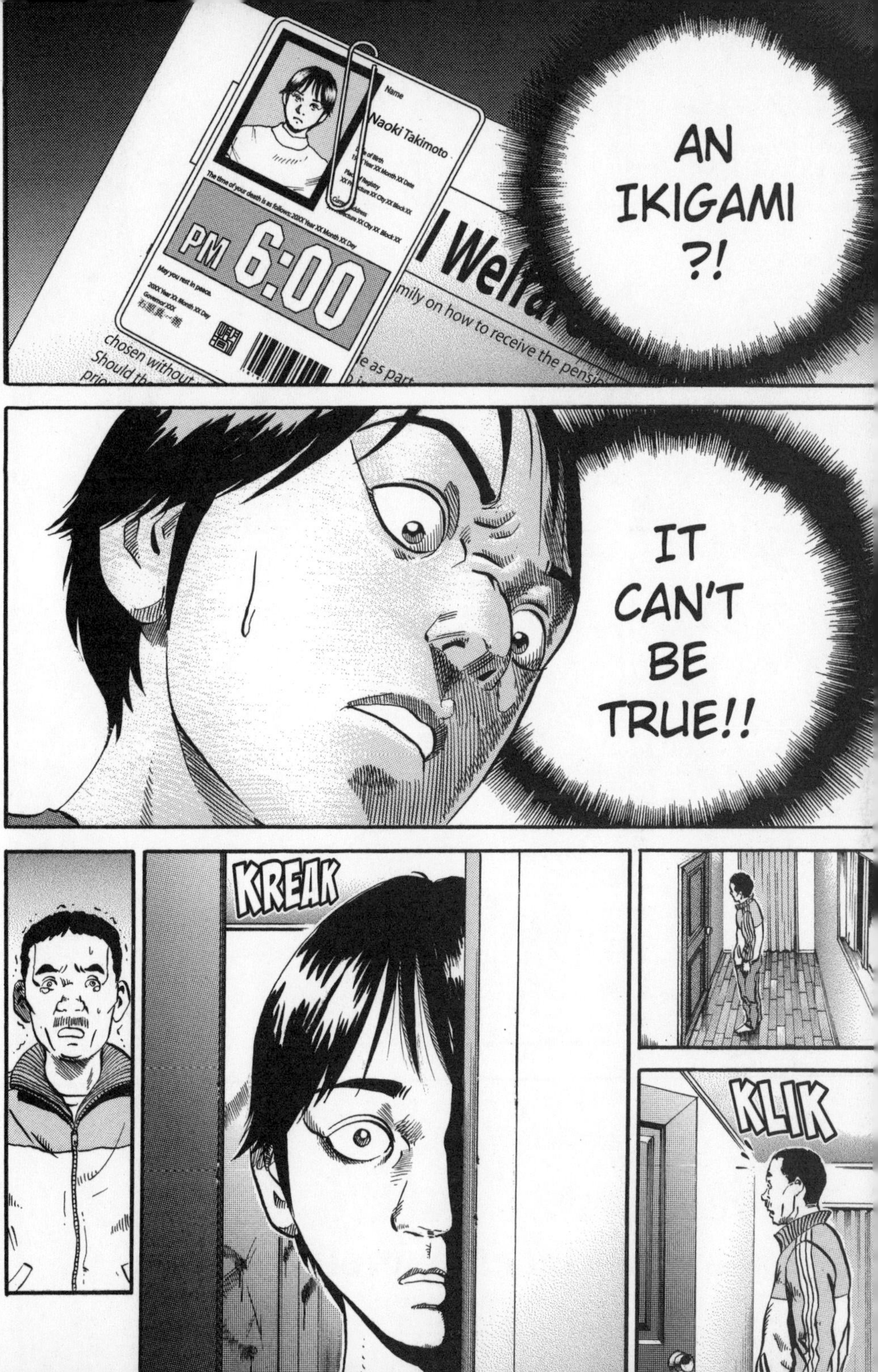
Name
Naoki Takimoto
PM 6:00
May you rest in peace.
l Welfare
mily on how to receive the pensi
chosen without
AN IKIGAMI ?!
IT CAN'T BE TRUE!!
KLIK
KREAK

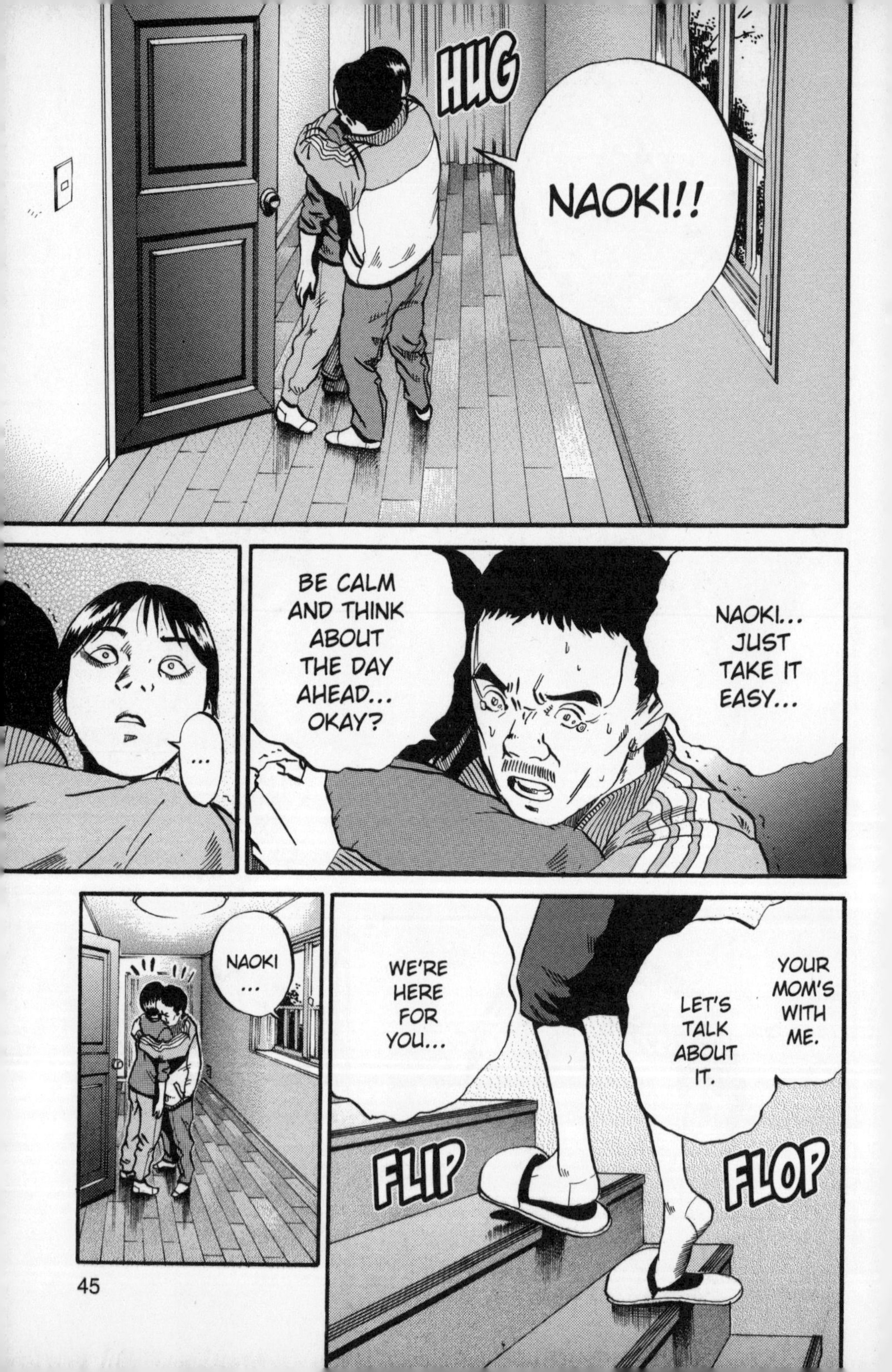
HUG
NAOKI!!
NAOKI... JUST TAKE IT EASY...
BE CALM AND THINK ABOUT THE DAY AHEAD... OKAY?
...
YOUR MOM'S WITH ME.
LET'S TALK ABOUT IT.
WE'RE HERE FOR YOU...
FLIP
FLOP
NAOKI ...

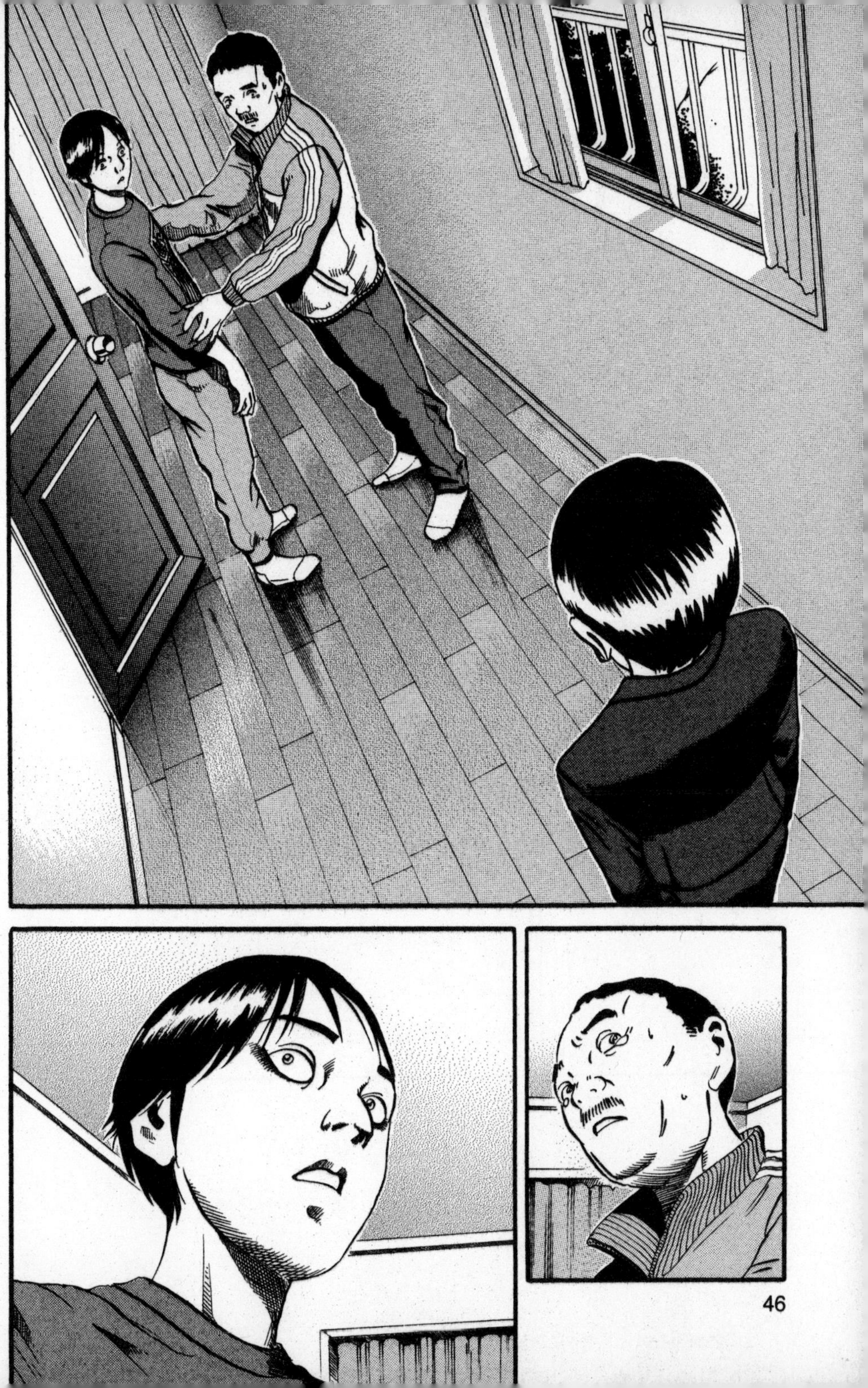

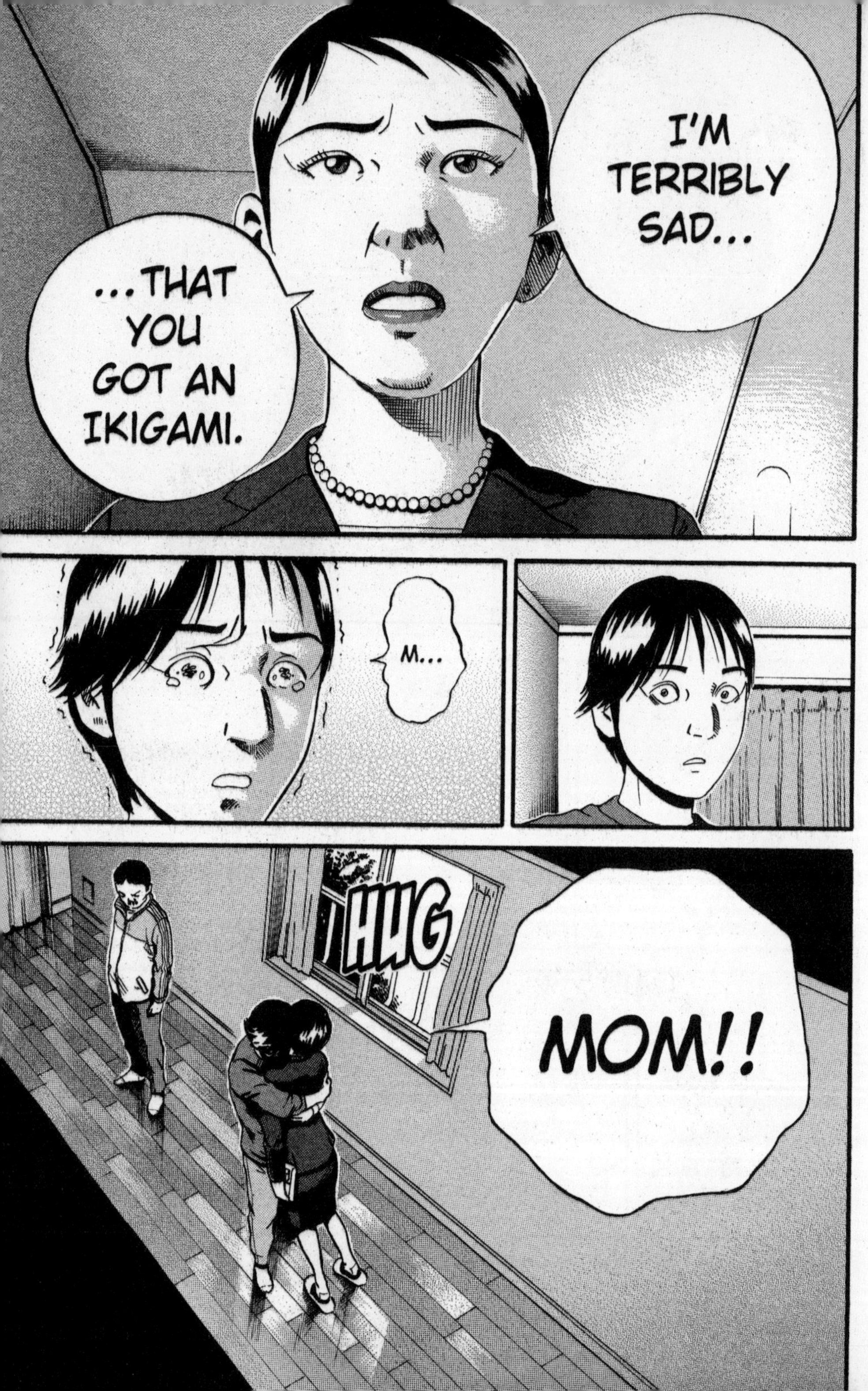
I'M TERRIBLY SAD...
...THAT YOU GOT AN IKIGAMI.
M...
HUG
MOM!!

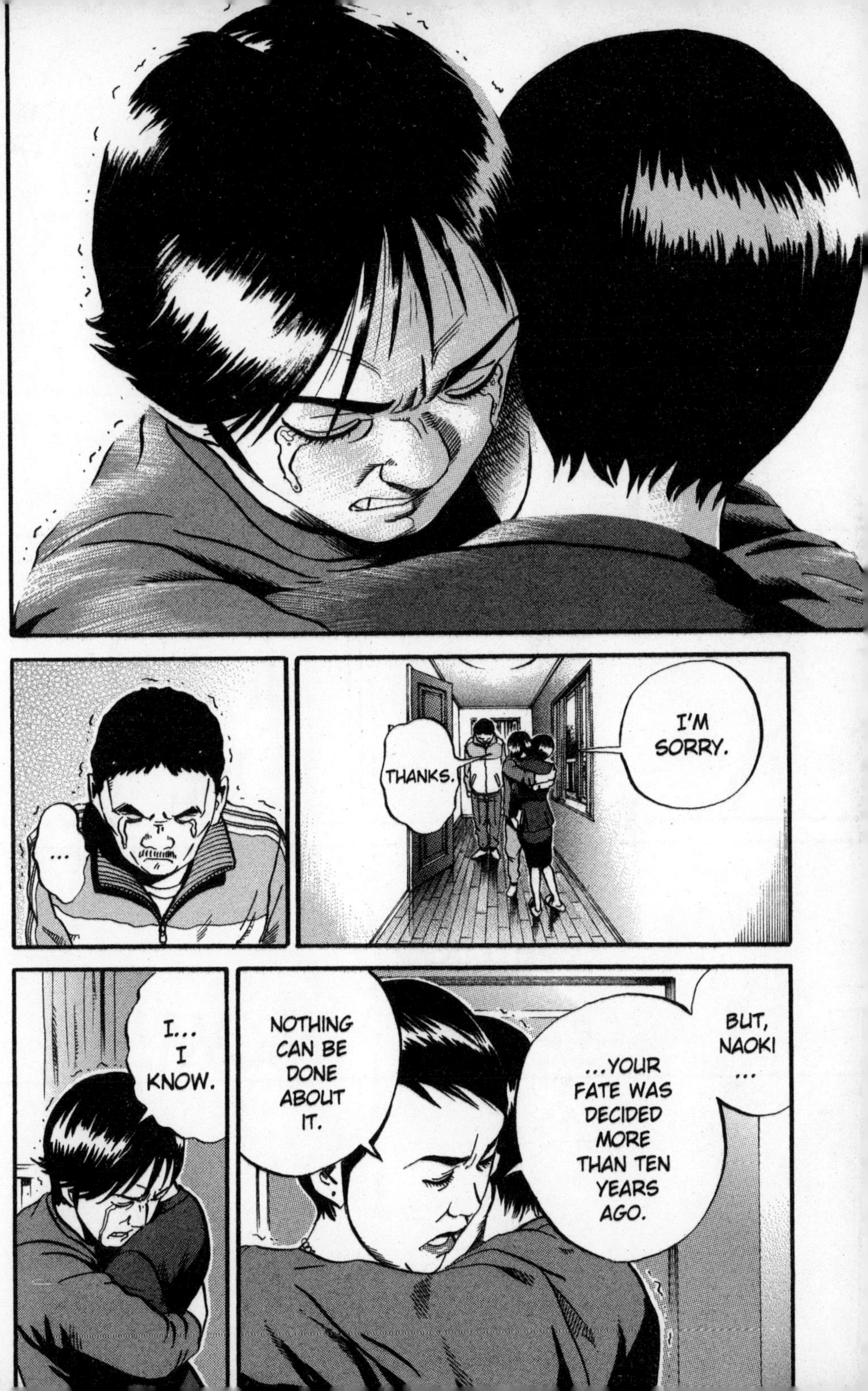
I'M SORRY.
THANKS.
...
BUT, NAOKI...
...YOUR FATE WAS DECIDED MORE THAN TEN YEARS AGO.
NOTHING CAN BE DONE ABOUT IT.
I... I KNOW.

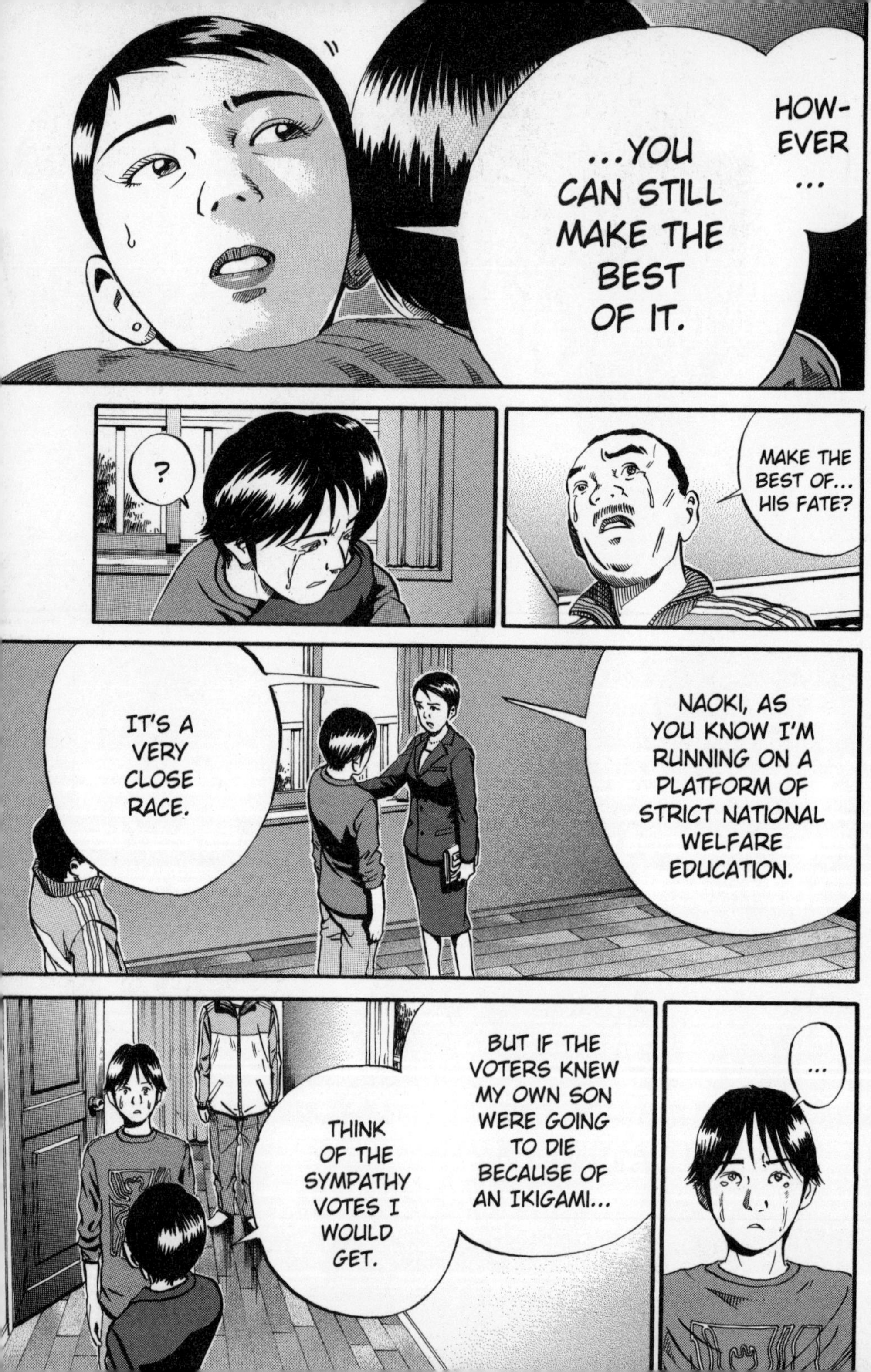
HOW-EVER...
...YOU CAN STILL MAKE THE BEST OF IT.
MAKE THE BEST OF... HIS FATE?
?
NAOKI, AS YOU KNOW I'M RUNNING ON A PLATFORM OF STRICT NATIONAL WELFARE EDUCATION.
IT'S A VERY CLOSE RACE.
...
BUT IF THE VOTERS KNEW MY OWN SON WERE GOING TO DIE BECAUSE OF AN IKIGAMI...
THINK OF THE SYMPATHY VOTES I WOULD GET.

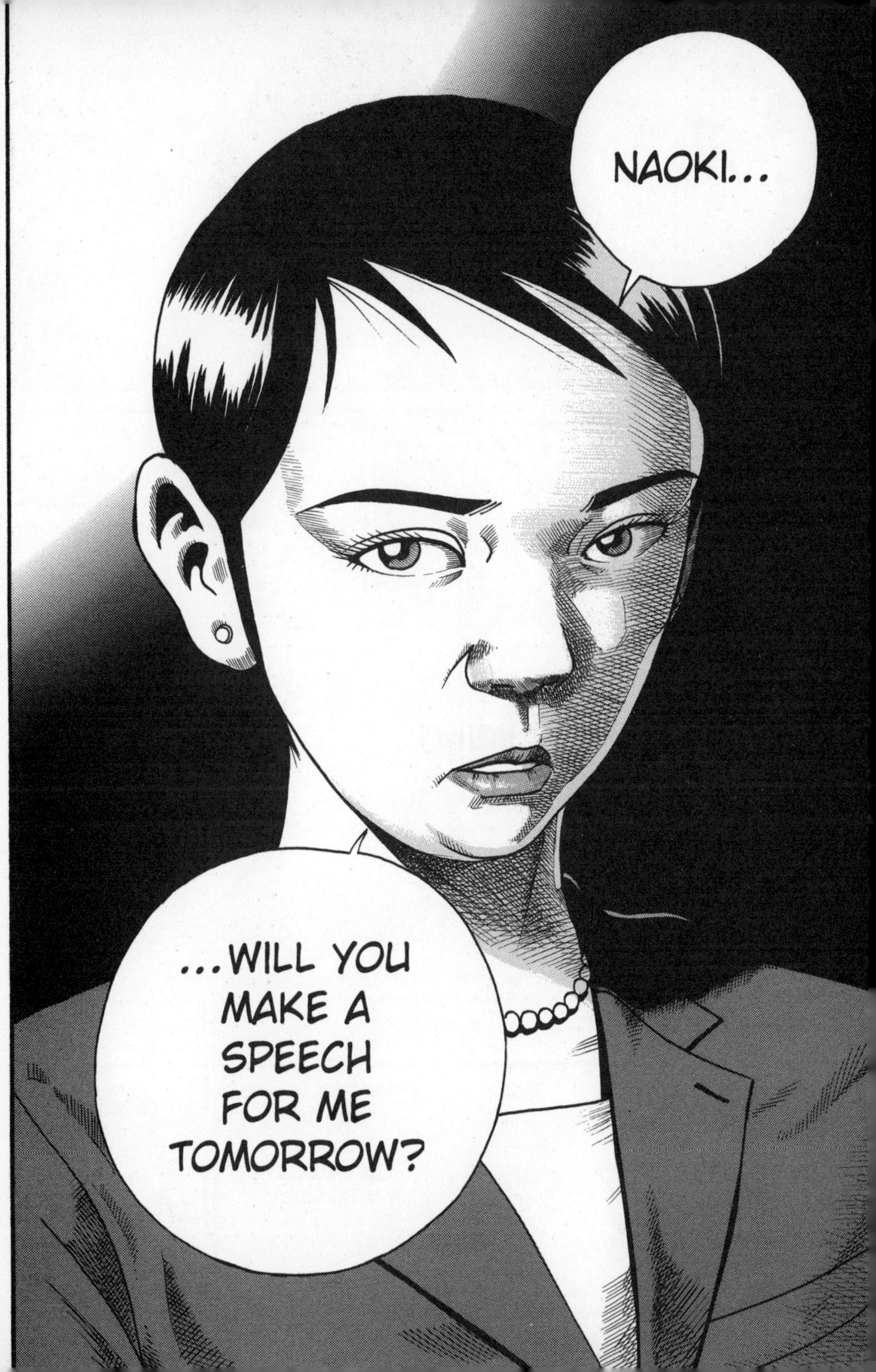
NAOKI...
...WILL YOU MAKE A SPEECH FOR ME TOMORROW?

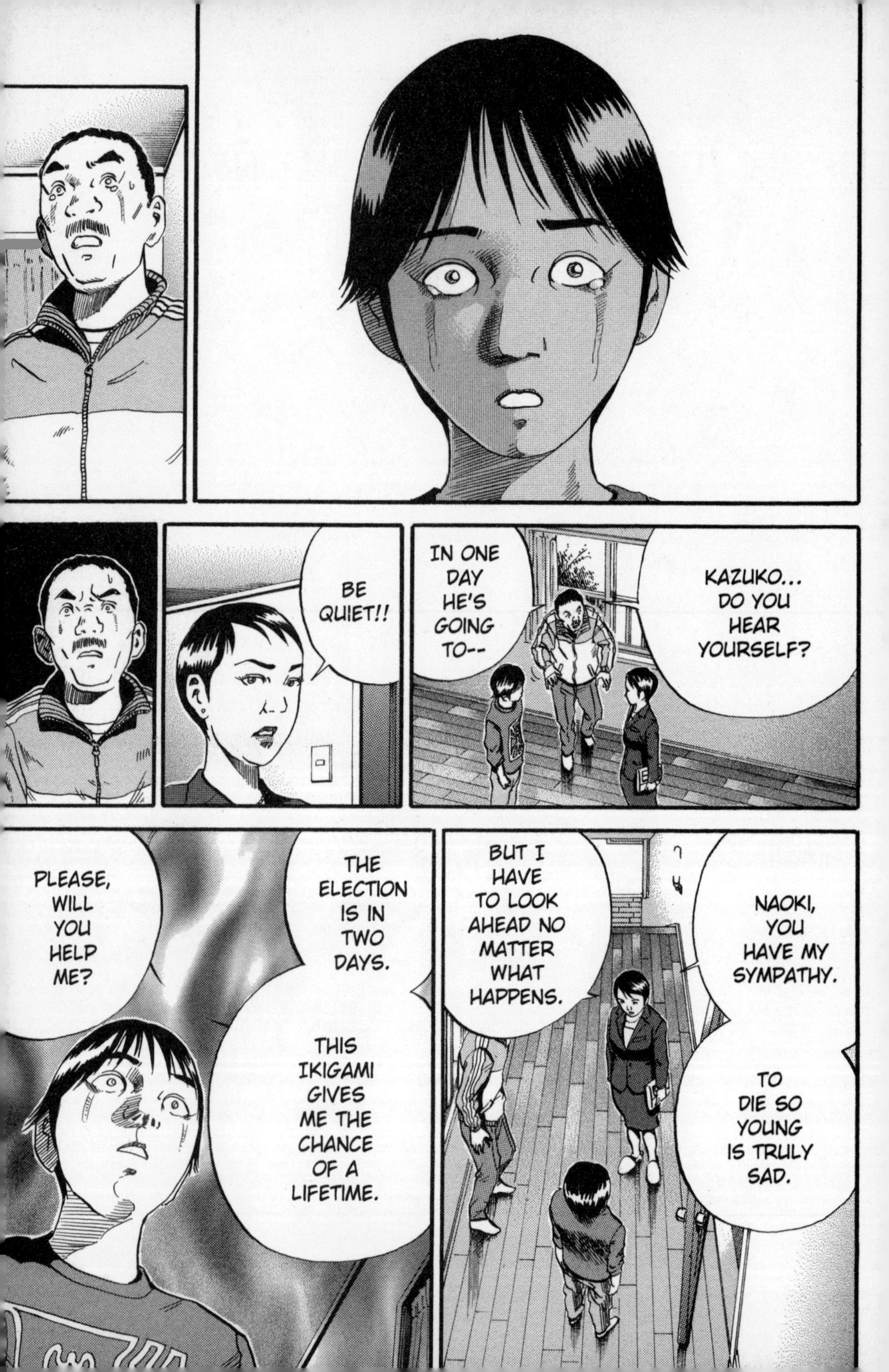
KAZUKO... DO YOU HEAR YOURSELF?
IN ONE DAY HE'S GOING TO--
BE QUIET!!
NAOKI, YOU HAVE MY SYMPATHY.
TO DIE SO YOUNG IS TRULY SAD.
BUT I HAVE TO LOOK AHEAD NO MATTER WHAT HAPPENS.
THE ELECTION IS IN TWO DAYS.
THIS IKIGAMI GIVES ME THE CHANCE OF A LIFETIME.
PLEASE, WILL YOU HELP ME?

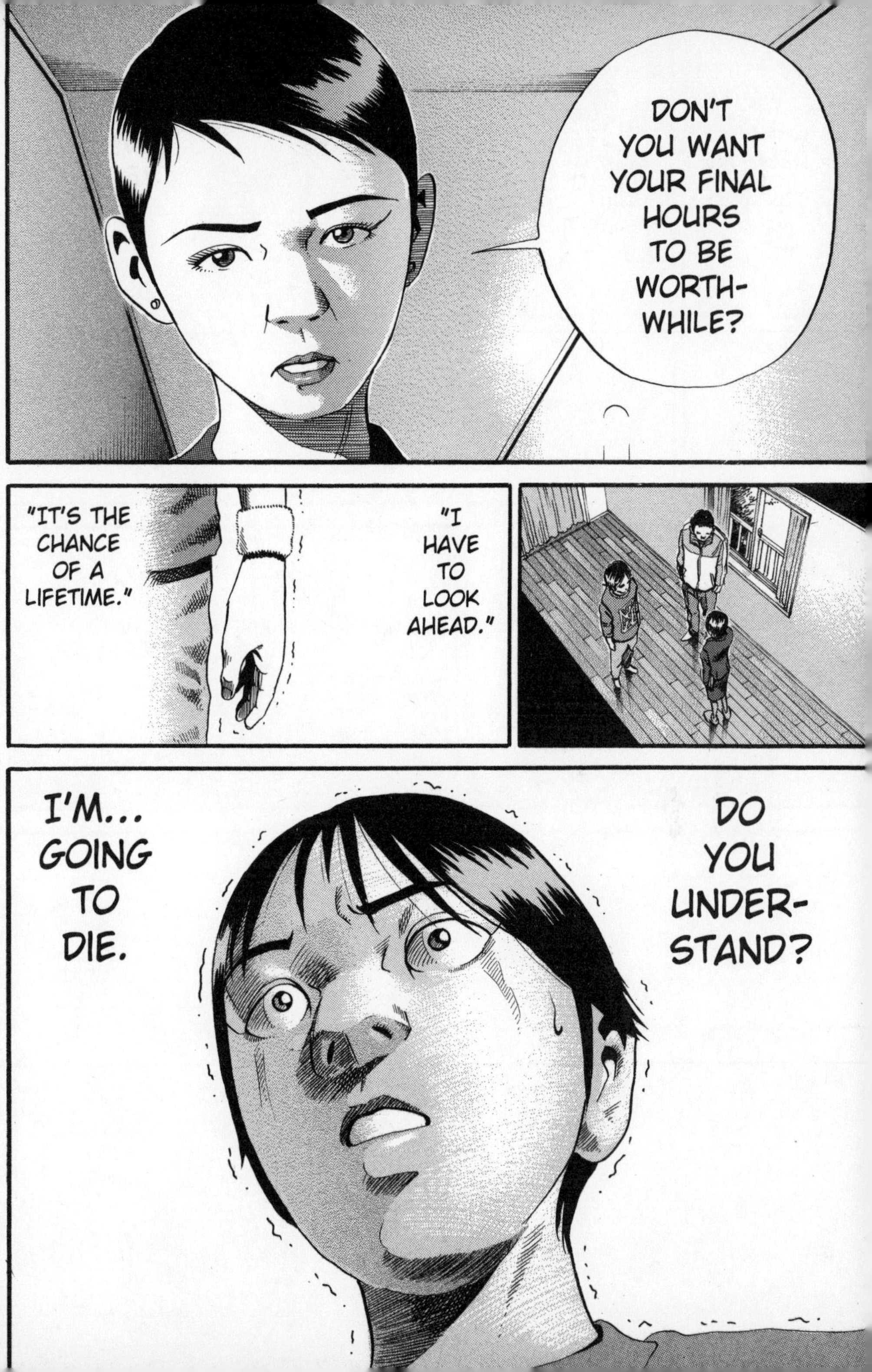
DON'T YOU WANT YOUR FINAL HOURS TO BE WORTH-WHILE?
"I HAVE TO LOOK AHEAD."
"IT'S THE CHANCE OF A LIFETIME."
DO YOU UNDER-STAND?
I'M... GOING TO DIE.

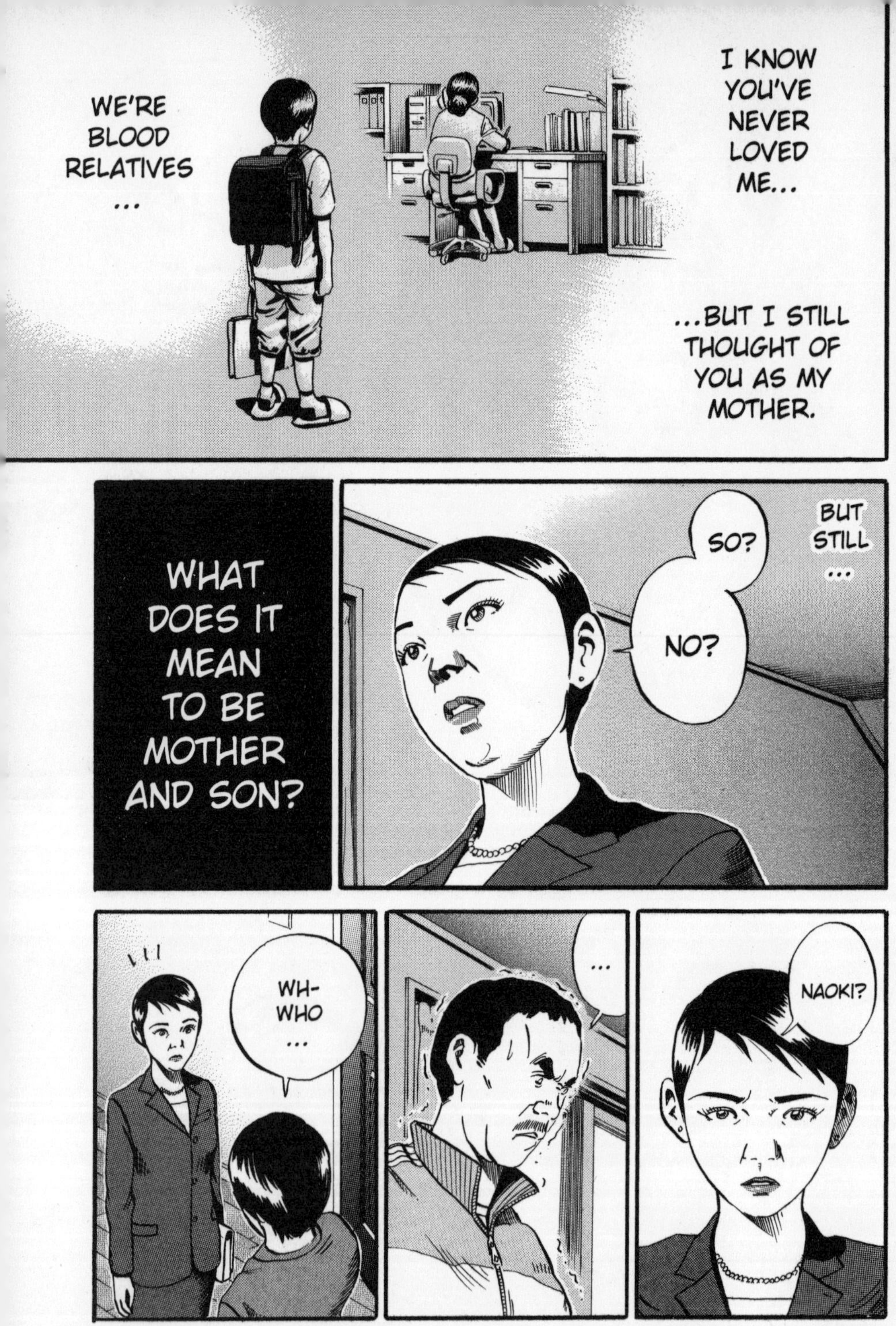

I KNOW YOU'VE NEVER LOVED ME...
WE'RE BLOOD RELATIVES...
...BUT I STILL THOUGHT OF YOU AS MY MOTHER.
BUT STILL...
SO?
NO?
WHAT DOES IT MEAN TO BE MOTHER AND SON?
NAOKI?
...
WH-WHO...

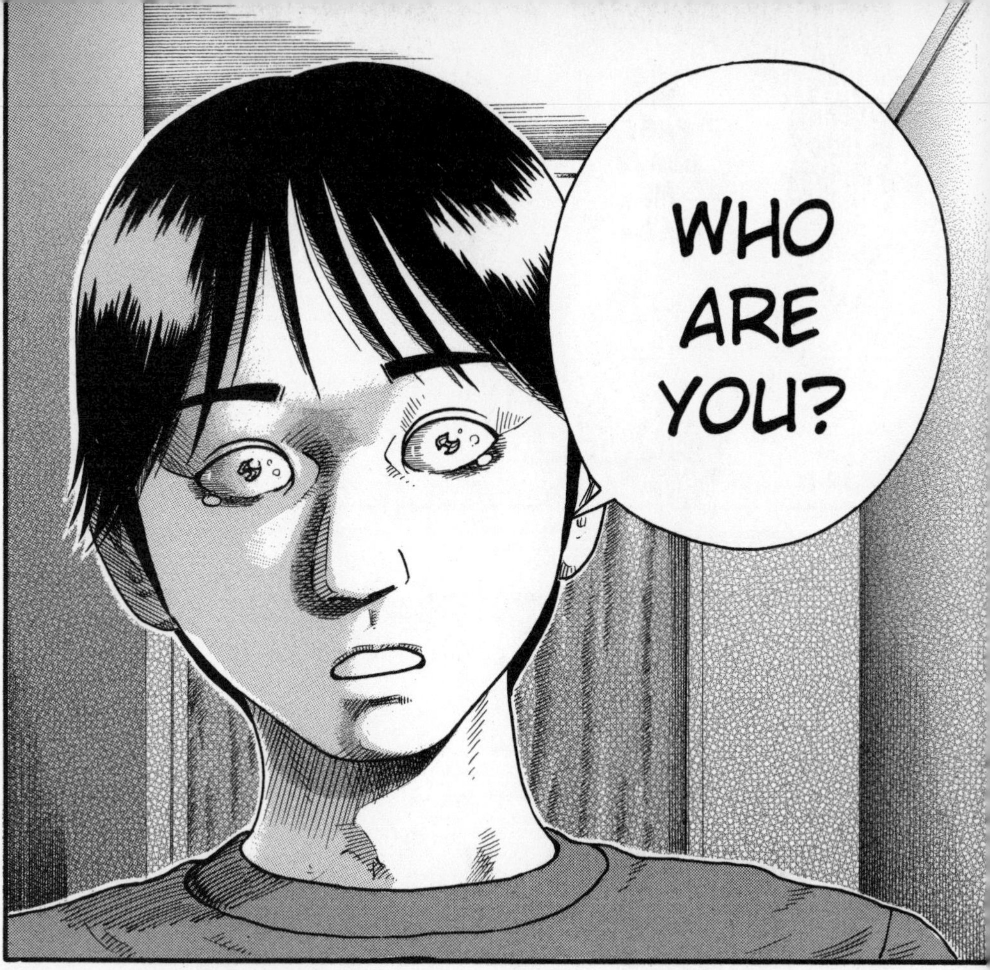
WHO ARE YOU?

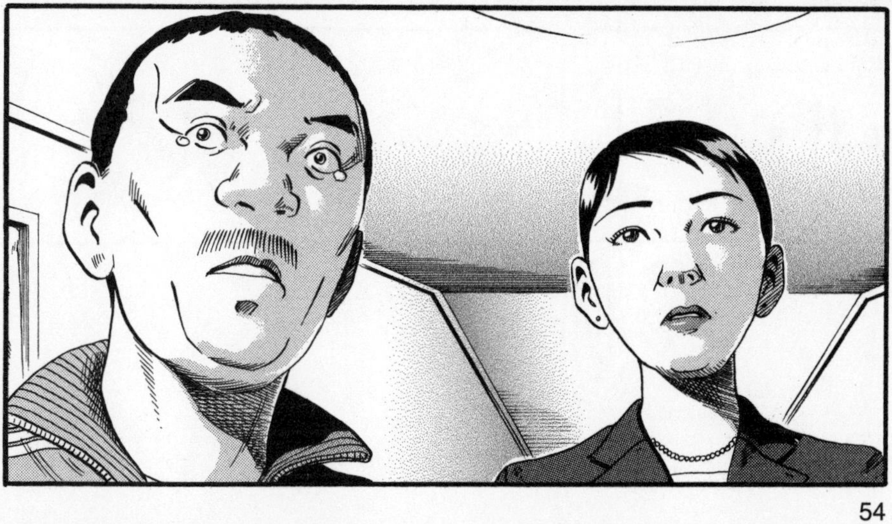

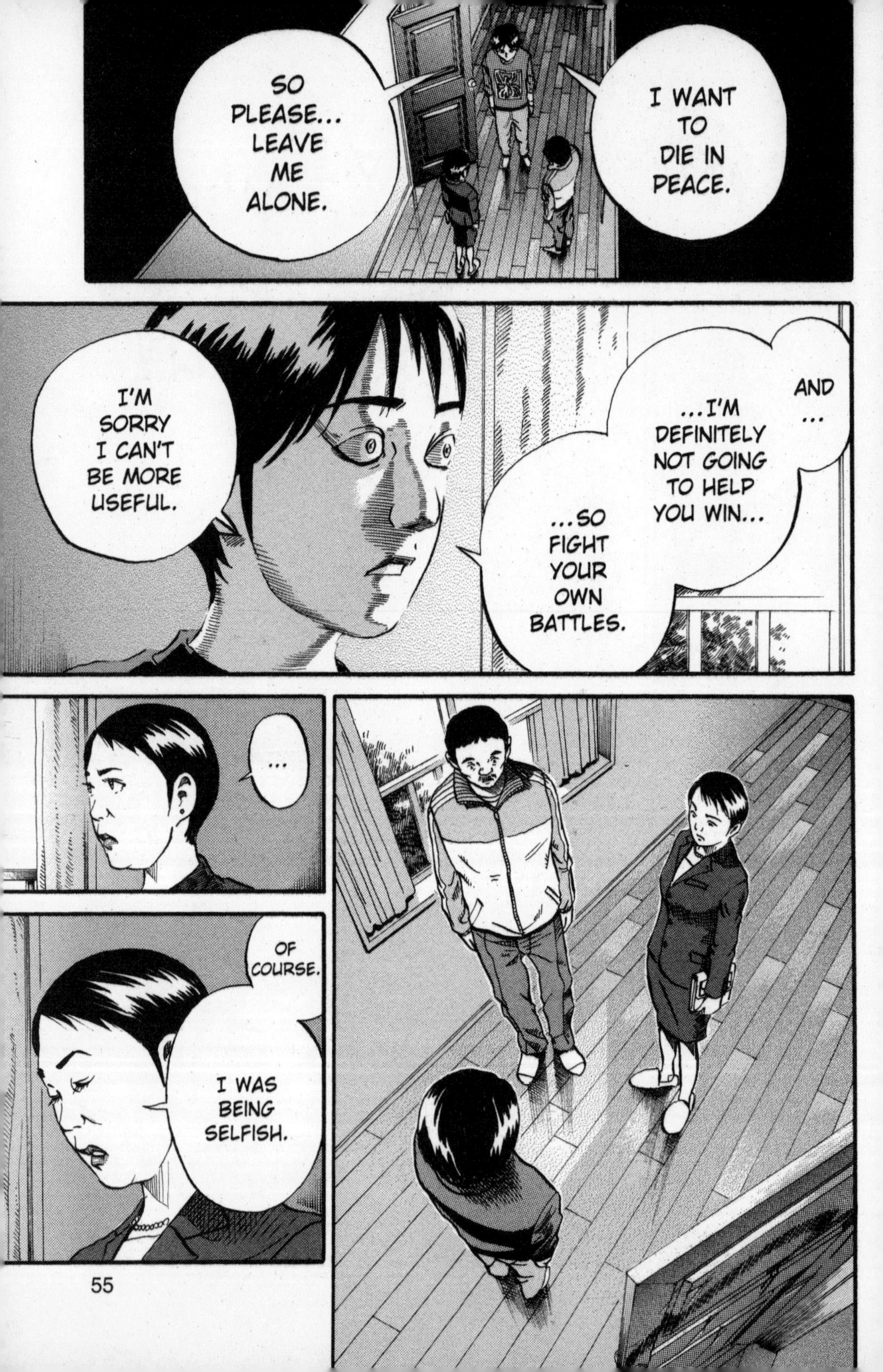
I WANT TO DIE IN PEACE.
SO PLEASE... LEAVE ME ALONE.
AND ...
...I'M DEFINITELY NOT GOING TO HELP YOU WIN...
...SO FIGHT YOUR OWN BATTLES.
I'M SORRY I CAN'T BE MORE USEFUL.
...
OF COURSE.
I WAS BEING SELFISH.

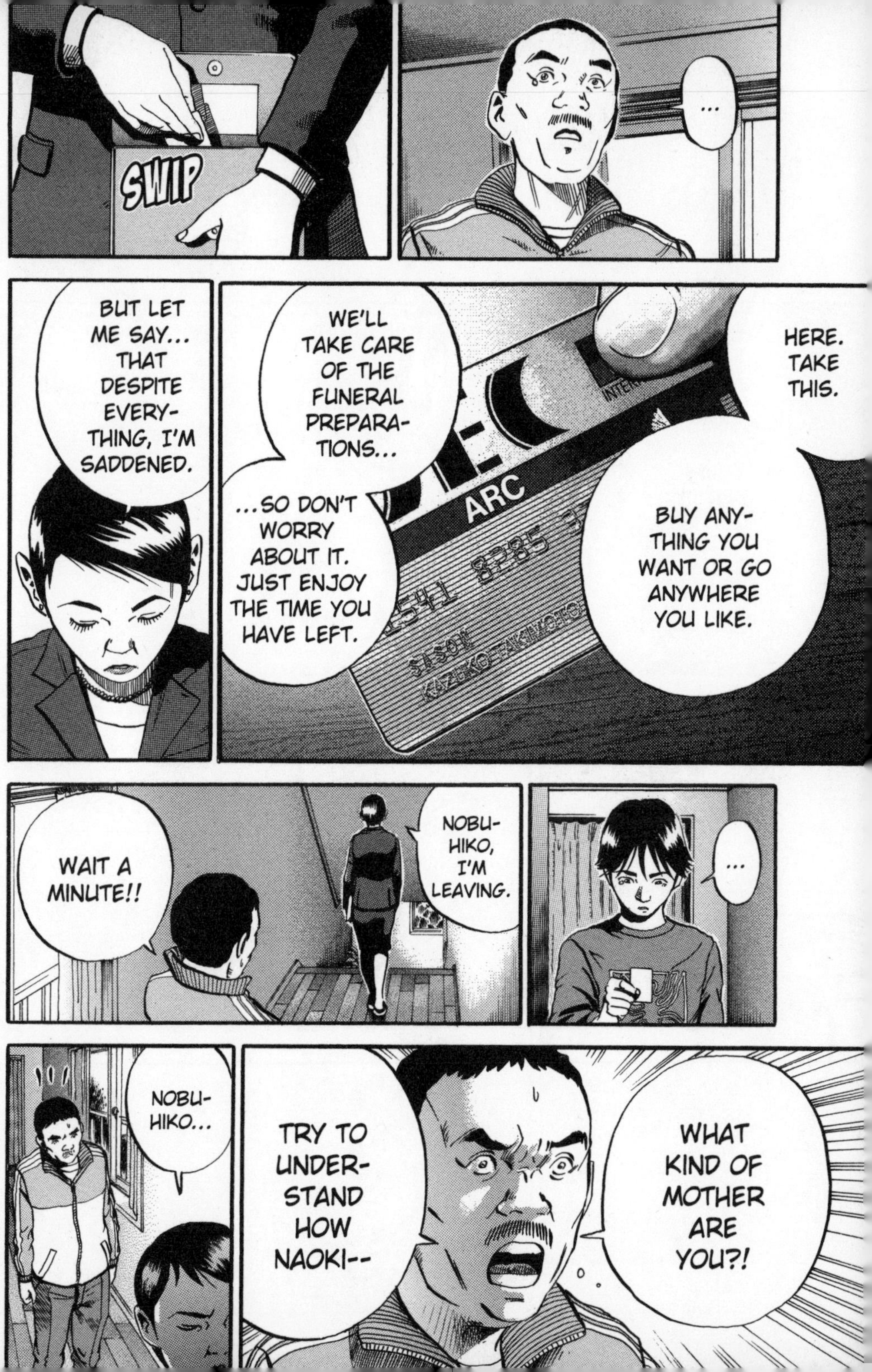
...
SWIP
HERE. TAKE THIS.
BUY ANYTHING YOU WANT OR GO ANYWHERE YOU LIKE.
ARC
WE'LL TAKE CARE OF THE FUNERAL PREPARATIONS...
...SO DON'T WORRY ABOUT IT. JUST ENJOY THE TIME YOU HAVE LEFT.
BUT LET ME SAY... THAT DESPITE EVERYTHING, I'M SADDENED.
...
NOBUHIKO, I'M LEAVING.
WAIT A MINUTE!!
WHAT KIND OF MOTHER ARE YOU?!
TRY TO UNDERSTAND HOW NAOKI--
NOBUHIKO...

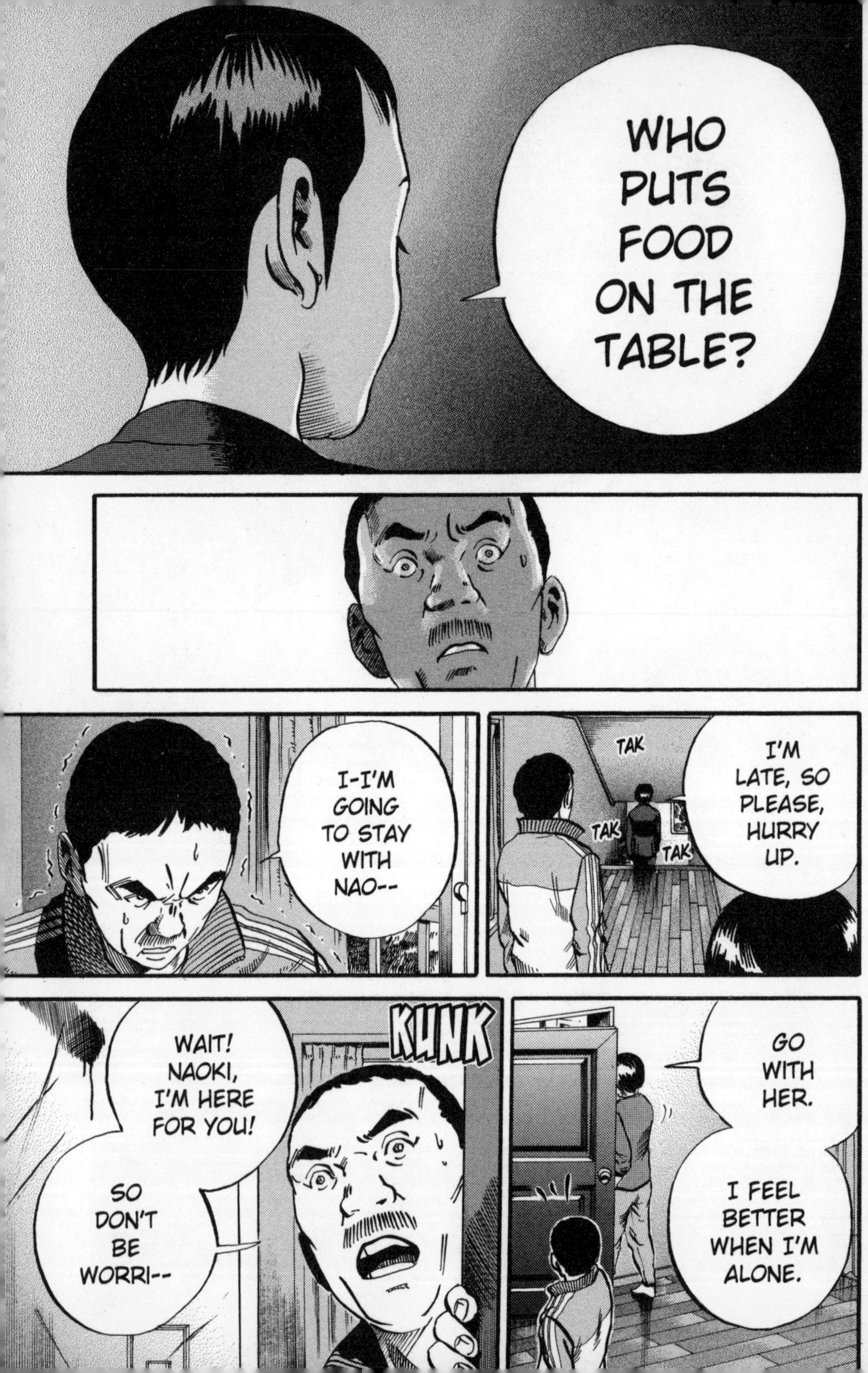
WHO PUTS FOOD ON THE TABLE?
I'M LATE, SO PLEASE, HURRY UP.
TAK
TAK
TAK
I-I'M GOING TO STAY WITH NAO--
GO WITH HER.
I FEEL BETTER WHEN I'M ALONE.
KUNK
WAIT! NAOKI, I'M HERE FOR YOU!
SO DON'T BE WORRI--

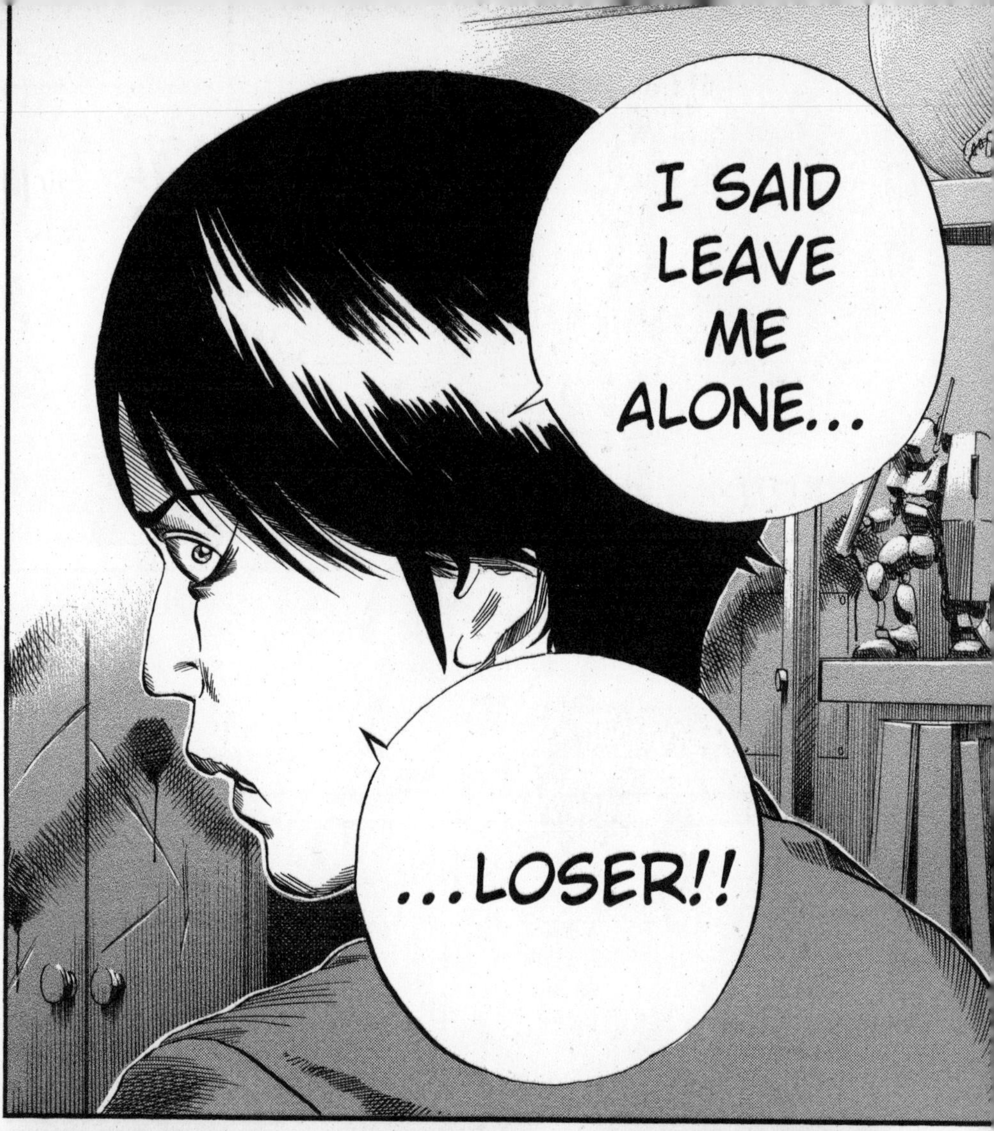
I SAID LEAVE ME ALONE...
...LOSER!!
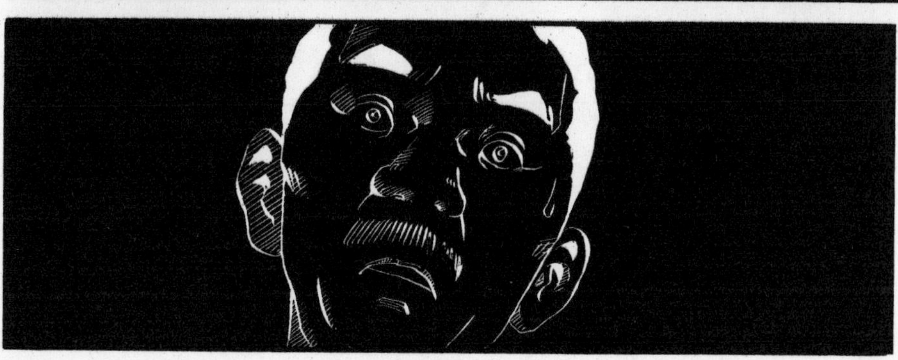

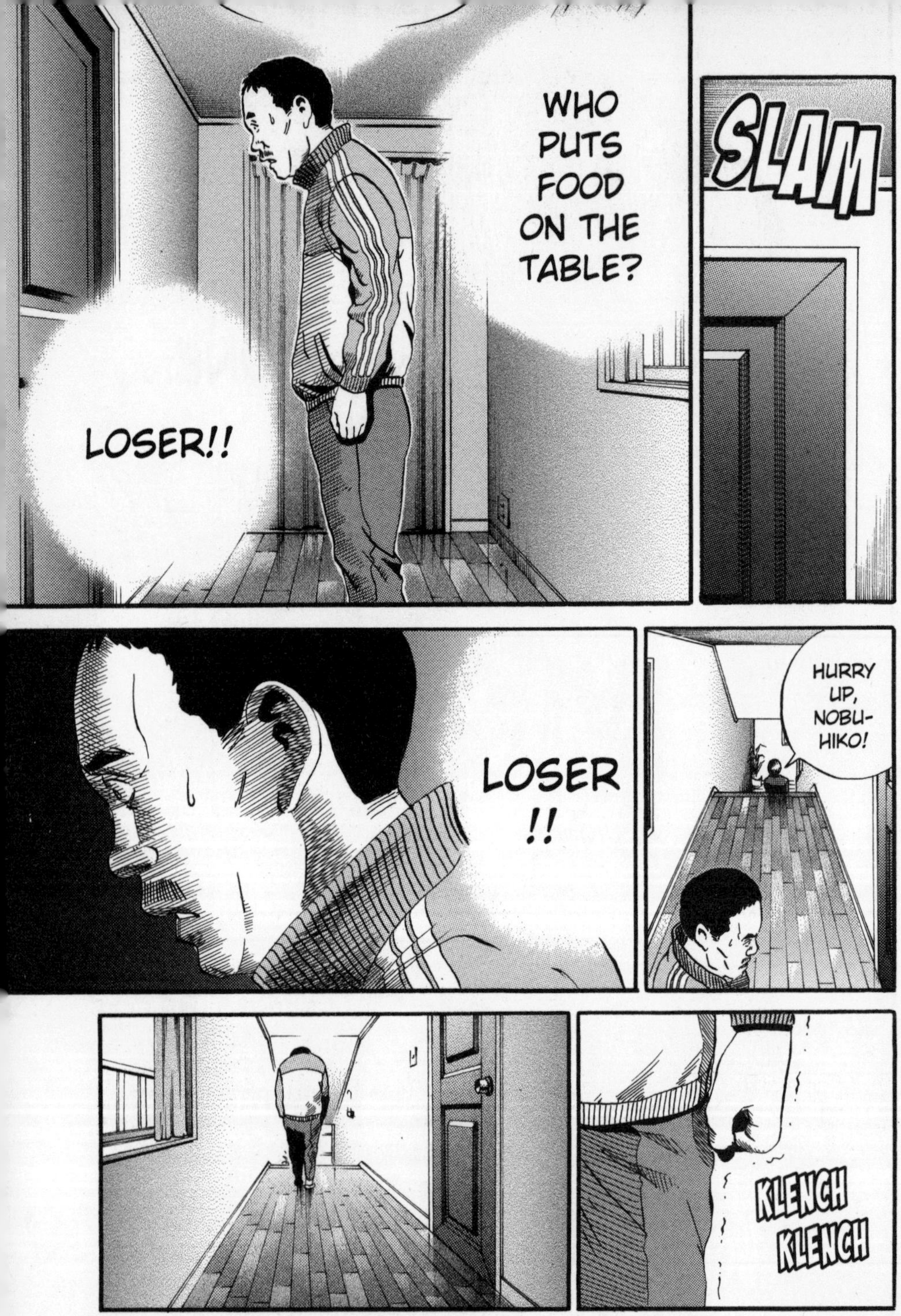
SLAM
WHO PUTS FOOD ON THE TABLE?
LOSER!!
HURRY UP, NOBUHIKO!
LOSER !!
KLENCH KLENCH

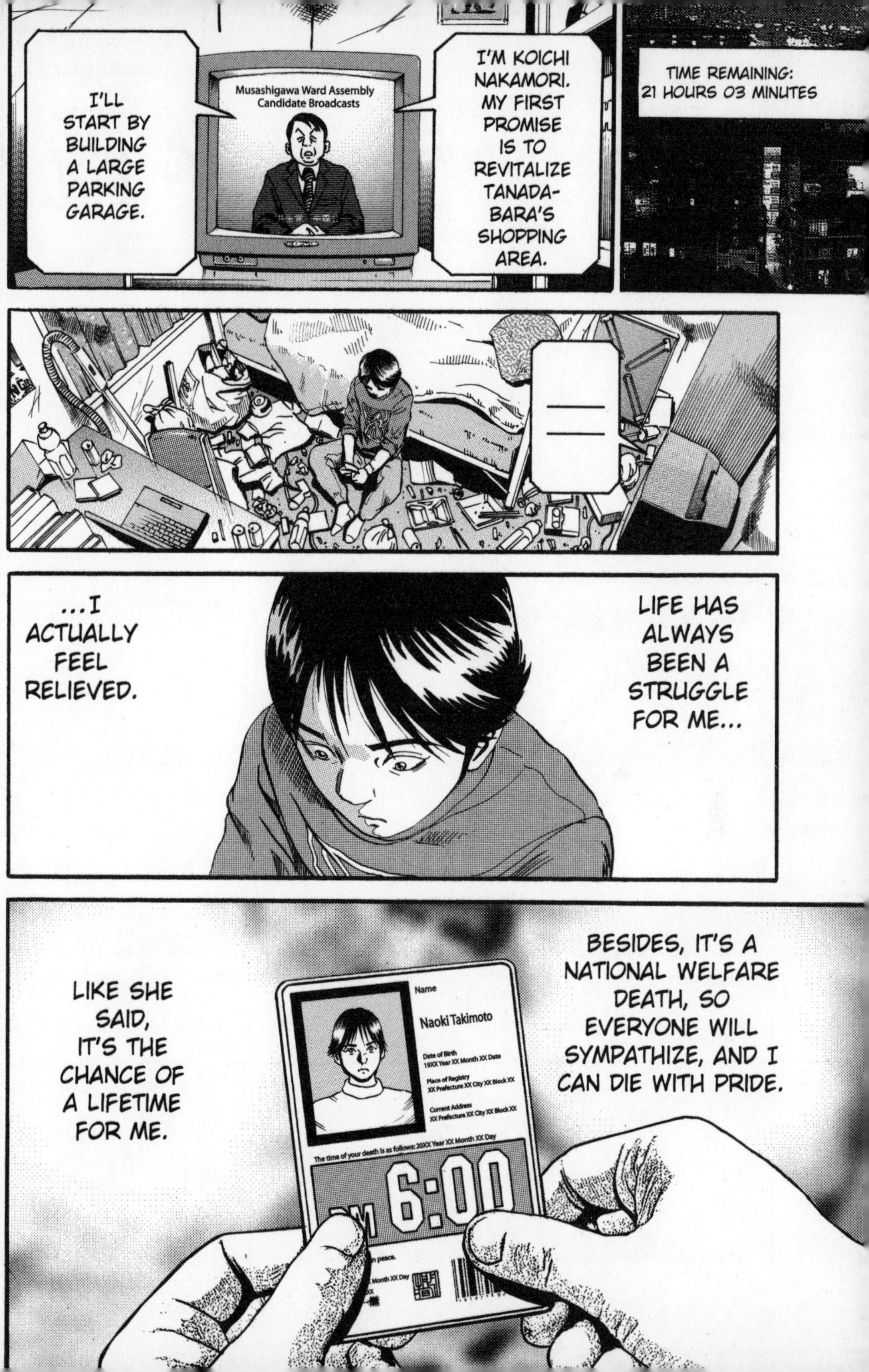
TIME REMAINING: 21 HOURS 03 MINUTES
Musashigawa Ward Assembly Candidate Broadcasts
I'M KOICHI NAKAMORI. MY FIRST PROMISE IS TO REVITALIZE TANADA-BARA'S SHOPPING AREA.
I'LL START BY BUILDING A LARGE PARKING GARAGE.
——
LIFE HAS ALWAYS BEEN A STRUGGLE FOR ME...
...I ACTUALLY FEEL RELIEVED.
BESIDES, IT'S A NATIONAL WELFARE DEATH, SO EVERYONE WILL SYMPATHIZE, AND I CAN DIE WITH PRIDE.
Name
Naoki Takimoto
Date of Birth
19XX Year XX Month XX Date
Place of Registry
XX Prefecture XX City XX Block XX
Current Address
XX Prefecture XX City XX Block XX
The time of your death is as follows: 20XX Year XX Month XX Day
6:00
LIKE SHE SAID, IT'S THE CHANCE OF A LIFETIME FOR ME.

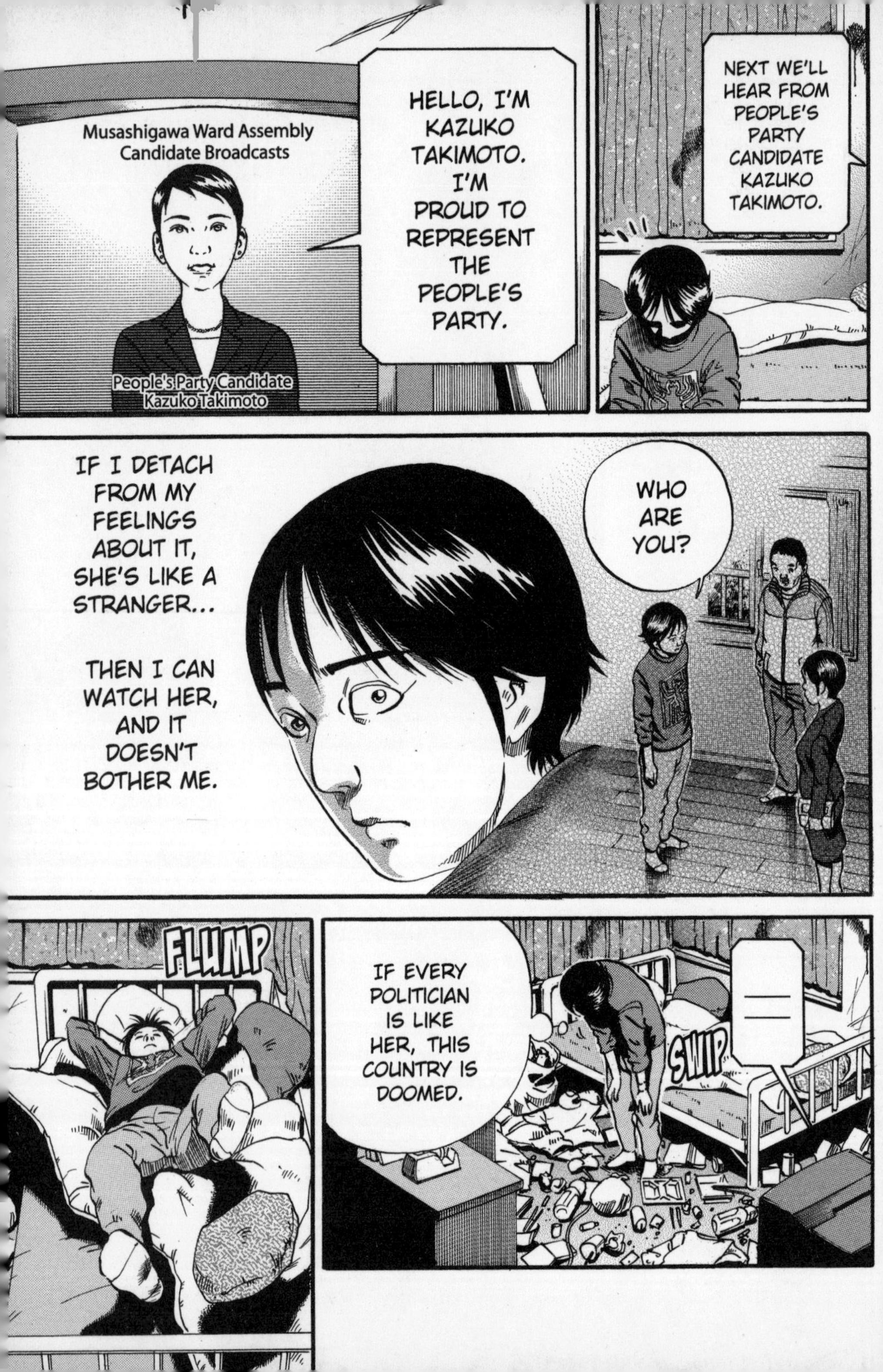
NEXT WE'LL HEAR FROM PEOPLE'S PARTY CANDIDATE KAZUKO TAKIMOTO.
HELLO, I'M KAZUKO TAKIMOTO. I'M PROUD TO REPRESENT THE PEOPLE'S PARTY.
Musashigawa Ward Assembly Candidate Broadcasts
People's Party Candidate Kazuko Takimoto
WHO ARE YOU?
IF I DETACH FROM MY FEELINGS ABOUT IT, SHE'S LIKE A STRANGER...
THEN I CAN WATCH HER, AND IT DOESN'T BOTHER ME.
——
SWIP
IF EVERY POLITICIAN IS LIKE HER, THIS COUNTRY IS DOOMED.
FLUMP

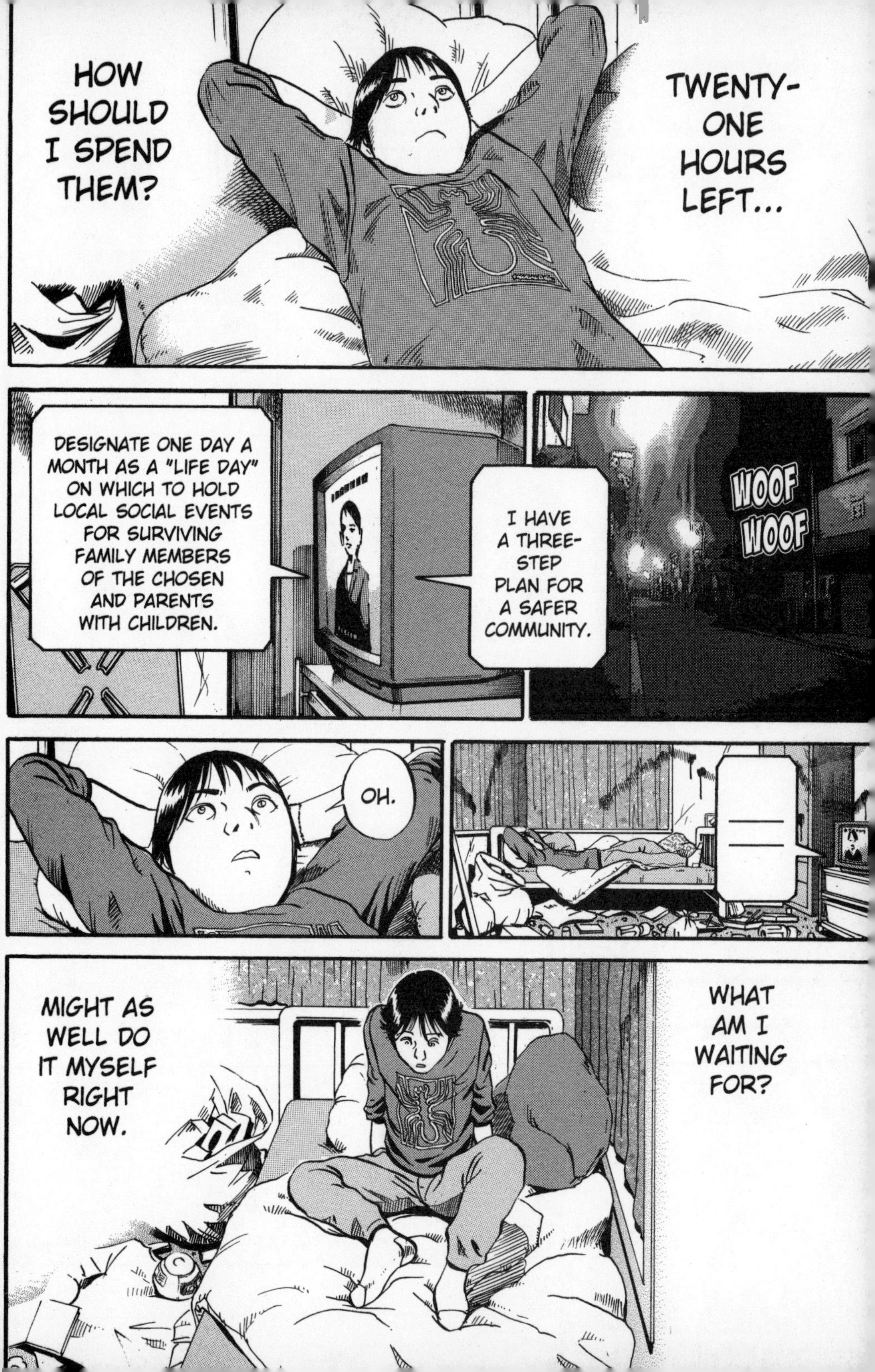
TWENTY-ONE HOURS LEFT...
HOW SHOULD I SPEND THEM?
WOOF WOOF
I HAVE A THREE-STEP PLAN FOR A SAFER COMMUNITY.
DESIGNATE ONE DAY A MONTH AS A "LIFE DAY" ON WHICH TO HOLD LOCAL SOCIAL EVENTS FOR SURVIVING FAMILY MEMBERS OF THE CHOSEN AND PARENTS WITH CHILDREN.
——
OH.
WHAT AM I WAITING FOR?
MIGHT AS WELL DO IT MYSELF RIGHT NOW.

FLIK
I'LL NEVER GET THE ARTERY LIKE THIS.
SWP
TAP
THIS'LL WORK.

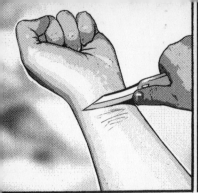

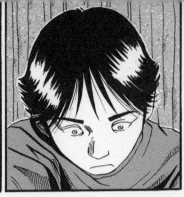

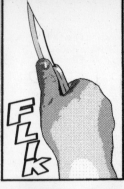

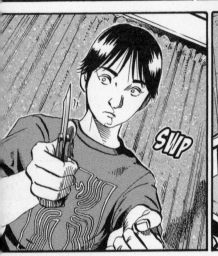

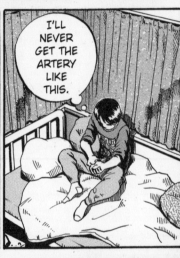

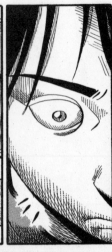

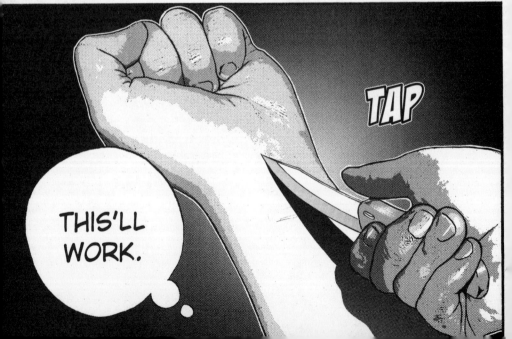

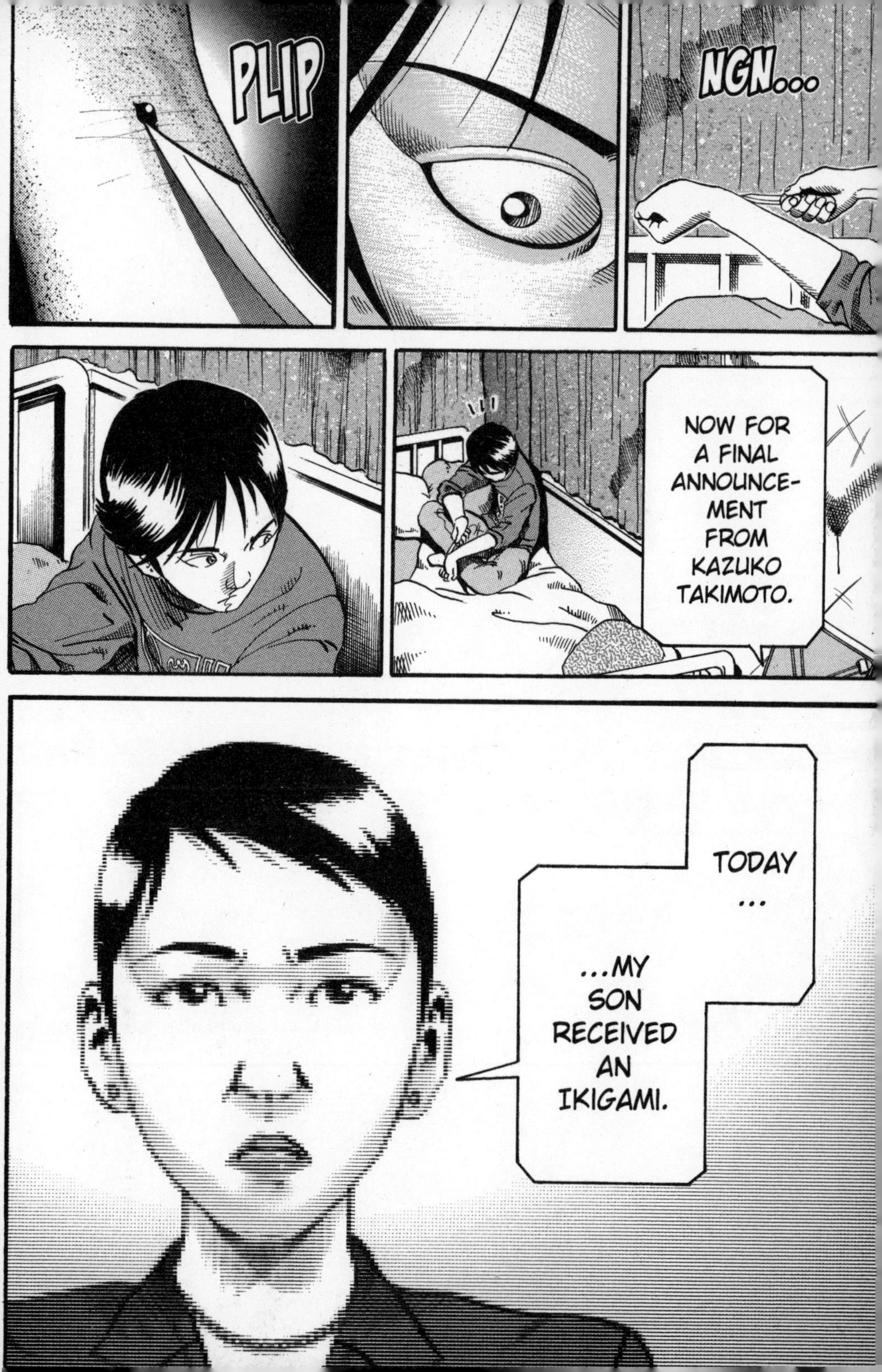
NGN...
PLIP
NOW FOR A FINAL ANNOUNCEMENT FROM KAZUKO TAKIMOTO.
TODAY...
...MY SON RECEIVED AN IKIGAMI.

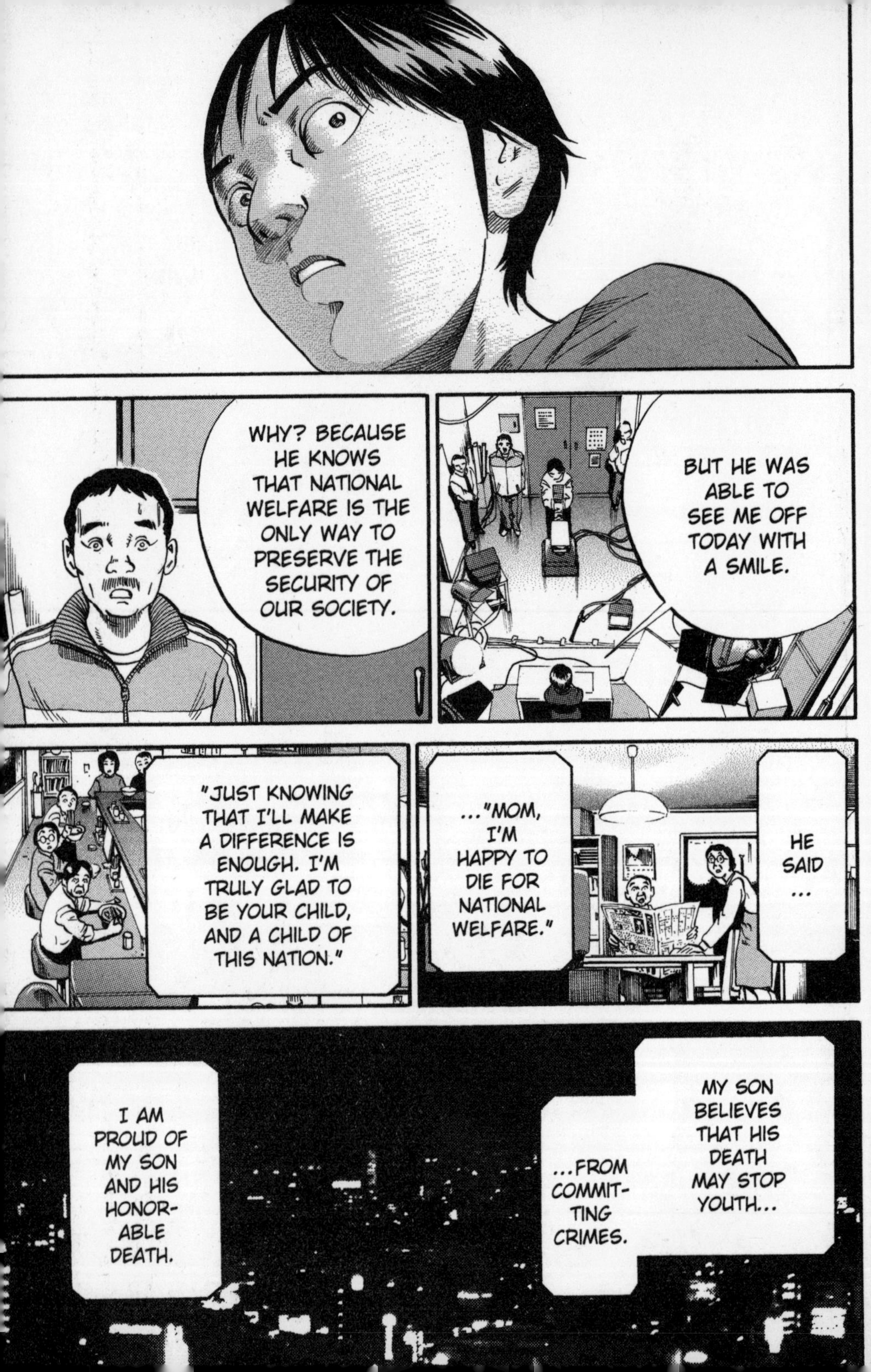
BUT HE WAS ABLE TO SEE ME OFF TODAY WITH A SMILE.
WHY? BECAUSE HE KNOWS THAT NATIONAL WELFARE IS THE ONLY WAY TO PRESERVE THE SECURITY OF OUR SOCIETY.
HE SAID ...
..."MOM, I'M HAPPY TO DIE FOR NATIONAL WELFARE."
"JUST KNOWING THAT I'LL MAKE A DIFFERENCE IS ENOUGH. I'M TRULY GLAD TO BE YOUR CHILD, AND A CHILD OF THIS NATION."
MY SON BELIEVES THAT HIS DEATH MAY STOP YOUTH...
...FROM COMMIT-TING CRIMES.
I AM PROUD OF MY SON AND HIS HONOR-ABLE DEATH.

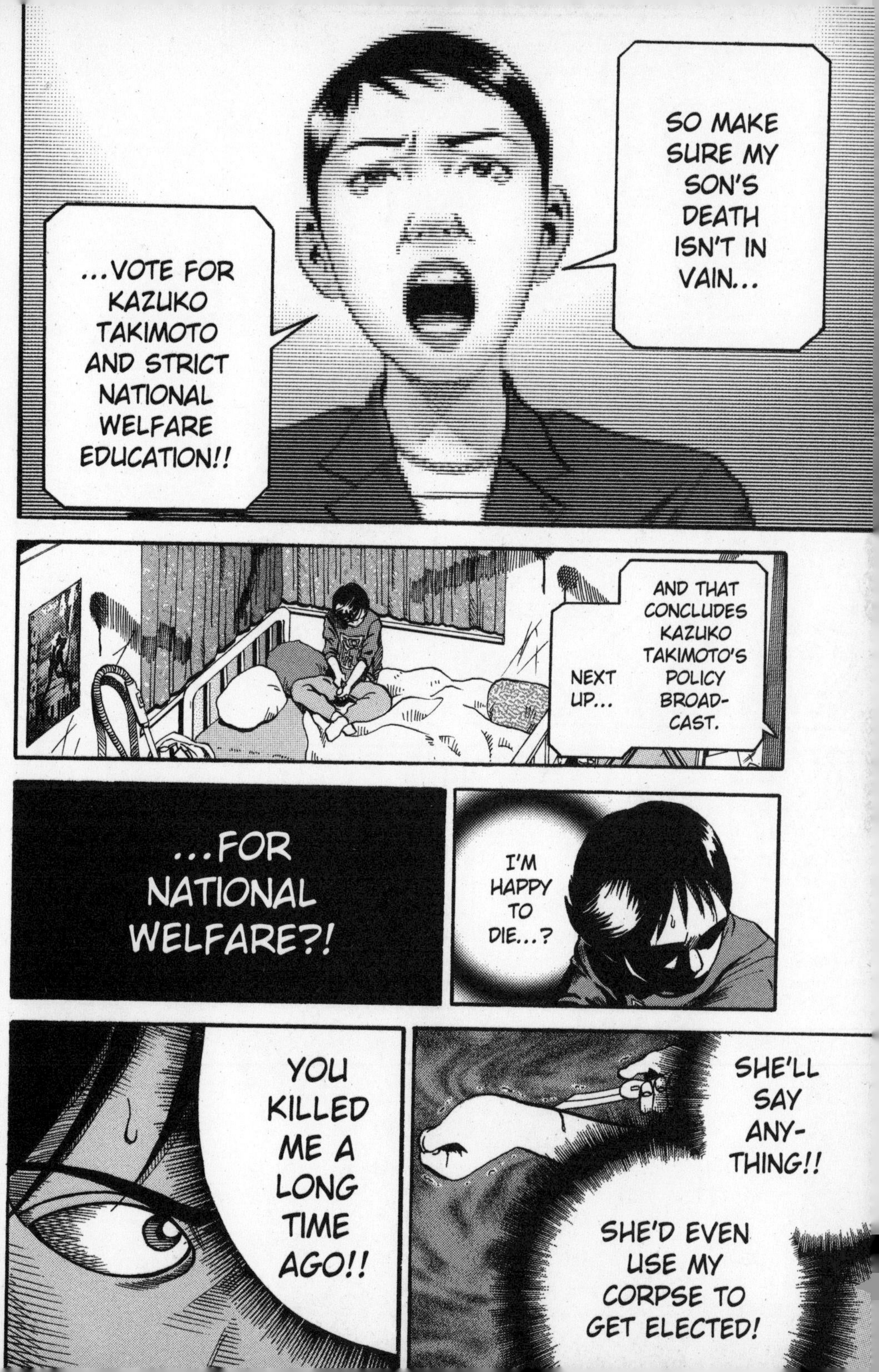
SO MAKE SURE MY SON'S DEATH ISN'T IN VAIN...
...VOTE FOR KAZUKO TAKIMOTO AND STRICT NATIONAL WELFARE EDUCATION!!
AND THAT CONCLUDES KAZUKO TAKIMOTO'S POLICY BROADCAST.
NEXT UP...
I'M HAPPY TO DIE...?
...FOR NATIONAL WELFARE?!
SHE'LL SAY ANY-THING!!
SHE'D EVEN USE MY CORPSE TO GET ELECTED!
YOU KILLED ME A LONG TIME AGO!!

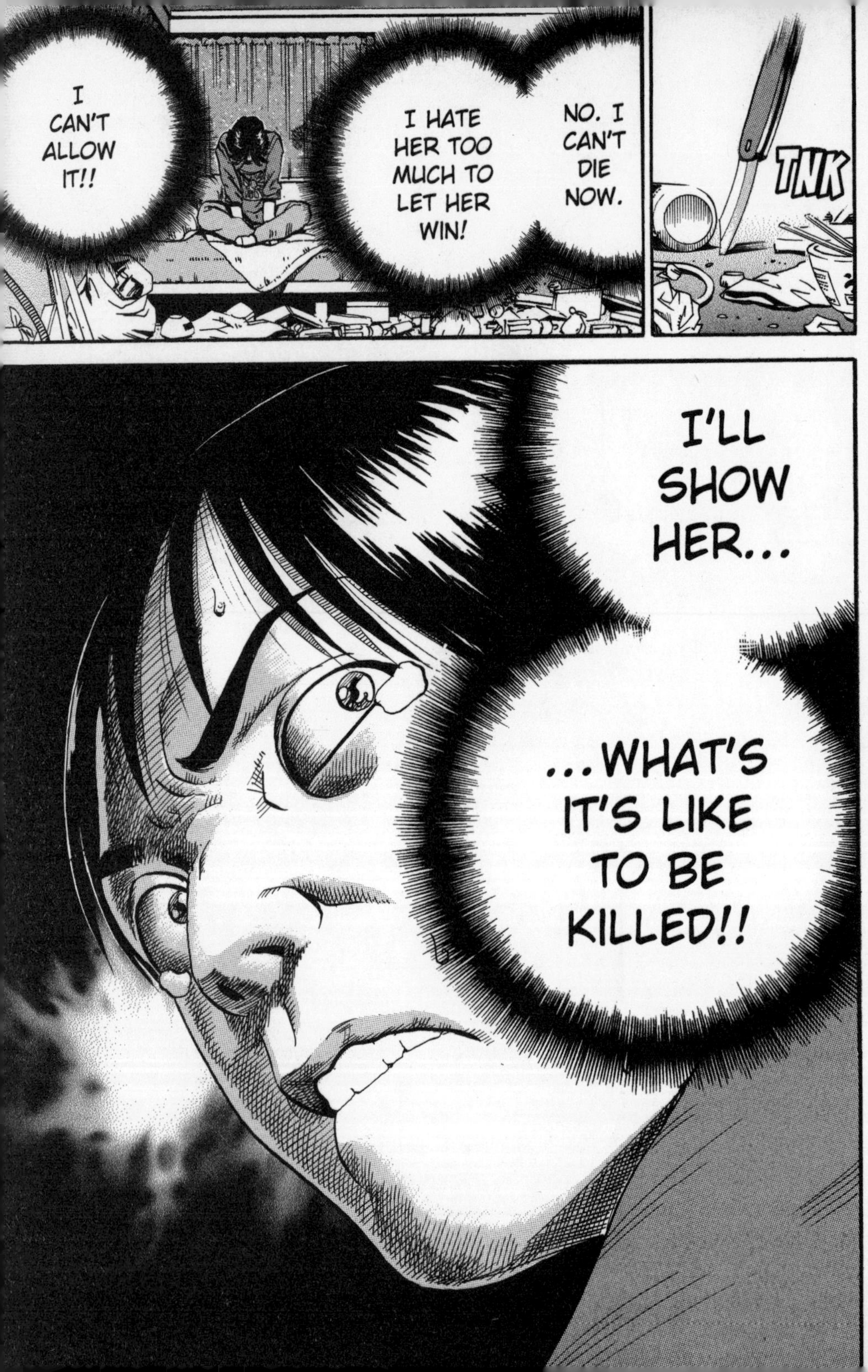
TNK
NO. I CAN'T DIE NOW.
I HATE HER TOO MUCH TO LET HER WIN!
I CAN'T ALLOW IT!!
I'LL SHOW HER...
...WHAT'S IT'S LIKE TO BE KILLED!!

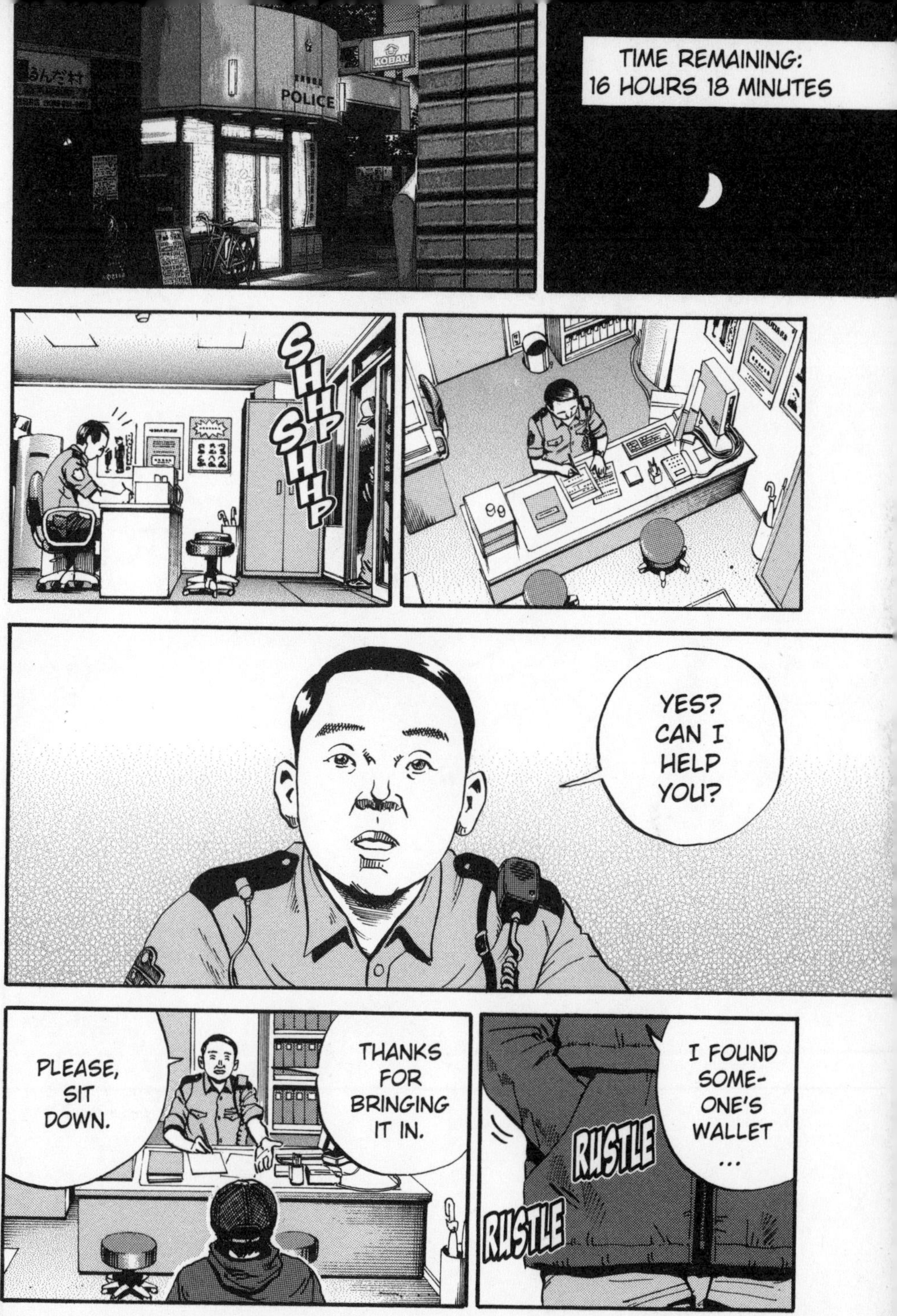
TIME REMAINING:
16 HOURS 18 MINUTES
KOBAN
POLICE
SHHP
SHHP
YES? CAN I HELP YOU?
I FOUND SOME-ONE'S WALLET ...
RUSTLE
RUSTLE
THANKS FOR BRINGING IT IN.
PLEASE, SIT DOWN.

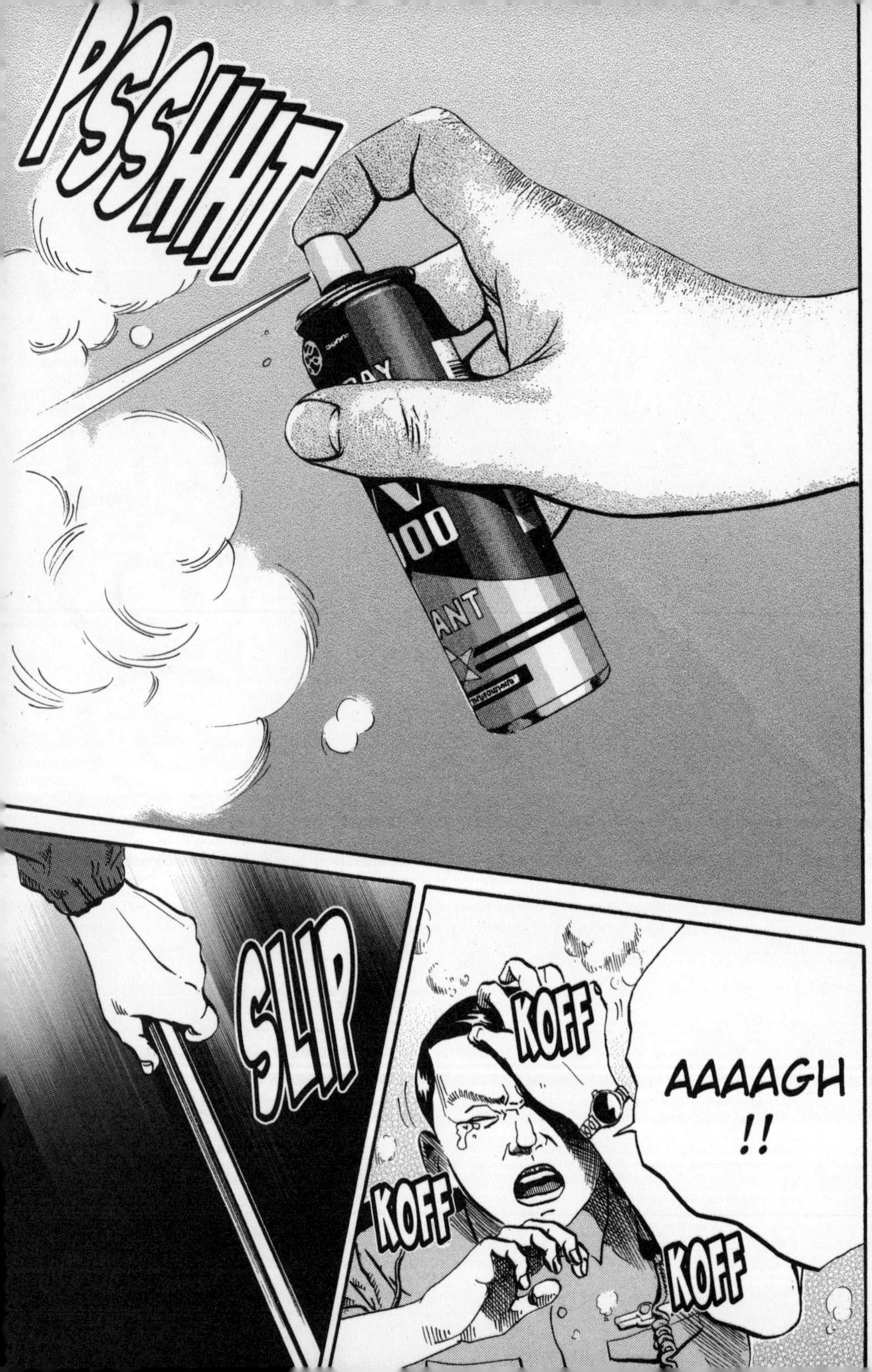
PSSHHT
AAAAGH !!
KOFF
KOFF
KOFF
SLIP

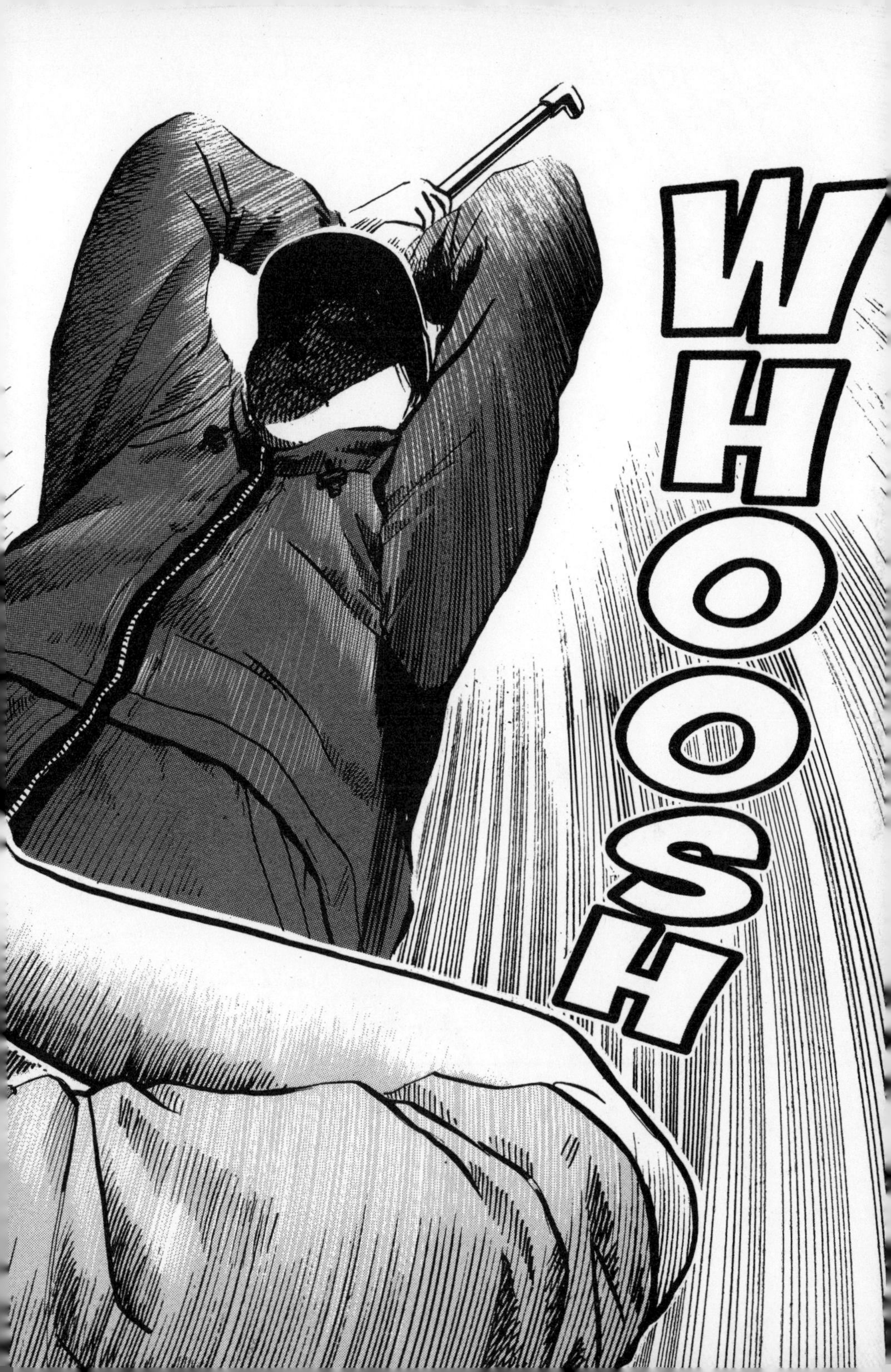
WHOOSH

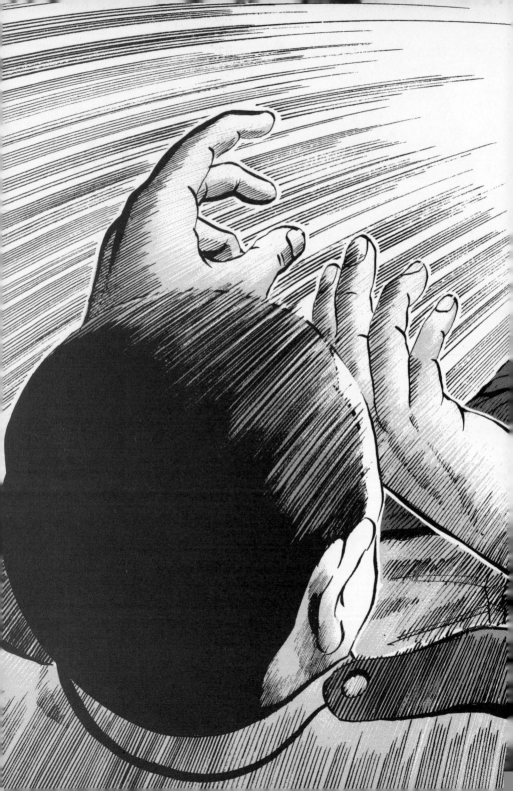

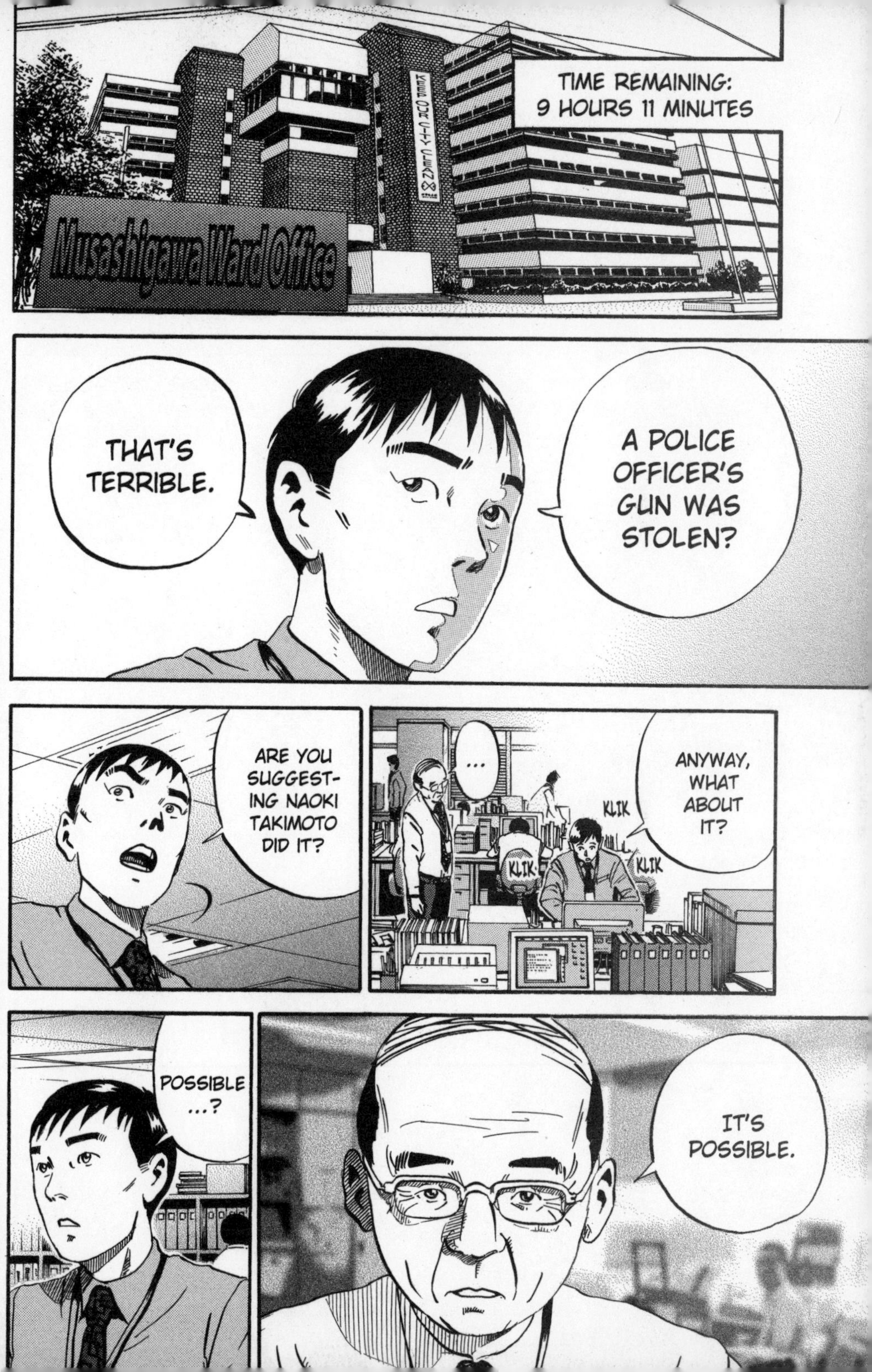
TIME REMAINING:
9 HOURS 11 MINUTES
KEEP OUR CITY CLEAN
Musashigawa Ward Office
A POLICE OFFICER'S GUN WAS STOLEN?
THAT'S TERRIBLE.
ANYWAY, WHAT ABOUT IT?
...
KLIK
KLIK
KLIK
ARE YOU SUGGEST-ING NAOKI TAKIMOTO DID IT?
IT'S POSSIBLE.
POSSIBLE ...?

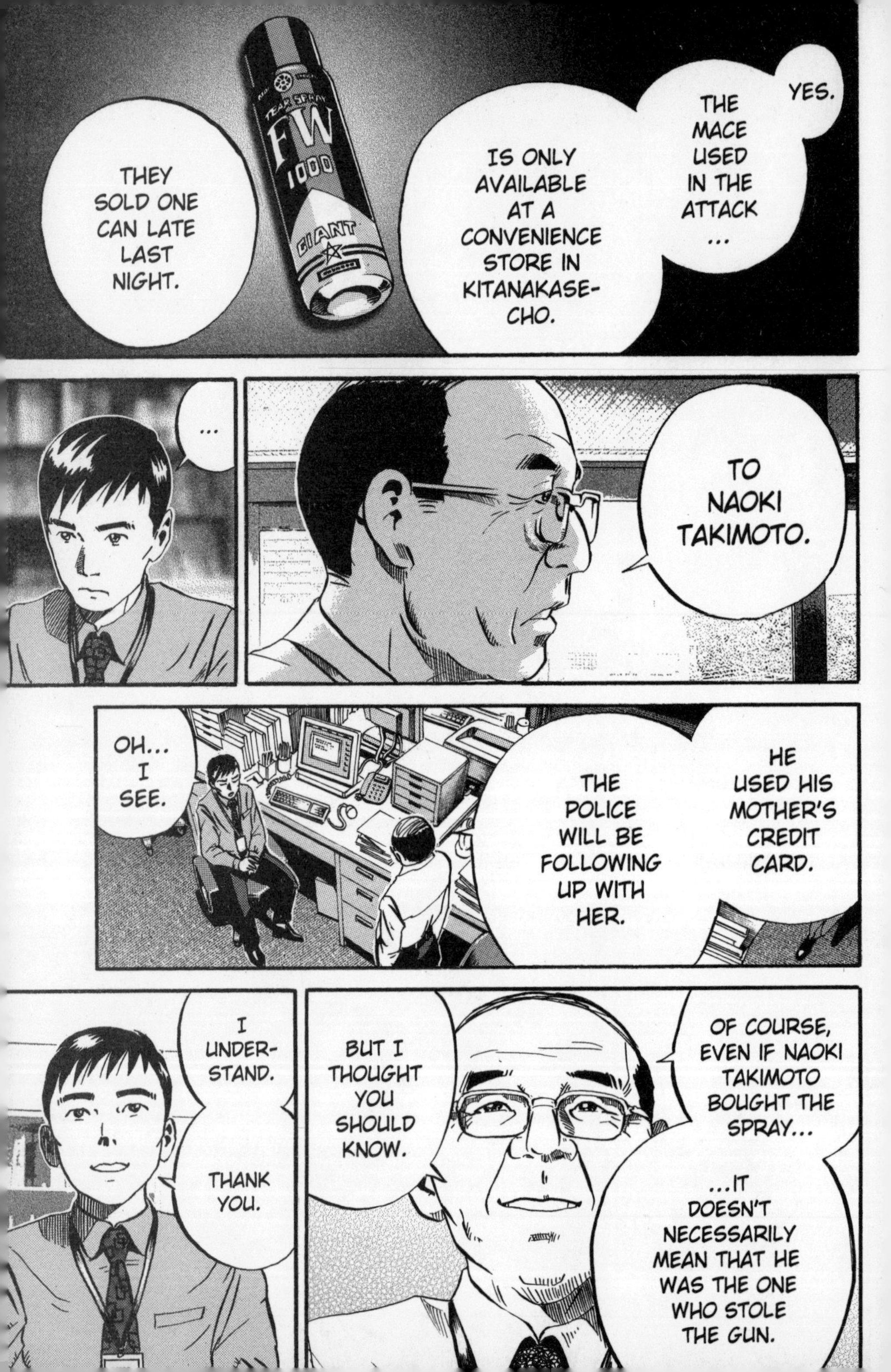
YES.
THE MACE USED IN THE ATTACK ...
IS ONLY AVAILABLE AT A CONVENIENCE STORE IN KITANAKASE-CHO.
TEAR SPRAY
FW 1000
GIANT
THEY SOLD ONE CAN LATE LAST NIGHT.
TO NAOKI TAKIMOTO.
...
HE USED HIS MOTHER'S CREDIT CARD.
THE POLICE WILL BE FOLLOWING UP WITH HER.
OH... I SEE.
OF COURSE, EVEN IF NAOKI TAKIMOTO BOUGHT THE SPRAY...
...IT DOESN'T NECESSARILY MEAN THAT HE WAS THE ONE WHO STOLE THE GUN.
BUT I THOUGHT YOU SHOULD KNOW.
I UNDER-STAND.
THANK YOU.

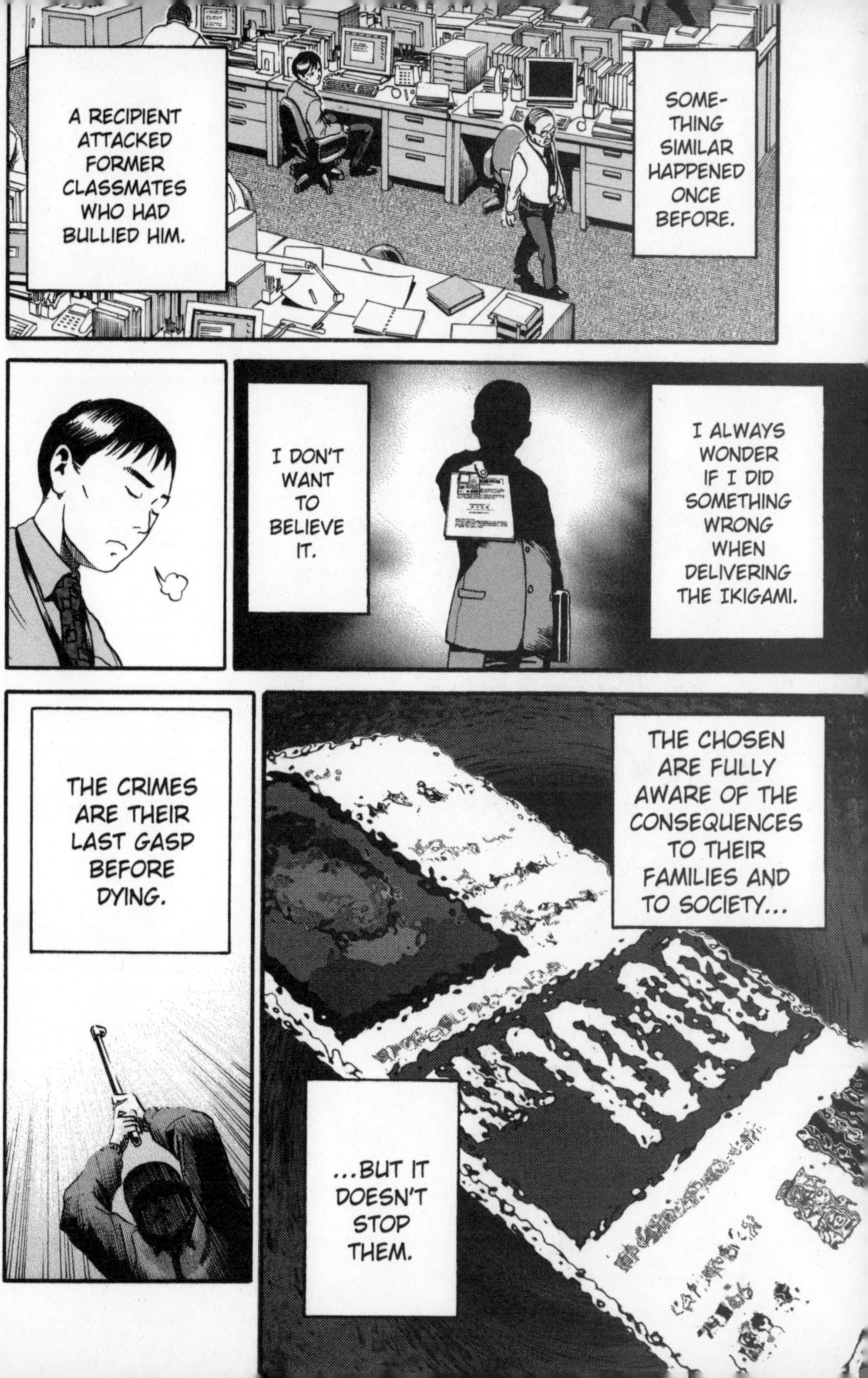
SOME-THING SIMILAR HAPPENED ONCE BEFORE.
A RECIPIENT ATTACKED FORMER CLASSMATES WHO HAD BULLIED HIM.
I ALWAYS WONDER IF I DID SOMETHING WRONG WHEN DELIVERING THE IKIGAMI.
I DON'T WANT TO BELIEVE IT.
THE CHOSEN ARE FULLY AWARE OF THE CONSEQUENCES TO THEIR FAMILIES AND TO SOCIETY...
...BUT IT DOESN'T STOP THEM.
THE CRIMES ARE THEIR LAST GASP BEFORE DYING.

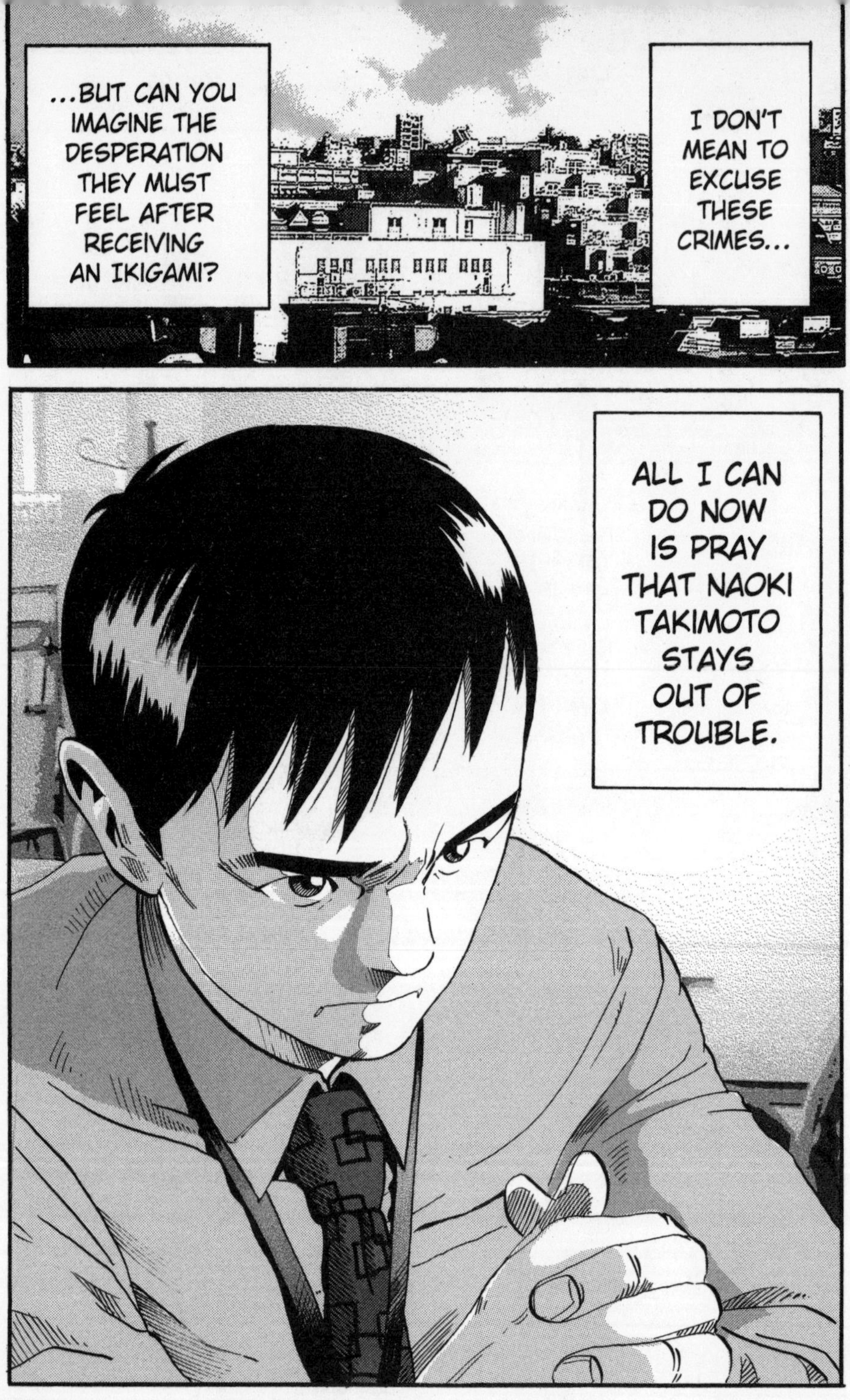
I DON'T MEAN TO EXCUSE THESE CRIMES...
...BUT CAN YOU IMAGINE THE DESPERATION THEY MUST FEEL AFTER RECEIVING AN IKIGAMI?
ALL I CAN DO NOW IS PRAY THAT NAOKI TAKIMOTO STAYS OUT OF TROUBLE.

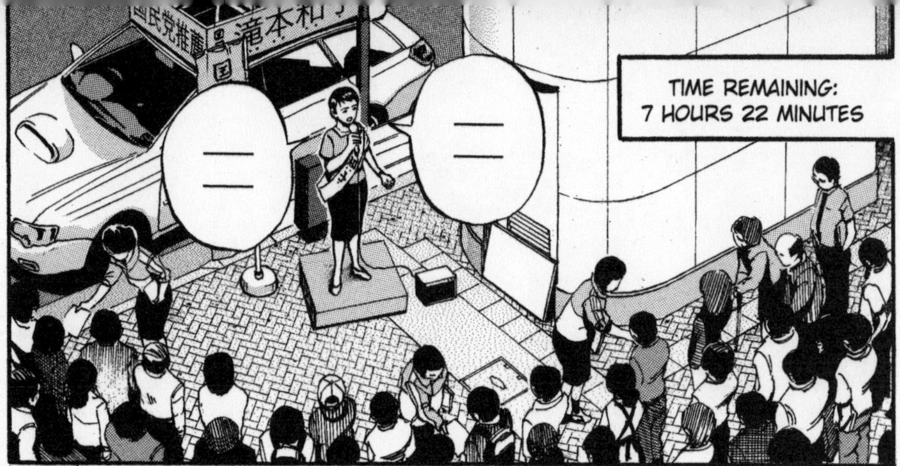
TIME REMAINING:
7 HOURS 22 MINUTES
*Signs & banners: People's Party, Vote for Kazuko Takimoto

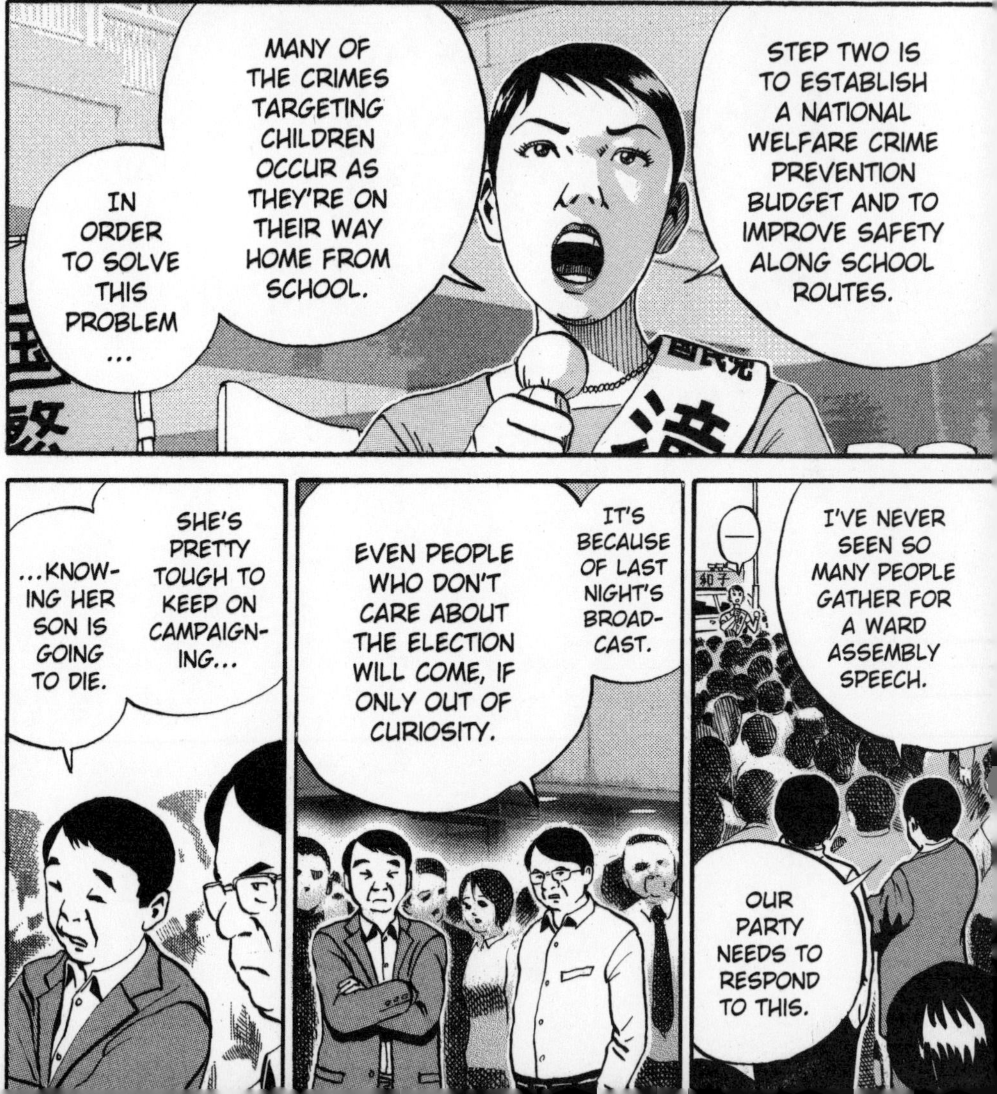
STEP TWO IS TO ESTABLISH A NATIONAL WELFARE CRIME PREVENTION BUDGET AND TO IMPROVE SAFETY ALONG SCHOOL ROUTES.
MANY OF THE CRIMES TARGETING CHILDREN OCCUR AS THEY'RE ON THEIR WAY HOME FROM SCHOOL.
IN ORDER TO SOLVE THIS PROBLEM ...
I'VE NEVER SEEN SO MANY PEOPLE GATHER FOR A WARD ASSEMBLY SPEECH.
OUR PARTY NEEDS TO RESPOND TO THIS.
IT'S BECAUSE OF LAST NIGHT'S BROAD-CAST.
EVEN PEOPLE WHO DON'T CARE ABOUT THE ELECTION WILL COME, IF ONLY OUT OF CURIOSITY.
SHE'S PRETTY TOUGH TO KEEP ON CAMPAIGN-ING...
...KNOW-ING HER SON IS GOING TO DIE.

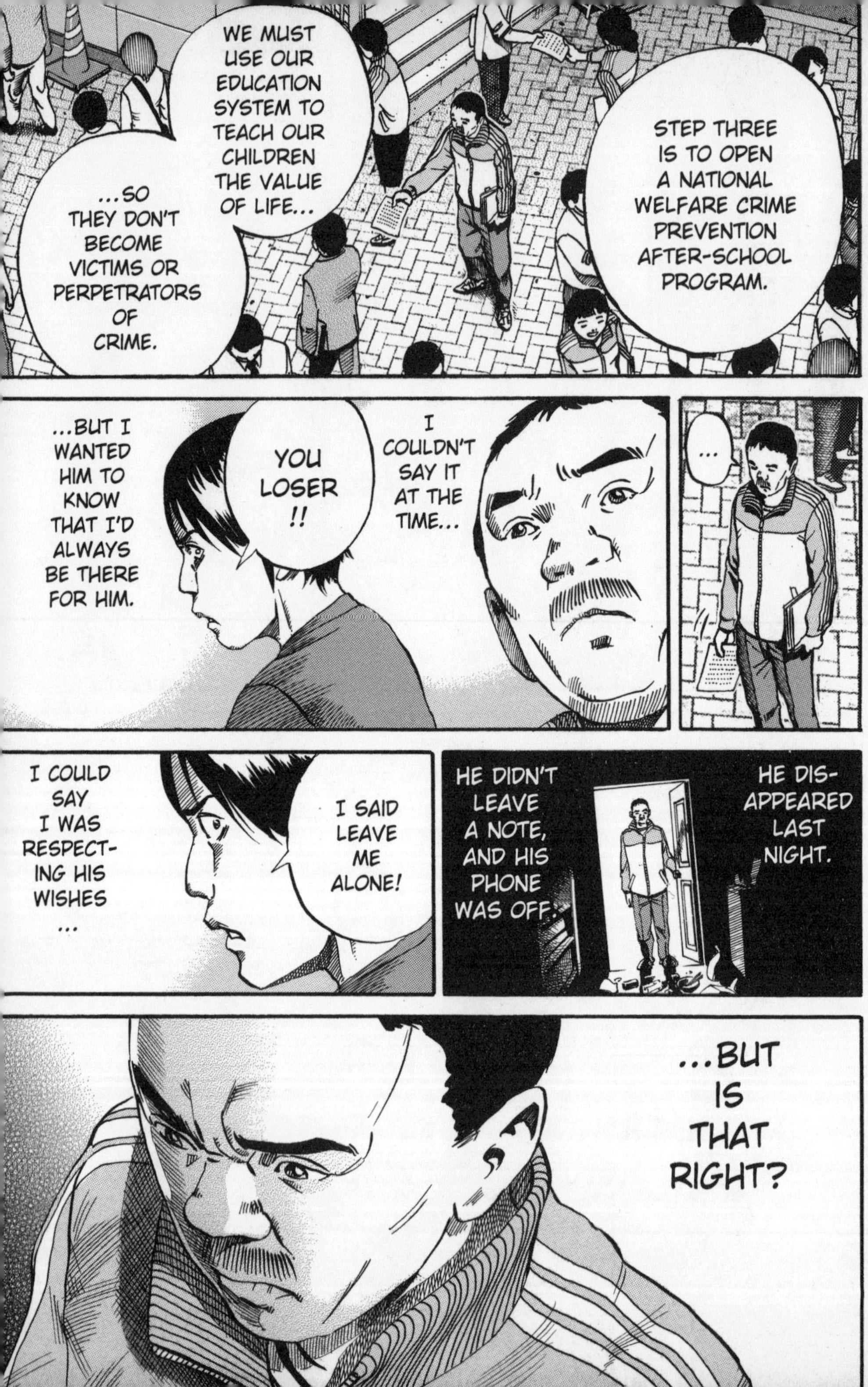
STEP THREE IS TO OPEN A NATIONAL WELFARE CRIME PREVENTION AFTER-SCHOOL PROGRAM.
WE MUST USE OUR EDUCATION SYSTEM TO TEACH OUR CHILDREN THE VALUE OF LIFE...
...SO THEY DON'T BECOME VICTIMS OR PERPETRATORS OF CRIME.
...
I COULDN'T SAY IT AT THE TIME...
YOU LOSER !!
...BUT I WANTED HIM TO KNOW THAT I'D ALWAYS BE THERE FOR HIM.
HE DIS-APPEARED LAST NIGHT.
HE DIDN'T LEAVE A NOTE, AND HIS PHONE WAS OFF.
I SAID LEAVE ME ALONE!
I COULD SAY I WAS RESPECT-ING HIS WISHES ...
...BUT IS THAT RIGHT?

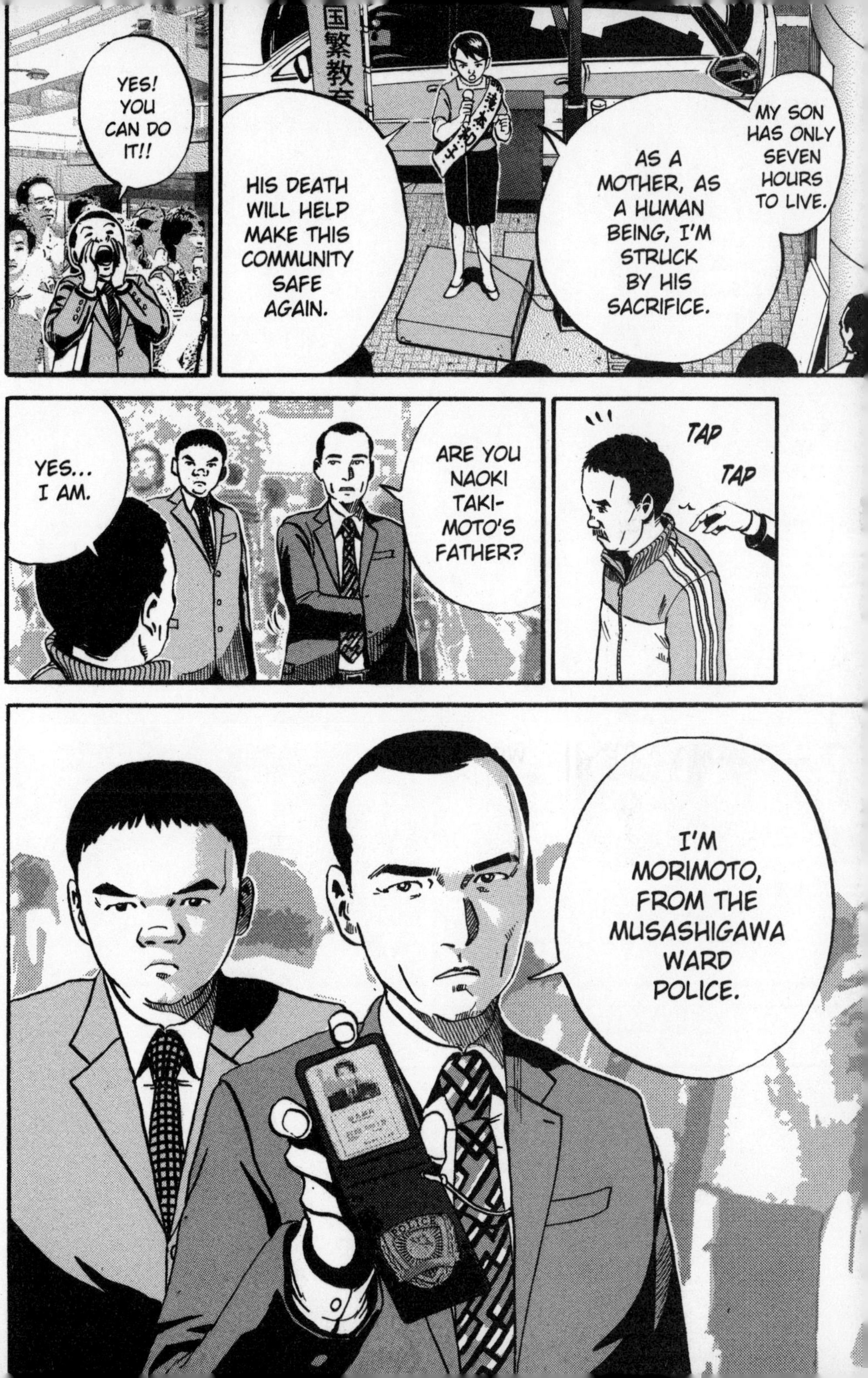

MY SON HAS ONLY SEVEN HOURS TO LIVE.
AS A MOTHER, AS A HUMAN BEING, I'M STRUCK BY HIS SACRIFICE.
HIS DEATH WILL HELP MAKE THIS COMMUNITY SAFE AGAIN.
YES! YOU CAN DO IT!!
TAP
TAP
ARE YOU NAOKI TAKI-MOTO'S FATHER?
YES... I AM.
I'M MORIMOTO, FROM THE MUSASHIGAWA WARD POLICE.

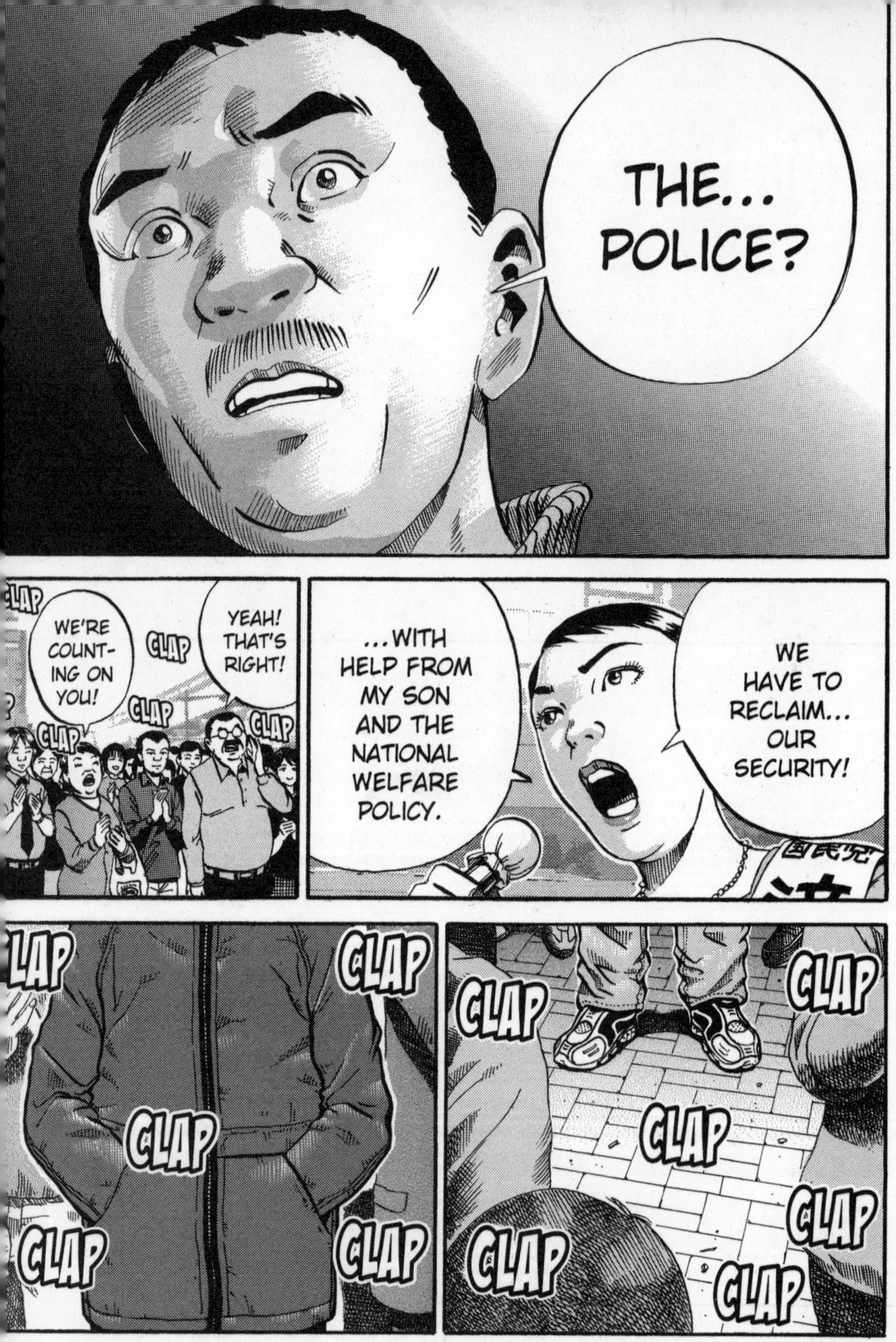
THE... POLICE?
WE HAVE TO RECLAIM... OUR SECURITY!
...WITH HELP FROM MY SON AND THE NATIONAL WELFARE POLICY.
YEAH! THAT'S RIGHT!
CLAP
CLAP
WE'RE COUNTING ON YOU!
CLAP
CLAP
CLAP
CLAP
CLAP
CLAP
CLAP
CLAP
CLAP
CLAP
CLAP
CLAP
CLAP
CLAP

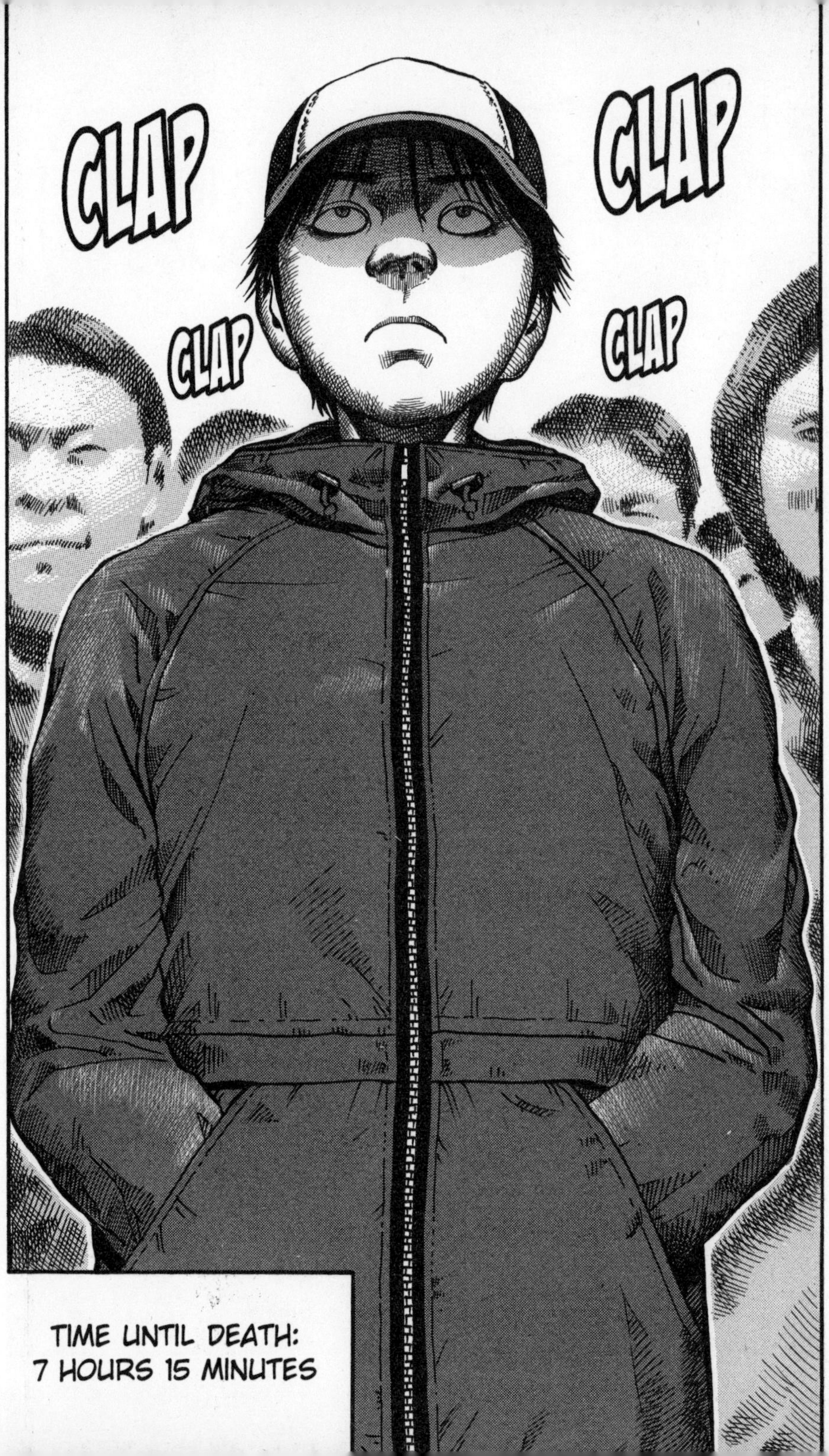
CLAP
CLAP
CLAP
CLAP
TIME UNTIL DEATH:
7 HOURS 15 MINUTES

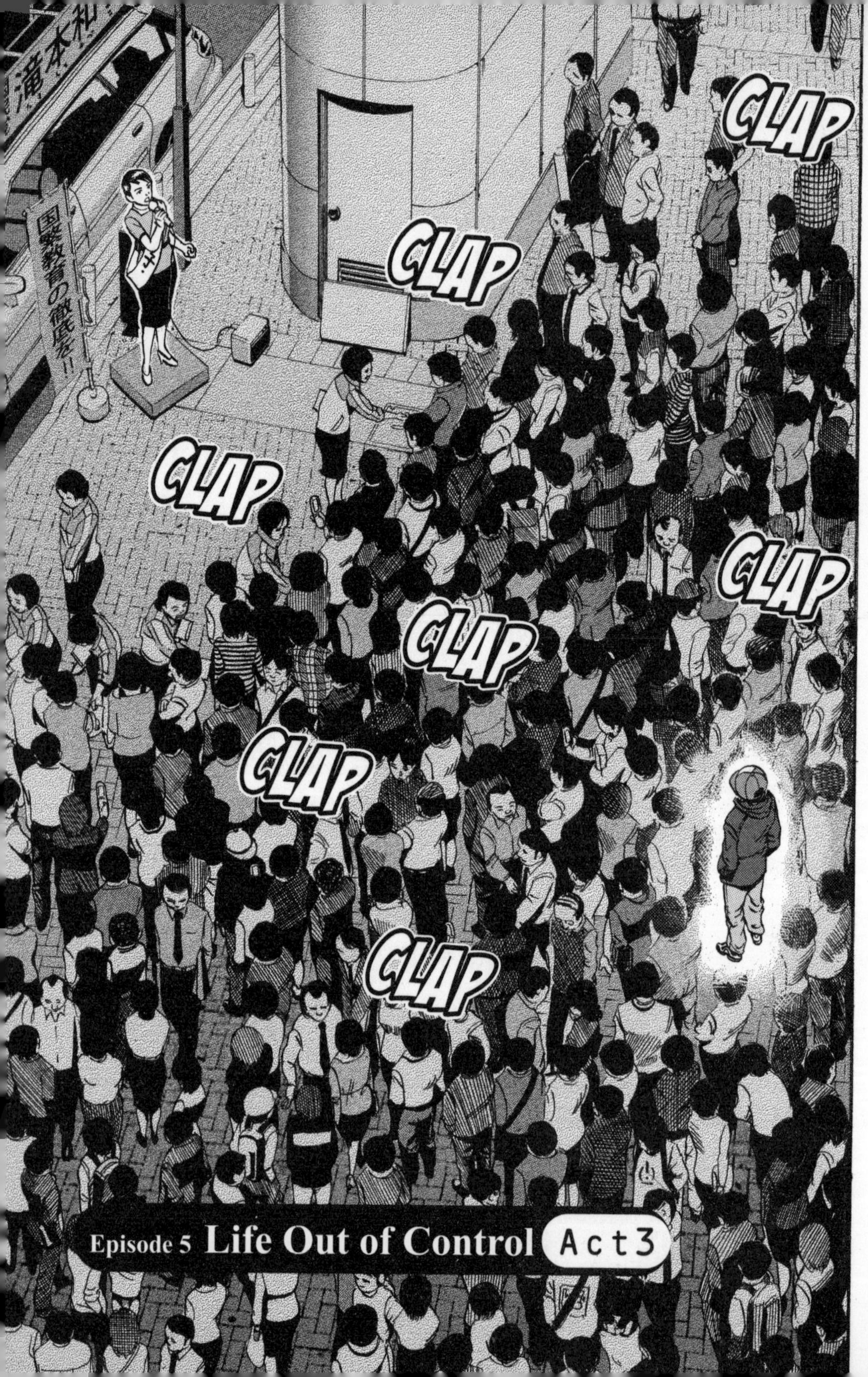
滝本和
CLAP
CLAP
CLAP
CLAP
CLAP
CLAP
CLAP

Episode 5 Life Out of Control Act3

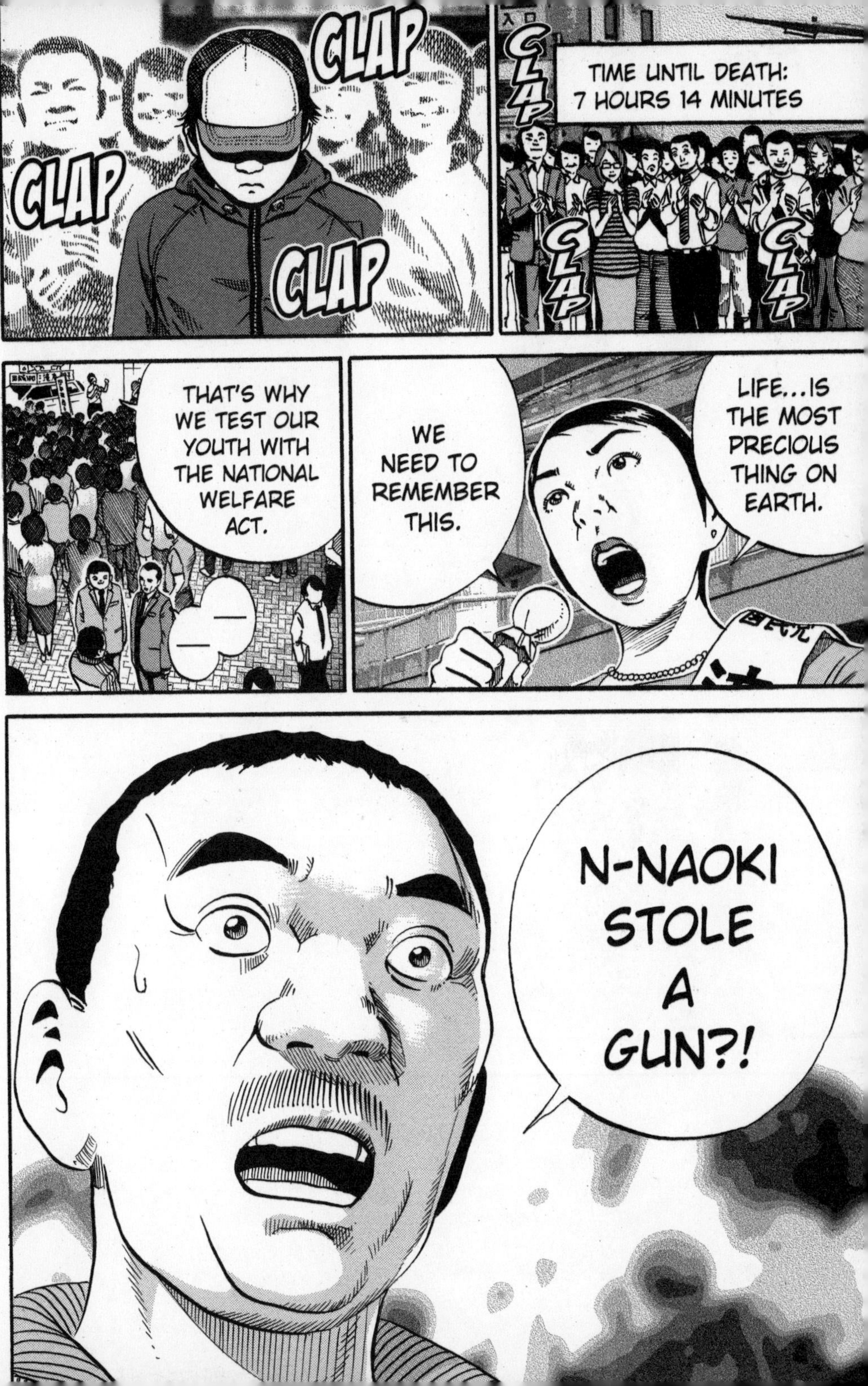
TIME UNTIL DEATH: 7 HOURS 14 MINUTES
CLAP
CLAP
CLAP
CLAP
CLAP
CLAP
LIFE...IS THE MOST PRECIOUS THING ON EARTH.
WE NEED TO REMEMBER THIS.
THAT'S WHY WE TEST OUR YOUTH WITH THE NATIONAL WELFARE ACT.
—
—
N-NAOKI STOLE A GUN?!

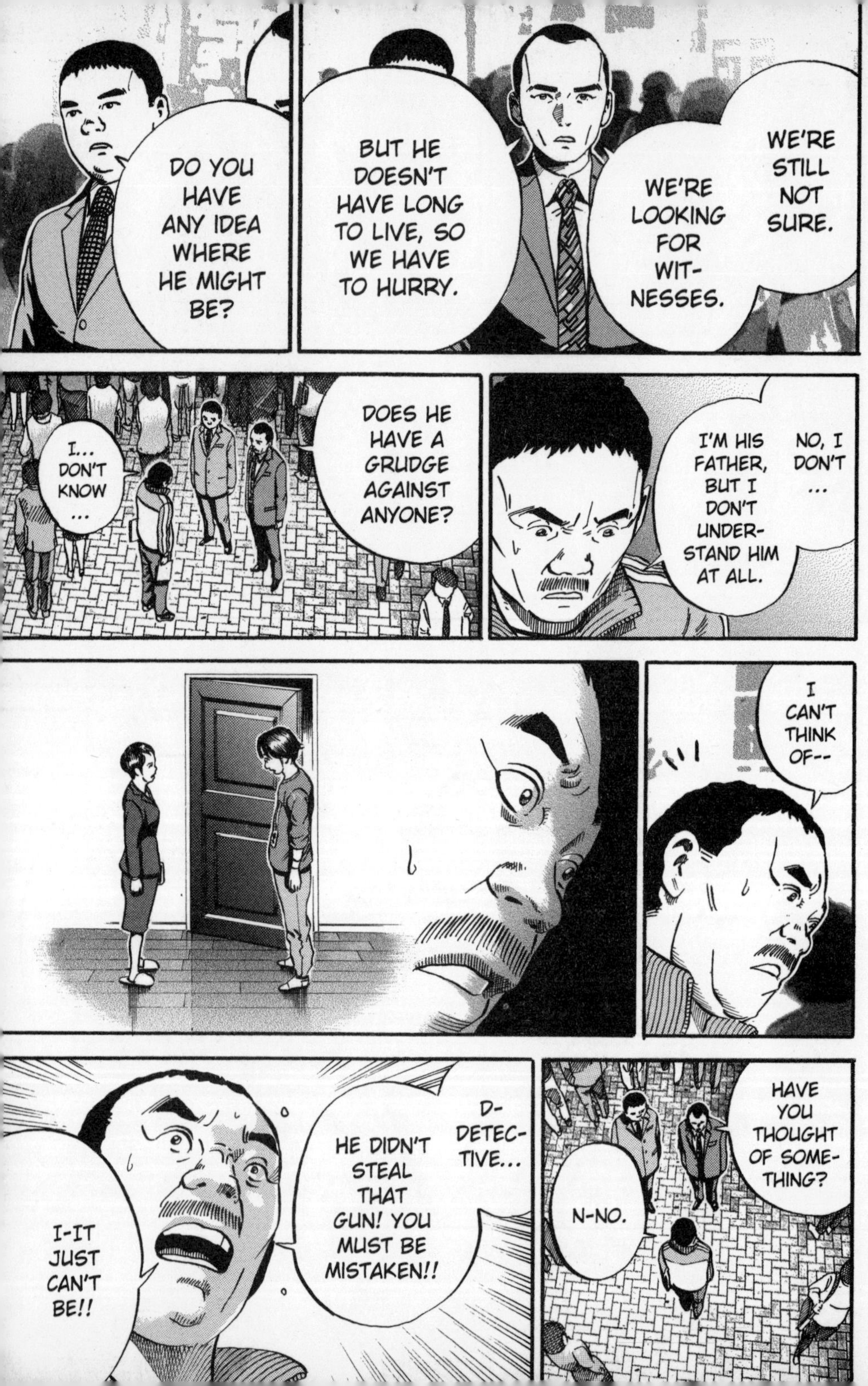
WE'RE STILL NOT SURE.
WE'RE LOOKING FOR WIT-NESSES.
BUT HE DOESN'T HAVE LONG TO LIVE, SO WE HAVE TO HURRY.
DO YOU HAVE ANY IDEA WHERE HE MIGHT BE?
NO, I DON'T ...
I'M HIS FATHER, BUT I DON'T UNDER-STAND HIM AT ALL.
DOES HE HAVE A GRUDGE AGAINST ANYONE?
I... DON'T KNOW ...
I CAN'T THINK OF--
HAVE YOU THOUGHT OF SOME-THING?
N-NO.
D-DETEC-TIVE...
HE DIDN'T STEAL THAT GUN! YOU MUST BE MISTAKEN!!
I-IT JUST CAN'T BE!!

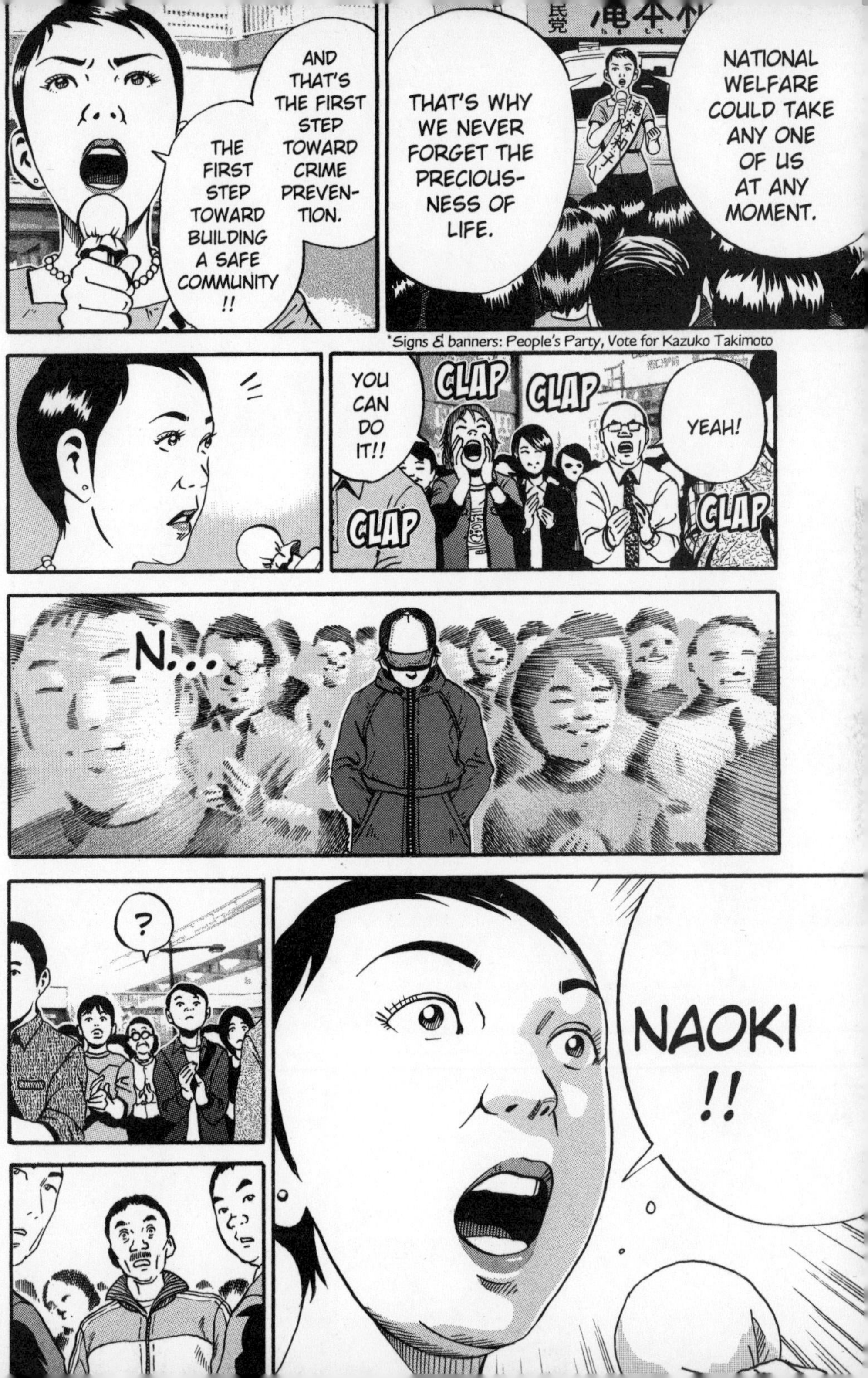
NATIONAL WELFARE COULD TAKE ANY ONE OF US AT ANY MOMENT.
THAT'S WHY WE NEVER FORGET THE PRECIOUSNESS OF LIFE.
AND THAT'S THE FIRST STEP TOWARD CRIME PREVENTION.
THE FIRST STEP TOWARD BUILDING A SAFE COMMUNITY!!
*Signs & banners: People's Party, Vote for Kazuko Takimoto
YEAH!
CLAP
CLAP
CLAP
YOU CAN DO IT!!
CLAP
N...
NAOKI!!
?

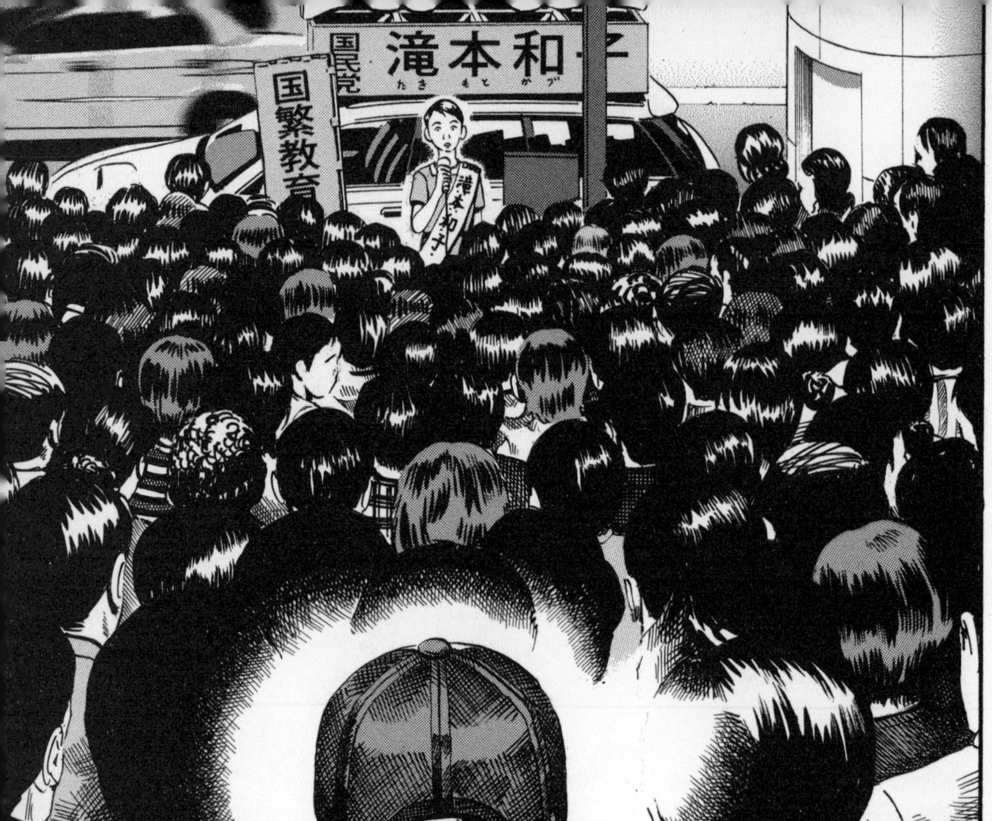
国民党
滝本和子
国繁教育

*Signs & banners: People's Party, Vote for Kazuko Takimoto

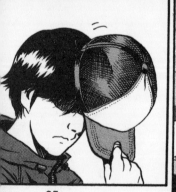

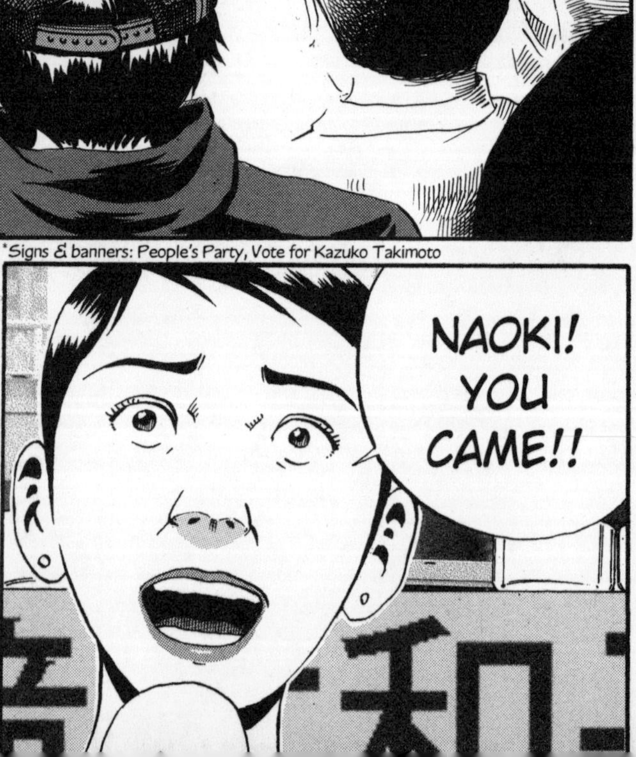
NAOKI! YOU CAME!!

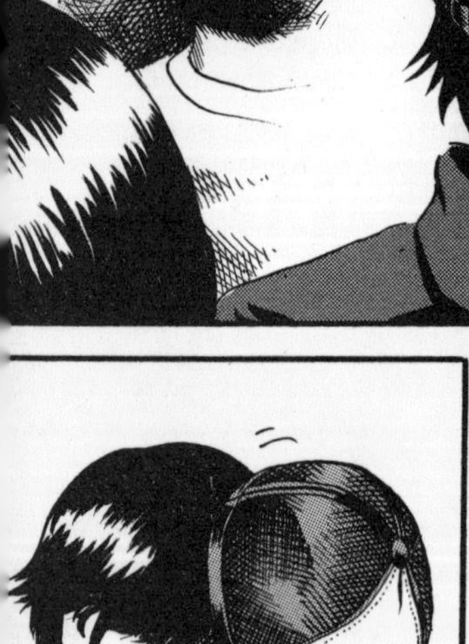

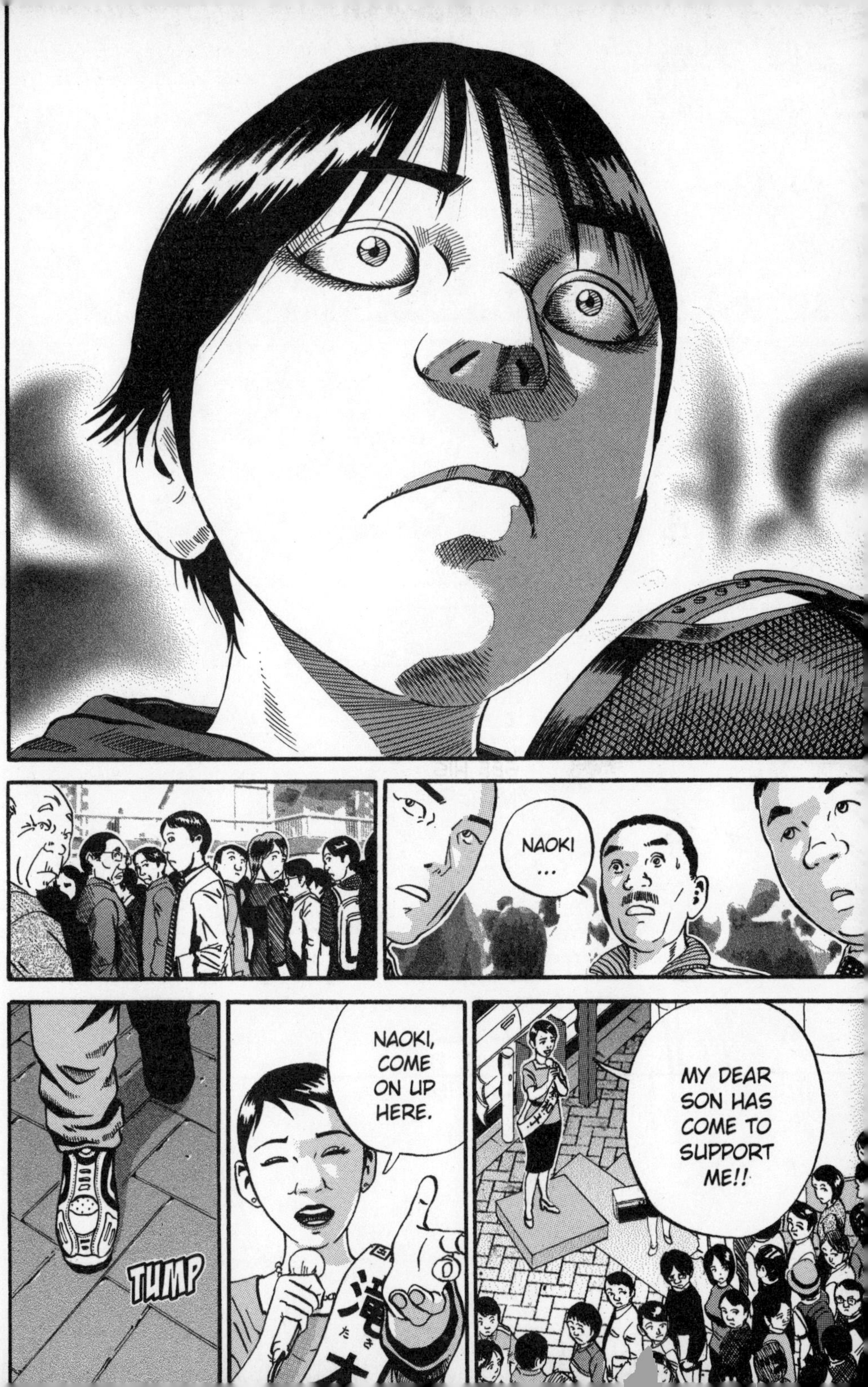
NAOKI ...
MY DEAR SON HAS COME TO SUPPORT ME!!
NAOKI, COME ON UP HERE.
滝
TUMP

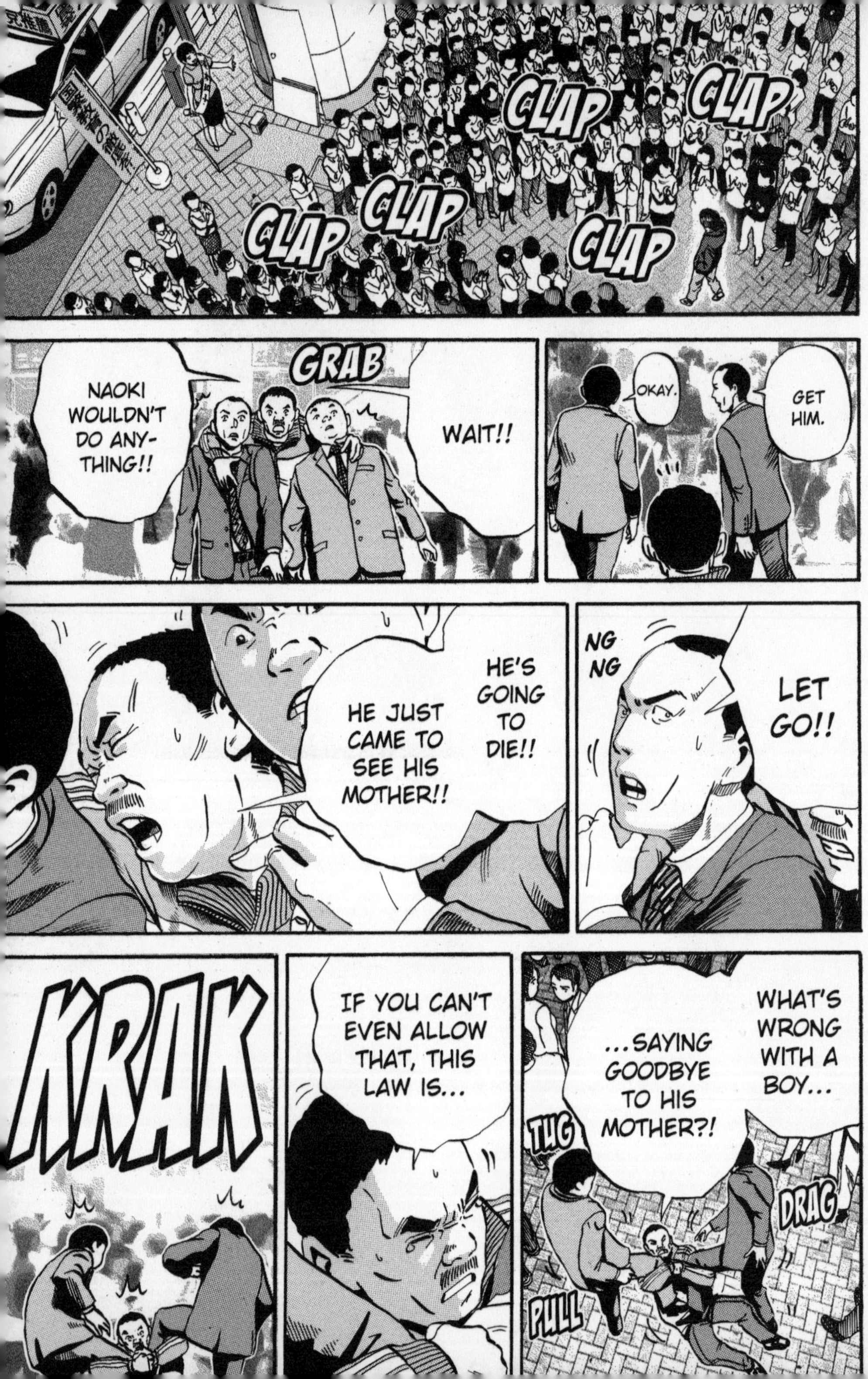
CLAP
CLAP
CLAP
CLAP
CLAP
GET HIM.
OKAY.
WAIT!!
GRAB
NAOKI WOULDN'T DO ANYTHING!!
LET GO!!
NG NG
HE'S GOING TO DIE!!
HE JUST CAME TO SEE HIS MOTHER!!
WHAT'S WRONG WITH A BOY...
...SAYING GOODBYE TO HIS MOTHER?!
TUG
DRAG
PULL
IF YOU CAN'T EVEN ALLOW THAT, THIS LAW IS...
KRAK

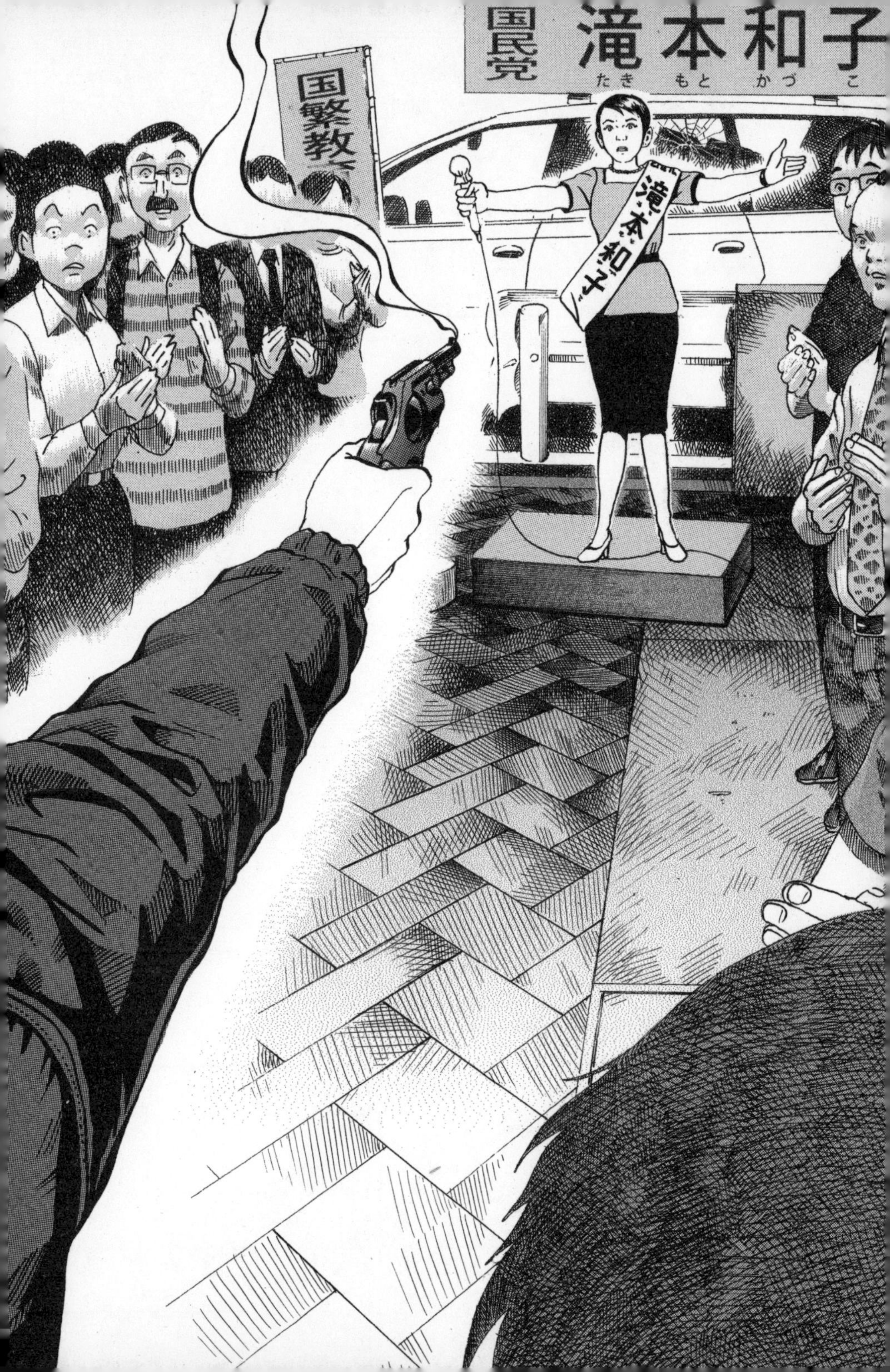
国民党
滝本和子
たきもと かづこ
滝本和子
国繁教

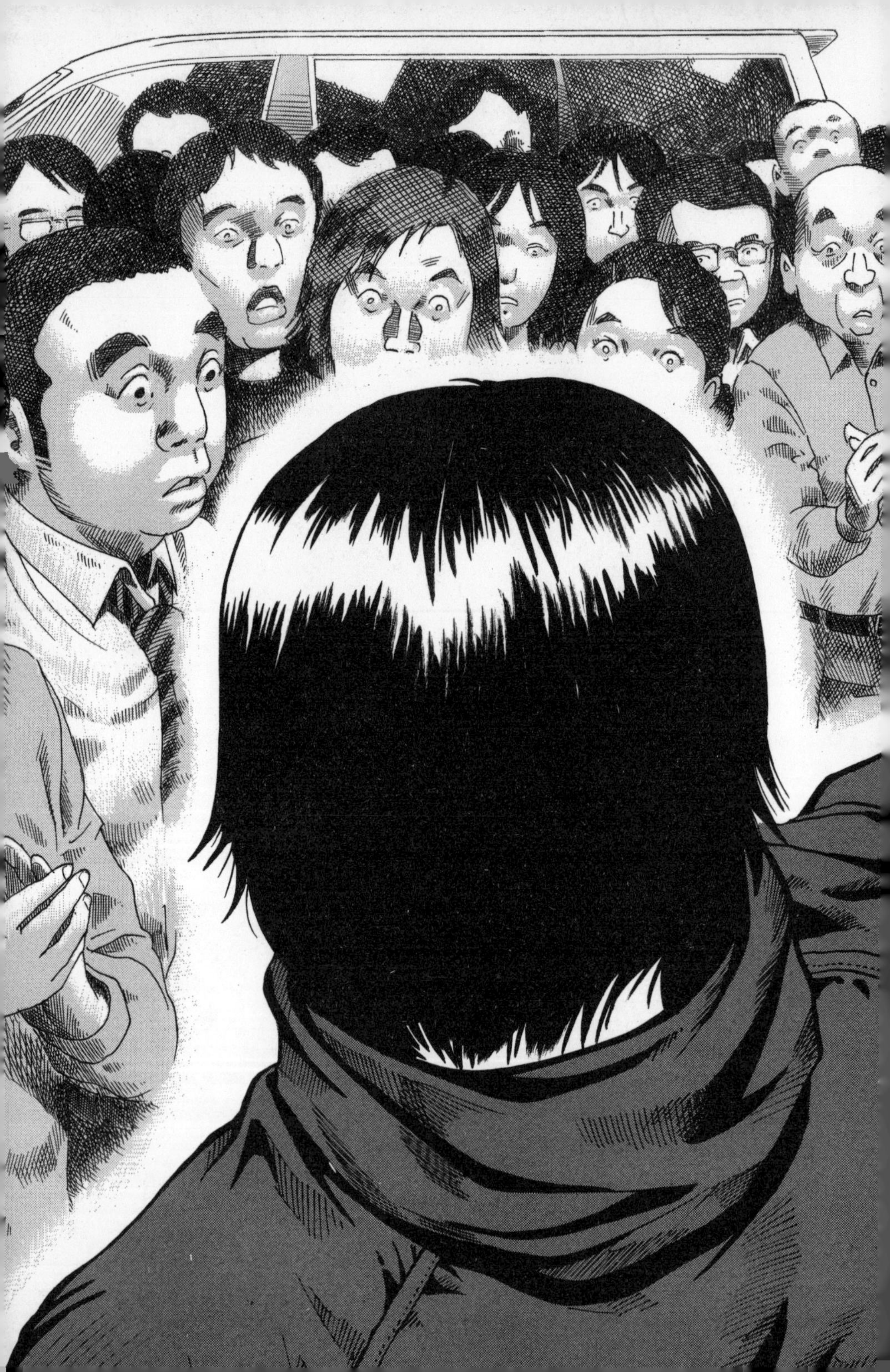

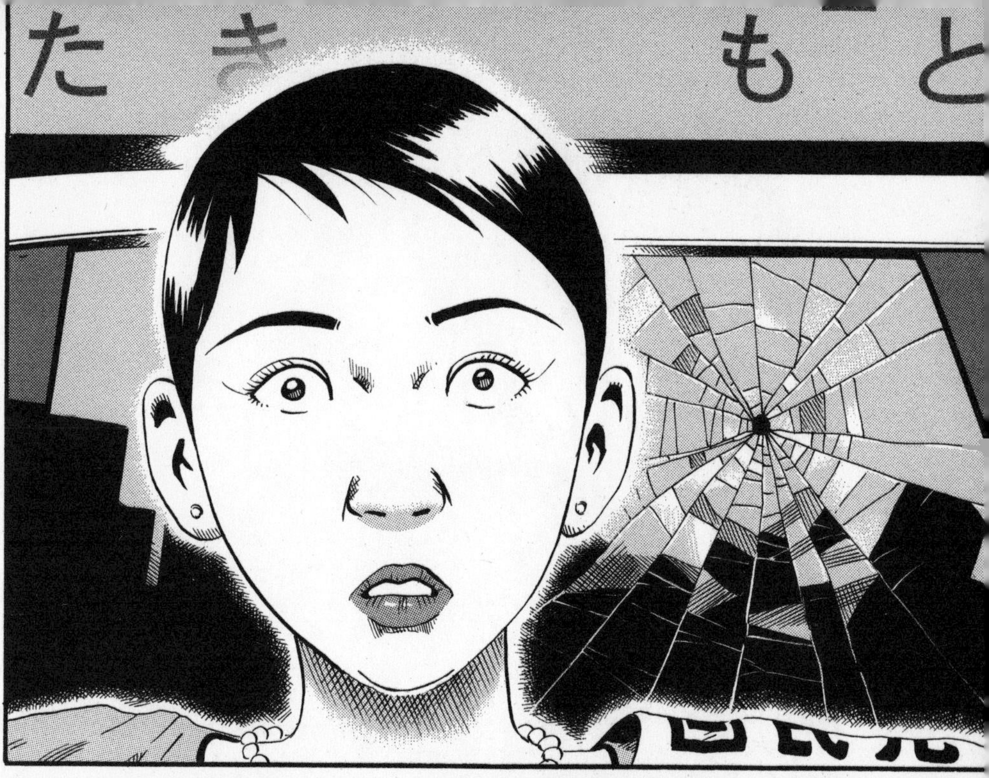
たき　もと

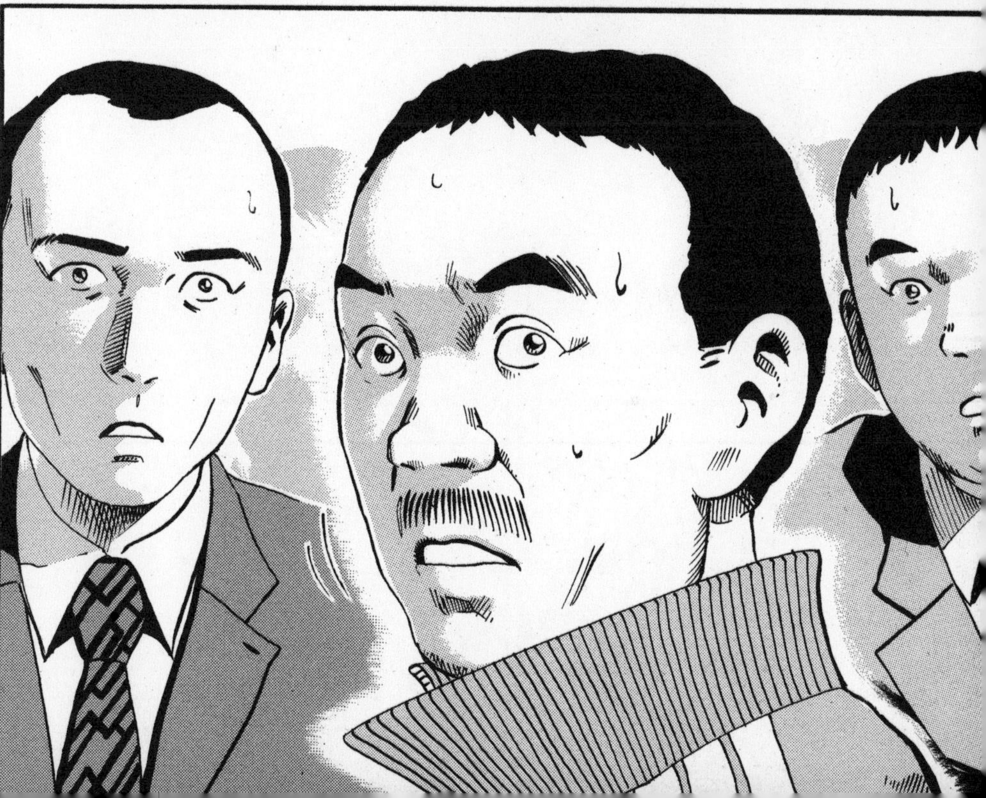

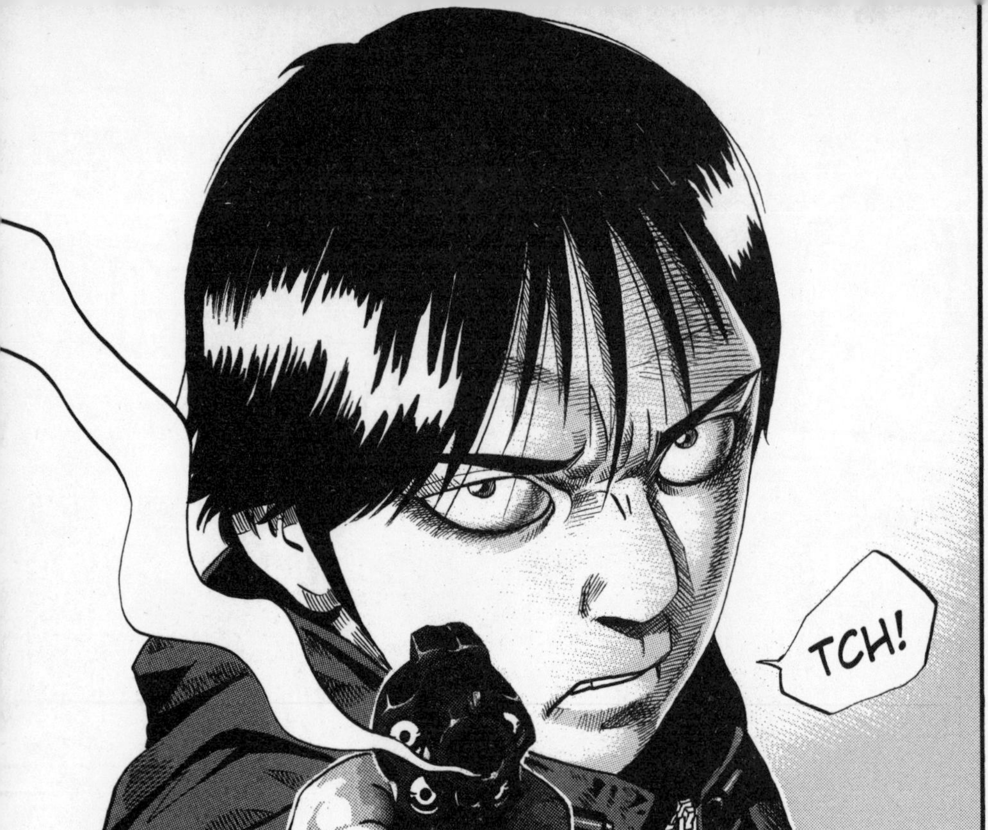
TCH!
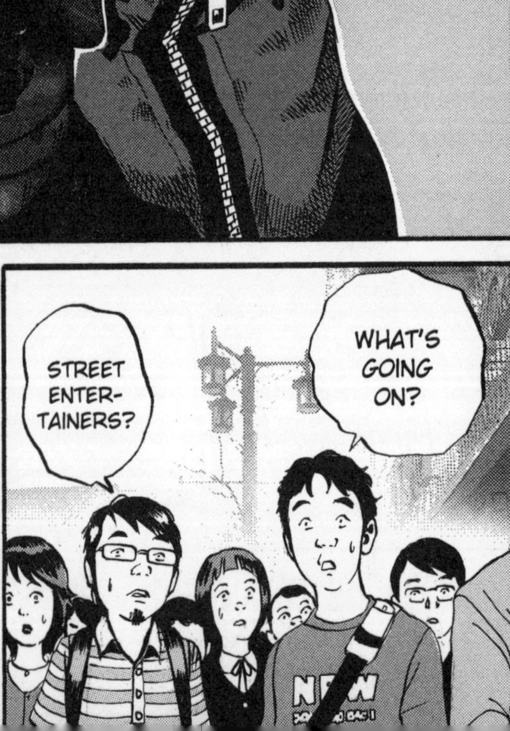
WHAT'S GOING ON?
STREET ENTER-TAINERS?
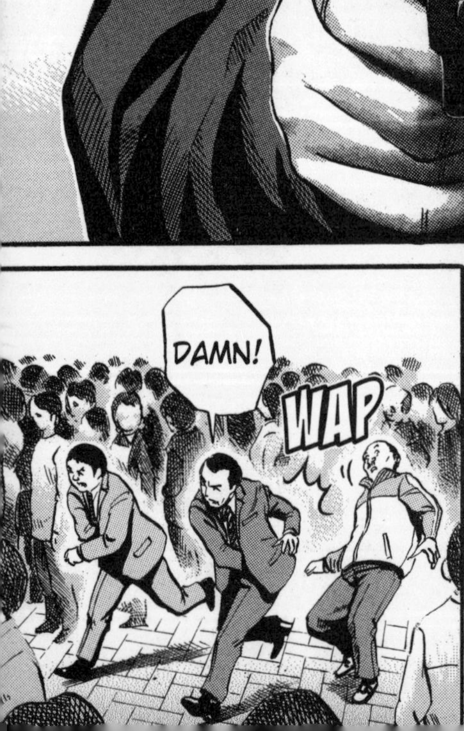
DAMN!
WAP

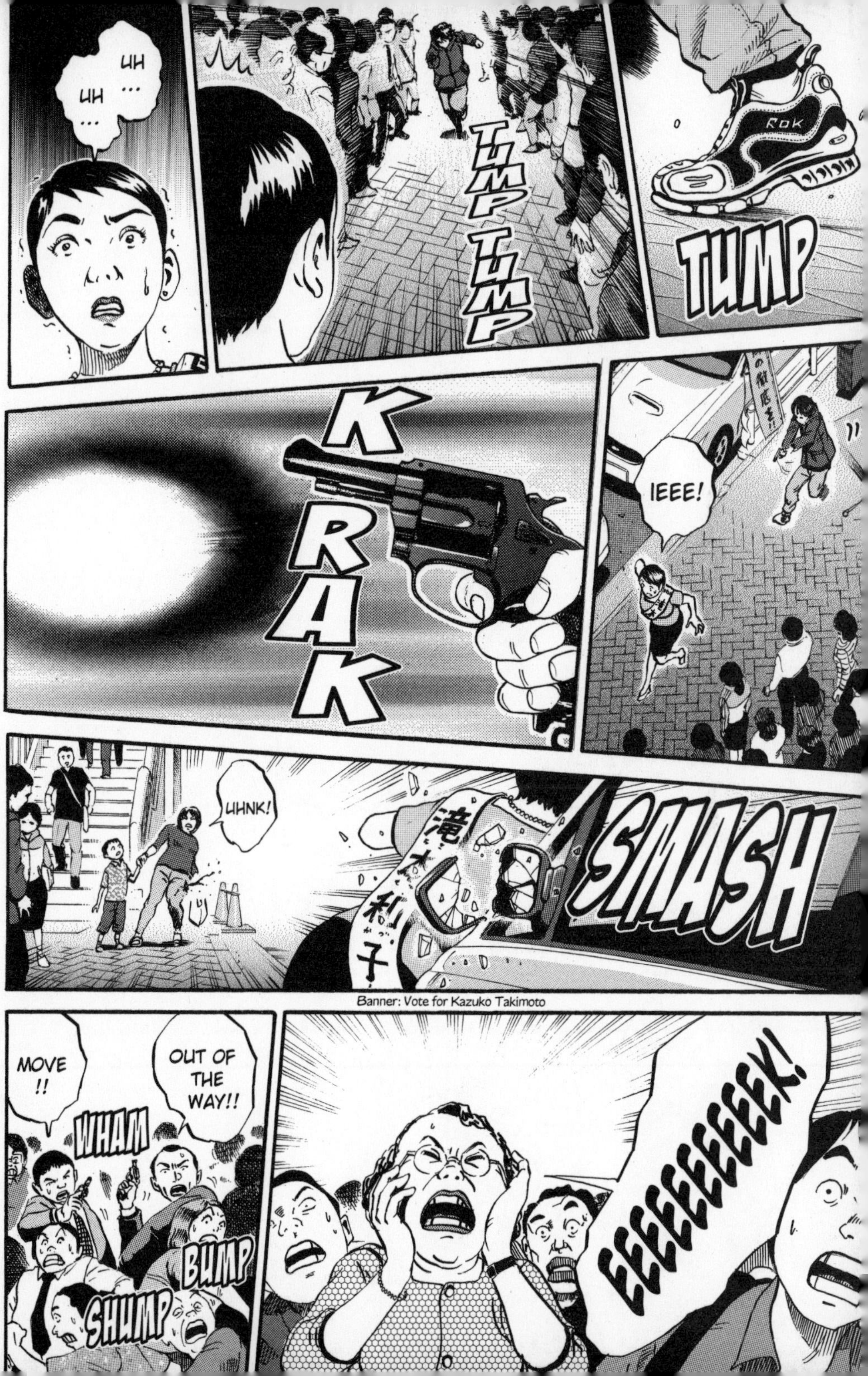

ROK
TUMP
TUMP TUMP TUMP
UH ... UH ...
IEEE!
KRAK
SMASH
UHNK!
Banner: Vote for Kazuko Takimoto
EEEEEEEEEK!
OUT OF THE WAY!!
MOVE !!
WHAM
BUMP
SHUMP

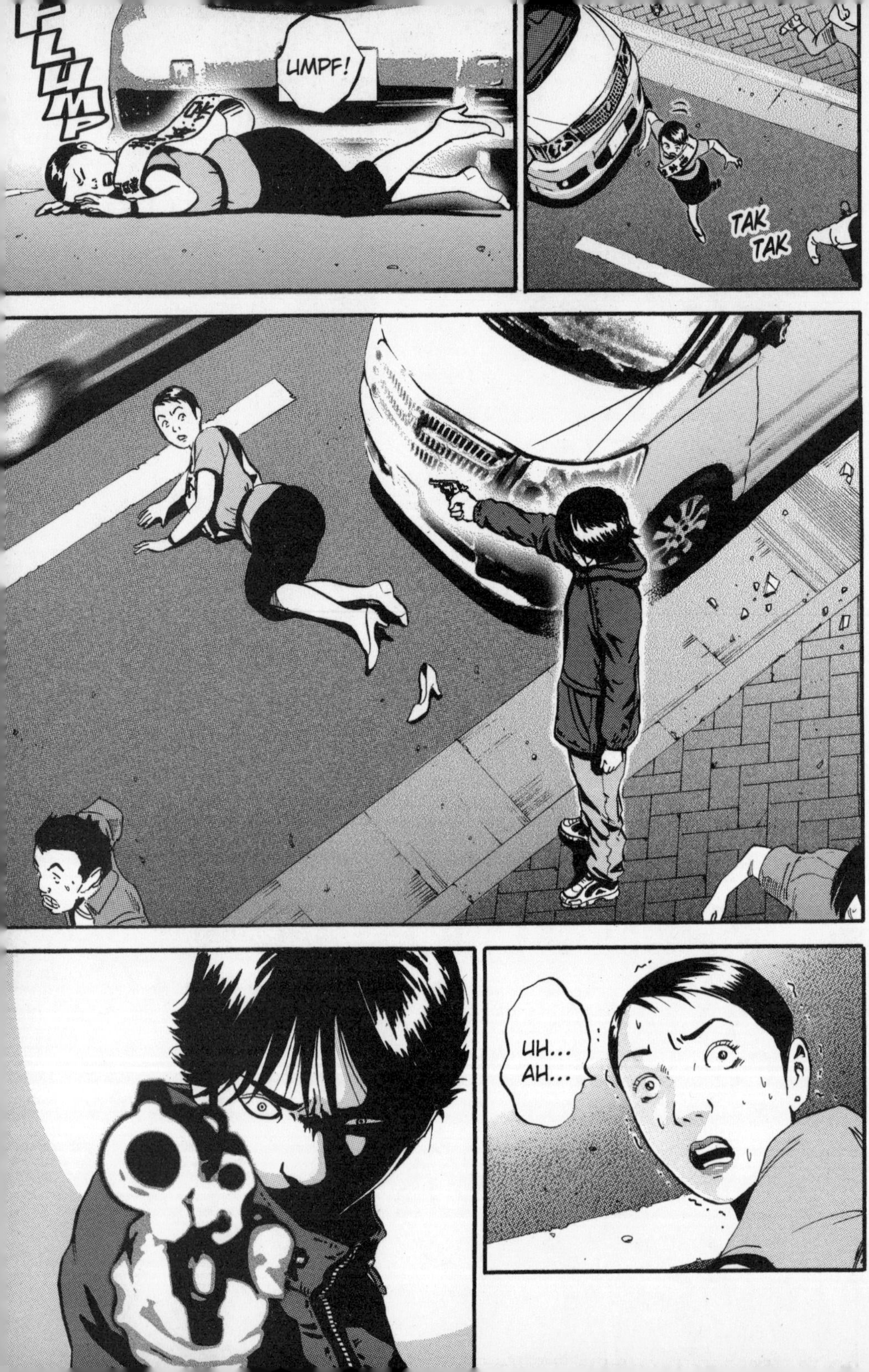
TAK
TAK
FLUMP
UMPF!
UH...
AH...

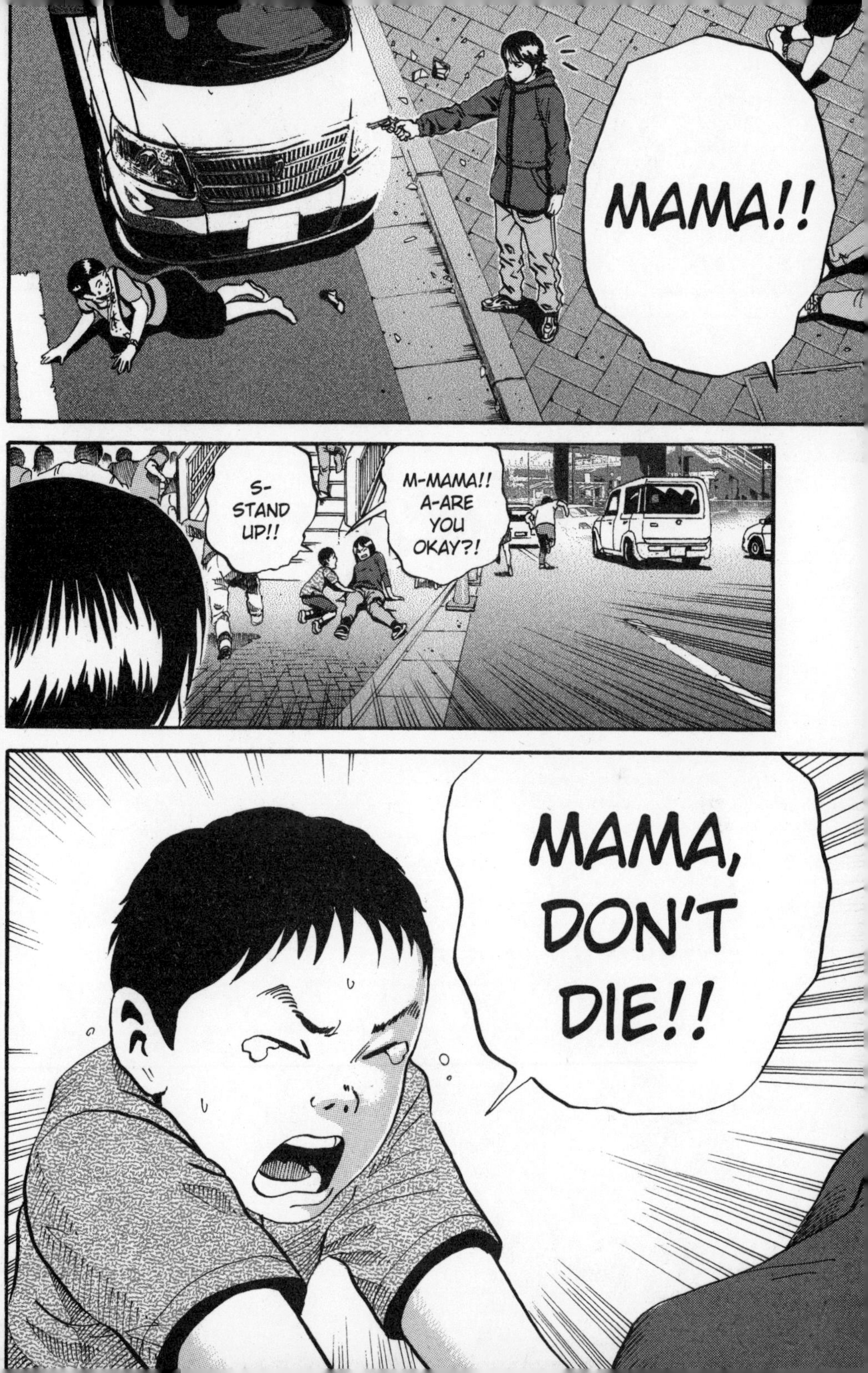
MAMA!!
M-MAMA!! A-ARE YOU OKAY?!
S-STAND UP!!
MAMA, DON'T DIE!!

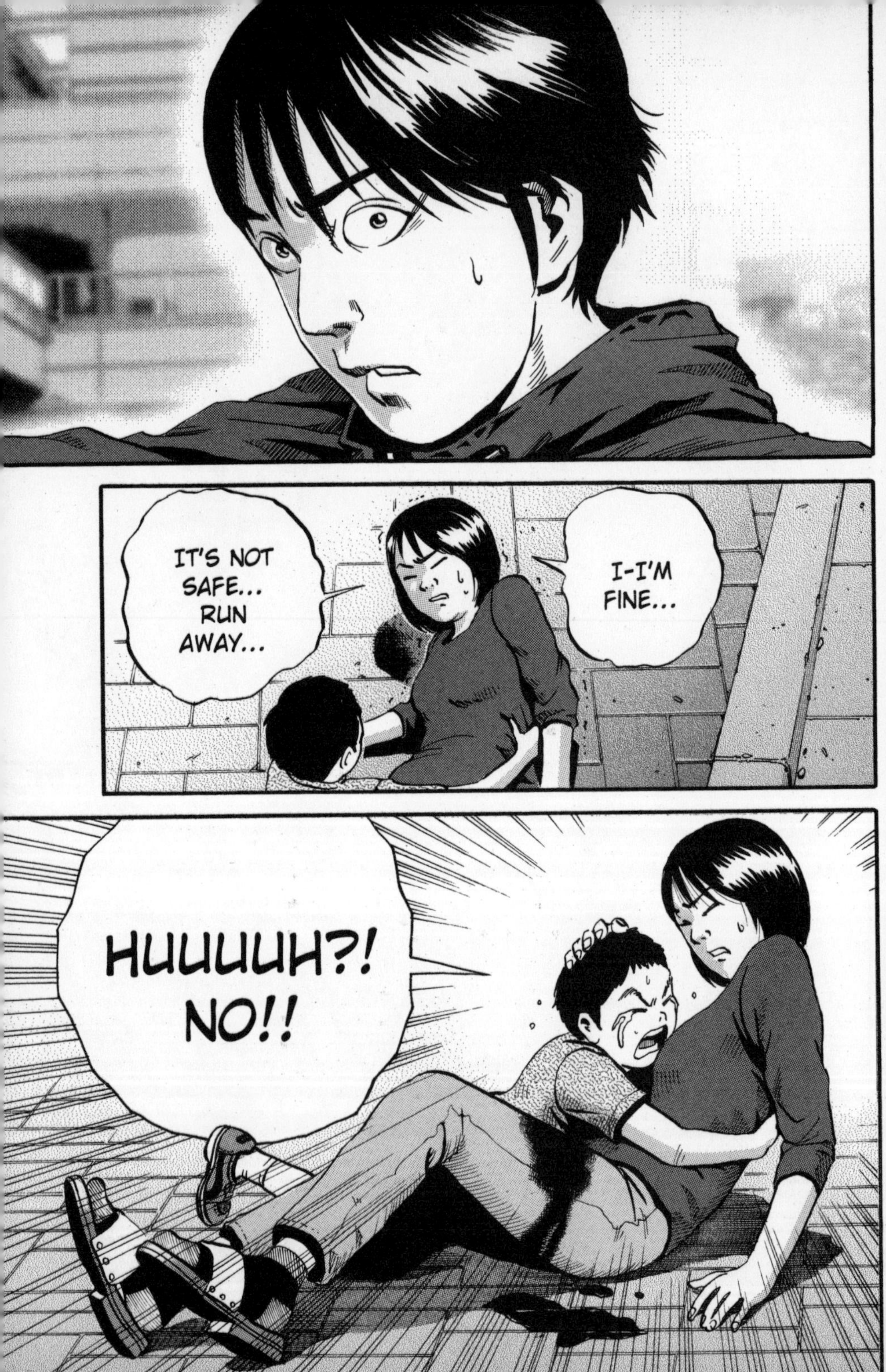
I-I'M FINE...
IT'S NOT SAFE... RUN AWAY...
HUUUUH?! NO!!

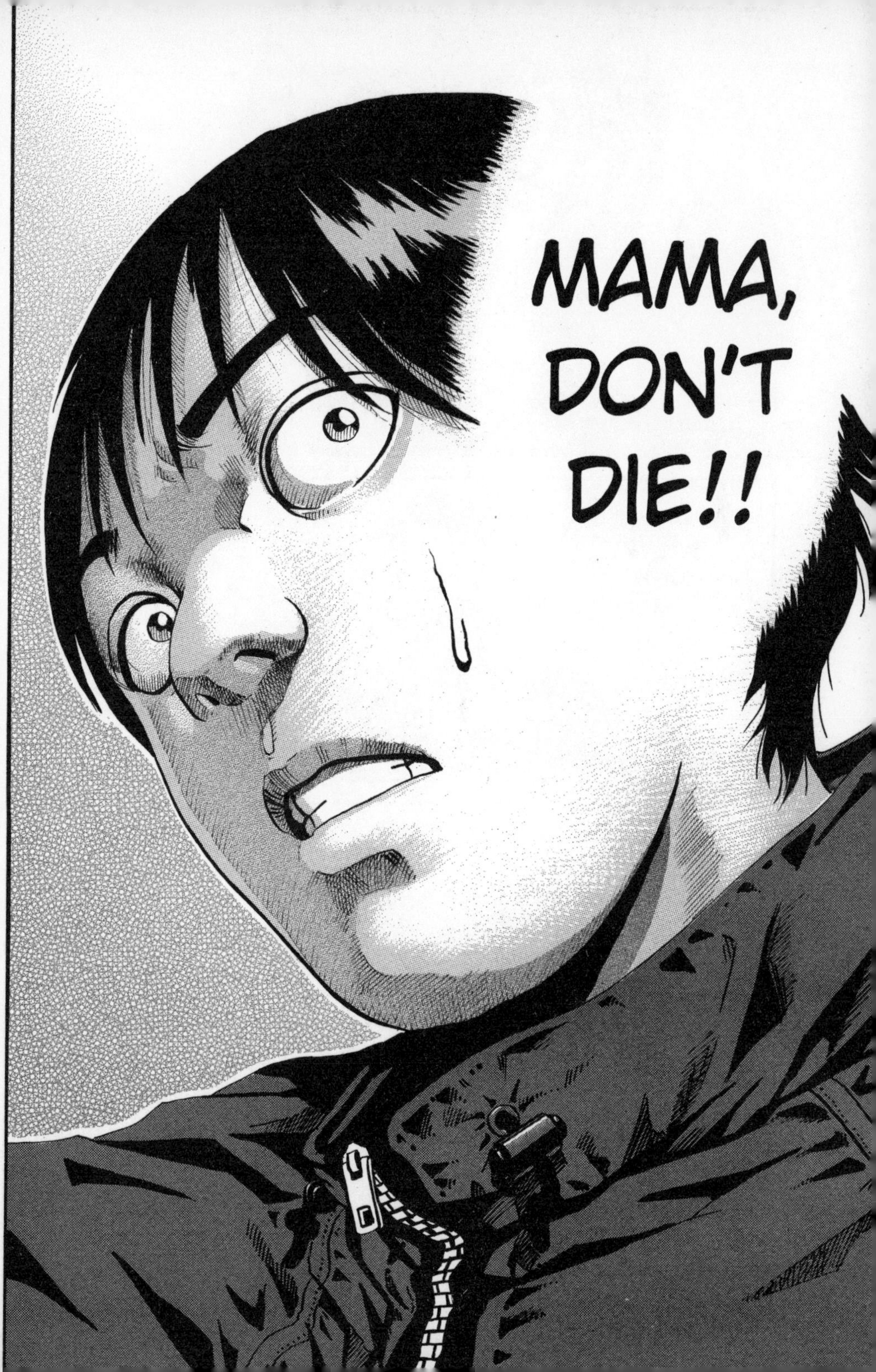
MAMA, DON'T DIE!!

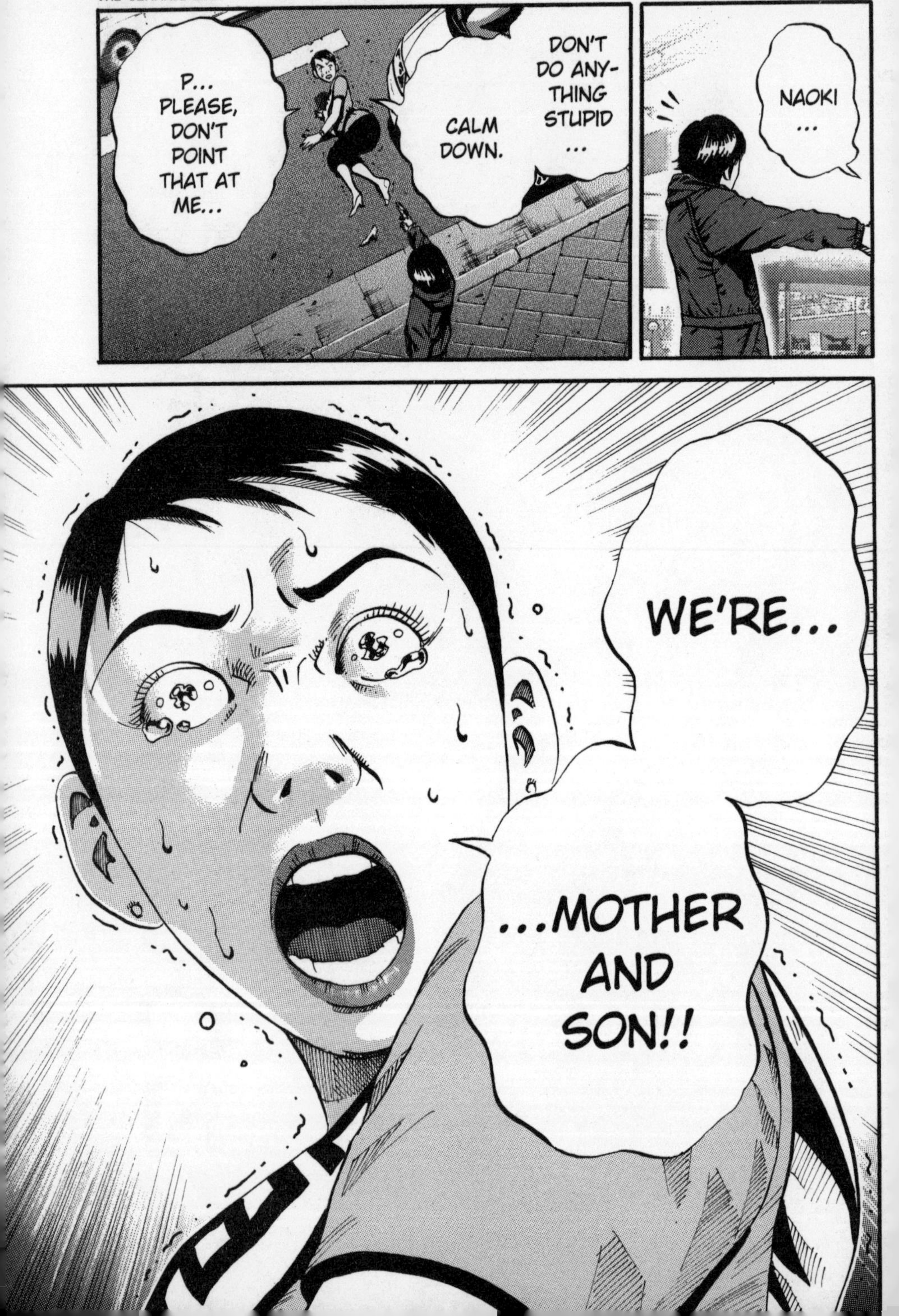
NAOKI ...
DON'T DO ANY-THING STUPID ...
CALM DOWN.
P... PLEASE, DON'T POINT THAT AT ME...
WE'RE...
...MOTHER AND SON!!

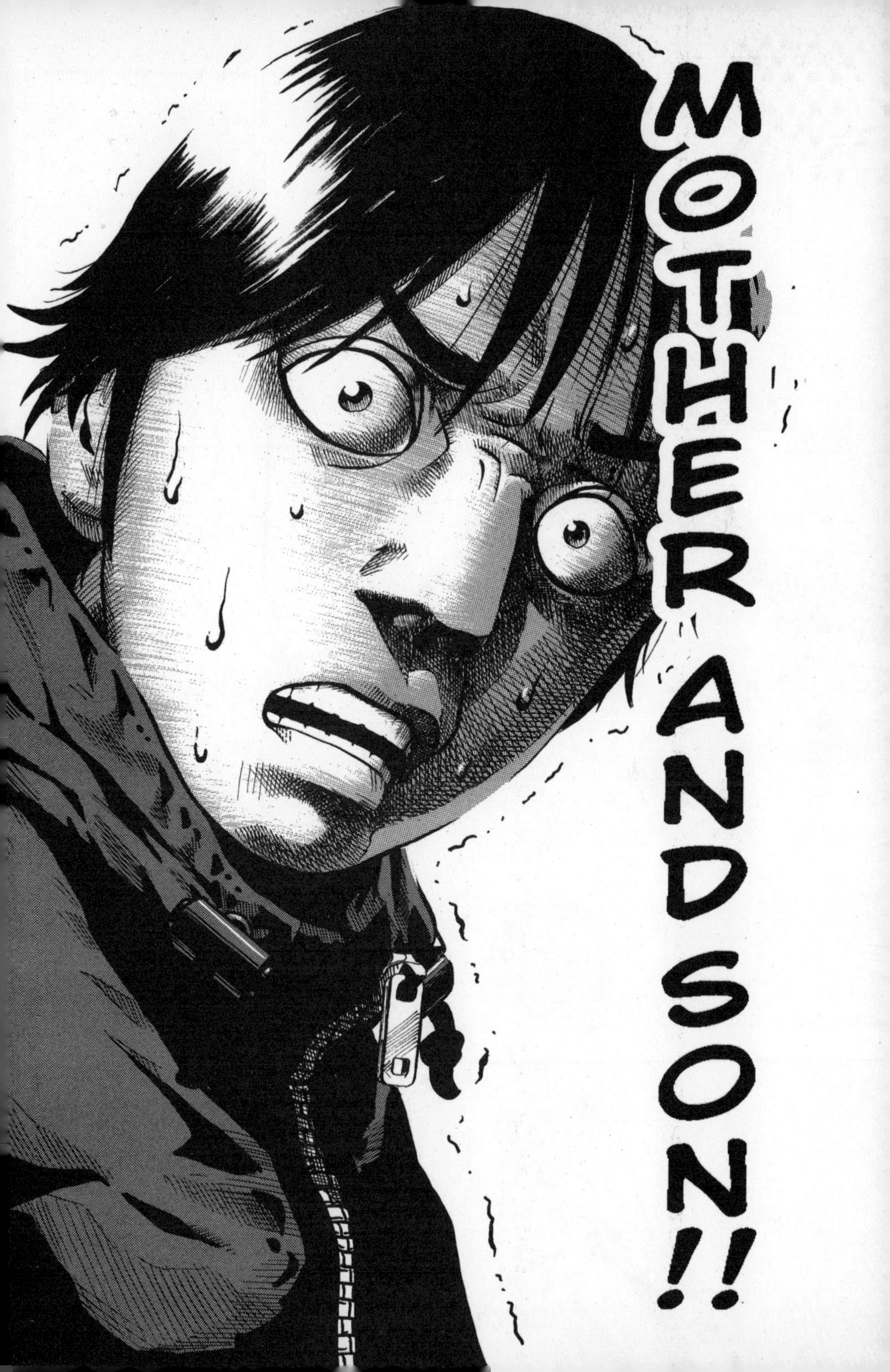
MOTHER AND SON!!

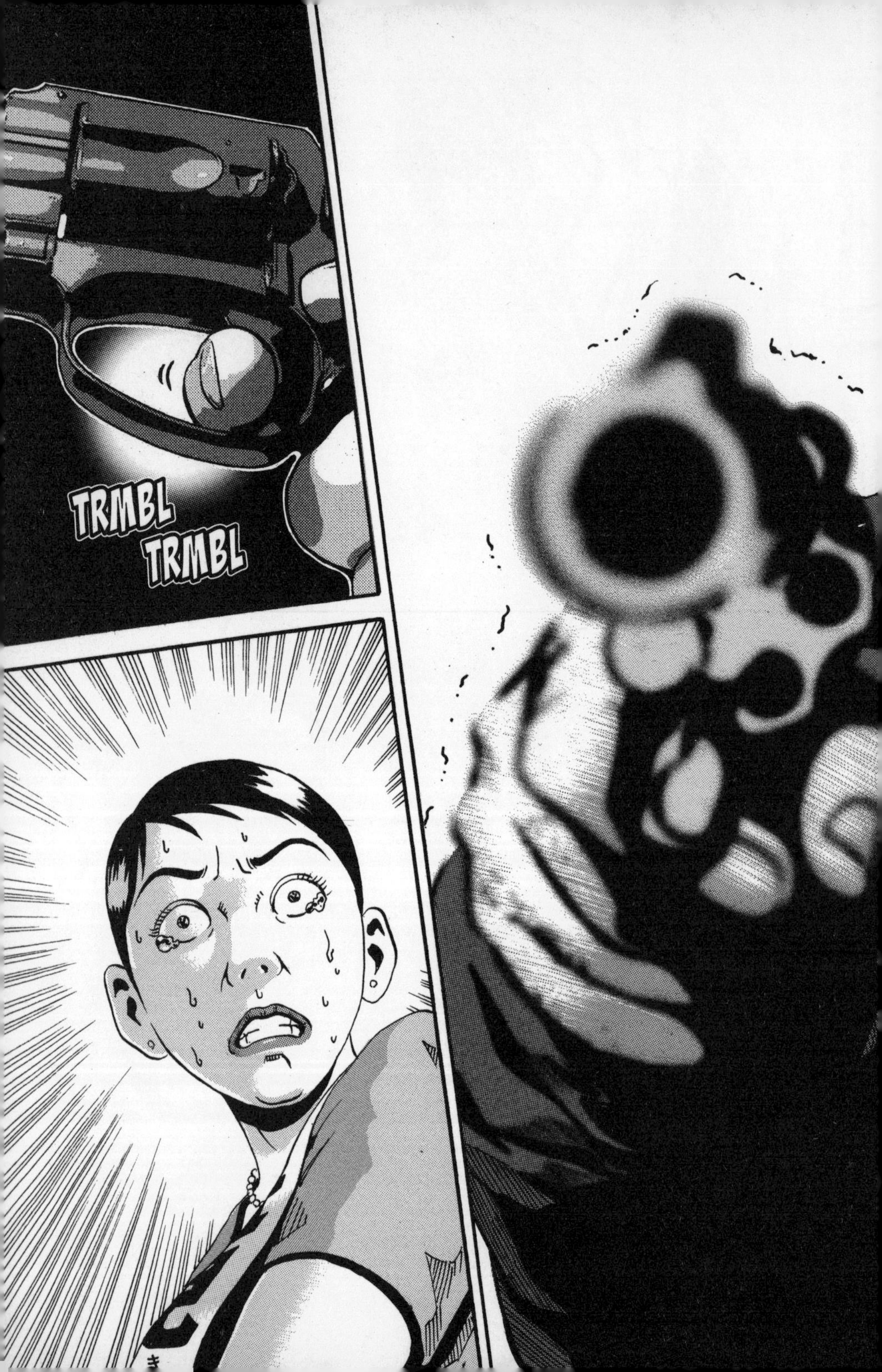
TRMBL
TRMBL

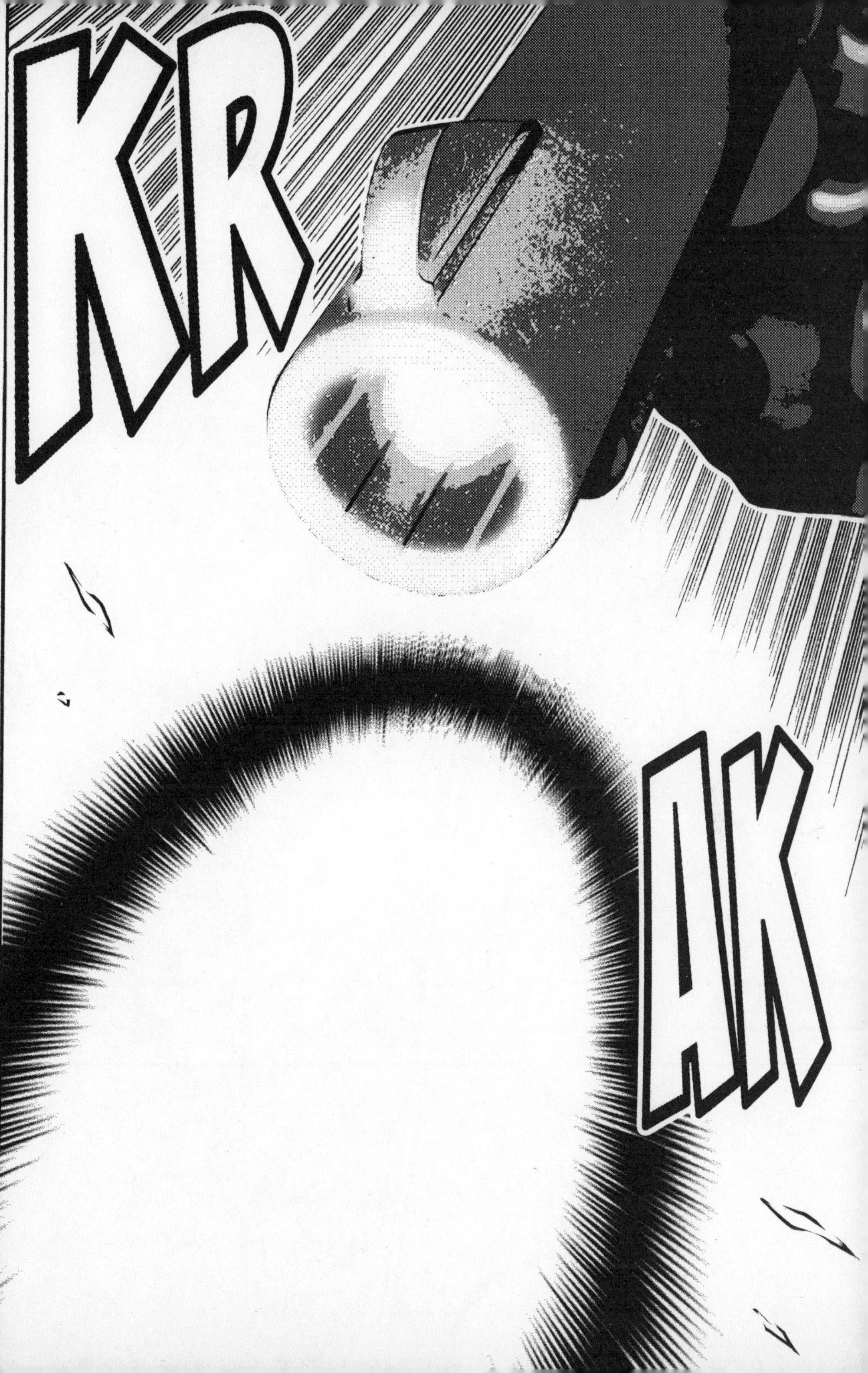
KR
AK

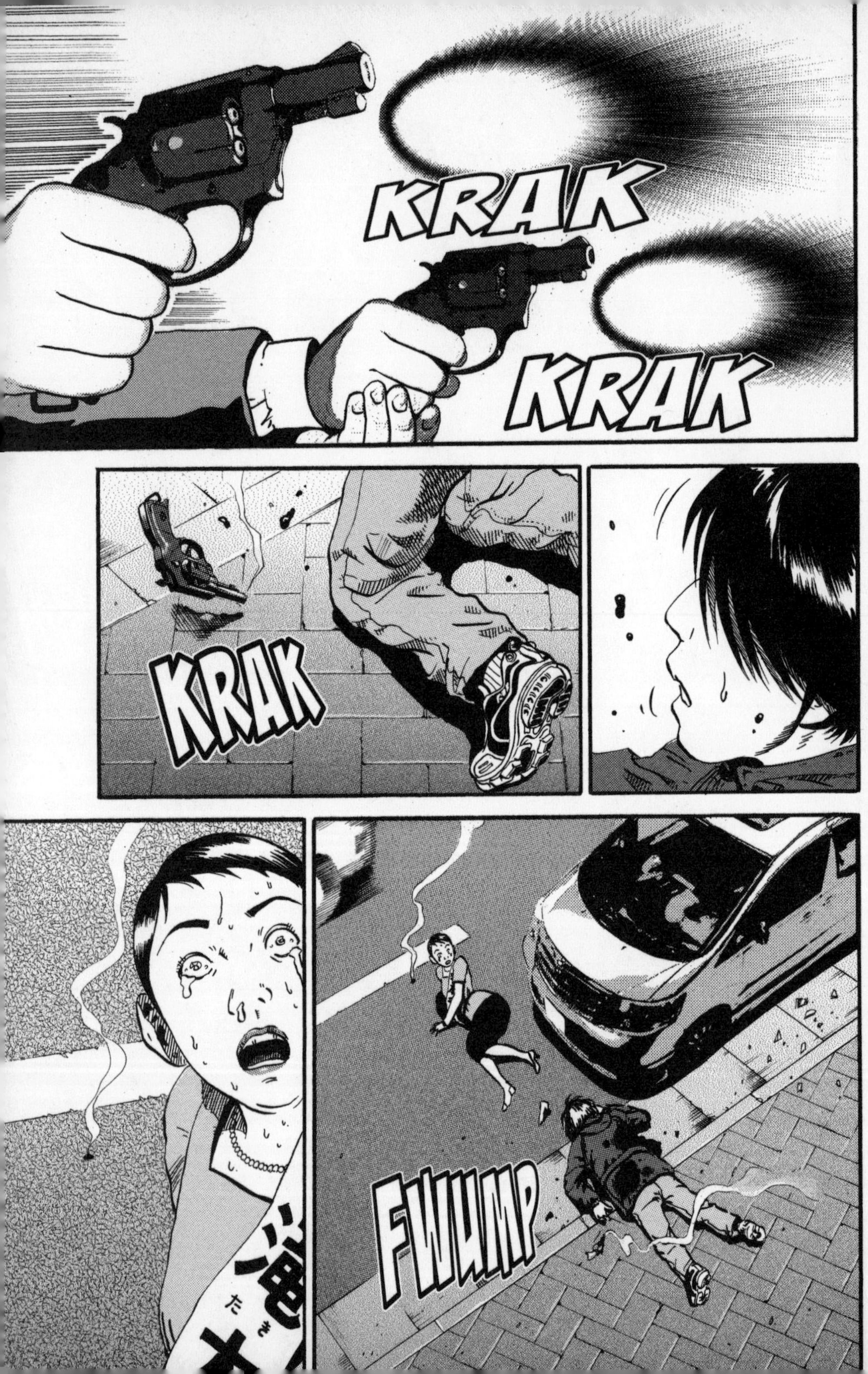
KRAK
KRAK
KRAK
FWUMP

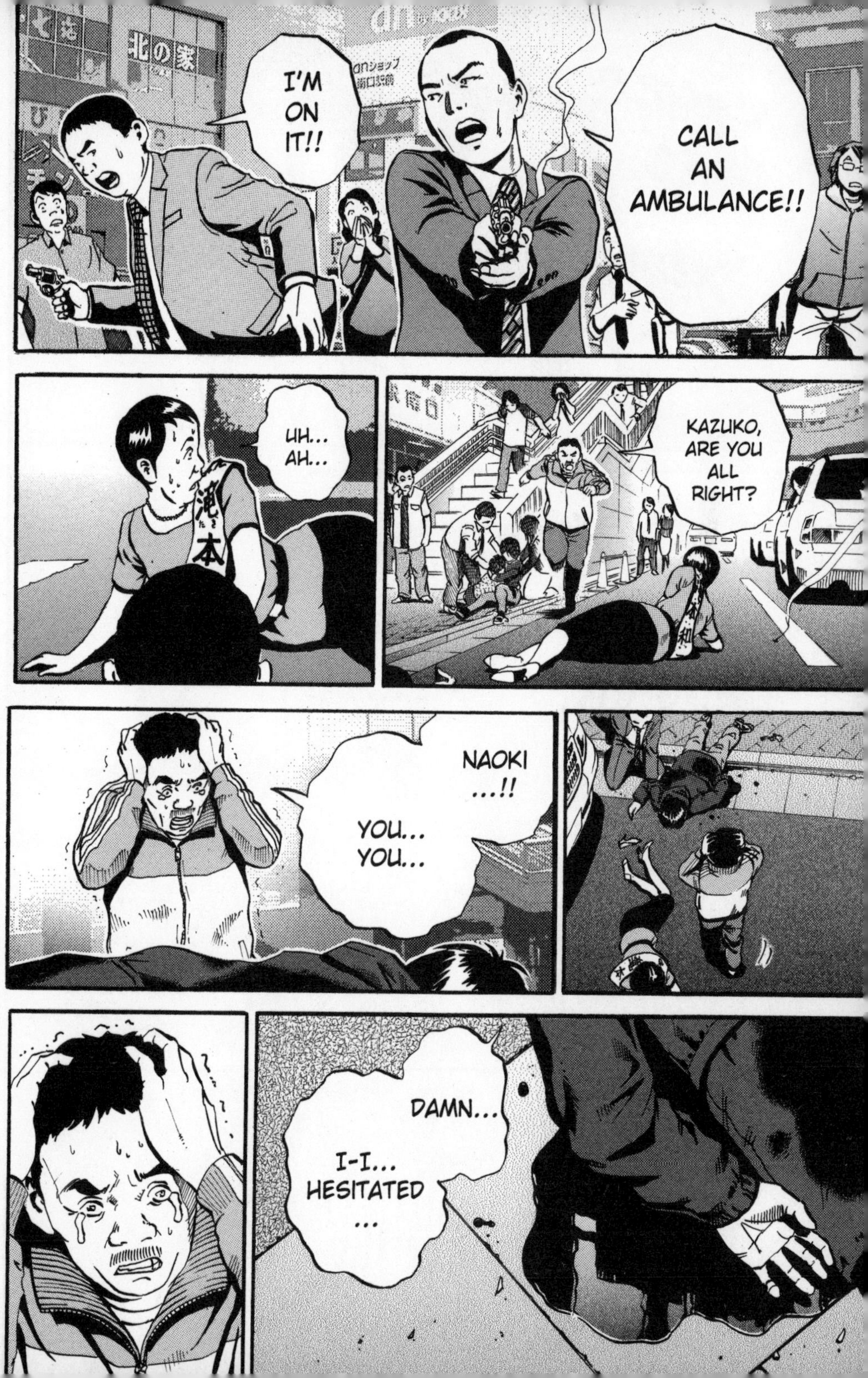
CALL AN AMBULANCE!!
I'M ON IT!!
KAZUKO, ARE YOU ALL RIGHT?
UH... AH...
NAOKI ...!!
YOU... YOU...
DAMN...
I-I... HESITATED ...

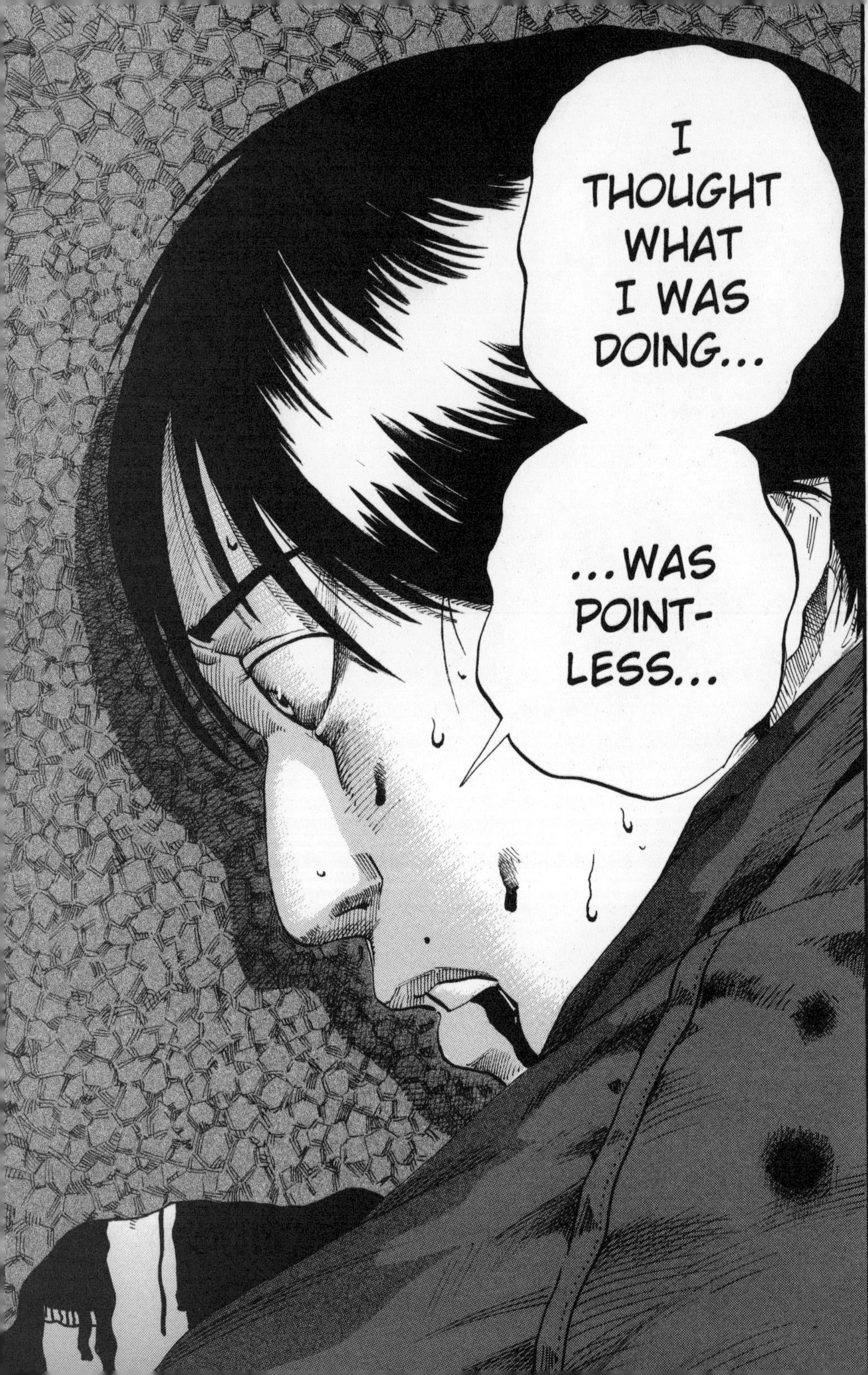
I THOUGHT WHAT I WAS DOING...
...WAS POINT-LESS...

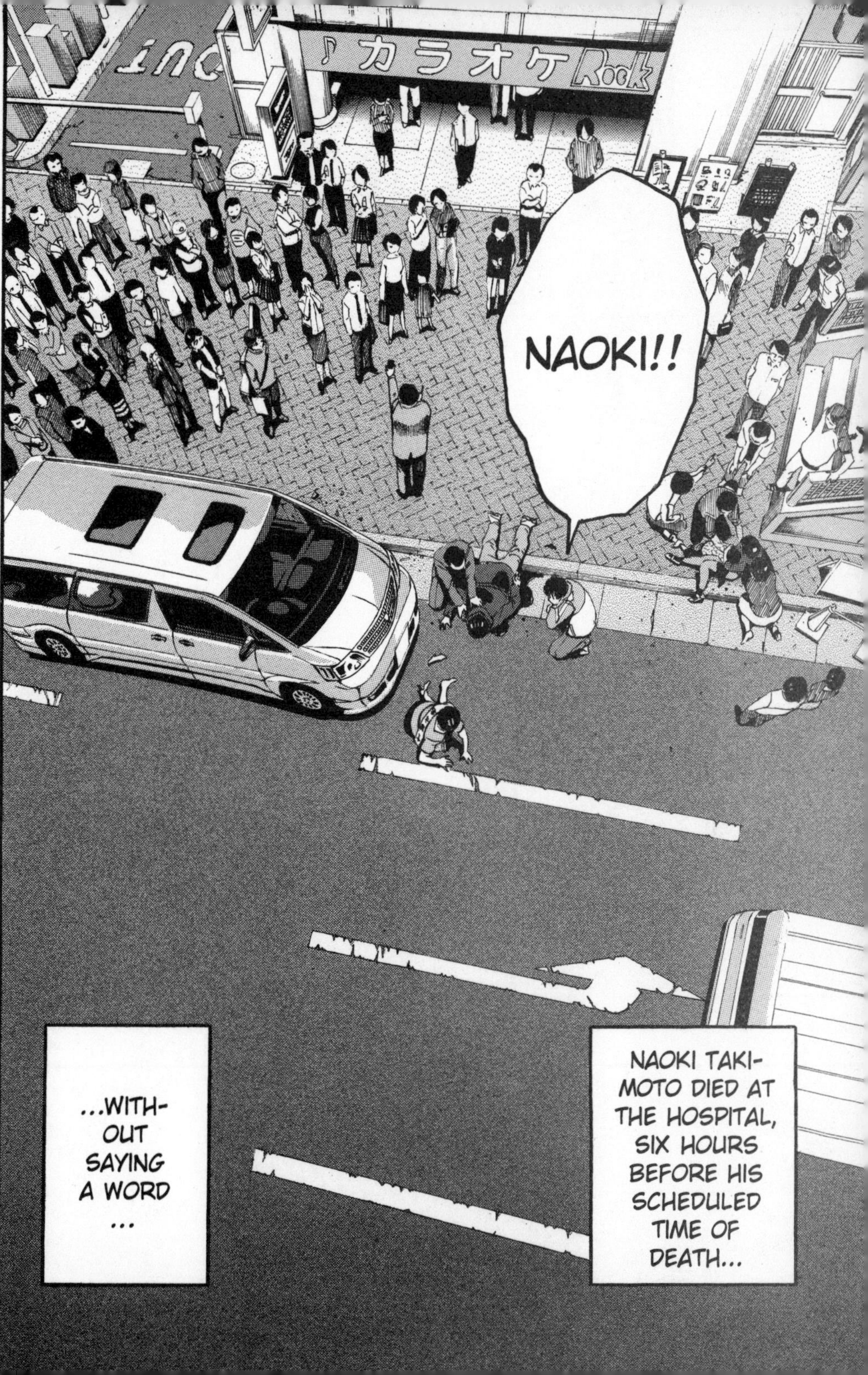

♪カラオケ Rock
NAOKI!!
NAOKI TAKI-MOTO DIED AT THE HOSPITAL, SIX HOURS BEFORE HIS SCHEDULED TIME OF DEATH...
...WITH-OUT SAYING A WORD ...

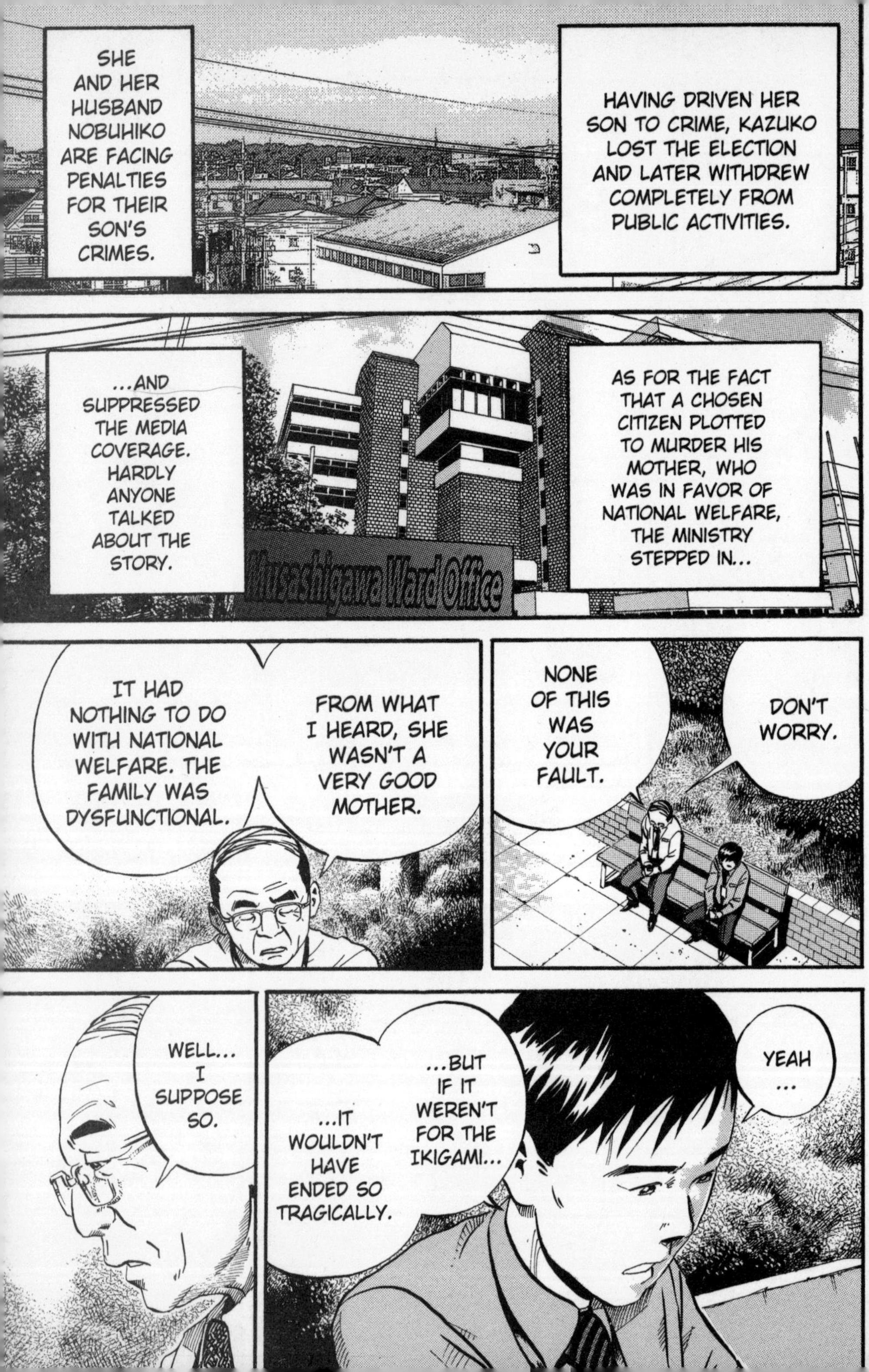
HAVING DRIVEN HER SON TO CRIME, KAZUKO LOST THE ELECTION AND LATER WITHDREW COMPLETELY FROM PUBLIC ACTIVITIES.
SHE AND HER HUSBAND NOBUHIKO ARE FACING PENALTIES FOR THEIR SON'S CRIMES.
AS FOR THE FACT THAT A CHOSEN CITIZEN PLOTTED TO MURDER HIS MOTHER, WHO WAS IN FAVOR OF NATIONAL WELFARE, THE MINISTRY STEPPED IN...
...AND SUPPRESSED THE MEDIA COVERAGE. HARDLY ANYONE TALKED ABOUT THE STORY.
Musashigawa Ward Office
DON'T WORRY.
NONE OF THIS WAS YOUR FAULT.
FROM WHAT I HEARD, SHE WASN'T A VERY GOOD MOTHER.
IT HAD NOTHING TO DO WITH NATIONAL WELFARE. THE FAMILY WAS DYSFUNCTIONAL.
YEAH...
...BUT IF IT WEREN'T FOR THE IKIGAMI...
...IT WOULDN'T HAVE ENDED SO TRAGICALLY.
WELL... I SUPPOSE SO.

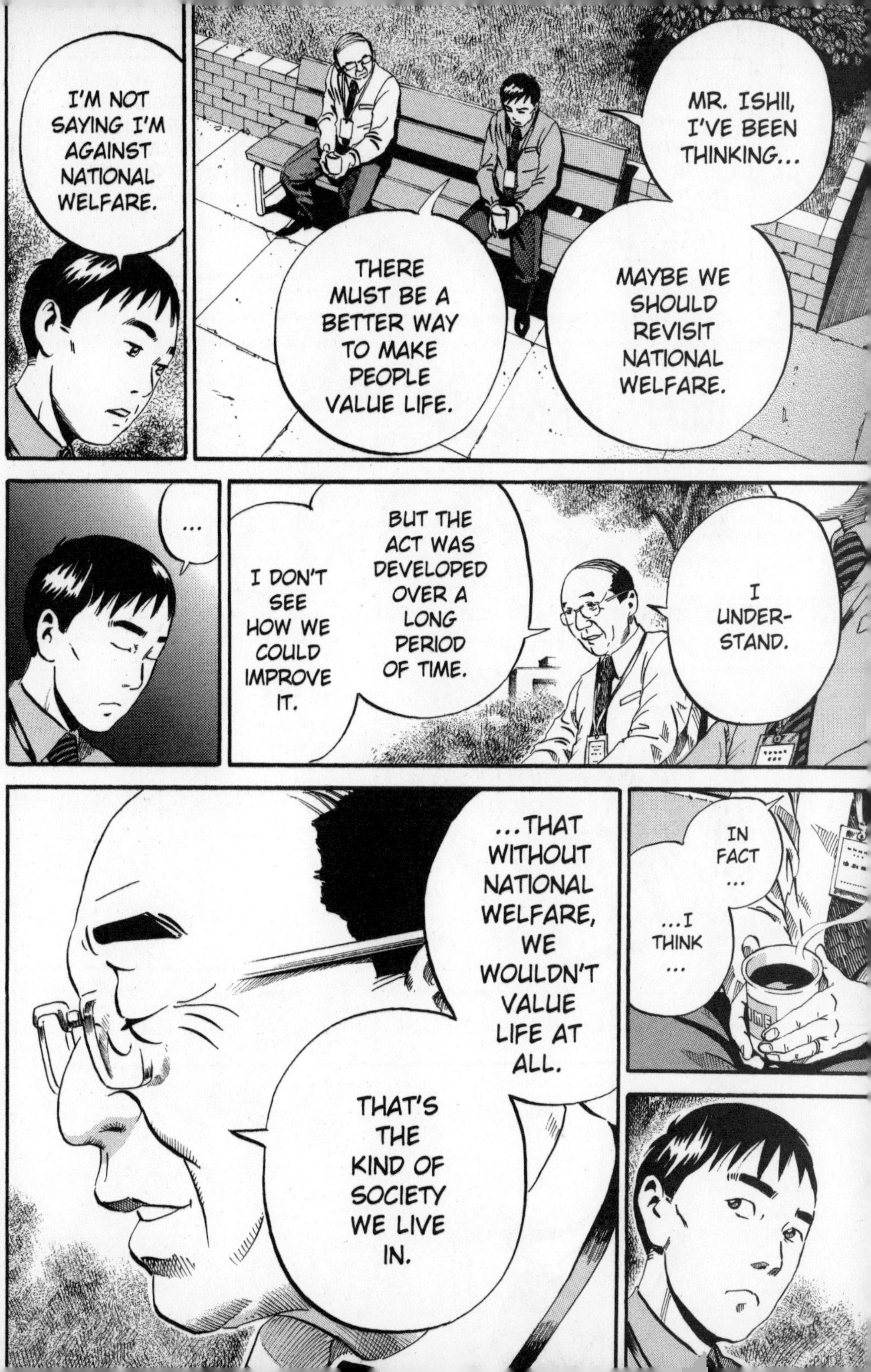
MR. ISHII, I'VE BEEN THINKING...
MAYBE WE SHOULD REVISIT NATIONAL WELFARE.
THERE MUST BE A BETTER WAY TO MAKE PEOPLE VALUE LIFE.
I'M NOT SAYING I'M AGAINST NATIONAL WELFARE.
I UNDER-STAND.
BUT THE ACT WAS DEVELOPED OVER A LONG PERIOD OF TIME.
I DON'T SEE HOW WE COULD IMPROVE IT.
...
IN FACT...
...I THINK...
...THAT WITHOUT NATIONAL WELFARE, WE WOULDN'T VALUE LIFE AT ALL.
THAT'S THE KIND OF SOCIETY WE LIVE IN.

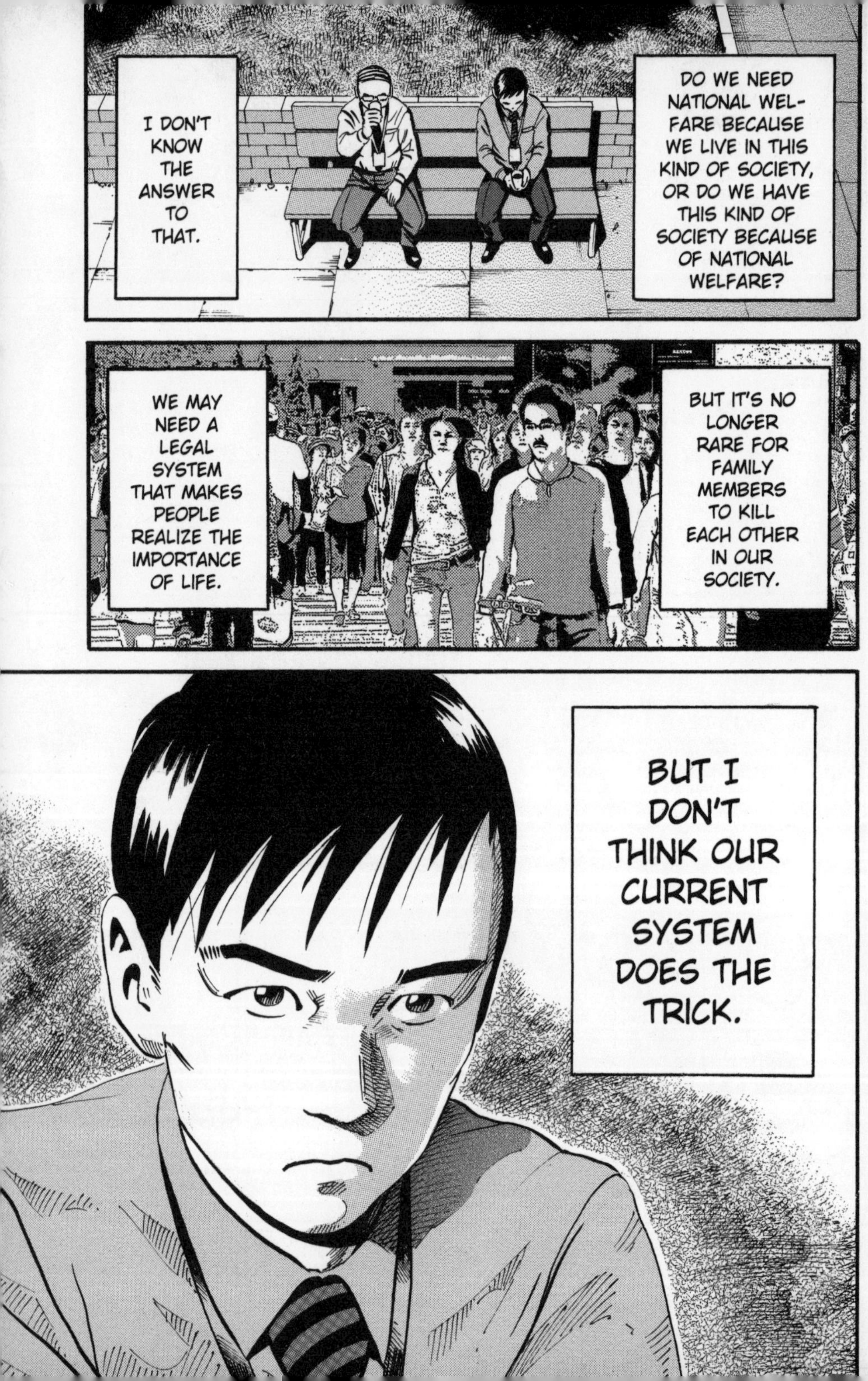
DO WE NEED NATIONAL WEL-FARE BECAUSE WE LIVE IN THIS KIND OF SOCIETY, OR DO WE HAVE THIS KIND OF SOCIETY BECAUSE OF NATIONAL WELFARE?
I DON'T KNOW THE ANSWER TO THAT.
BUT IT'S NO LONGER RARE FOR FAMILY MEMBERS TO KILL EACH OTHER IN OUR SOCIETY.
WE MAY NEED A LEGAL SYSTEM THAT MAKES PEOPLE REALIZE THE IMPORTANCE OF LIFE.
BUT I DON'T THINK OUR CURRENT SYSTEM DOES THE TRICK.

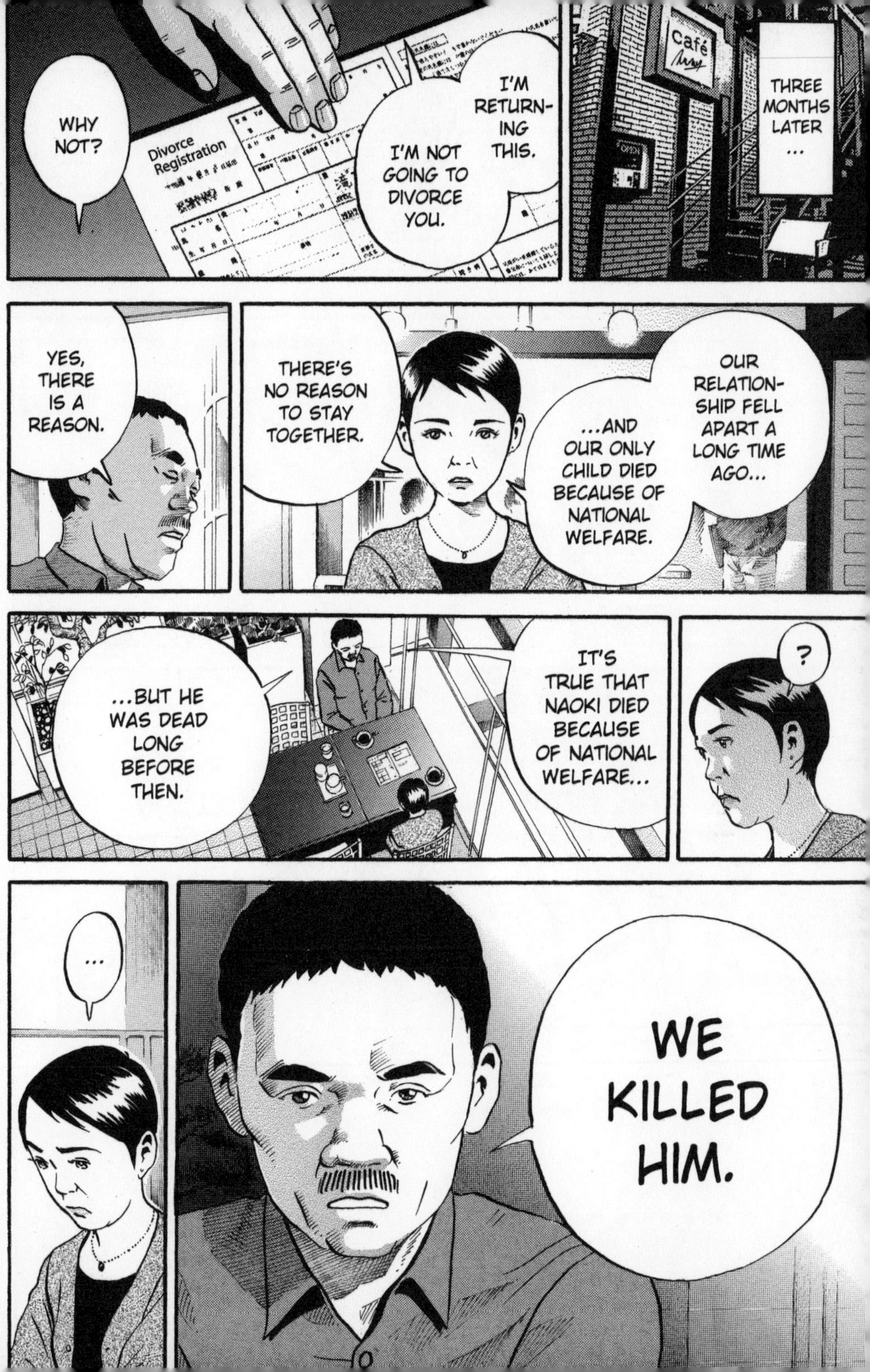
Café
THREE MONTHS LATER...
OPEN
I'M RETURNING THIS.
I'M NOT GOING TO DIVORCE YOU.
Divorce Registration
WHY NOT?
OUR RELATIONSHIP FELL APART A LONG TIME AGO...
...AND OUR ONLY CHILD DIED BECAUSE OF NATIONAL WELFARE.
THERE'S NO REASON TO STAY TOGETHER.
YES, THERE IS A REASON.
?
IT'S TRUE THAT NAOKI DIED BECAUSE OF NATIONAL WELFARE...
...BUT HE WAS DEAD LONG BEFORE THEN.
WE KILLED HIM.
...

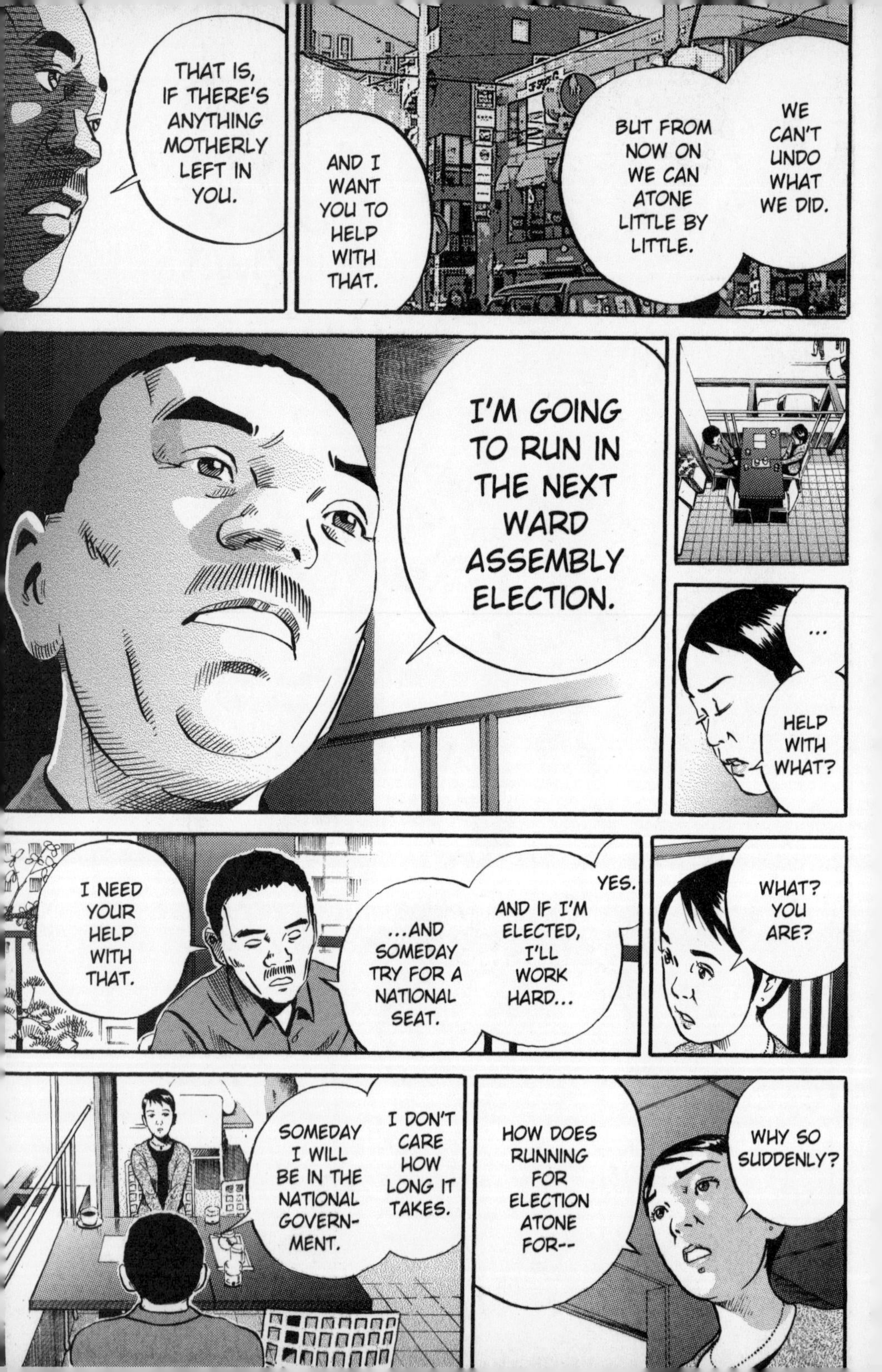
WE CAN'T UNDO WHAT WE DID.
BUT FROM NOW ON WE CAN ATONE LITTLE BY LITTLE.
AND I WANT YOU TO HELP WITH THAT.
THAT IS, IF THERE'S ANYTHING MOTHERLY LEFT IN YOU.
...
HELP WITH WHAT?
I'M GOING TO RUN IN THE NEXT WARD ASSEMBLY ELECTION.
WHAT? YOU ARE?
YES.
AND IF I'M ELECTED, I'LL WORK HARD...
...AND SOMEDAY TRY FOR A NATIONAL SEAT.
I NEED YOUR HELP WITH THAT.
WHY SO SUDDENLY?
HOW DOES RUNNING FOR ELECTION ATONE FOR--
I DON'T CARE HOW LONG IT TAKES.
SOMEDAY I WILL BE IN THE NATIONAL GOVERNMENT.

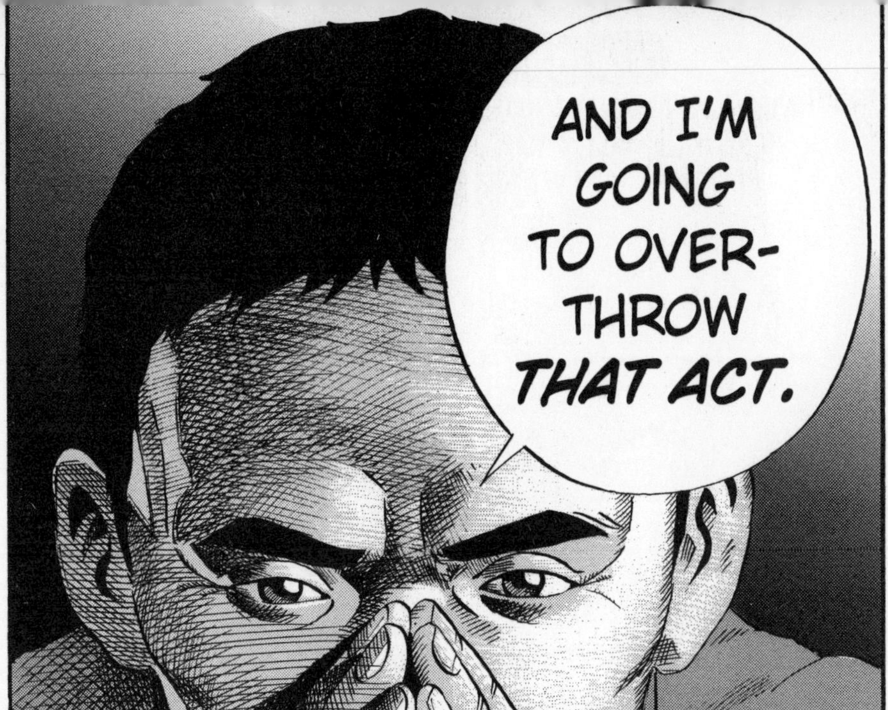
AND I'M GOING TO OVER-THROW THAT ACT.

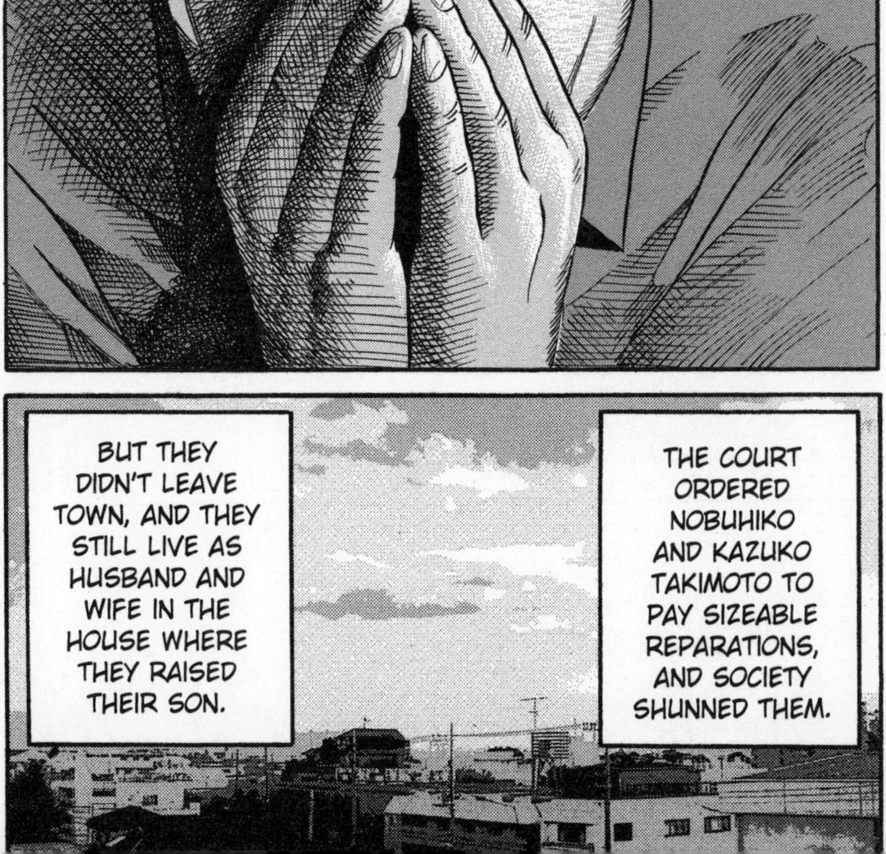
THE COURT ORDERED NOBUHIKO AND KAZUKO TAKIMOTO TO PAY SIZEABLE REPARATIONS, AND SOCIETY SHUNNED THEM.
BUT THEY DIDN'T LEAVE TOWN, AND THEY STILL LIVE AS HUSBAND AND WIFE IN THE HOUSE WHERE THEY RAISED THEIR SON.

Episode 6 The Loveliest Lie Act 1

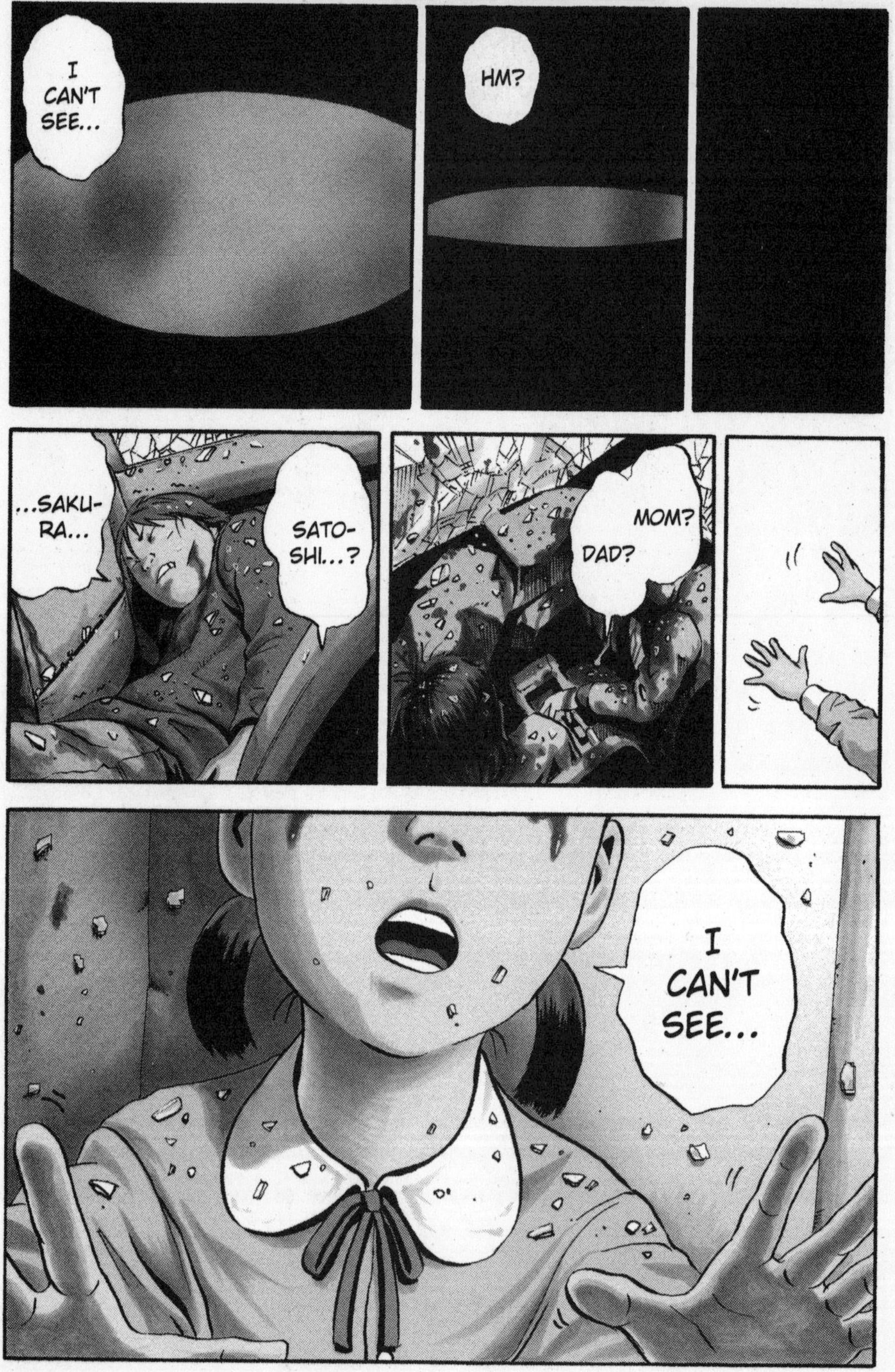
HM?
I CAN'T SEE...
MOM?
DAD?
SATO-SHI...?
...SAKU-RA...
I CAN'T SEE...

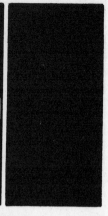

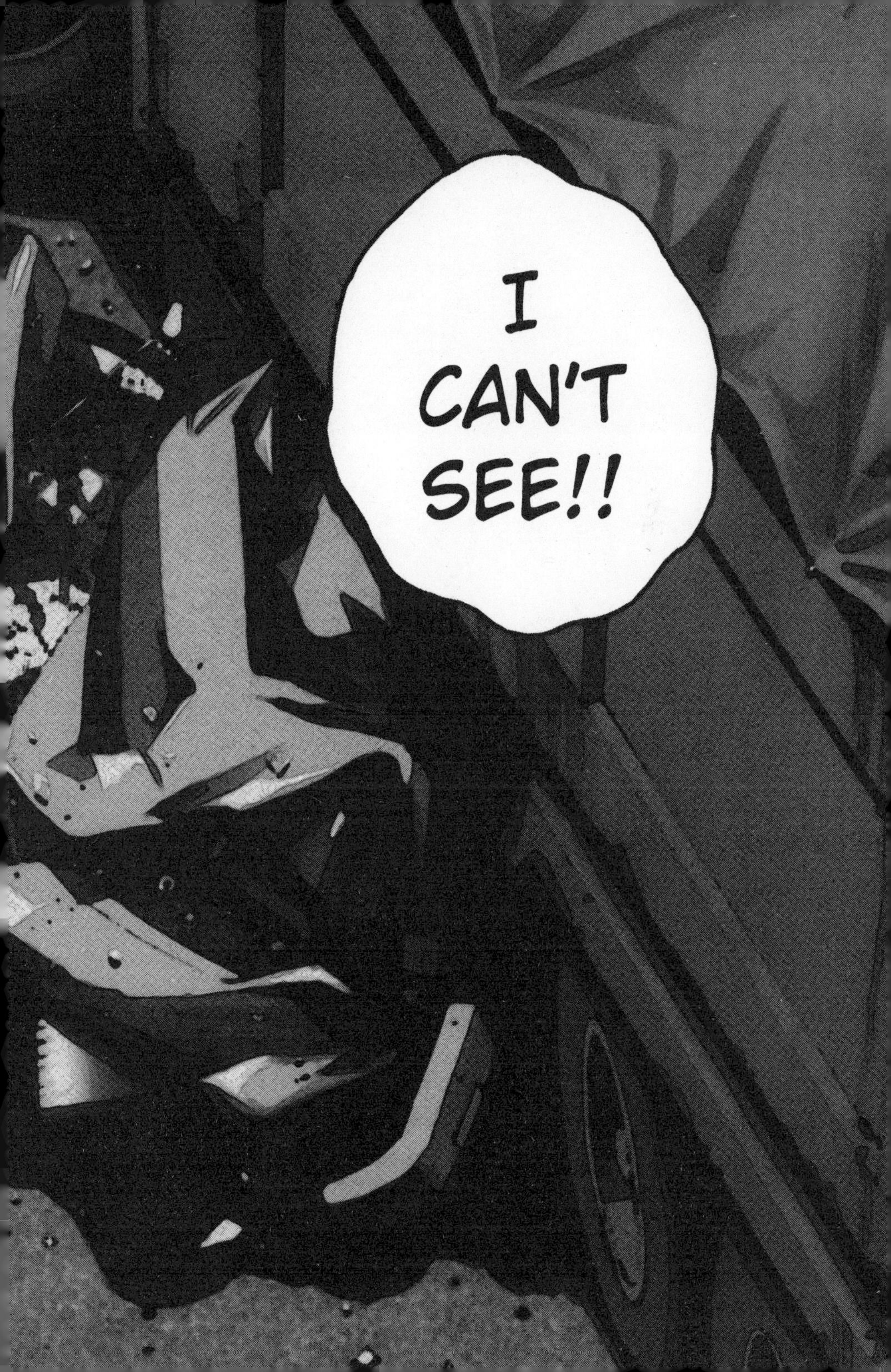
I CAN'T SEE!!

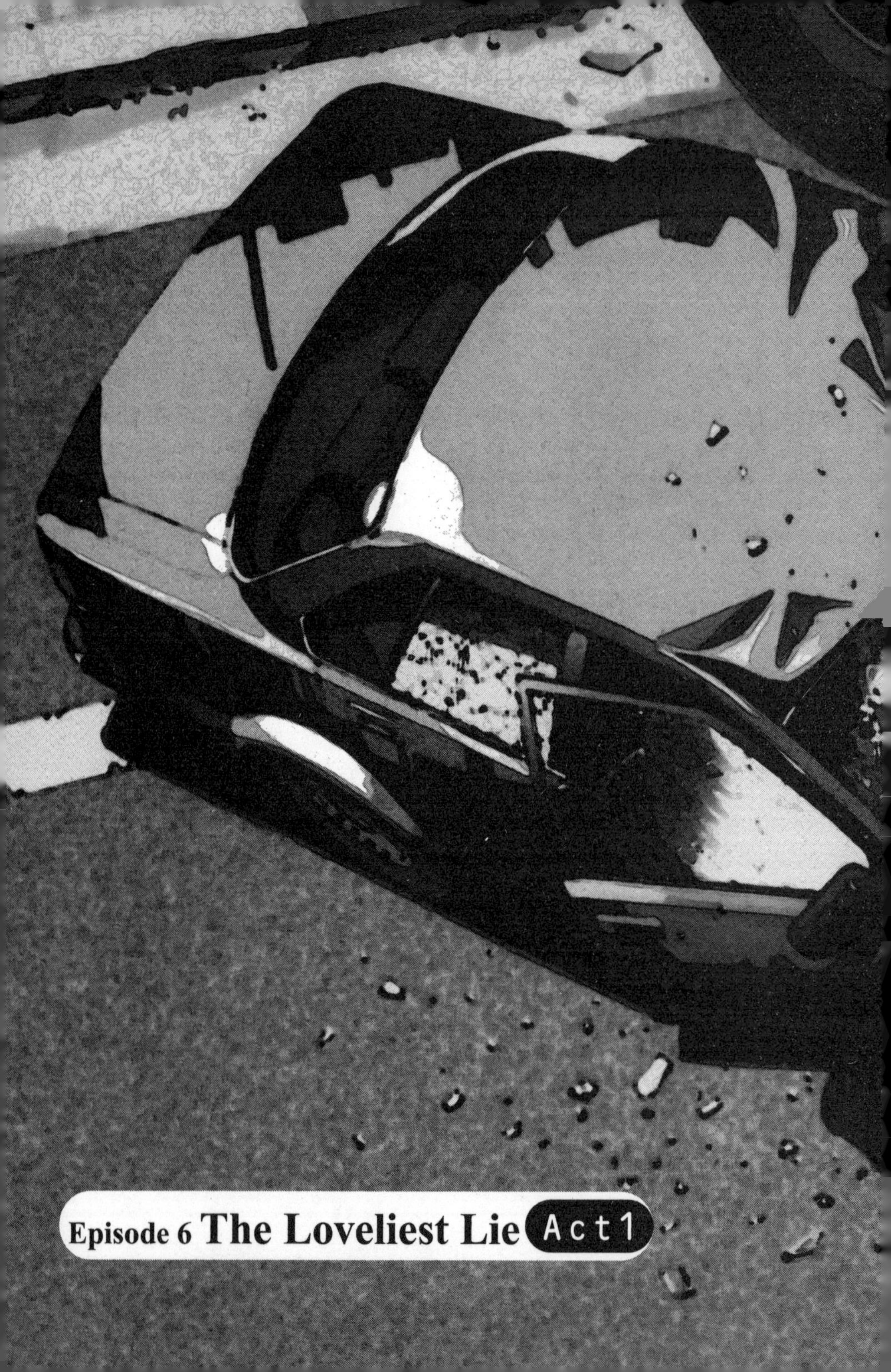
Episode 6 The Loveliest Lie Act 1

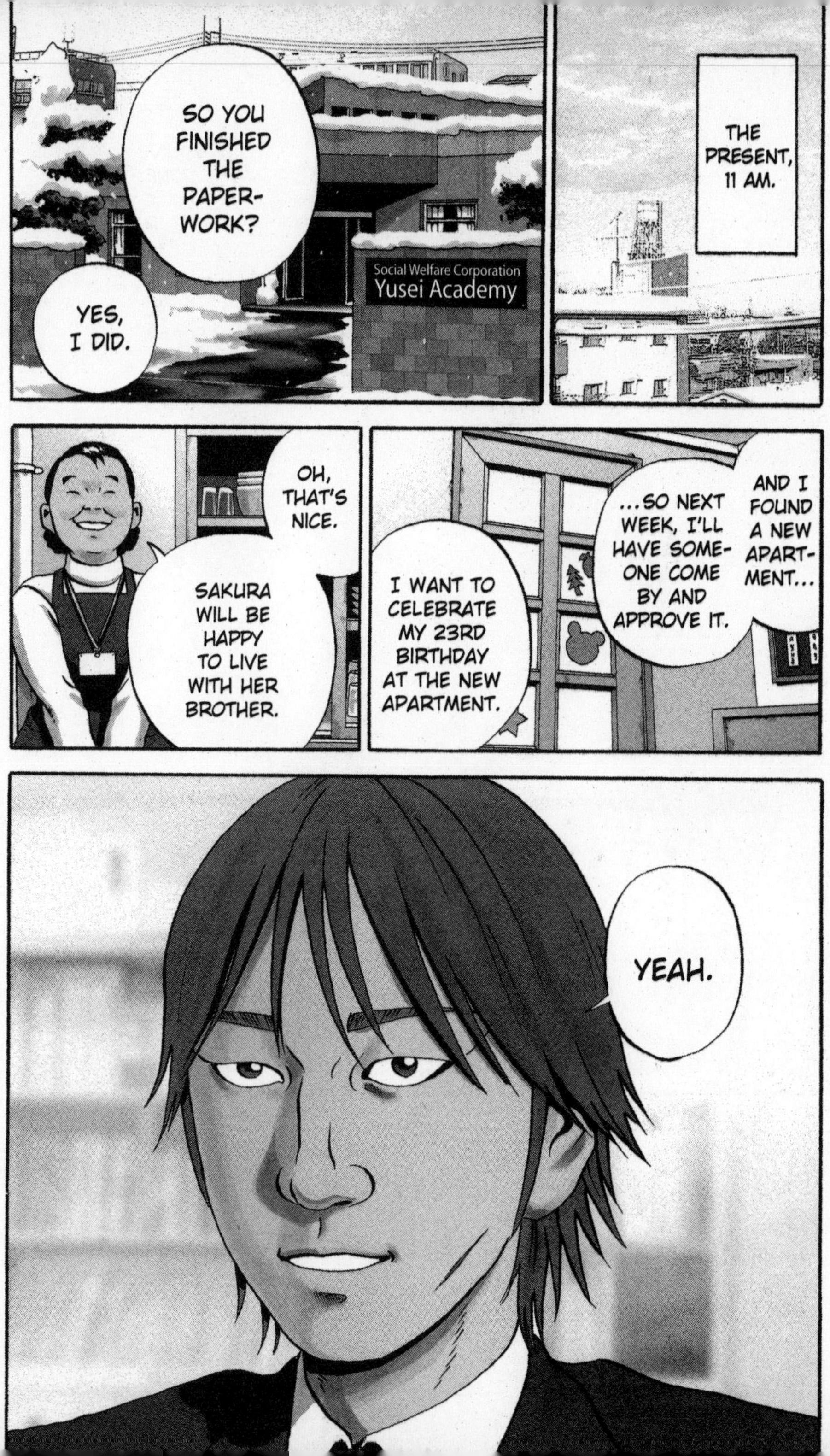
THE PRESENT, 11 AM.
SO YOU FINISHED THE PAPER-WORK?
Social Welfare Corporation Yusei Academy
YES, I DID.
AND I FOUND A NEW APART-MENT...
...SO NEXT WEEK, I'LL HAVE SOME-ONE COME BY AND APPROVE IT.
I WANT TO CELEBRATE MY 23RD BIRTHDAY AT THE NEW APARTMENT.
OH, THAT'S NICE.
SAKURA WILL BE HAPPY TO LIVE WITH HER BROTHER.
YEAH.

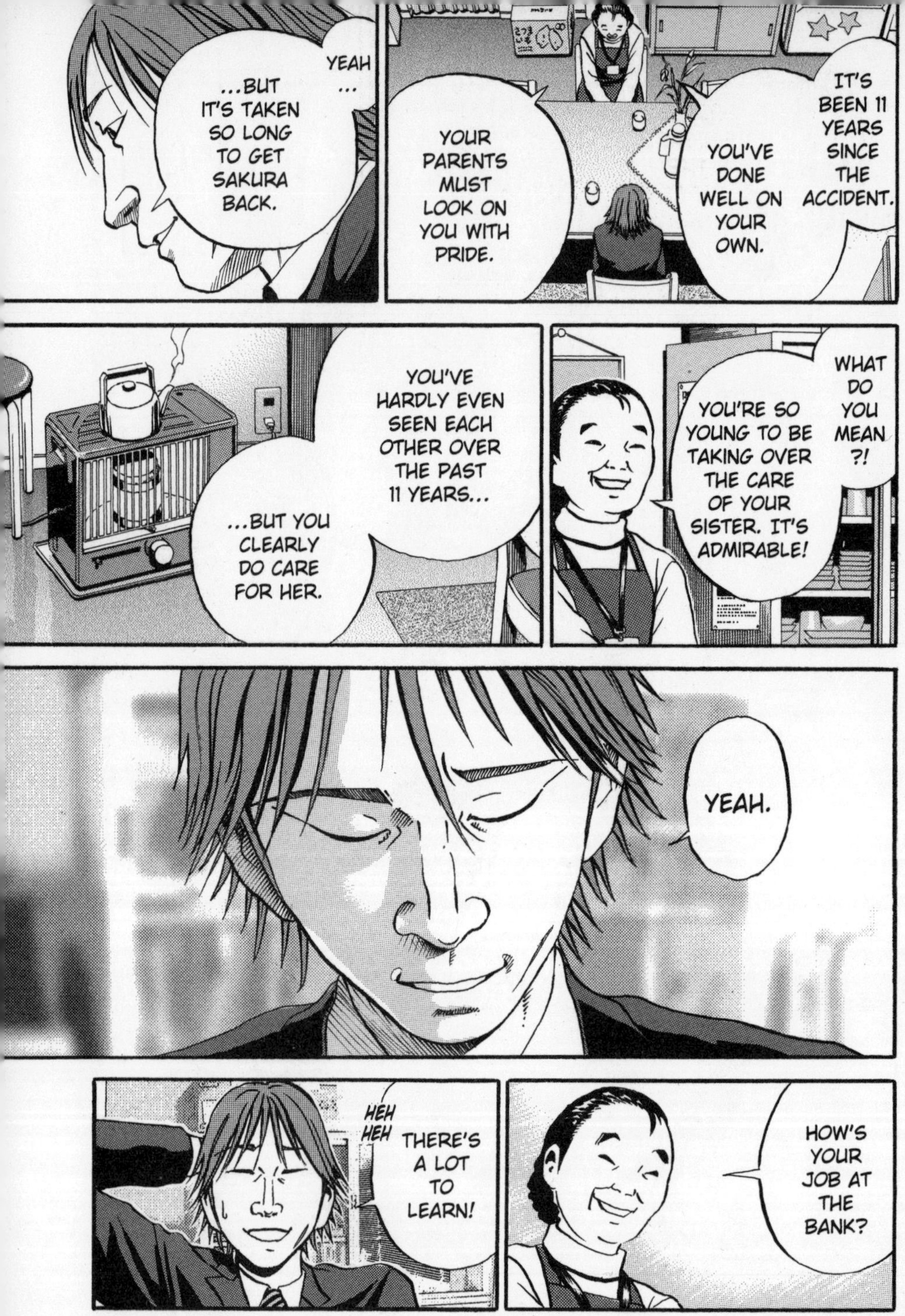
IT'S BEEN 11 YEARS SINCE THE ACCIDENT.
YOU'VE DONE WELL ON YOUR OWN.
YOUR PARENTS MUST LOOK ON YOU WITH PRIDE.
YEAH...
...BUT IT'S TAKEN SO LONG TO GET SAKURA BACK.
WHAT DO YOU MEAN?!
YOU'RE SO YOUNG TO BE TAKING OVER THE CARE OF YOUR SISTER. IT'S ADMIRABLE!
YOU'VE HARDLY EVEN SEEN EACH OTHER OVER THE PAST 11 YEARS...
...BUT YOU CLEARLY DO CARE FOR HER.
YEAH.
HOW'S YOUR JOB AT THE BANK?
HEH HEH
THERE'S A LOT TO LEARN!

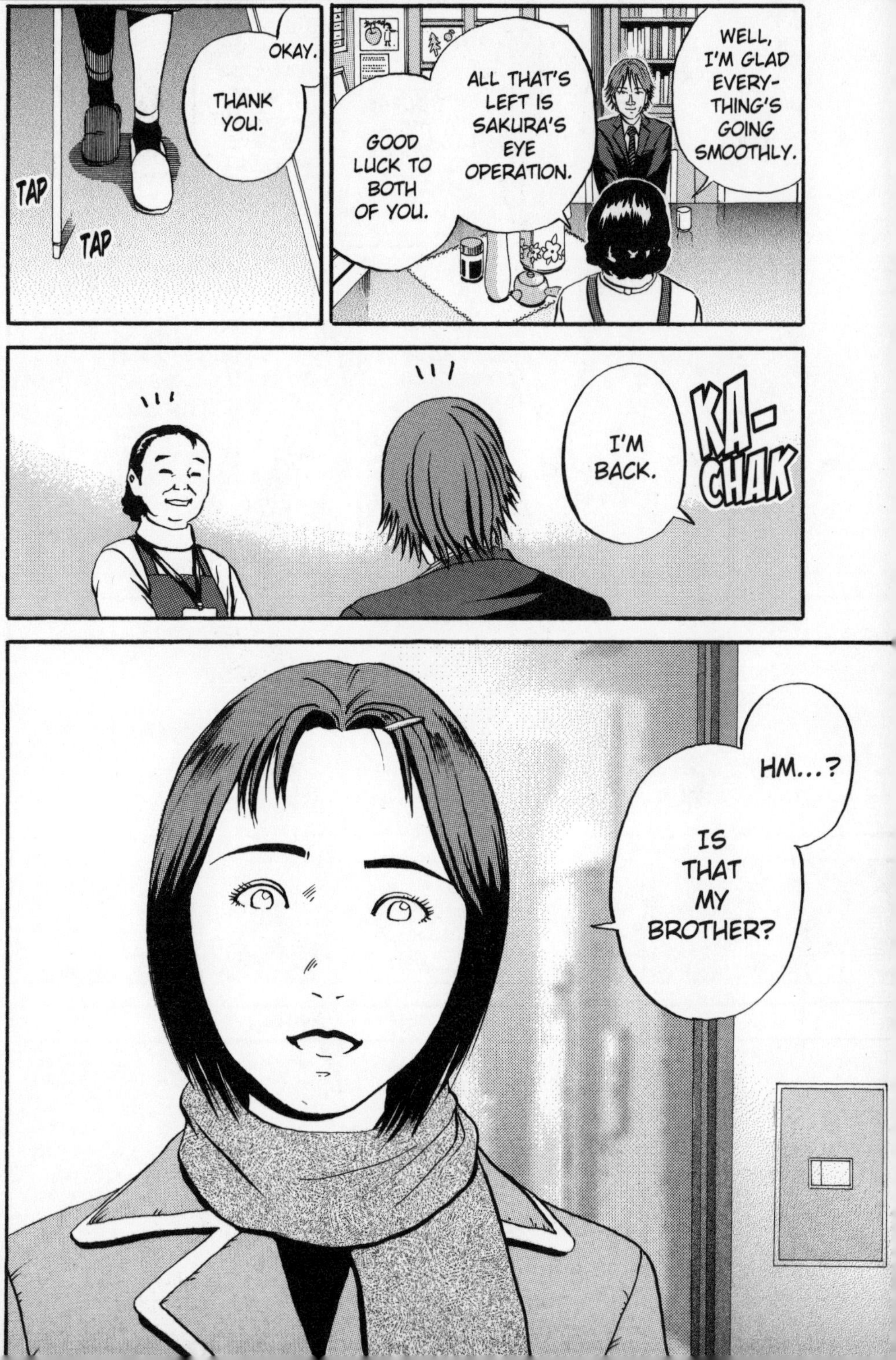
WELL, I'M GLAD EVERY-THING'S GOING SMOOTHLY.
ALL THAT'S LEFT IS SAKURA'S EYE OPERATION.
GOOD LUCK TO BOTH OF YOU.
OKAY.
THANK YOU.
TAP
TAP
KA-CHAK
I'M BACK.
HM...?
IS THAT MY BROTHER?

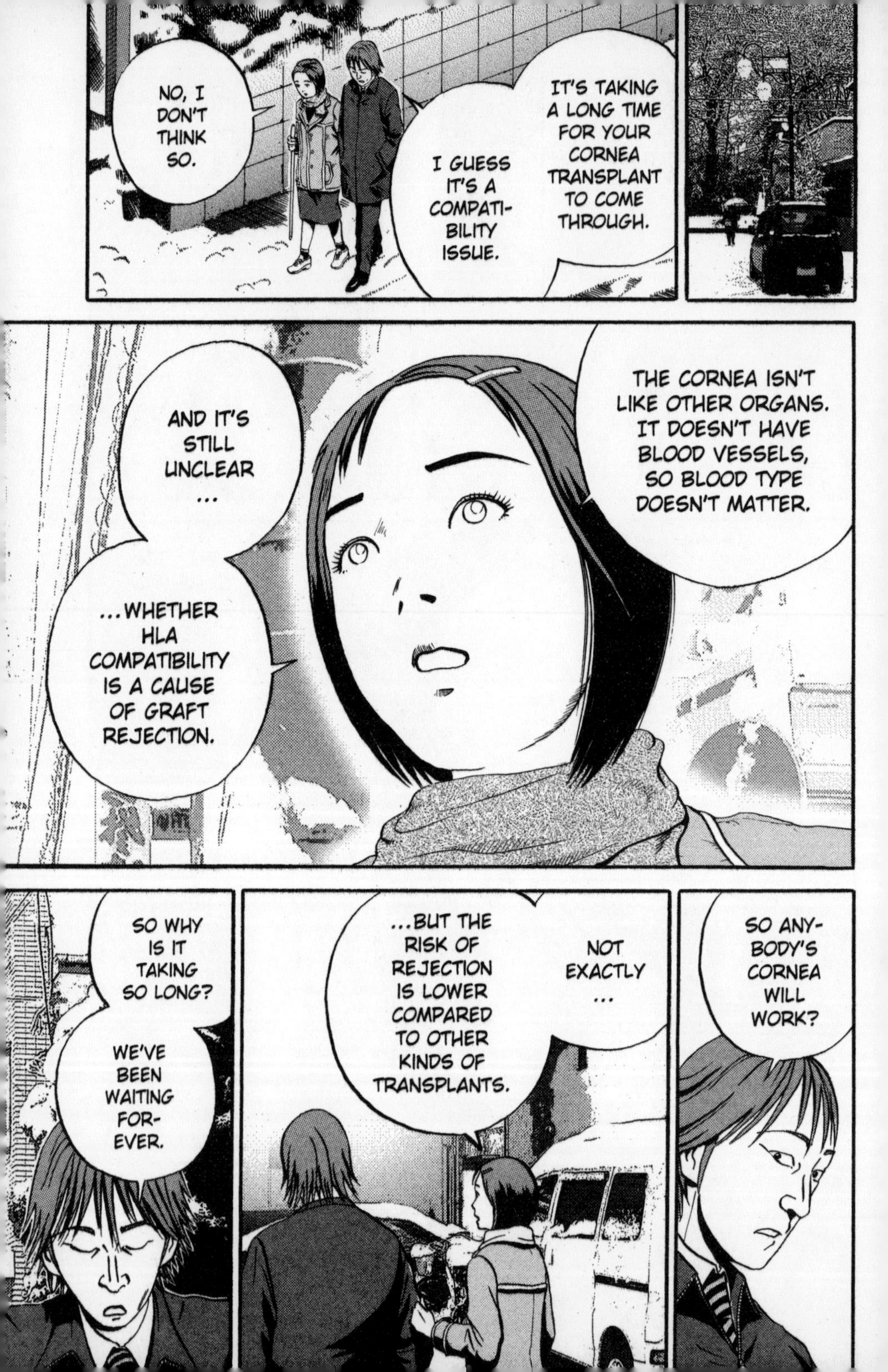
IT'S TAKING A LONG TIME FOR YOUR CORNEA TRANSPLANT TO COME THROUGH.
I GUESS IT'S A COMPATIBILITY ISSUE.
NO, I DON'T THINK SO.
THE CORNEA ISN'T LIKE OTHER ORGANS. IT DOESN'T HAVE BLOOD VESSELS, SO BLOOD TYPE DOESN'T MATTER.
AND IT'S STILL UNCLEAR ...
...WHETHER HLA COMPATIBILITY IS A CAUSE OF GRAFT REJECTION.
SO ANYBODY'S CORNEA WILL WORK?
NOT EXACTLY ...
...BUT THE RISK OF REJECTION IS LOWER COMPARED TO OTHER KINDS OF TRANSPLANTS.
SO WHY IS IT TAKING SO LONG?
WE'VE BEEN WAITING FOREVER.

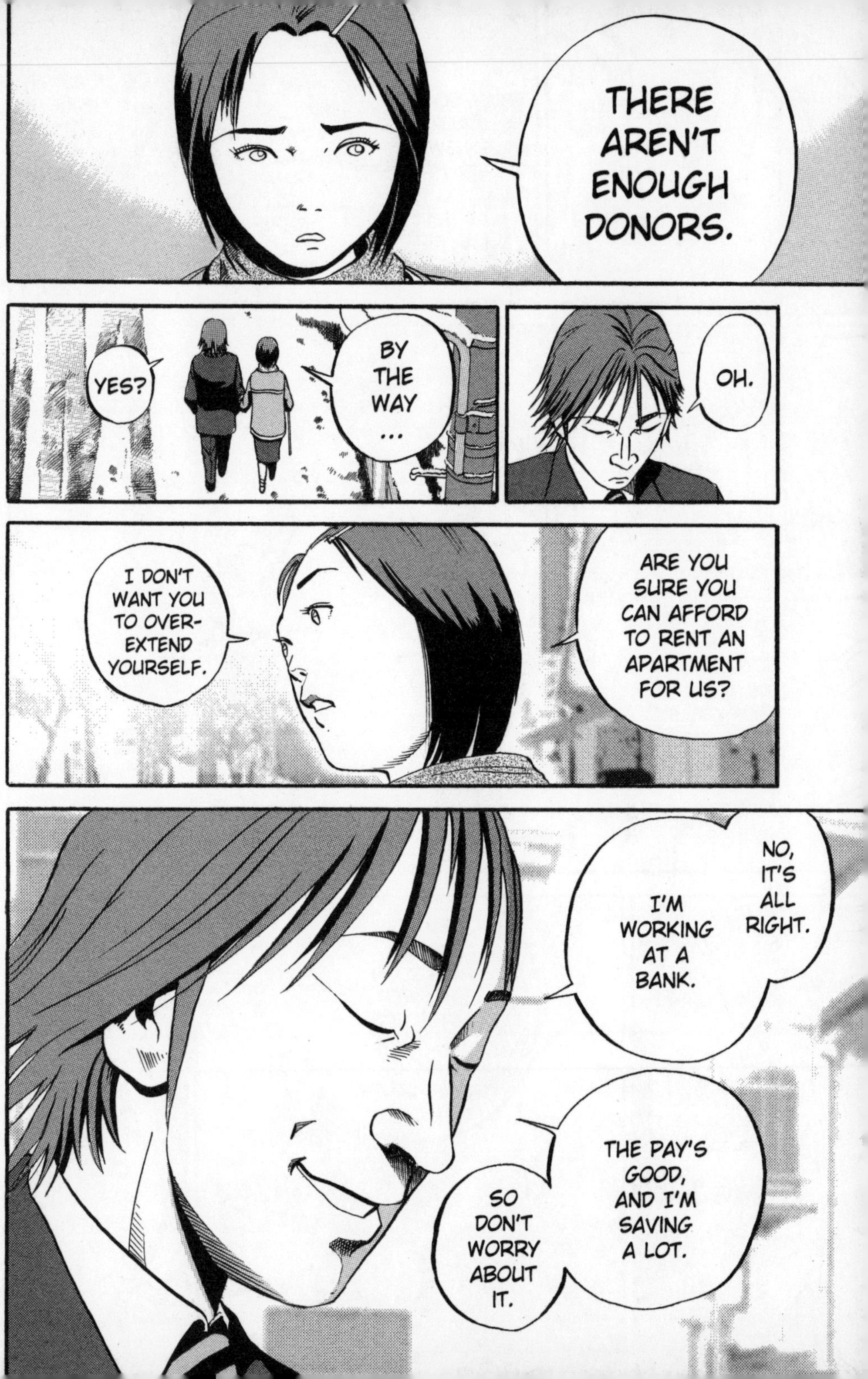
THERE AREN'T ENOUGH DONORS.
OH.
BY THE WAY ...
YES?
ARE YOU SURE YOU CAN AFFORD TO RENT AN APARTMENT FOR US?
I DON'T WANT YOU TO OVER-EXTEND YOURSELF.
NO, IT'S ALL RIGHT.
I'M WORKING AT A BANK.
THE PAY'S GOOD, AND I'M SAVING A LOT.
SO DON'T WORRY ABOUT IT.

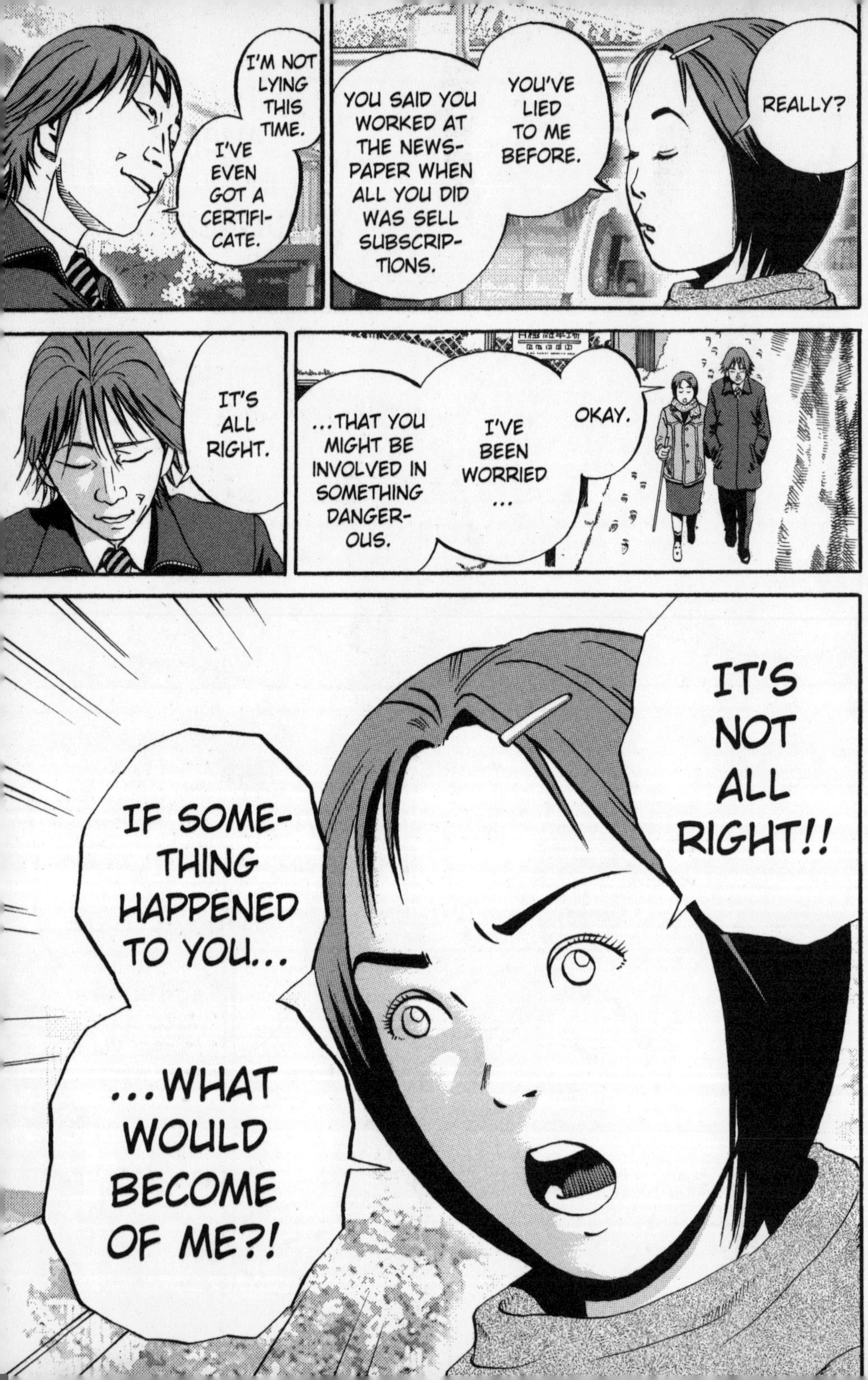
REALLY?
YOU'VE LIED TO ME BEFORE.
YOU SAID YOU WORKED AT THE NEWSPAPER WHEN ALL YOU DID WAS SELL SUBSCRIPTIONS.
I'M NOT LYING THIS TIME.
I'VE EVEN GOT A CERTIFICATE.
OKAY.
I'VE BEEN WORRIED ...
...THAT YOU MIGHT BE INVOLVED IN SOMETHING DANGEROUS.
IT'S ALL RIGHT.
IT'S NOT ALL RIGHT!!
IF SOMETHING HAPPENED TO YOU...
...WHAT WOULD BECOME OF ME?!

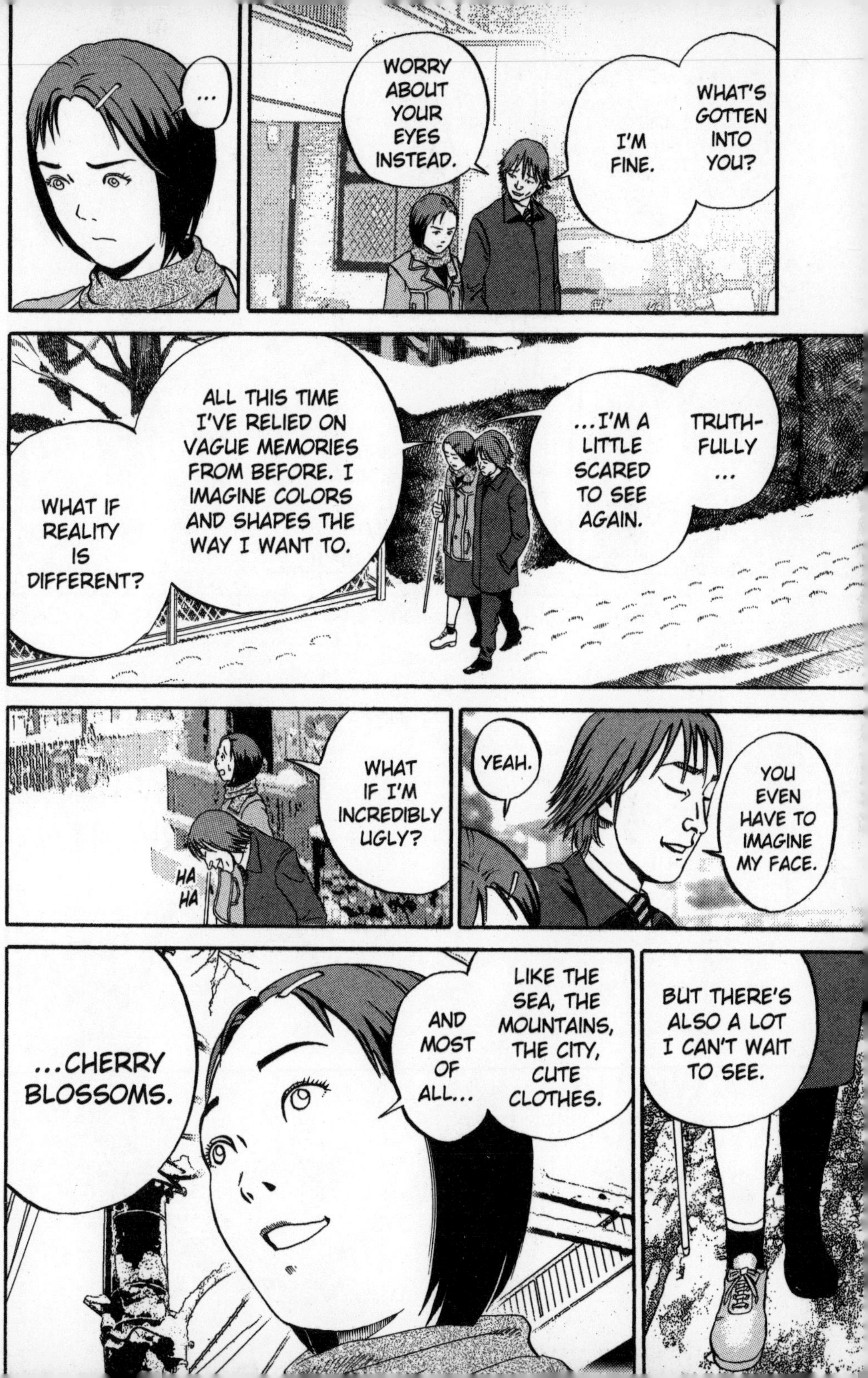
WHAT'S GOTTEN INTO YOU?
I'M FINE.
WORRY ABOUT YOUR EYES INSTEAD.
...
TRUTHFULLY...
...I'M A LITTLE SCARED TO SEE AGAIN.
ALL THIS TIME I'VE RELIED ON VAGUE MEMORIES FROM BEFORE. I IMAGINE COLORS AND SHAPES THE WAY I WANT TO.
WHAT IF REALITY IS DIFFERENT?
YOU EVEN HAVE TO IMAGINE MY FACE.
YEAH.
WHAT IF I'M INCREDIBLY UGLY?
HA HA
BUT THERE'S ALSO A LOT I CAN'T WAIT TO SEE.
LIKE THE SEA, THE MOUNTAINS, THE CITY, CUTE CLOTHES.
AND MOST OF ALL...
...CHERRY BLOSSOMS.

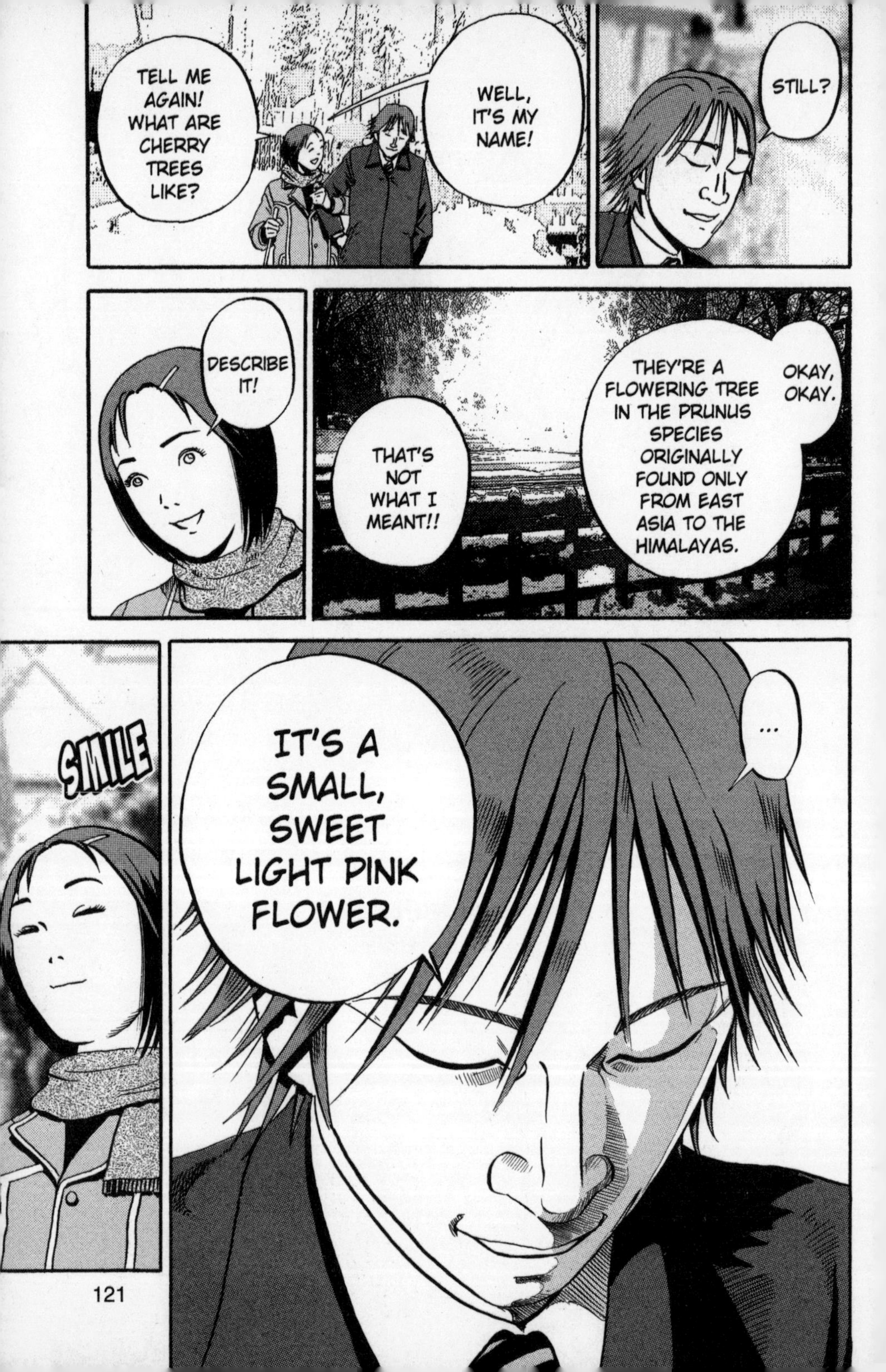
STILL?
WELL, IT'S MY NAME!
TELL ME AGAIN! WHAT ARE CHERRY TREES LIKE?
OKAY, OKAY.
THEY'RE A FLOWERING TREE IN THE PRUNUS SPECIES ORIGINALLY FOUND ONLY FROM EAST ASIA TO THE HIMALAYAS.
THAT'S NOT WHAT I MEANT!!
DESCRIBE IT!
...
IT'S A SMALL, SWEET LIGHT PINK FLOWER.
SMILE

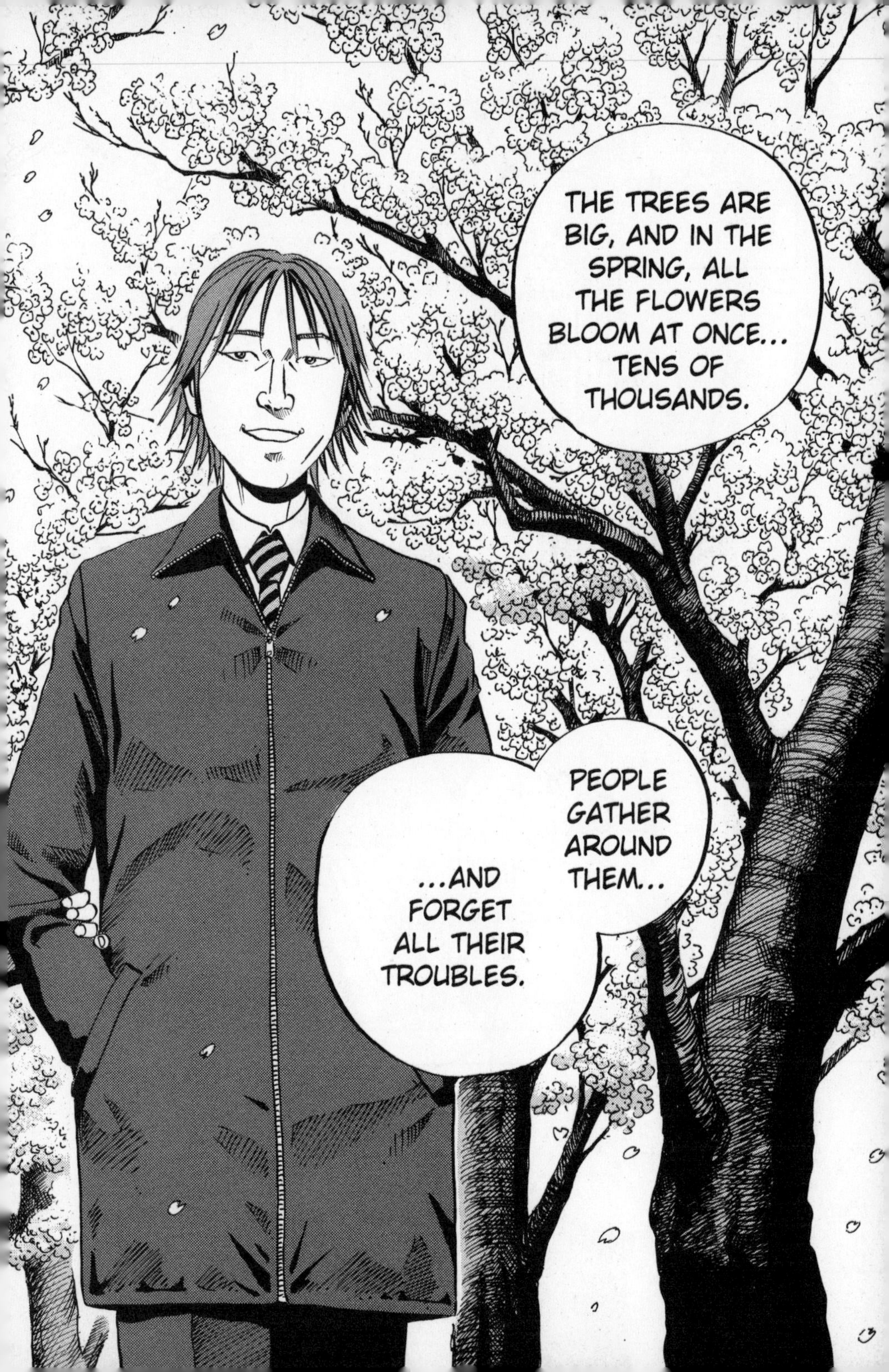
THE TREES ARE BIG, AND IN THE SPRING, ALL THE FLOWERS BLOOM AT ONCE... TENS OF THOUSANDS.
PEOPLE GATHER AROUND THEM...
...AND FORGET ALL THEIR TROUBLES.

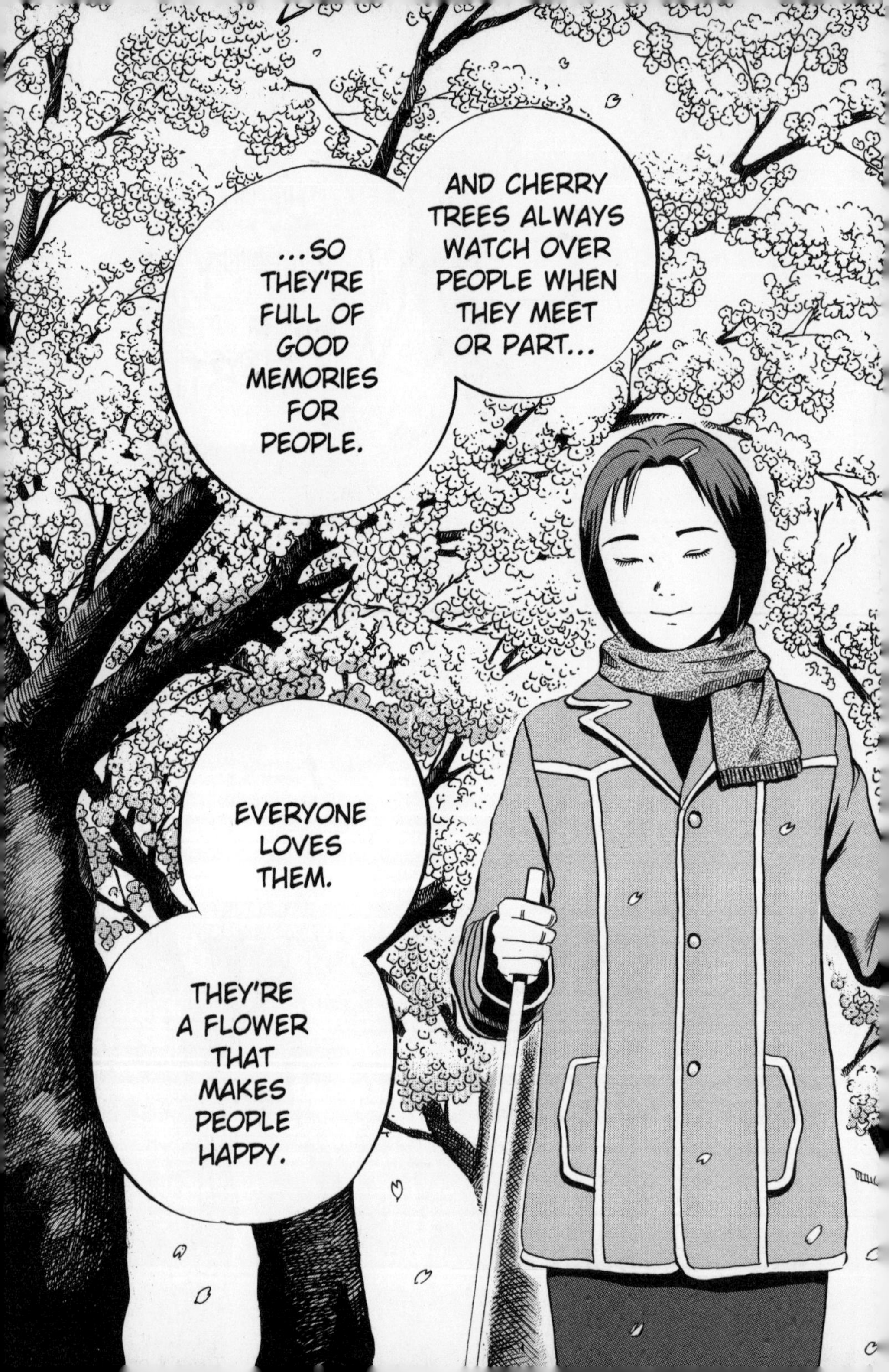
AND CHERRY TREES ALWAYS WATCH OVER PEOPLE WHEN THEY MEET OR PART...
...SO THEY'RE FULL OF GOOD MEMORIES FOR PEOPLE.
EVERYONE LOVES THEM.
THEY'RE A FLOWER THAT MAKES PEOPLE HAPPY.

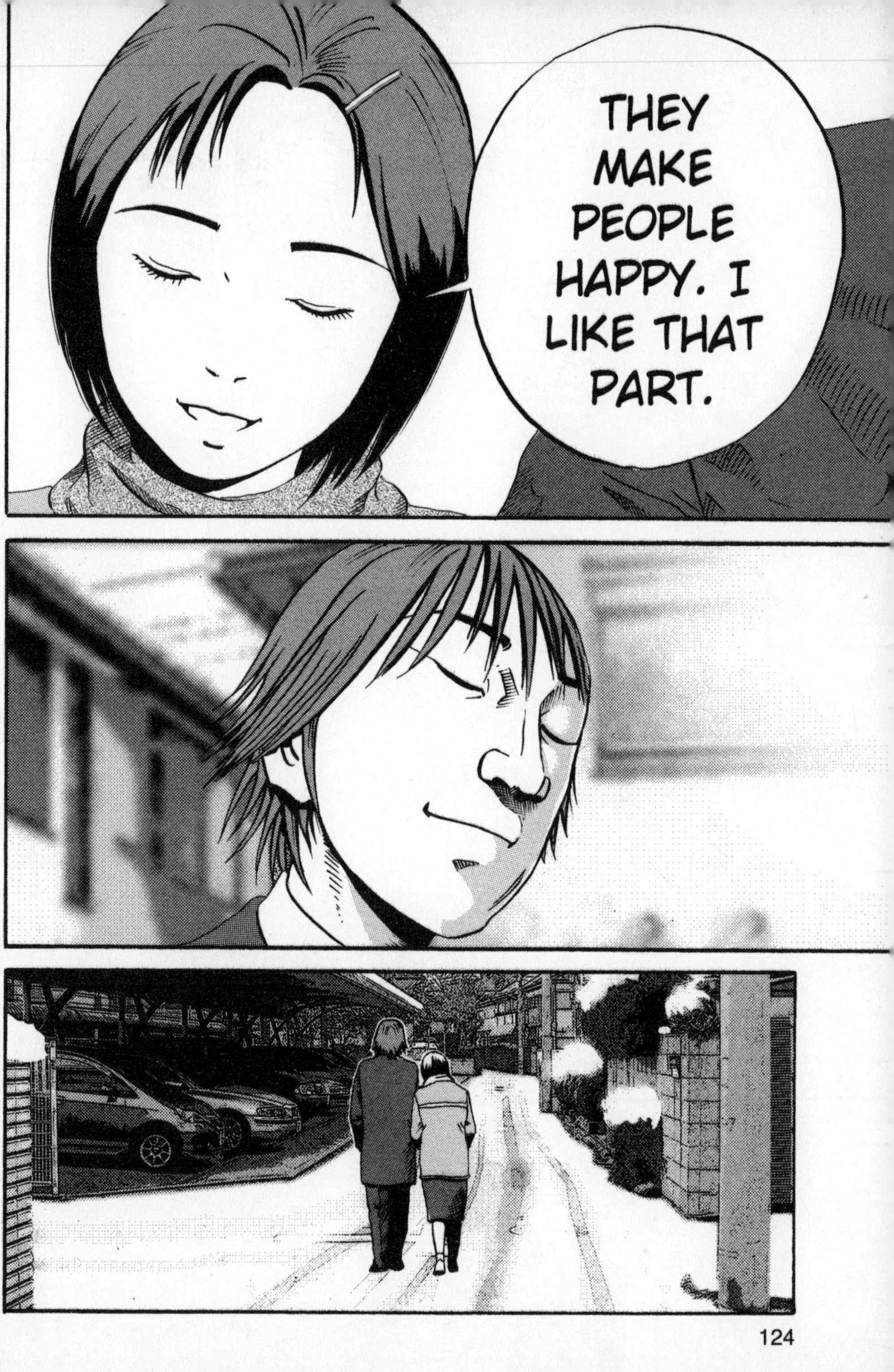
THEY MAKE PEOPLE HAPPY. I LIKE THAT PART.

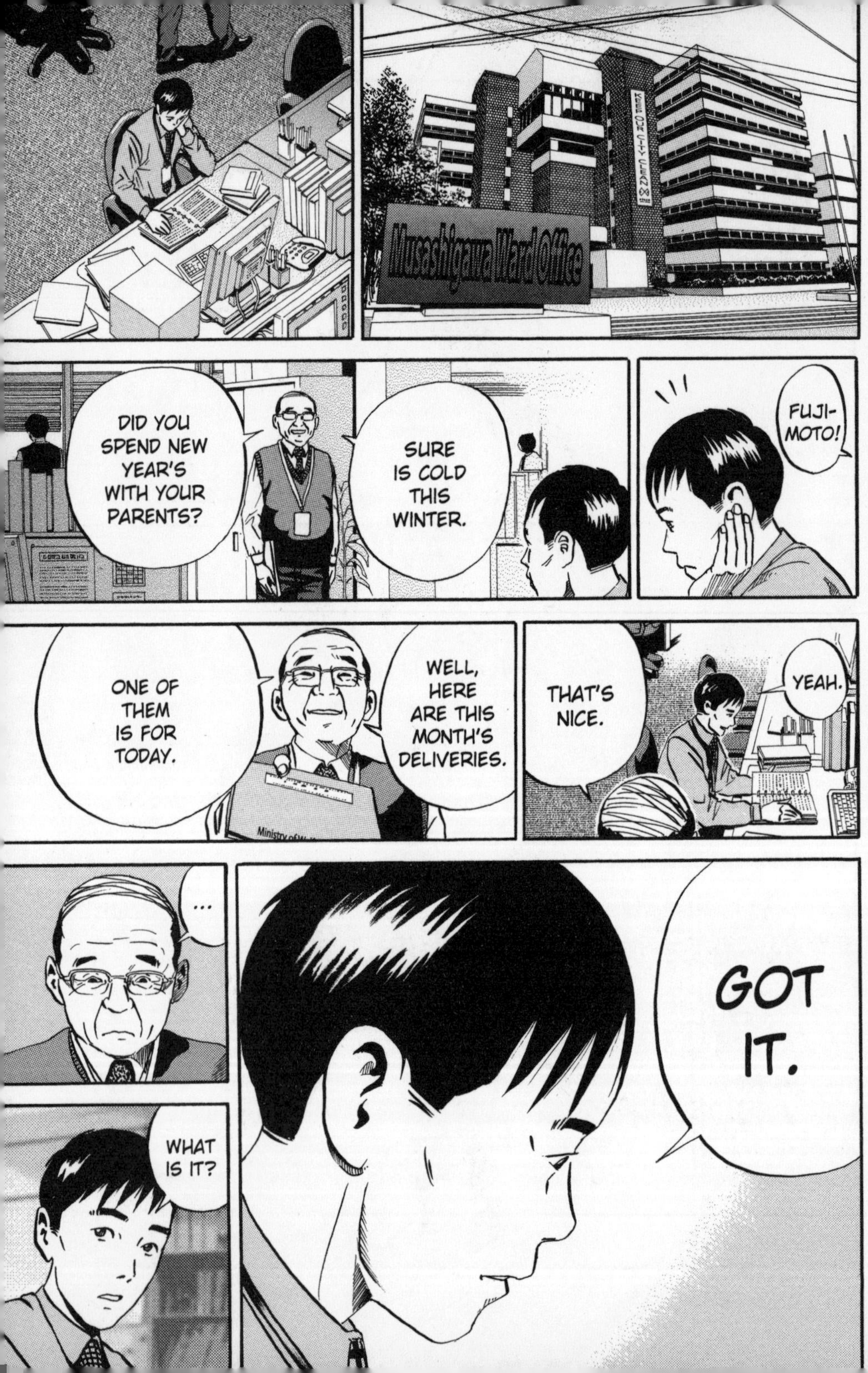
KEEP OUR CITY CLEAN
Musashigawa Ward Office
FUJI-MOTO!
SURE IS COLD THIS WINTER.
DID YOU SPEND NEW YEAR'S WITH YOUR PARENTS?
YEAH.
THAT'S NICE.
WELL, HERE ARE THIS MONTH'S DELIVERIES.
ONE OF THEM IS FOR TODAY.
GOT IT.
...
WHAT IS IT?

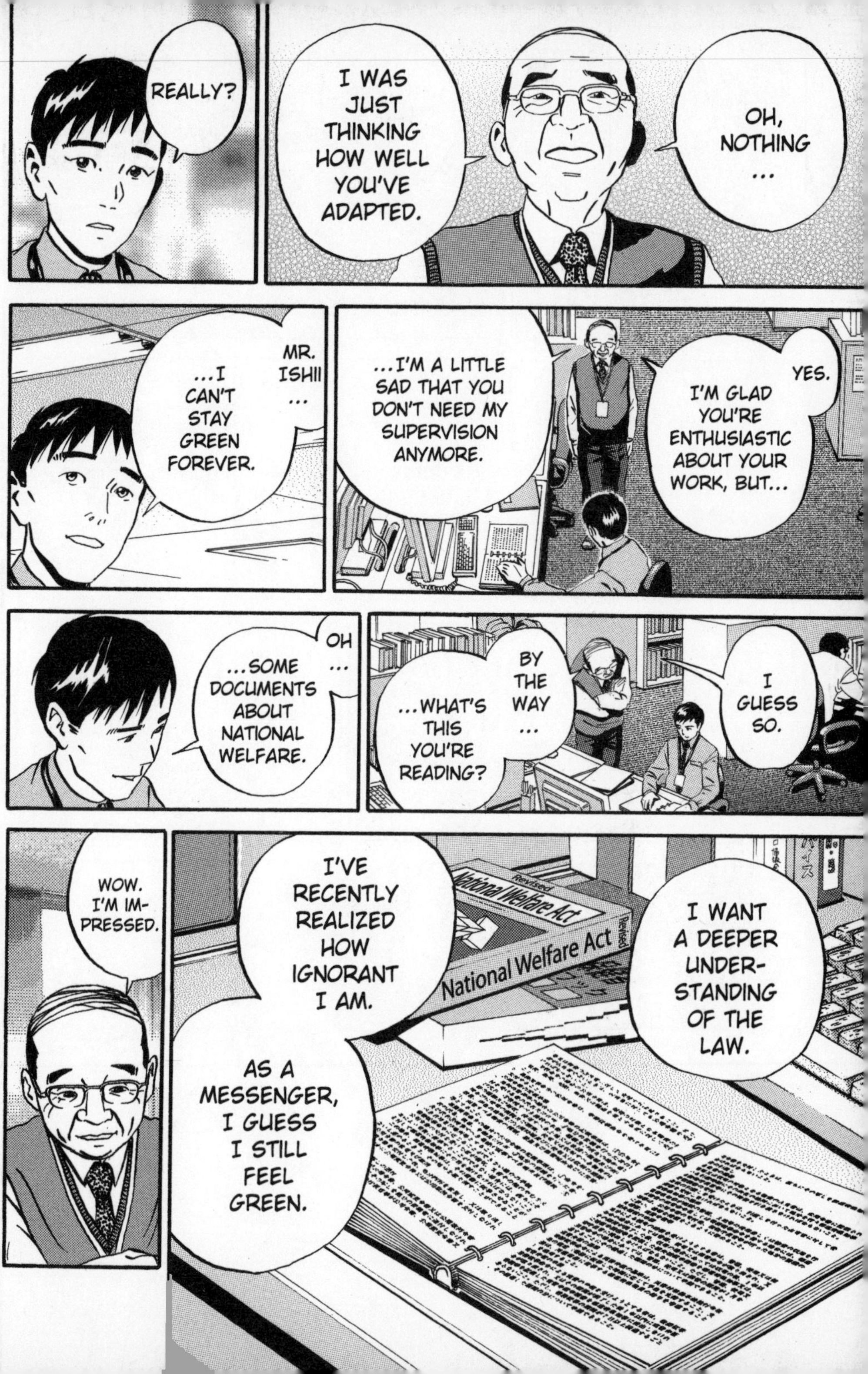
OH, NOTHING ...
I WAS JUST THINKING HOW WELL YOU'VE ADAPTED.
REALLY?
YES.
I'M GLAD YOU'RE ENTHUSIASTIC ABOUT YOUR WORK, BUT...
...I'M A LITTLE SAD THAT YOU DON'T NEED MY SUPERVISION ANYMORE.
MR. ISHII ...
...I CAN'T STAY GREEN FOREVER.
I GUESS SO.
BY THE WAY ...
...WHAT'S THIS YOU'RE READING?
OH ...
...SOME DOCUMENTS ABOUT NATIONAL WELFARE.
I WANT A DEEPER UNDERSTANDING OF THE LAW.
Revised
National Welfare Act
Revised
National Welfare Act
I'VE RECENTLY REALIZED HOW IGNORANT I AM.
AS A MESSENGER, I GUESS I STILL FEEL GREEN.
WOW. I'M IMPRESSED.

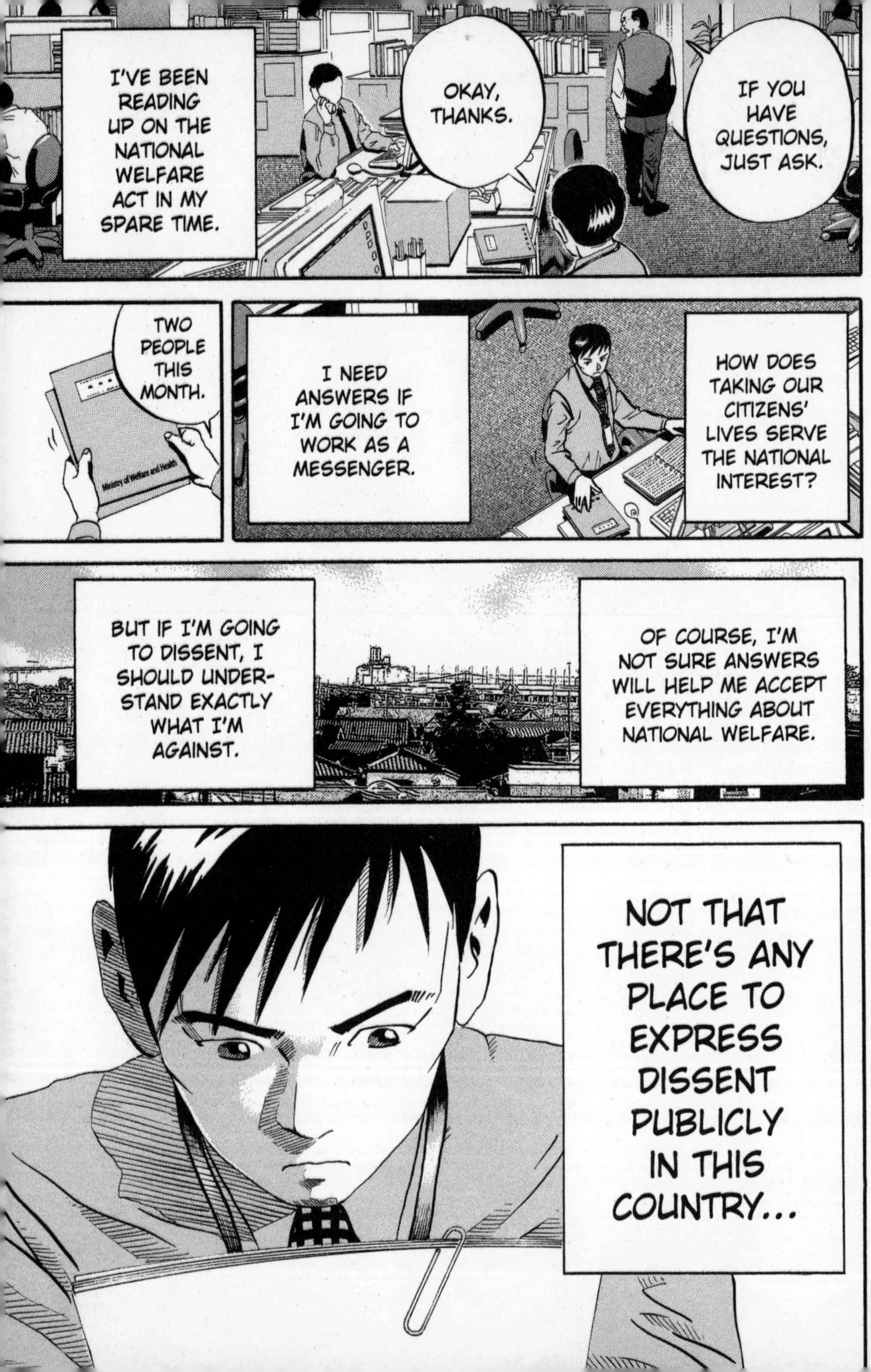
IF YOU HAVE QUESTIONS, JUST ASK.
OKAY, THANKS.
I'VE BEEN READING UP ON THE NATIONAL WELFARE ACT IN MY SPARE TIME.
HOW DOES TAKING OUR CITIZENS' LIVES SERVE THE NATIONAL INTEREST?
I NEED ANSWERS IF I'M GOING TO WORK AS A MESSENGER.
TWO PEOPLE THIS MONTH.
Ministry of Welfare and Health
OF COURSE, I'M NOT SURE ANSWERS WILL HELP ME ACCEPT EVERYTHING ABOUT NATIONAL WELFARE.
BUT IF I'M GOING TO DISSENT, I SHOULD UNDER-STAND EXACTLY WHAT I'M AGAINST.
NOT THAT THERE'S ANY PLACE TO EXPRESS DISSENT PUBLICLY IN THIS COUNTRY...

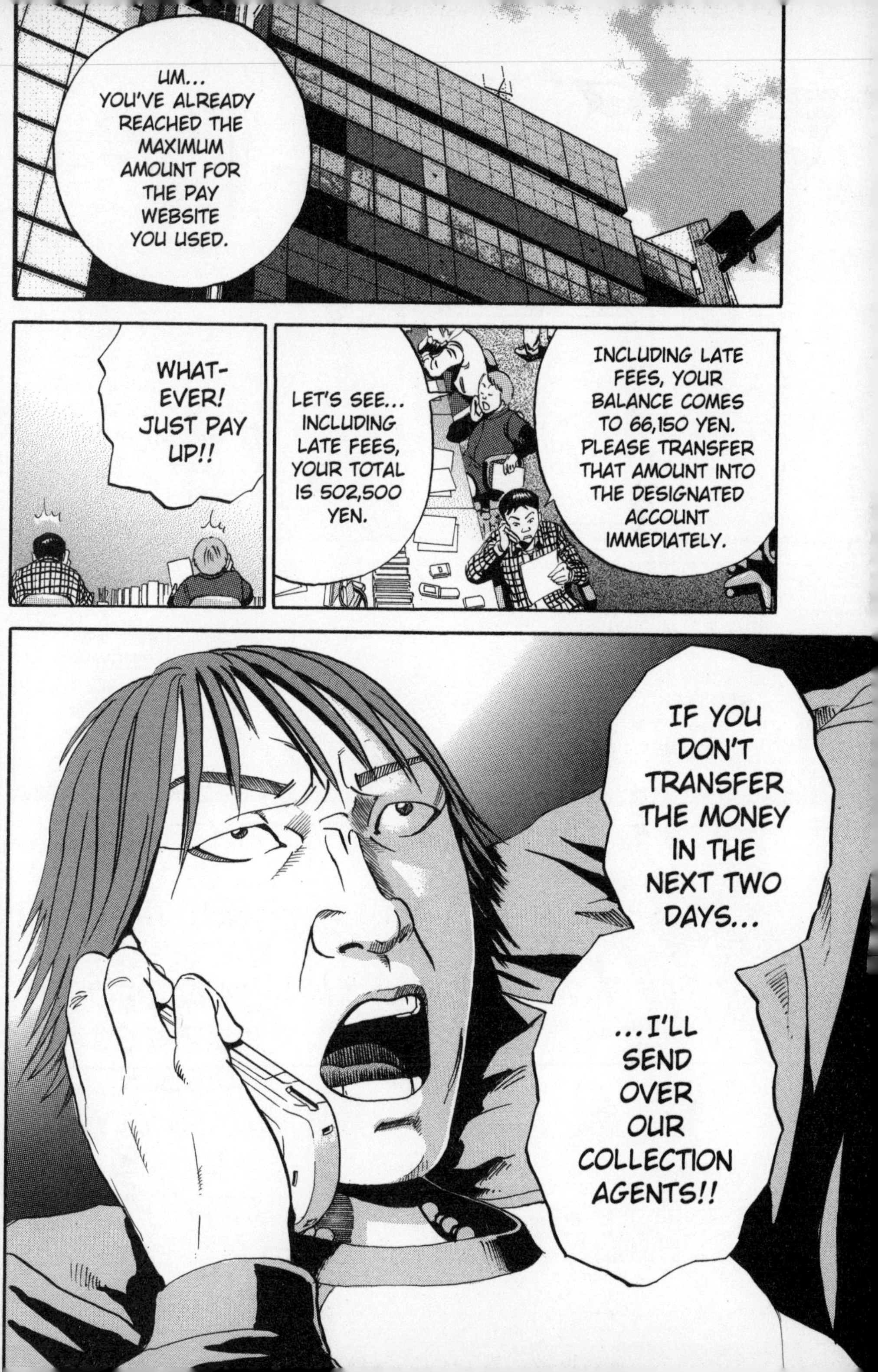
UM... YOU'VE ALREADY REACHED THE MAXIMUM AMOUNT FOR THE PAY WEBSITE YOU USED.
INCLUDING LATE FEES, YOUR BALANCE COMES TO 66,150 YEN. PLEASE TRANSFER THAT AMOUNT INTO THE DESIGNATED ACCOUNT IMMEDIATELY.
LET'S SEE... INCLUDING LATE FEES, YOUR TOTAL IS 502,500 YEN.
WHAT-EVER! JUST PAY UP!!
IF YOU DON'T TRANSFER THE MONEY IN THE NEXT TWO DAYS...
...I'LL SEND OVER OUR COLLECTION AGENTS!!

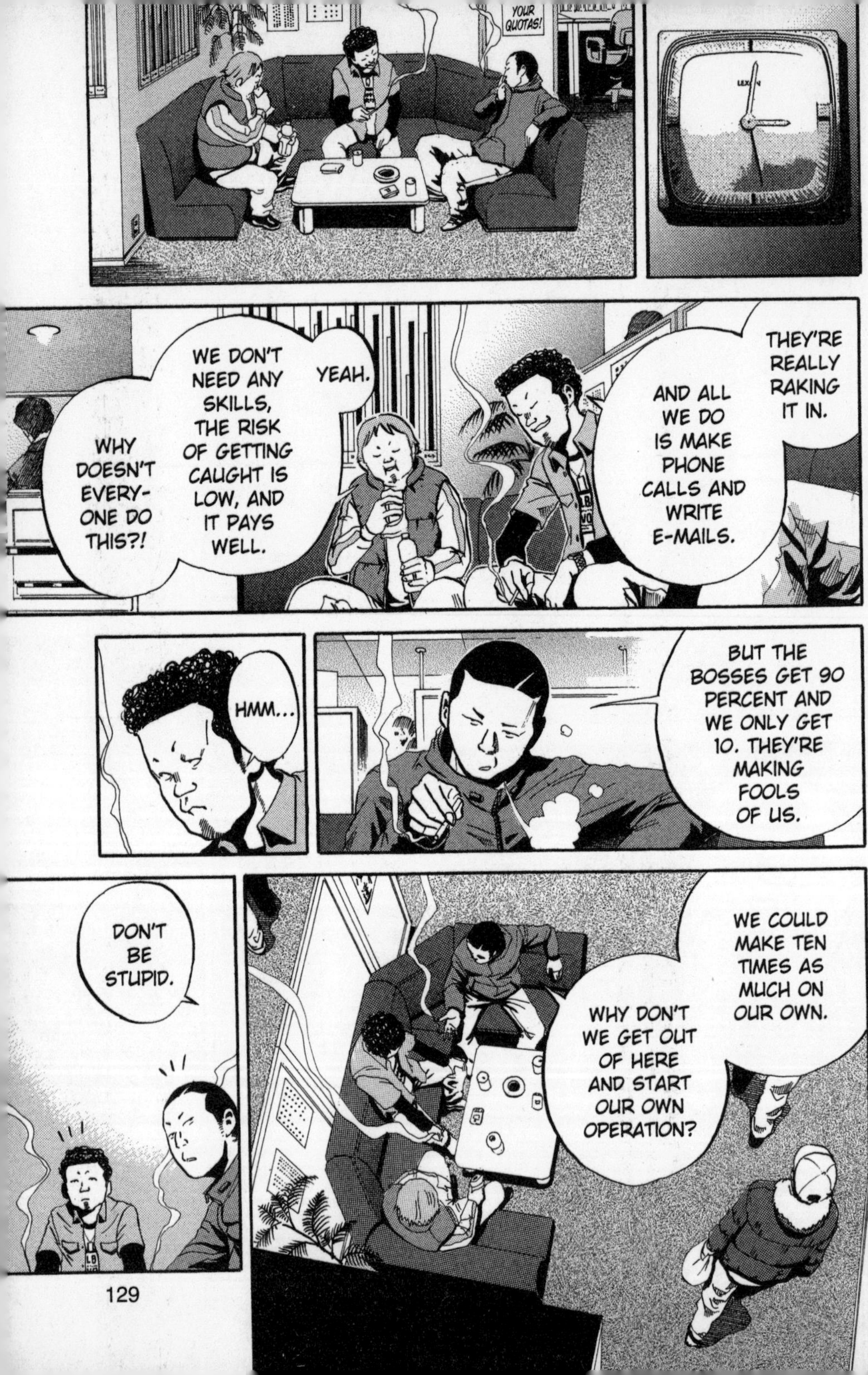
YOUR QUOTAS!
THEY'RE REALLY RAKING IT IN.
AND ALL WE DO IS MAKE PHONE CALLS AND WRITE E-MAILS.
YEAH.
WE DON'T NEED ANY SKILLS, THE RISK OF GETTING CAUGHT IS LOW, AND IT PAYS WELL.
WHY DOESN'T EVERY-ONE DO THIS?!
BUT THE BOSSES GET 90 PERCENT AND WE ONLY GET 10. THEY'RE MAKING FOOLS OF US.
HMM...
WE COULD MAKE TEN TIMES AS MUCH ON OUR OWN.
WHY DON'T WE GET OUT OF HERE AND START OUR OWN OPERATION?
DON'T BE STUPID.

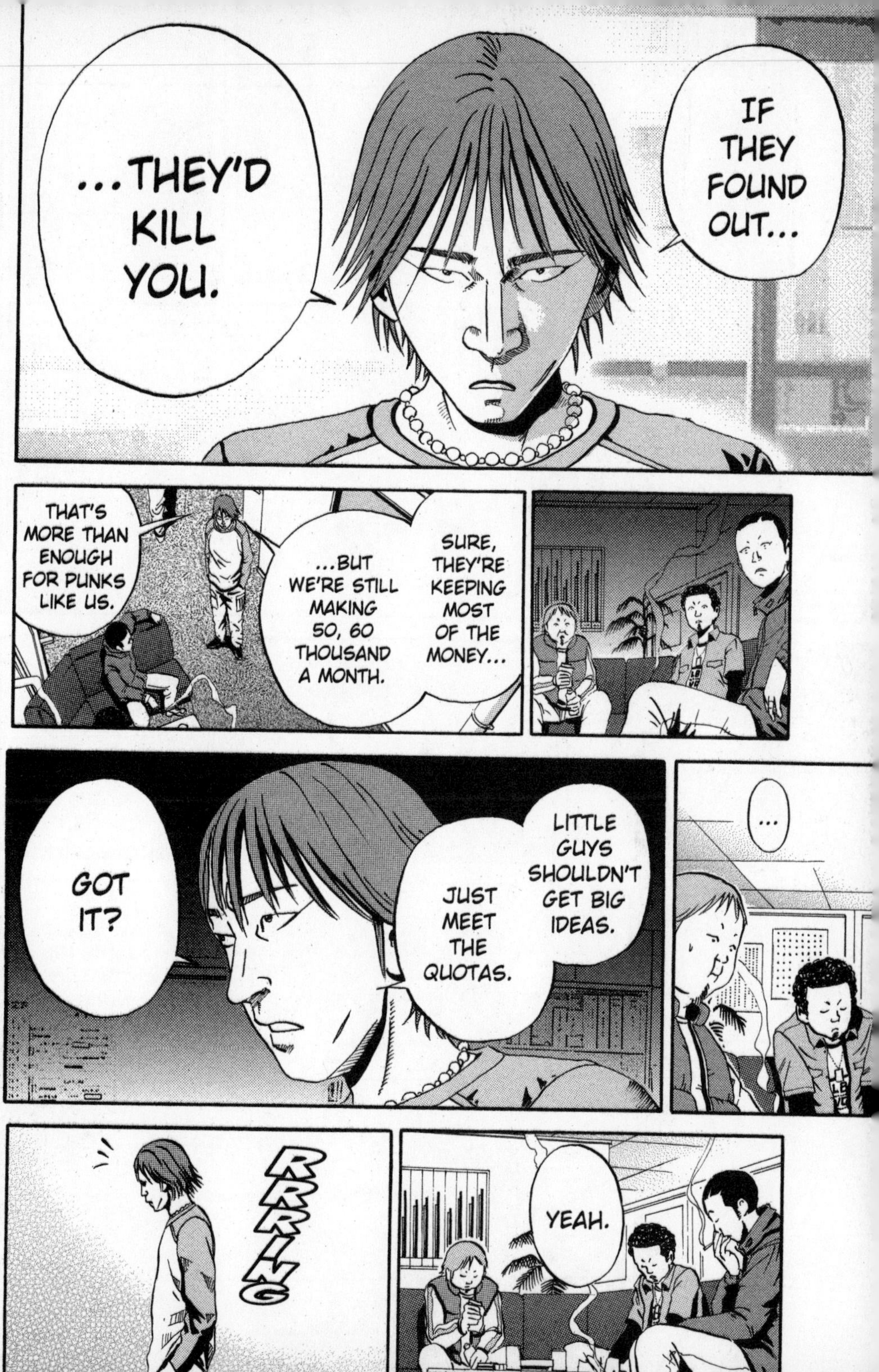
IF THEY FOUND OUT...
...THEY'D KILL YOU.
SURE, THEY'RE KEEPING MOST OF THE MONEY...
...BUT WE'RE STILL MAKING 50, 60 THOUSAND A MONTH.
THAT'S MORE THAN ENOUGH FOR PUNKS LIKE US.
...
LITTLE GUYS SHOULDN'T GET BIG IDEAS.
JUST MEET THE QUOTAS.
GOT IT?
YEAH.
RRRING

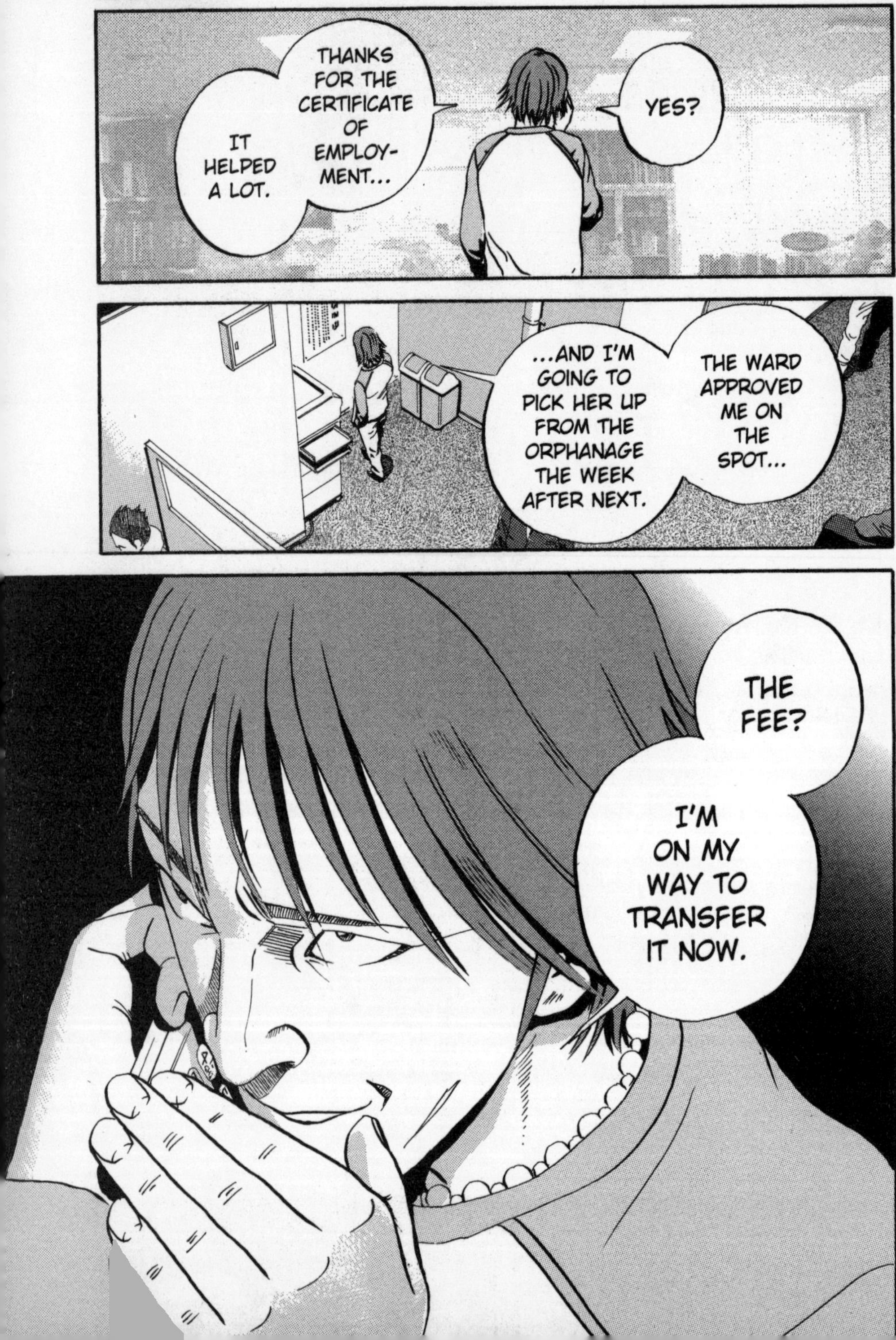
YES?
THANKS FOR THE CERTIFICATE OF EMPLOYMENT...
IT HELPED A LOT.
THE WARD APPROVED ME ON THE SPOT...
...AND I'M GOING TO PICK HER UP FROM THE ORPHANAGE THE WEEK AFTER NEXT.
THE FEE?
I'M ON MY WAY TO TRANSFER IT NOW.

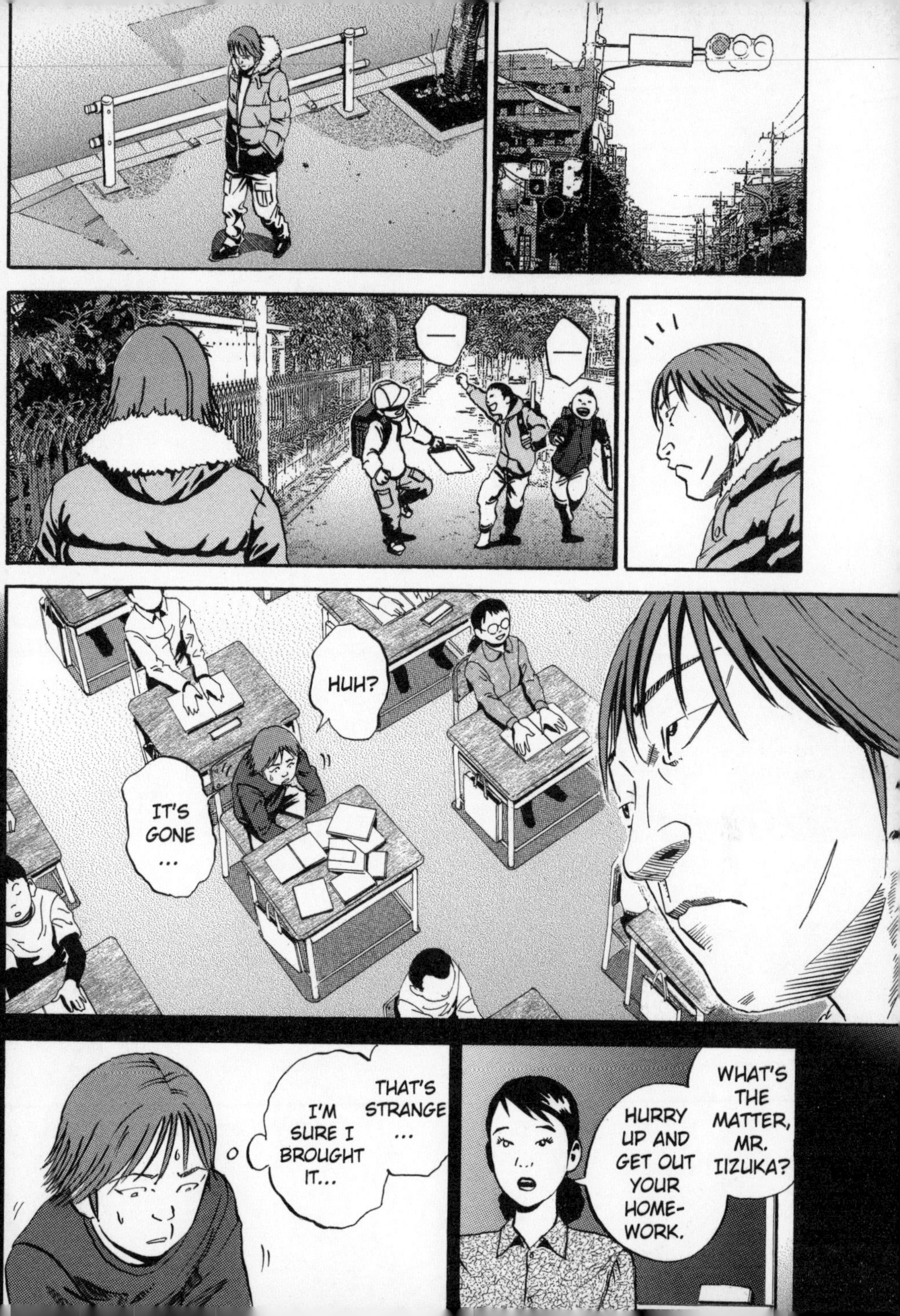
—
—
HUH?
IT'S GONE ...
WHAT'S THE MATTER, MR. IIZUKA?
HURRY UP AND GET OUT YOUR HOMEWORK.
THAT'S STRANGE ...
I'M SURE I BROUGHT IT...

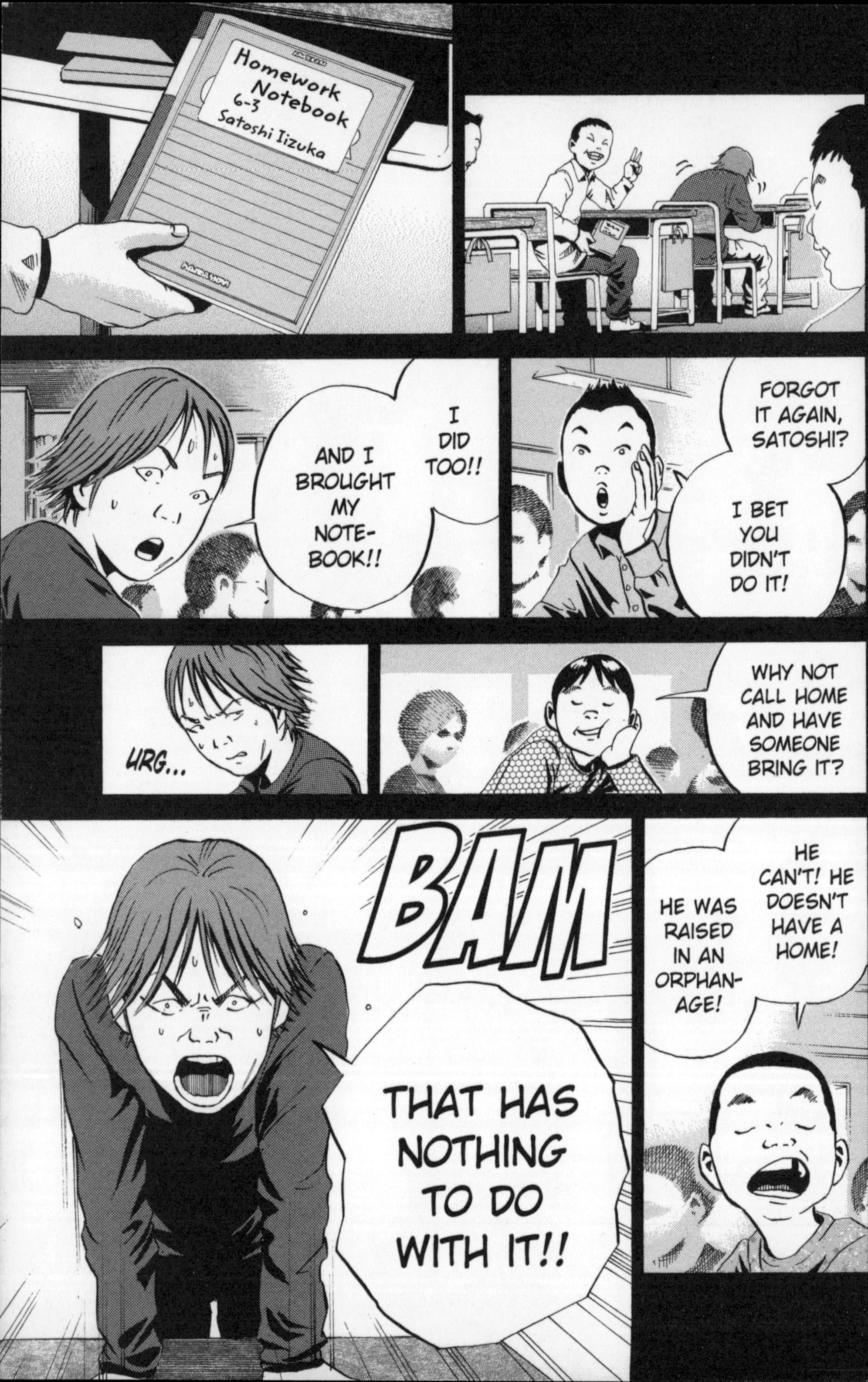
Homework Notebook 6-3 Satoshi Iizuka
FORGOT IT AGAIN, SATOSHI?
I BET YOU DIDN'T DO IT!
I DID TOO!!
AND I BROUGHT MY NOTEBOOK!!
WHY NOT CALL HOME AND HAVE SOMEONE BRING IT?
URG...
HE CAN'T! HE DOESN'T HAVE A HOME!
HE WAS RAISED IN AN ORPHANAGE!
BAM
THAT HAS NOTHING TO DO WITH IT!!

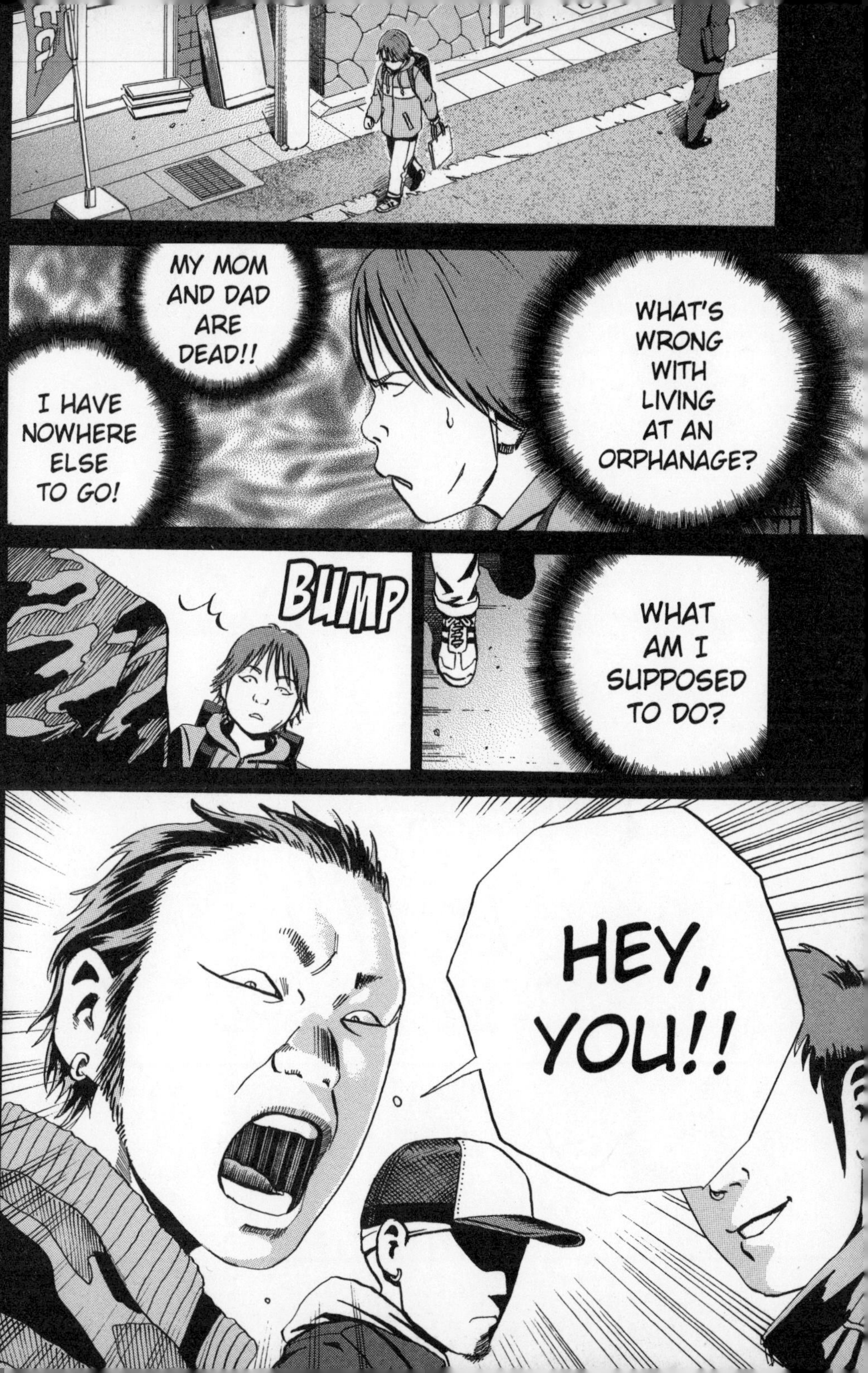
WHAT'S WRONG WITH LIVING AT AN ORPHANAGE?
MY MOM AND DAD ARE DEAD!!
I HAVE NOWHERE ELSE TO GO!
WHAT AM I SUPPOSED TO DO?
BUMP
HEY, YOU!!

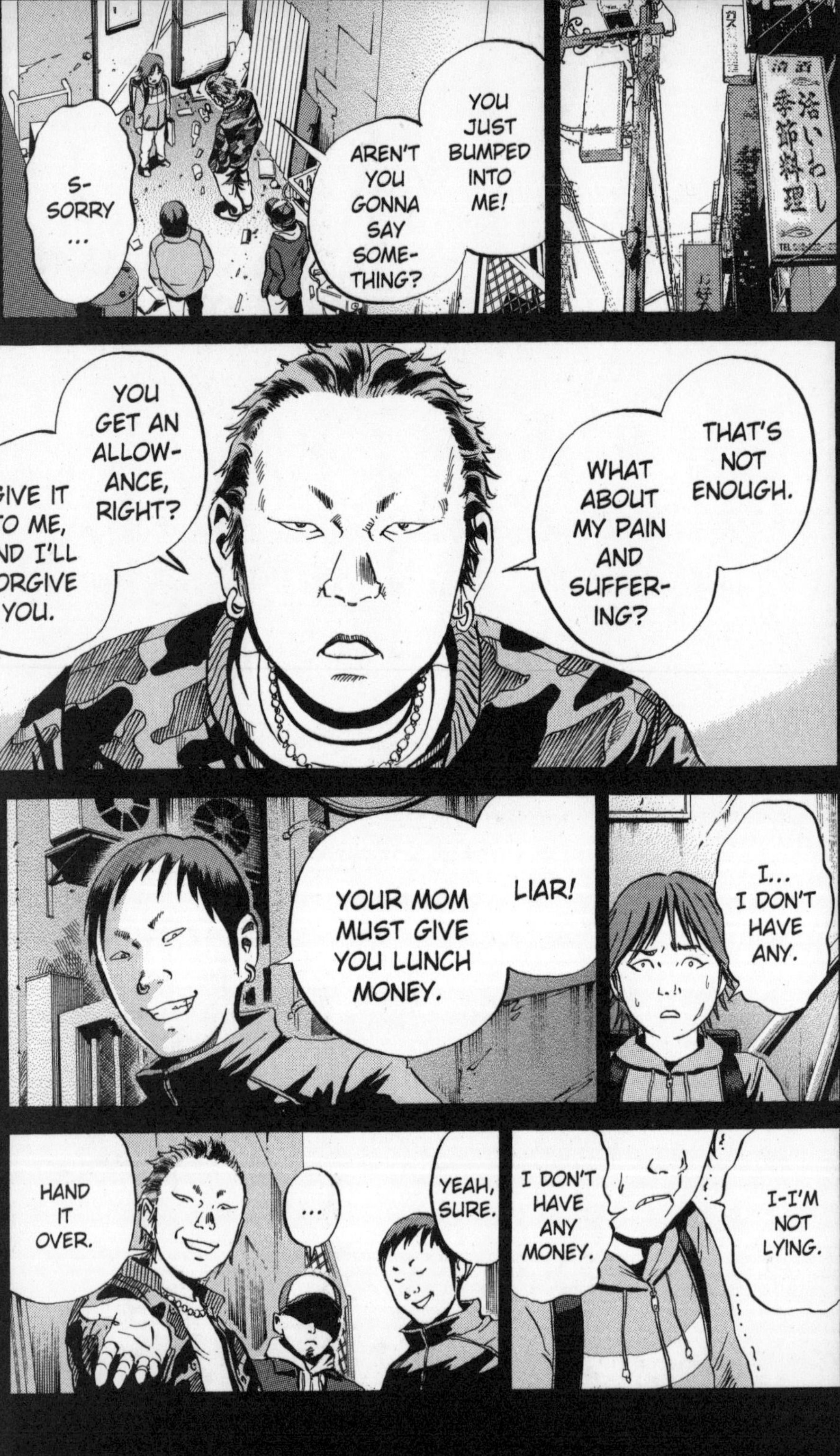
季節料理
YOU JUST BUMPED INTO ME!
AREN'T YOU GONNA SAY SOME-THING?
S-SORRY...
THAT'S NOT ENOUGH.
WHAT ABOUT MY PAIN AND SUFFER-ING?
YOU GET AN ALLOW-ANCE, RIGHT?
GIVE IT TO ME, AND I'LL FORGIVE YOU.
I... I DON'T HAVE ANY.
LIAR!
YOUR MOM MUST GIVE YOU LUNCH MONEY.
I-I'M NOT LYING.
I DON'T HAVE ANY MONEY.
YEAH, SURE.
...
HAND IT OVER.

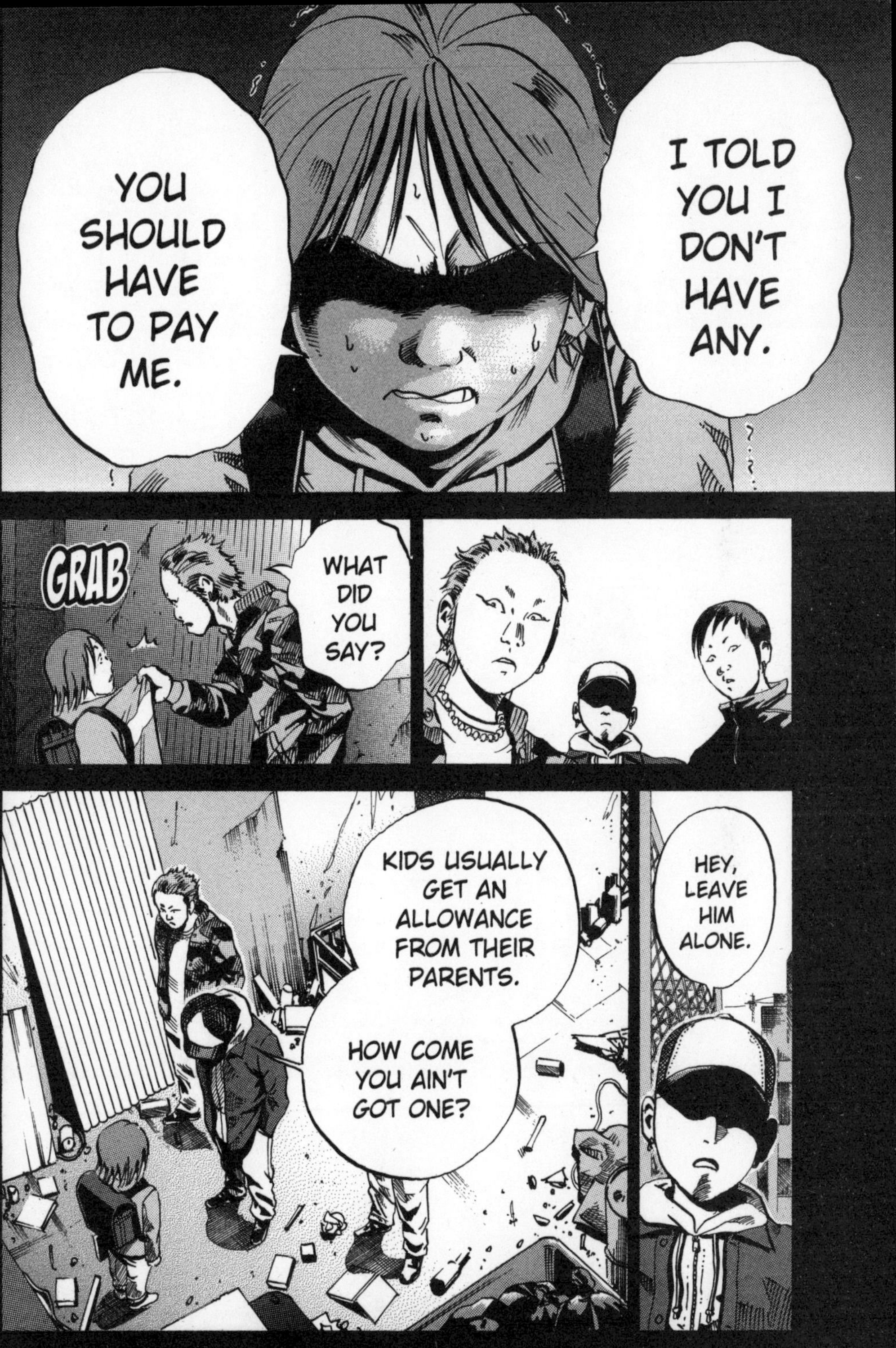
I TOLD YOU I DON'T HAVE ANY.
YOU SHOULD HAVE TO PAY ME.
WHAT DID YOU SAY?
GRAB
HEY, LEAVE HIM ALONE.
KIDS USUALLY GET AN ALLOWANCE FROM THEIR PARENTS.
HOW COME YOU AIN'T GOT ONE?

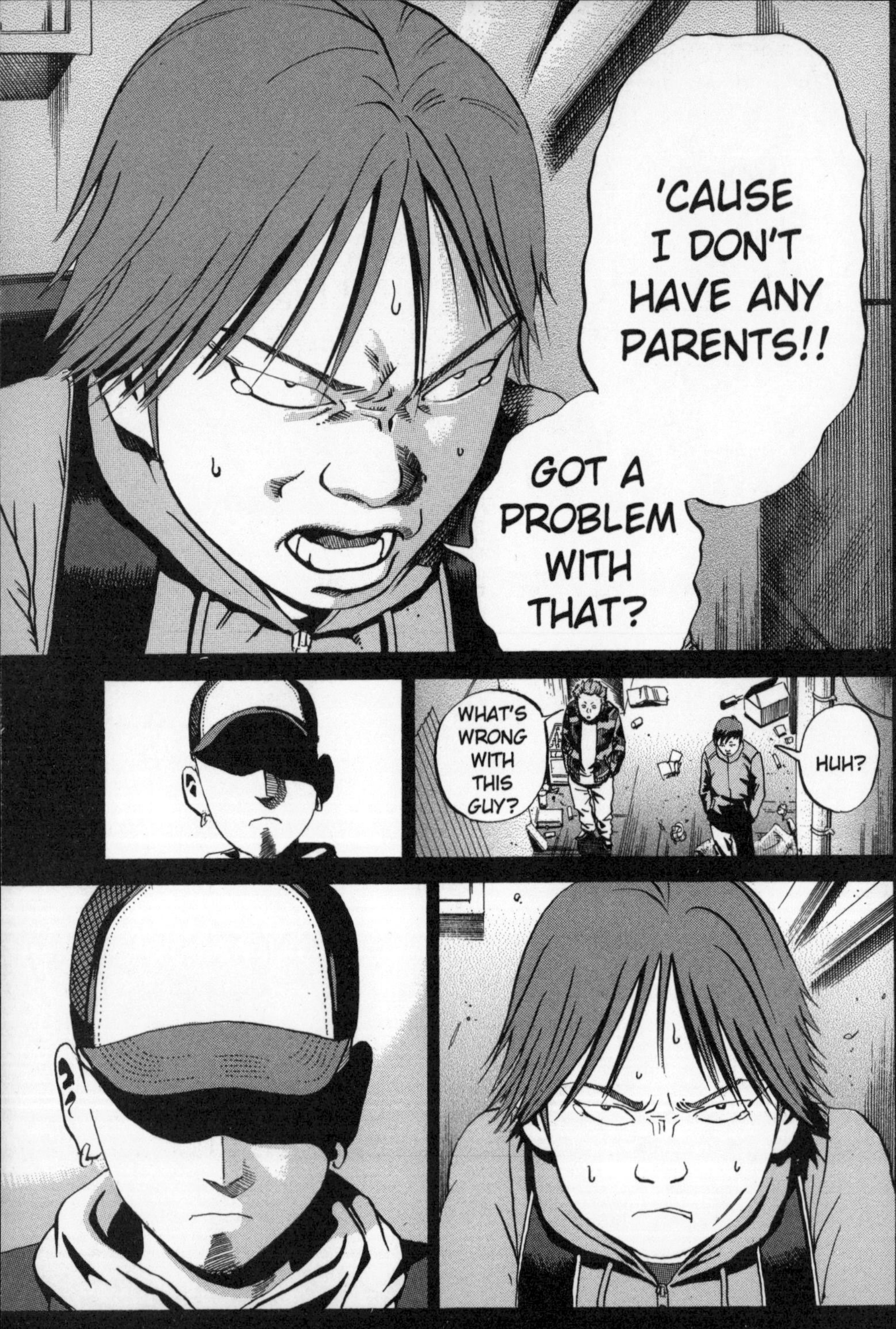
'CAUSE I DON'T HAVE ANY PARENTS!!
GOT A PROBLEM WITH THAT?
HUH?
WHAT'S WRONG WITH THIS GUY?

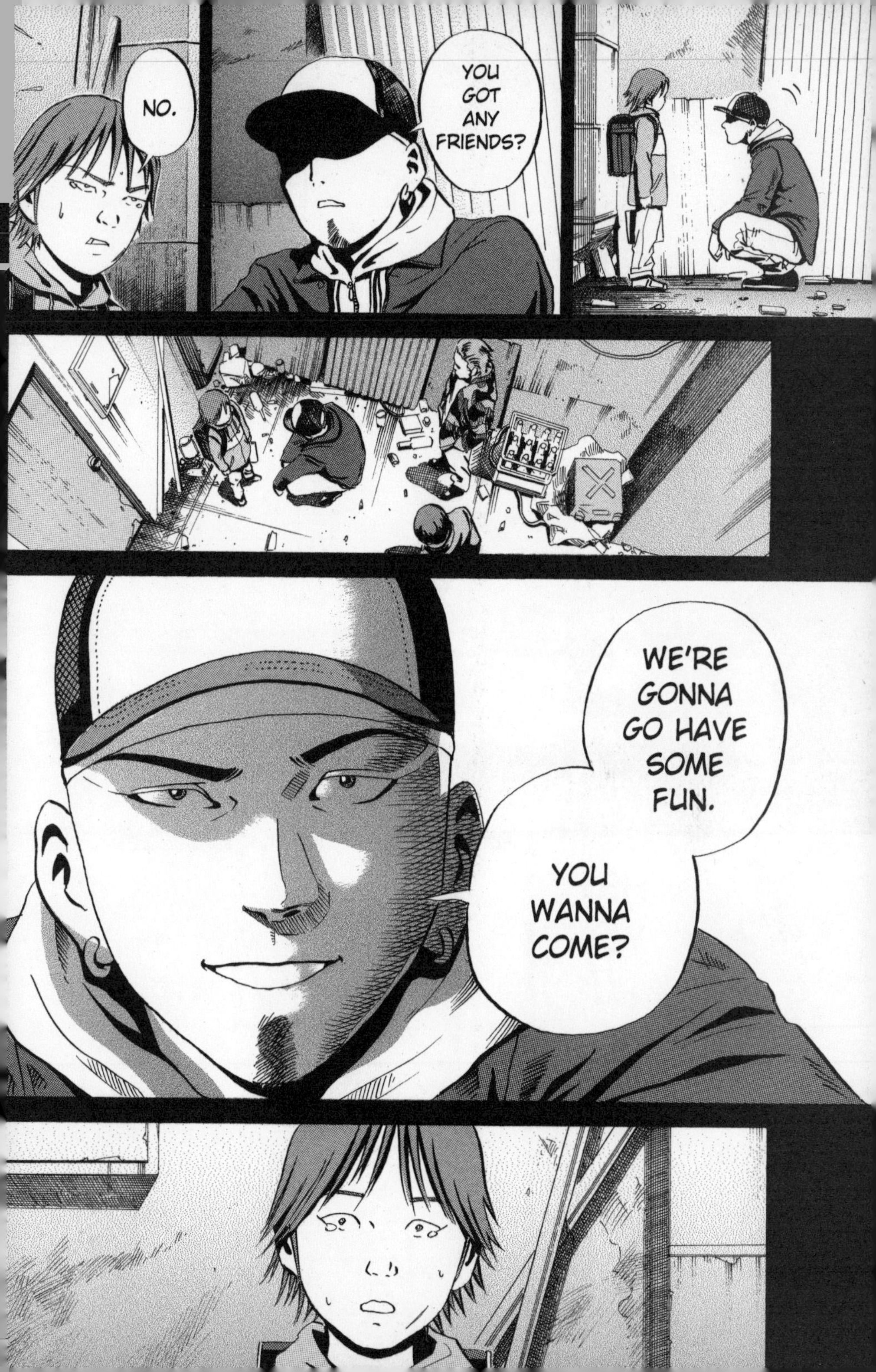
YOU GOT ANY FRIENDS?
NO.
WE'RE GONNA GO HAVE SOME FUN.
YOU WANNA COME?

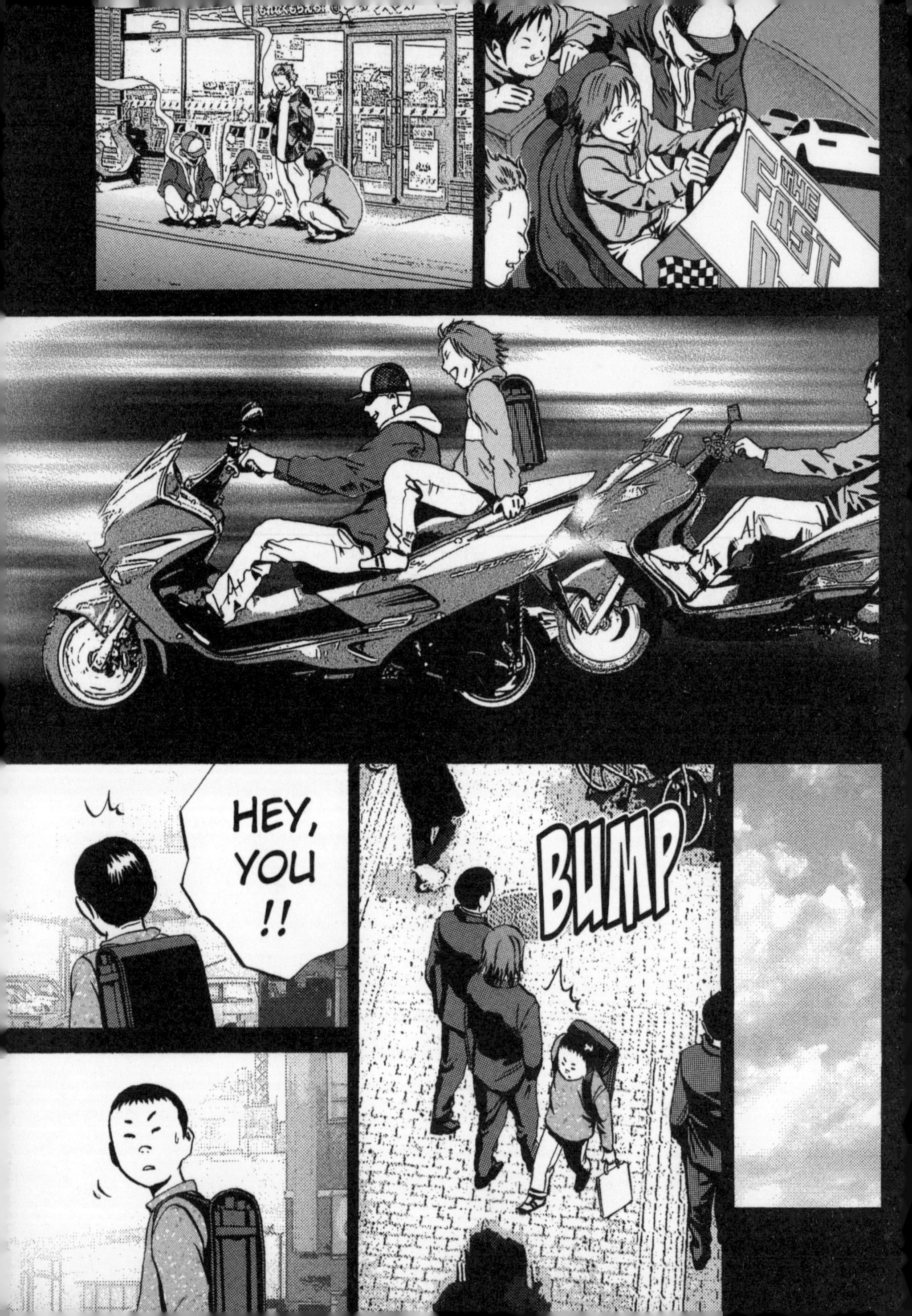
THE FAST
BUMP
HEY, YOU !!

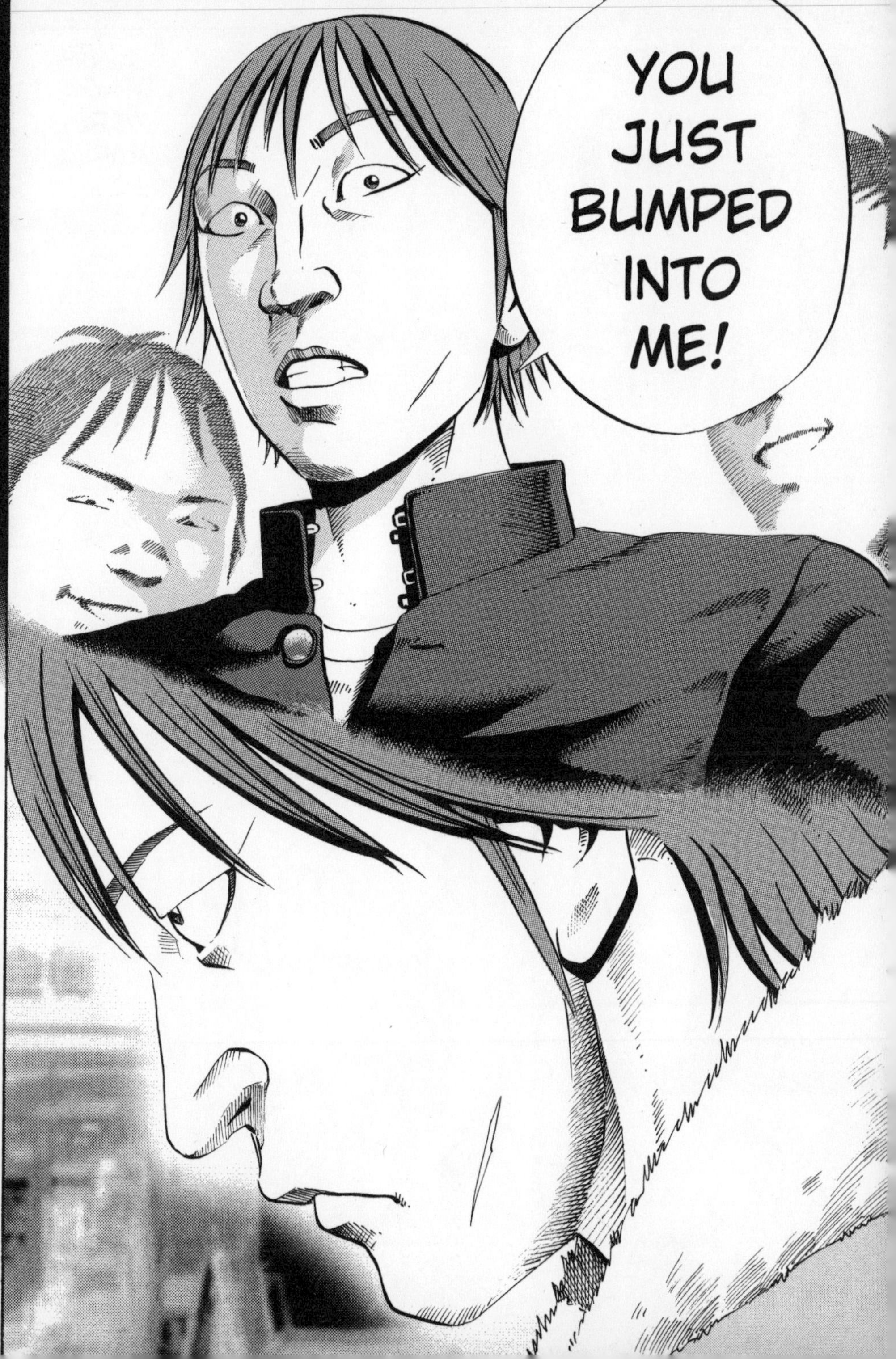
YOU JUST BUMPED INTO ME!

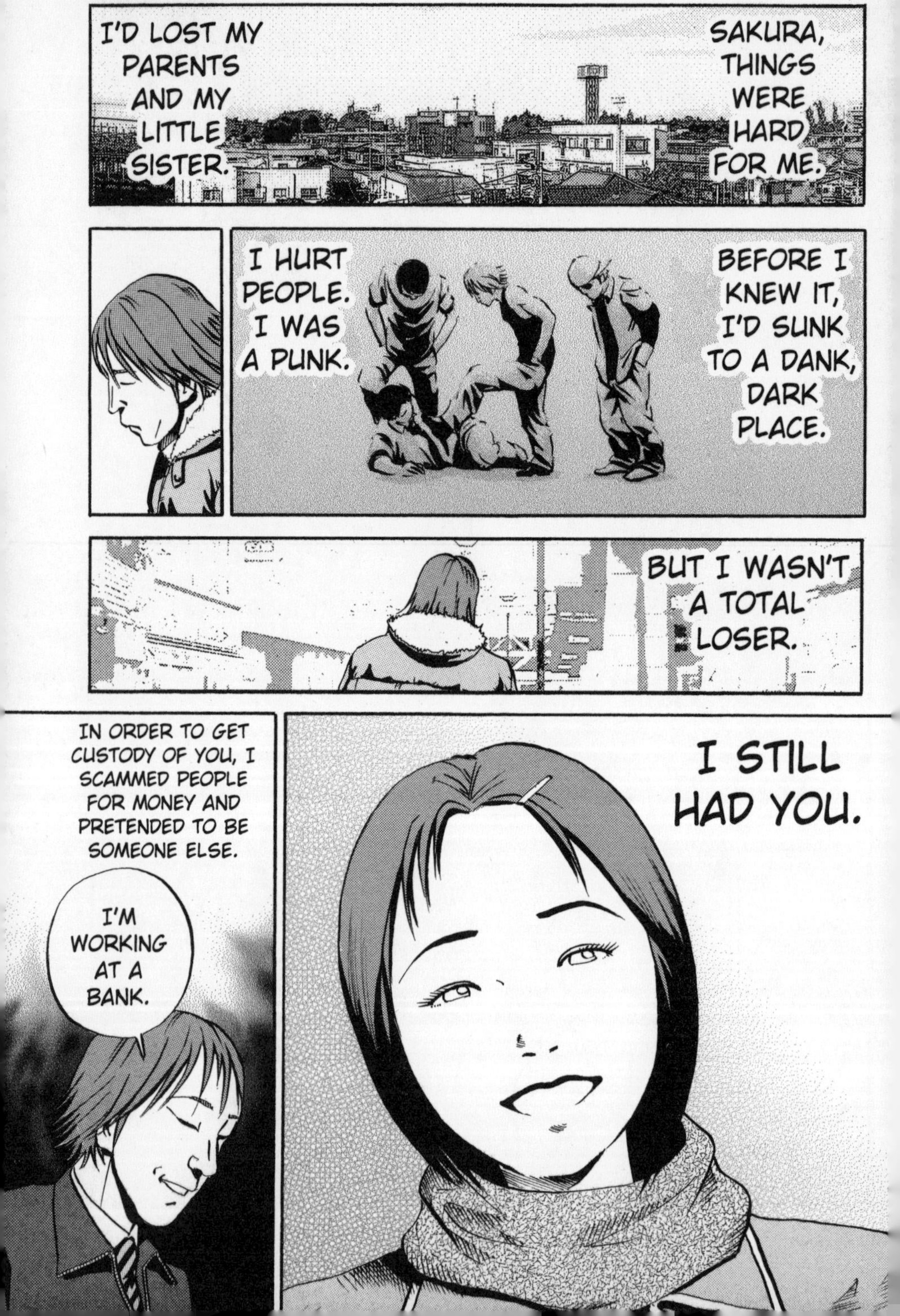
SAKURA, THINGS WERE HARD FOR ME.
I'D LOST MY PARENTS AND MY LITTLE SISTER.
BEFORE I KNEW IT, I'D SUNK TO A DANK, DARK PLACE.
I HURT PEOPLE. I WAS A PUNK.
BUT I WASN'T A TOTAL LOSER.
I STILL HAD YOU.
IN ORDER TO GET CUSTODY OF YOU, I SCAMMED PEOPLE FOR MONEY AND PRETENDED TO BE SOMEONE ELSE.
I'M WORKING AT A BANK.

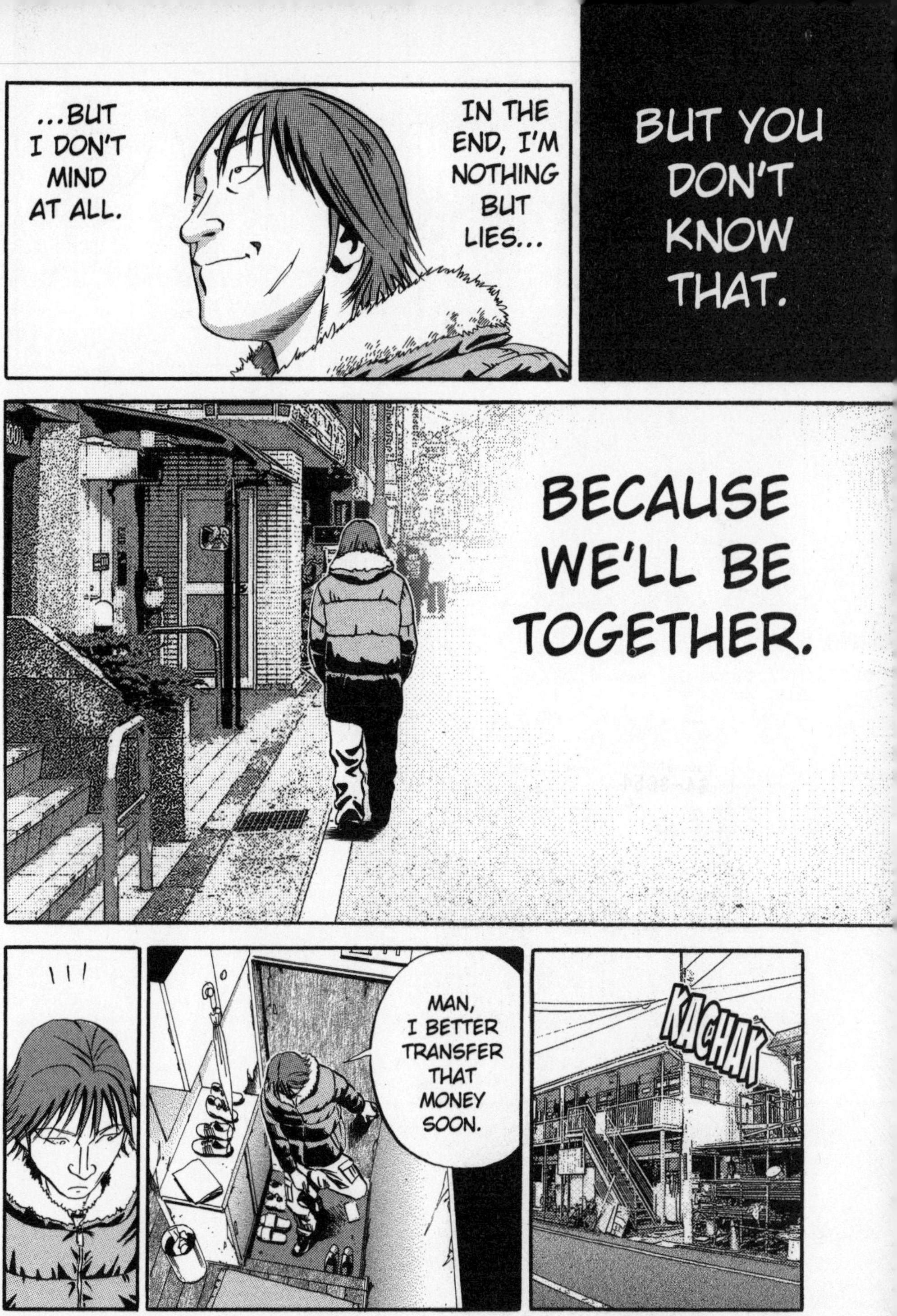
BUT YOU DON'T KNOW THAT.
IN THE END, I'M NOTHING BUT LIES...
...BUT I DON'T MIND AT ALL.
BECAUSE WE'LL BE TOGETHER.
KACHAK
MAN, I BETTER TRANSFER THAT MONEY SOON.

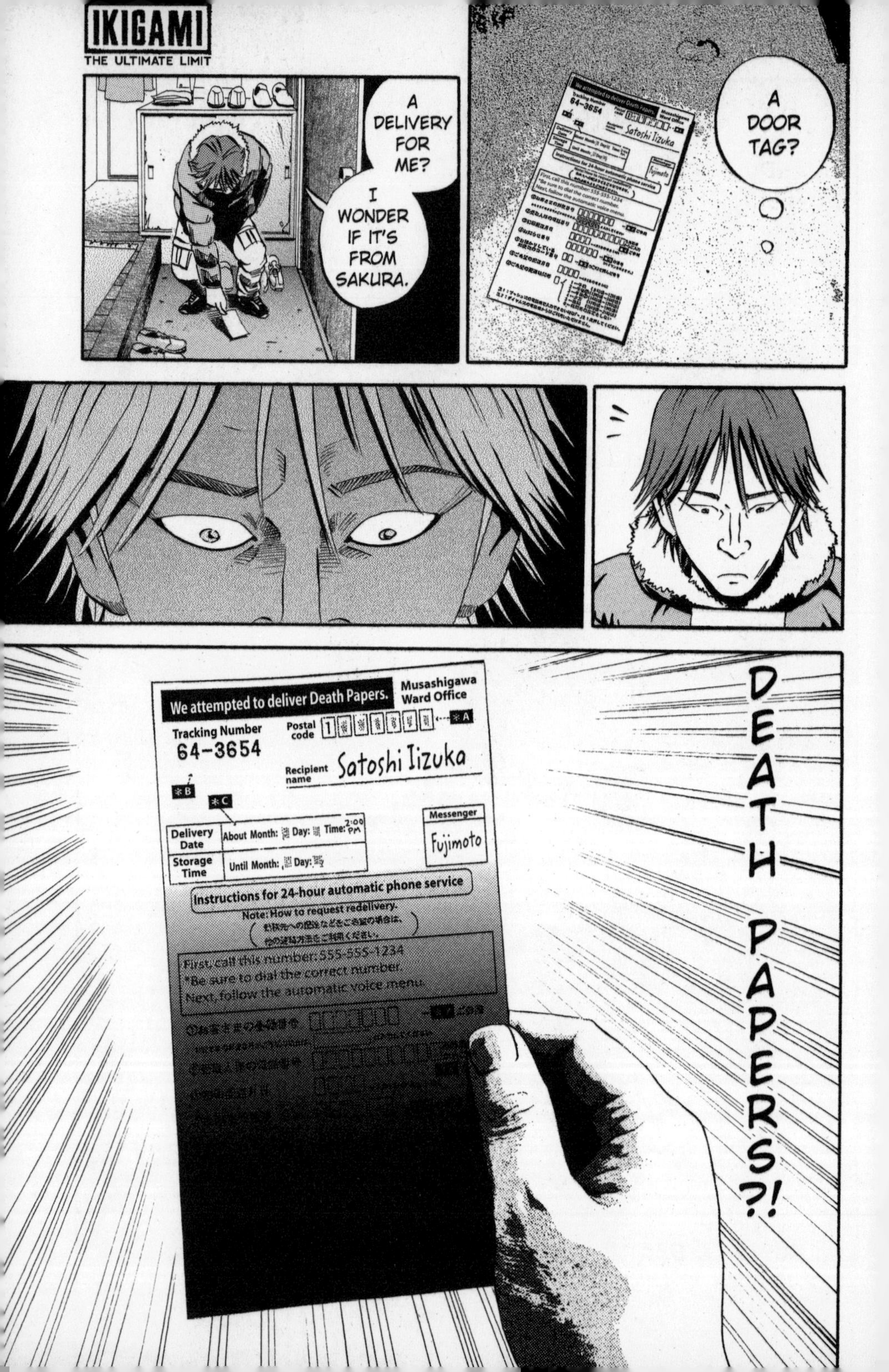
A DOOR TAG?
A DELIVERY FOR ME?
I WONDER IF IT'S FROM SAKURA.
We attempted to deliver Death Papers.
Musashigawa Ward Office
Tracking Number
64-3654
Postal code
*A
Recipient name
Satoshi Iizuka
*B
*C
Messenger
Fujimoto
Delivery Date
About Month: Day: Time: 2:00 PM
Storage Time
Until Month: Day:
Instructions for 24-hour automatic phone service
Note: How to request redelivery.
First, call this number: 555-555-1234
*Be sure to dial the correct number.
Next, follow the automatic voice menu.
DEATH PAPERS?!

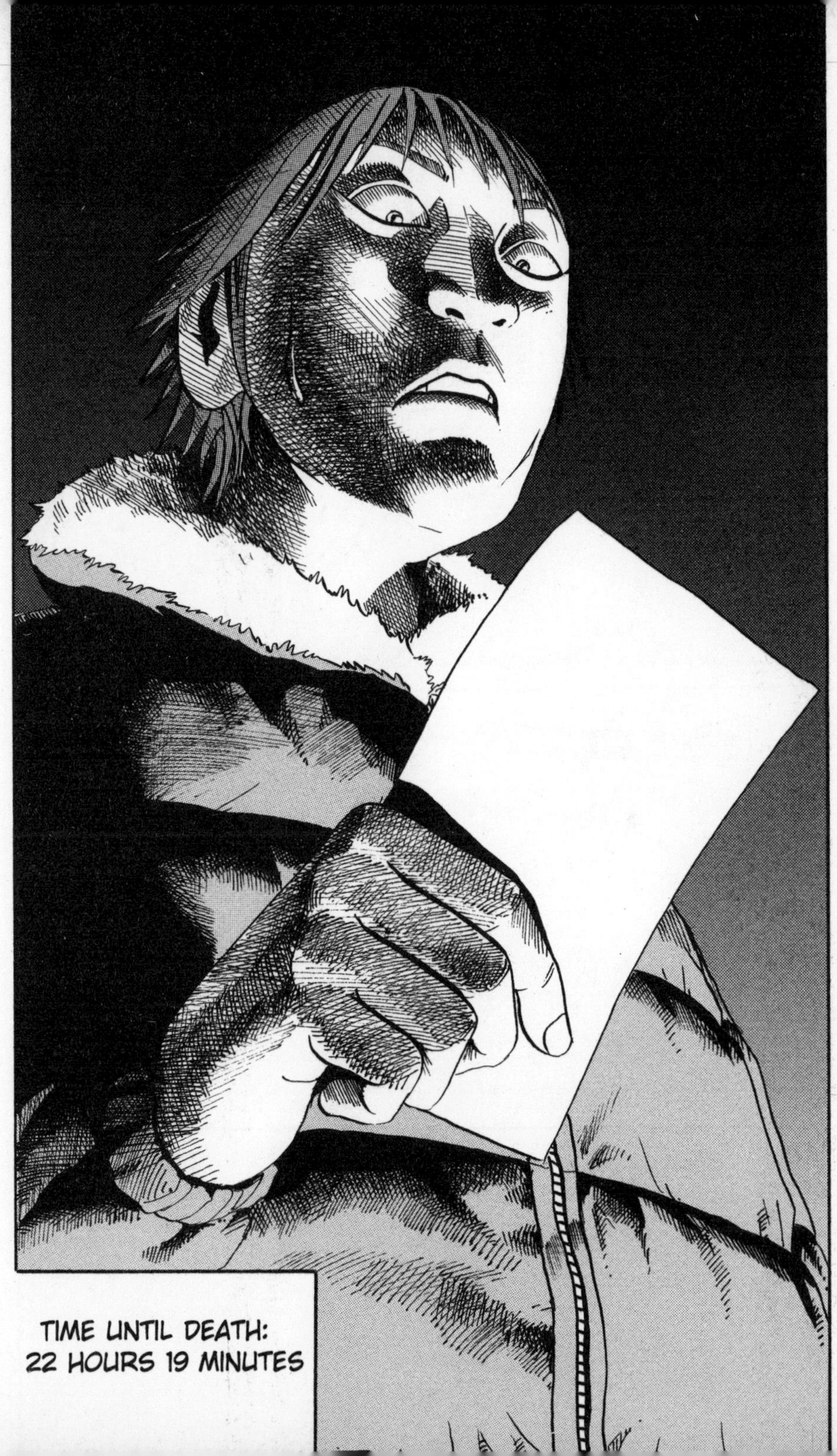
TIME UNTIL DEATH:
22 HOURS 19 MINUTES

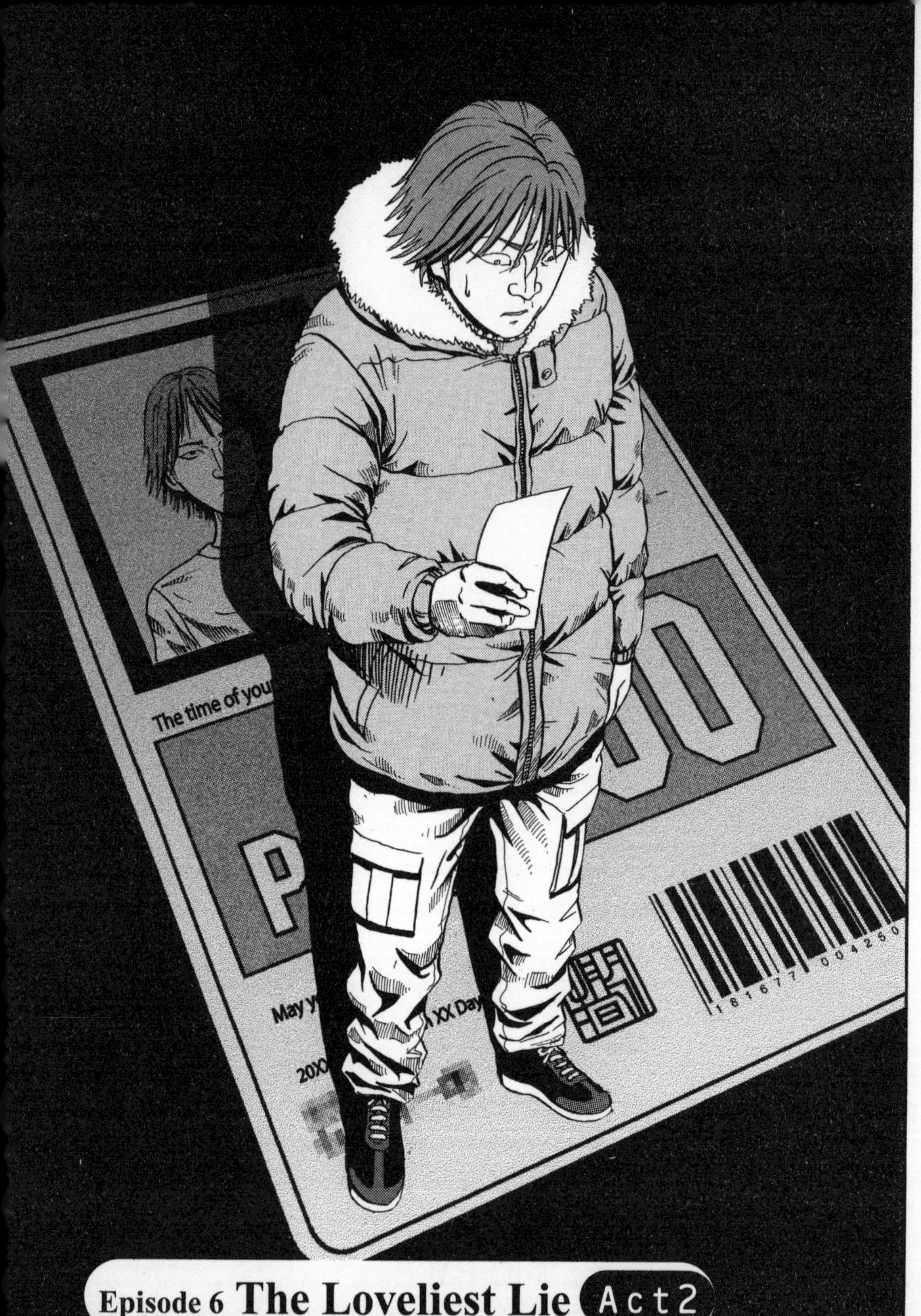
The time of you
May y
XX Day
20XX
181677 004250

Episode 6 The Loveliest Lie Act2

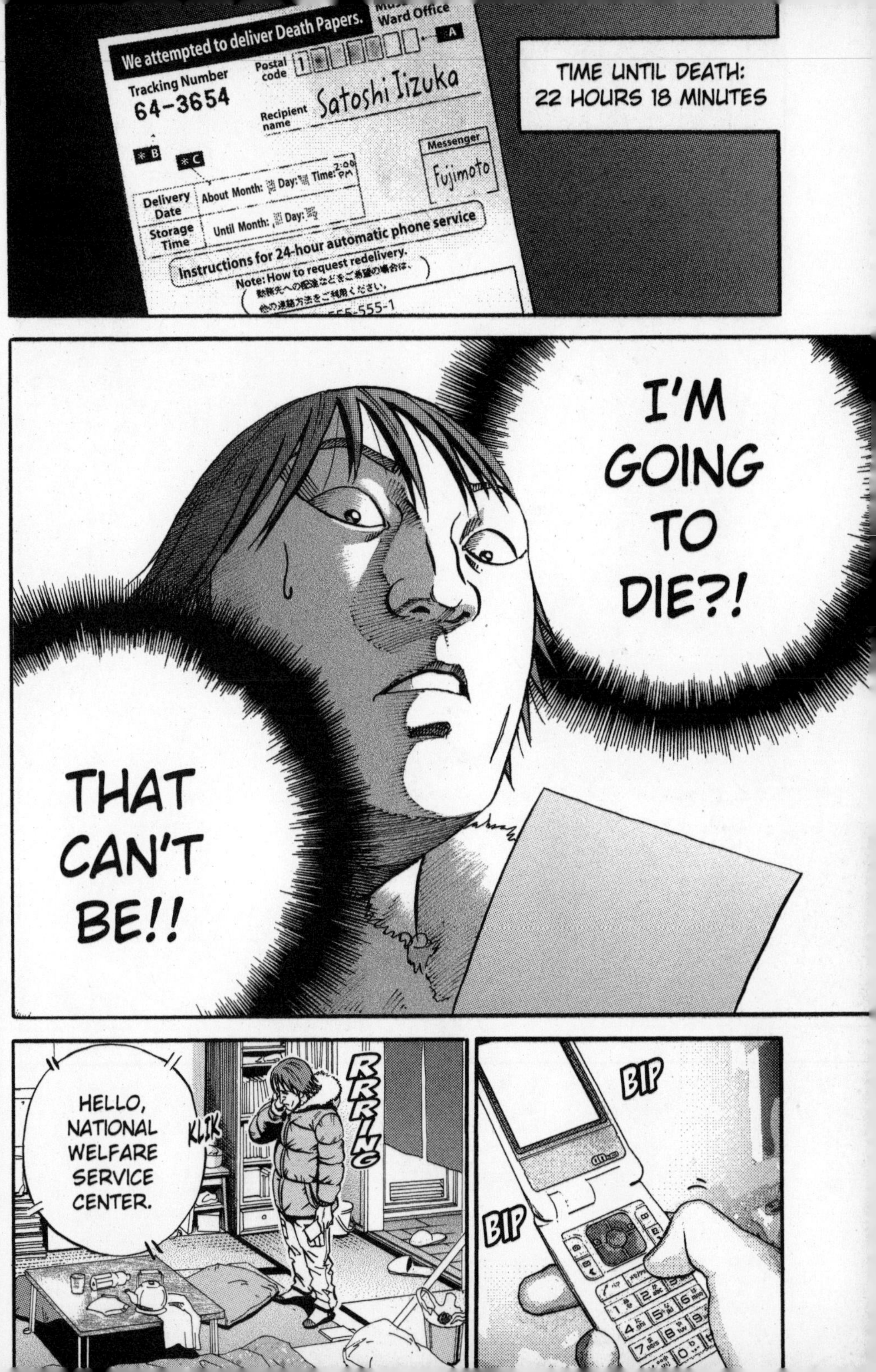

TIME UNTIL DEATH:
22 HOURS 18 MINUTES
We attempted to deliver Death Papers.
Ward Office
A
Postal code
1
Tracking Number
64-3654
Recipient name
Satoshi Iizuka
B
C
Messenger
Fujimoto
Delivery Date
About Month: Day: Time: 2:00 PM
Storage Time
Until Month: Day:
Instructions for 24-hour automatic phone service
Note: How to request redelivery.
I'M GOING TO DIE?!
THAT CAN'T BE!!
BIP
BIP
RRRING
KLIK
HELLO, NATIONAL WELFARE SERVICE CENTER.

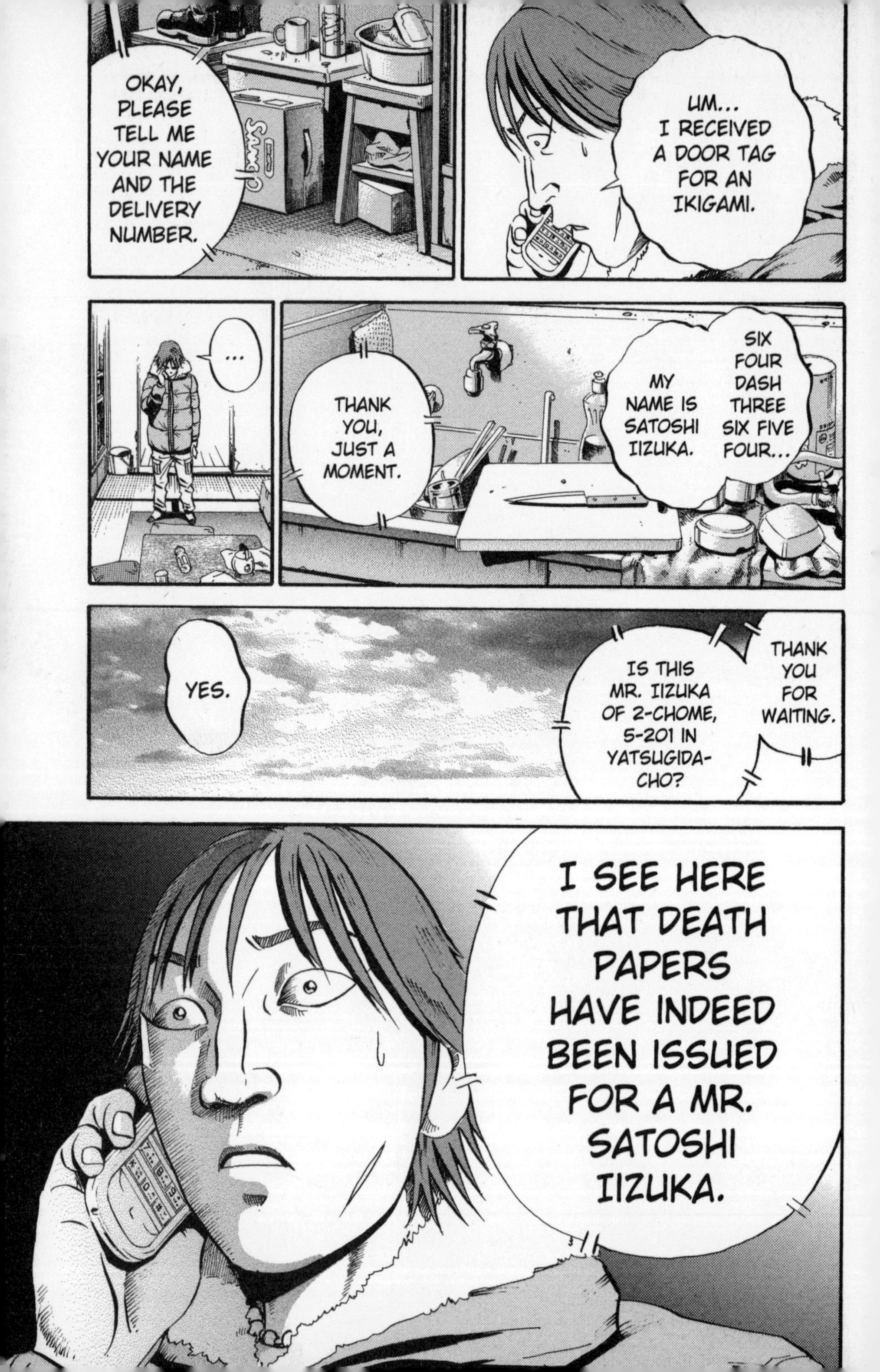
UM... I RECEIVED A DOOR TAG FOR AN IKIGAMI.
OKAY, PLEASE TELL ME YOUR NAME AND THE DELIVERY NUMBER.
SIX FOUR DASH THREE SIX FIVE FOUR...
MY NAME IS SATOSHI IIZUKA.
THANK YOU, JUST A MOMENT.
...
THANK YOU FOR WAITING.
IS THIS MR. IIZUKA OF 2-CHOME, 5-201 IN YATSUGIDA-CHO?
YES.
I SEE HERE THAT DEATH PAPERS HAVE INDEED BEEN ISSUED FOR A MR. SATOSHI IIZUKA.

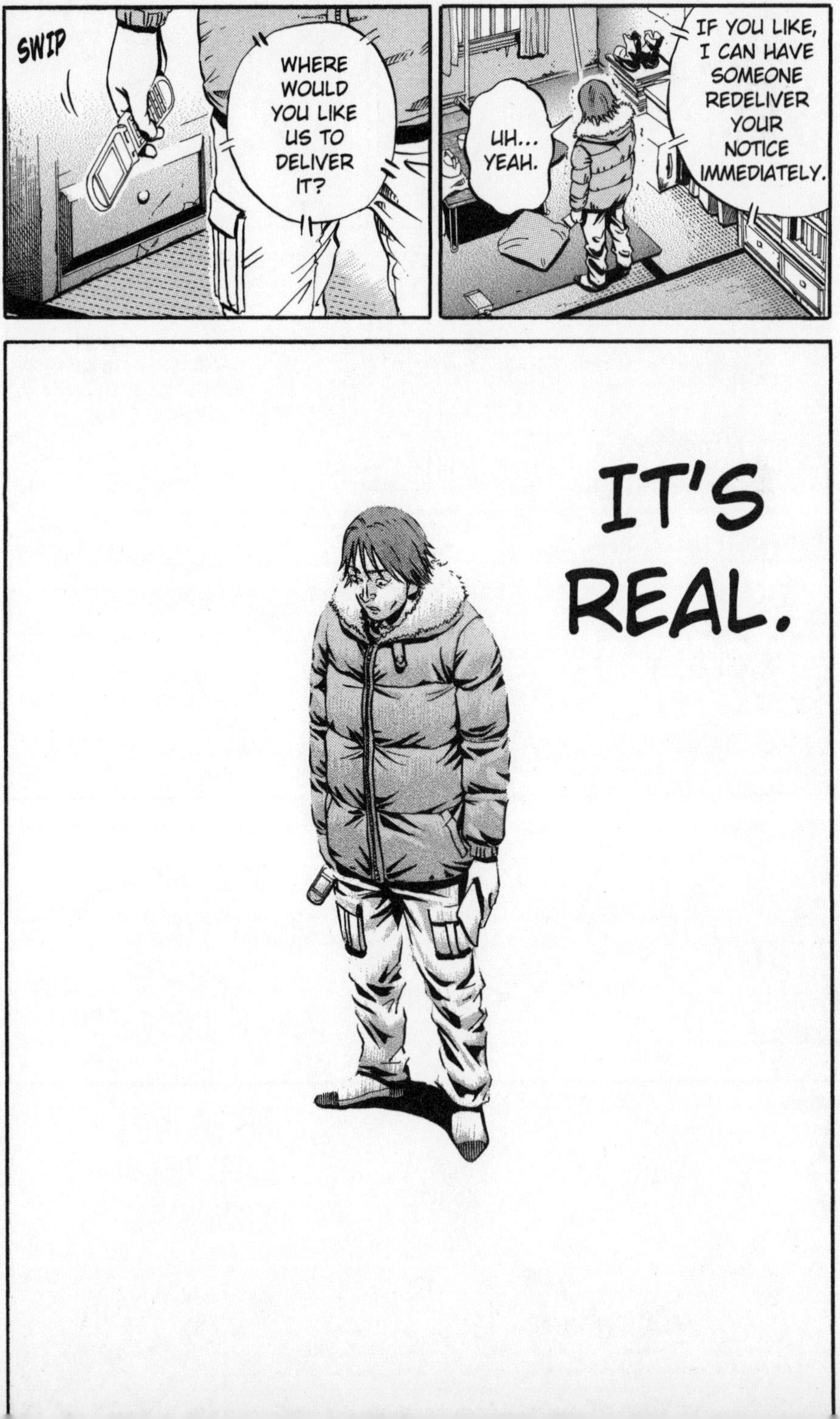
IF YOU LIKE, I CAN HAVE SOMEONE REDELIVER YOUR NOTICE IMMEDIATELY.
UH... YEAH.
WHERE WOULD YOU LIKE US TO DELIVER IT?
SWIP
IT'S REAL.

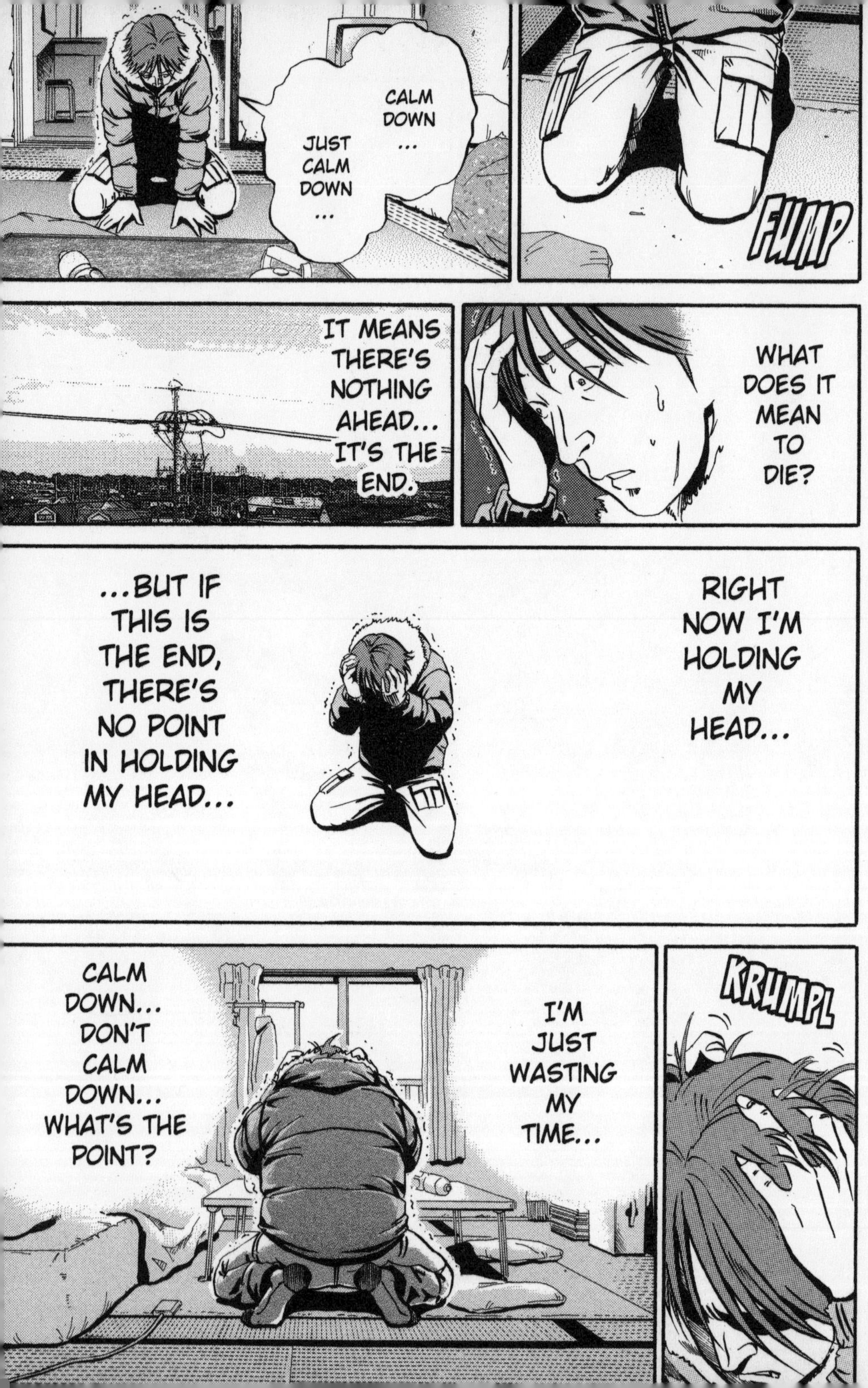
FUMP
CALM DOWN ...
JUST CALM DOWN ...
WHAT DOES IT MEAN TO DIE?
IT MEANS THERE'S NOTHING AHEAD... IT'S THE END.
RIGHT NOW I'M HOLDING MY HEAD...
...BUT IF THIS IS THE END, THERE'S NO POINT IN HOLDING MY HEAD...
KRUMPL
I'M JUST WASTING MY TIME...
CALM DOWN... DON'T CALM DOWN... WHAT'S THE POINT?

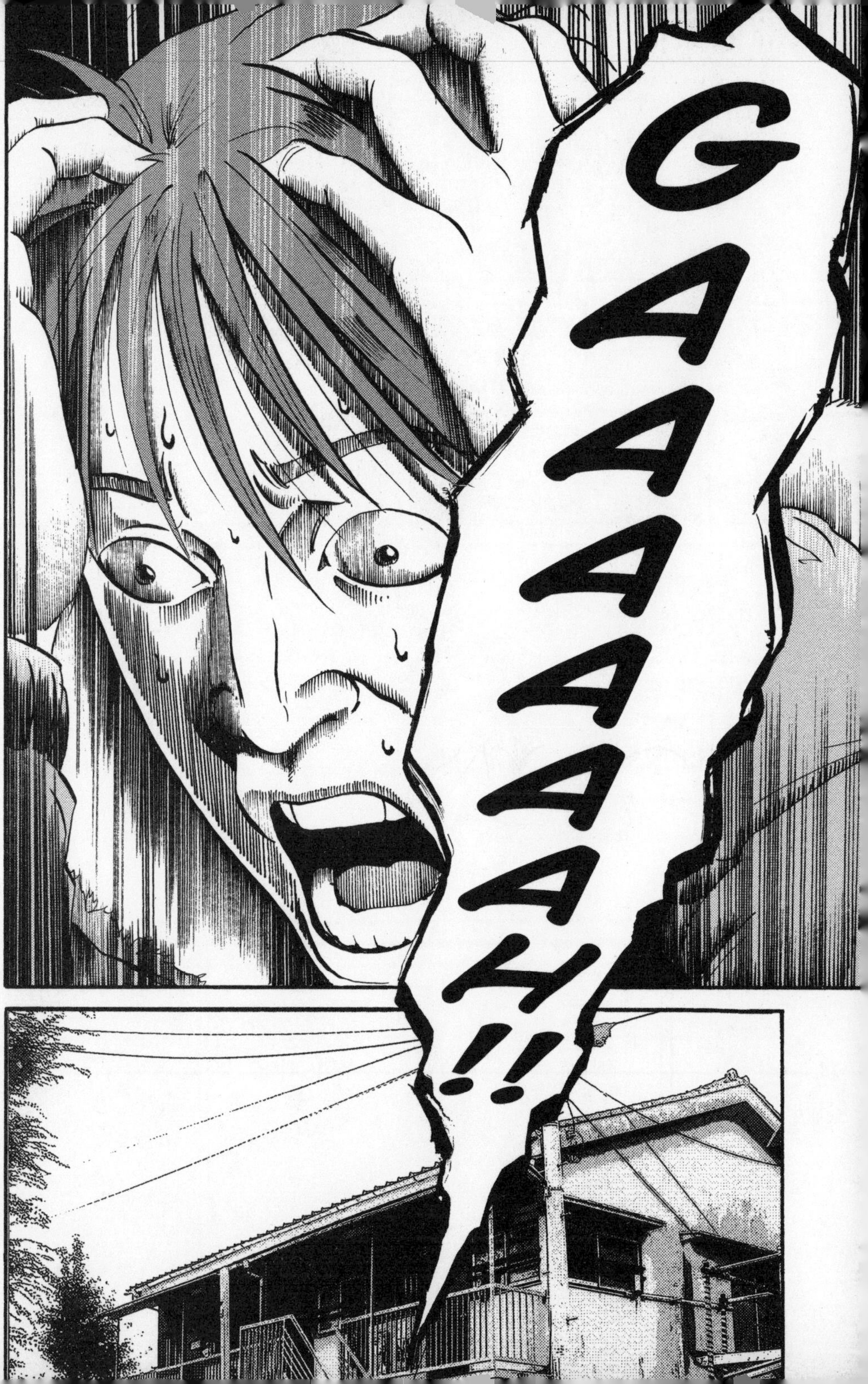
GAAAAAAH!!

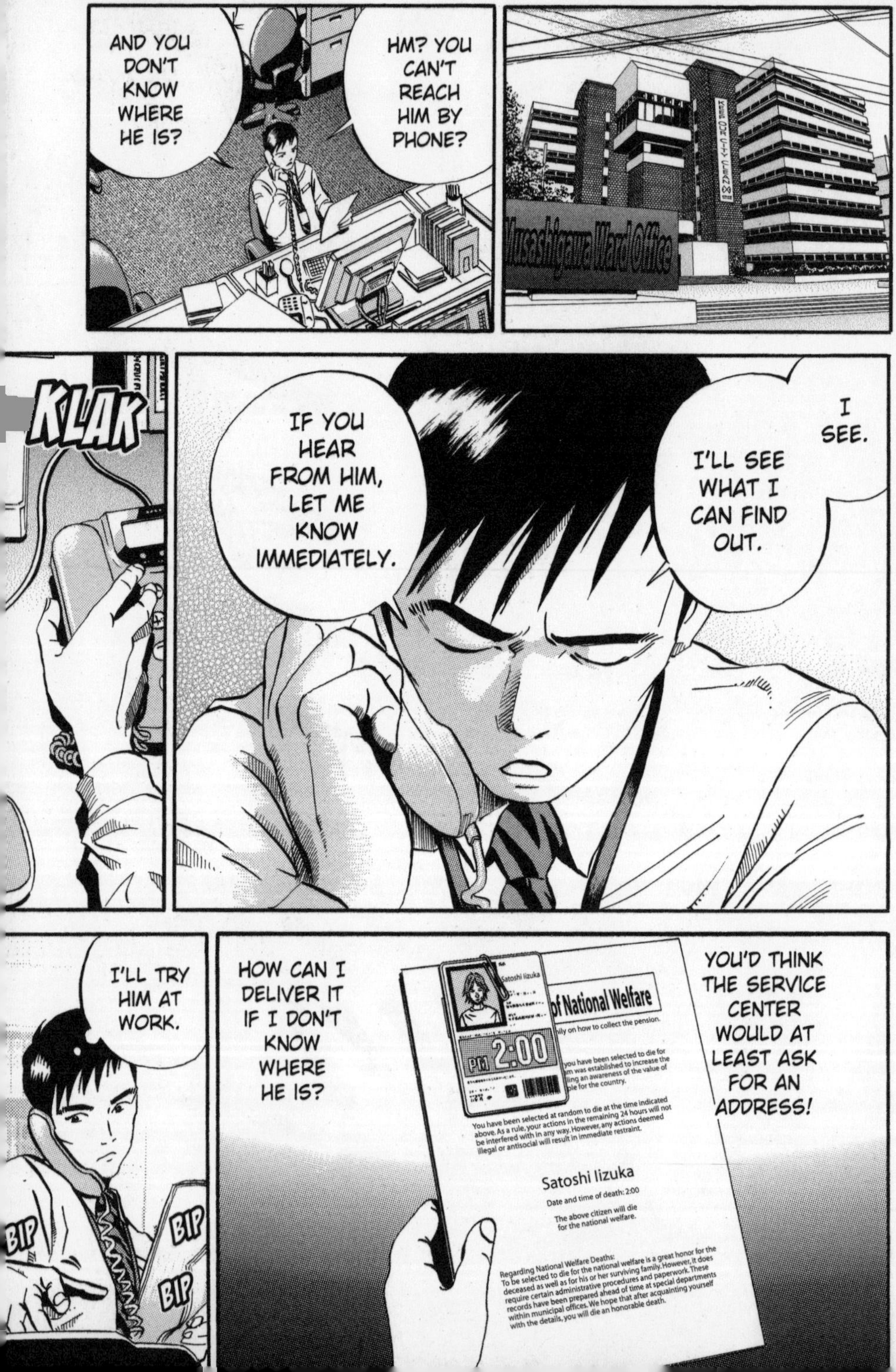
KEEP OUR CITY CLEAN
Musashigawa Ward Office
HM? YOU CAN'T REACH HIM BY PHONE?
AND YOU DON'T KNOW WHERE HE IS?
I SEE.
I'LL SEE WHAT I CAN FIND OUT.
IF YOU HEAR FROM HIM, LET ME KNOW IMMEDIATELY.
KLAK
YOU'D THINK THE SERVICE CENTER WOULD AT LEAST ASK FOR AN ADDRESS!
HOW CAN I DELIVER IT IF I DON'T KNOW WHERE HE IS?
Satoshi Iizuka
PM 2:00
of National Welfare
You have been selected at random to die at the time indicated above. As a rule, your actions in the remaining 24 hours will not be interfered with in any way. However, any actions deemed illegal or antisocial will result in immediate restraint.
Satoshi Iizuka
Date and time of death: 2:00
The above citizen will die for the national welfare.
Regarding National Welfare Deaths:
To be selected to die for the national welfare is a great honor for the deceased as well as for his or her surviving family. However, it does require certain administrative procedures and paperwork. These records have been prepared ahead of time at special departments within municipal offices. We hope that after acquainting yourself with the details, you will die an honorable death.
I'LL TRY HIM AT WORK.
BIP
BIP
BIP

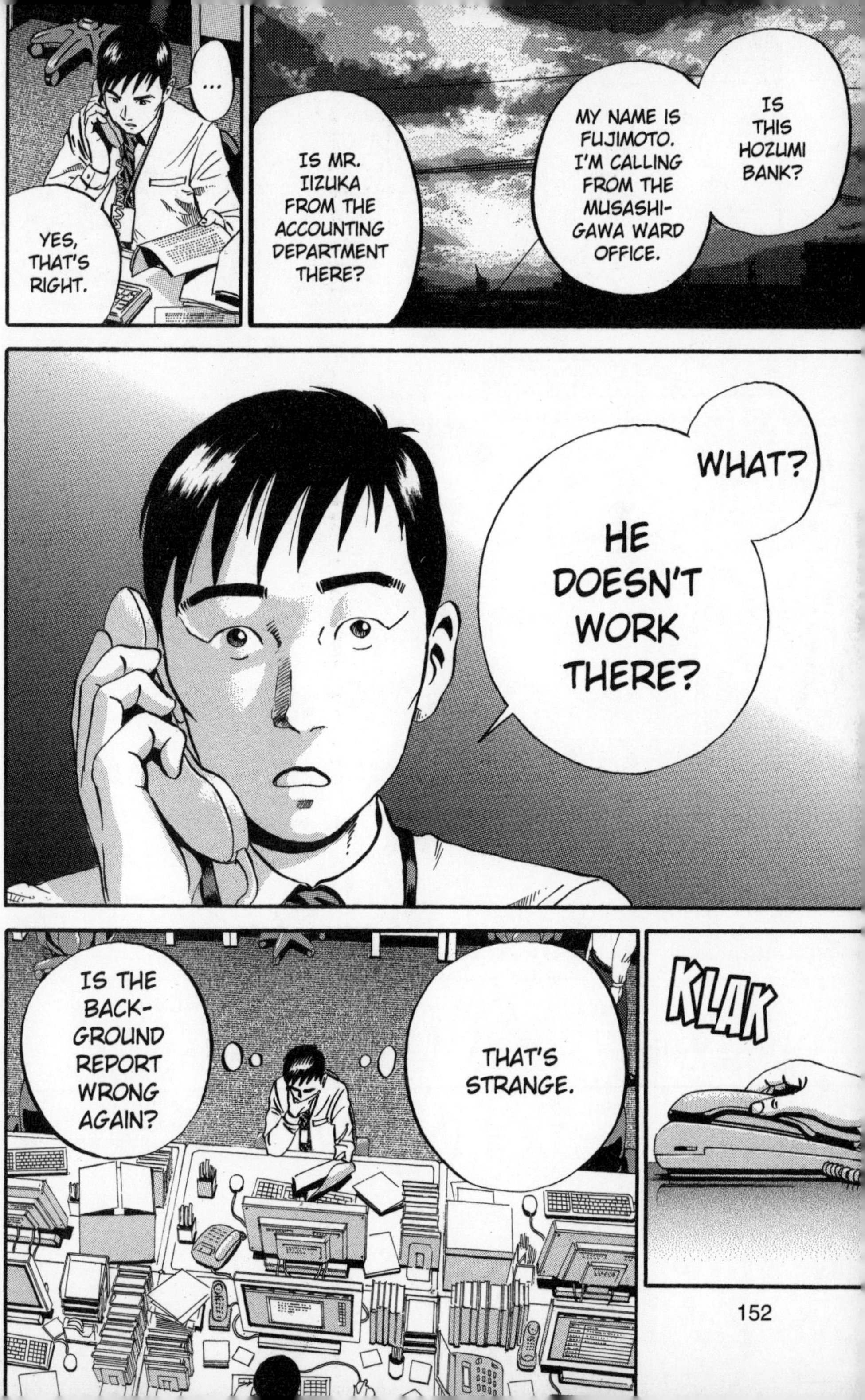
IS THIS HOZUMI BANK?
MY NAME IS FUJIMOTO. I'M CALLING FROM THE MUSASHI-GAWA WARD OFFICE.
IS MR. IIZUKA FROM THE ACCOUNTING DEPARTMENT THERE?
...
YES, THAT'S RIGHT.
WHAT?
HE DOESN'T WORK THERE?
KLAK
THAT'S STRANGE.
IS THE BACK-GROUND REPORT WRONG AGAIN?

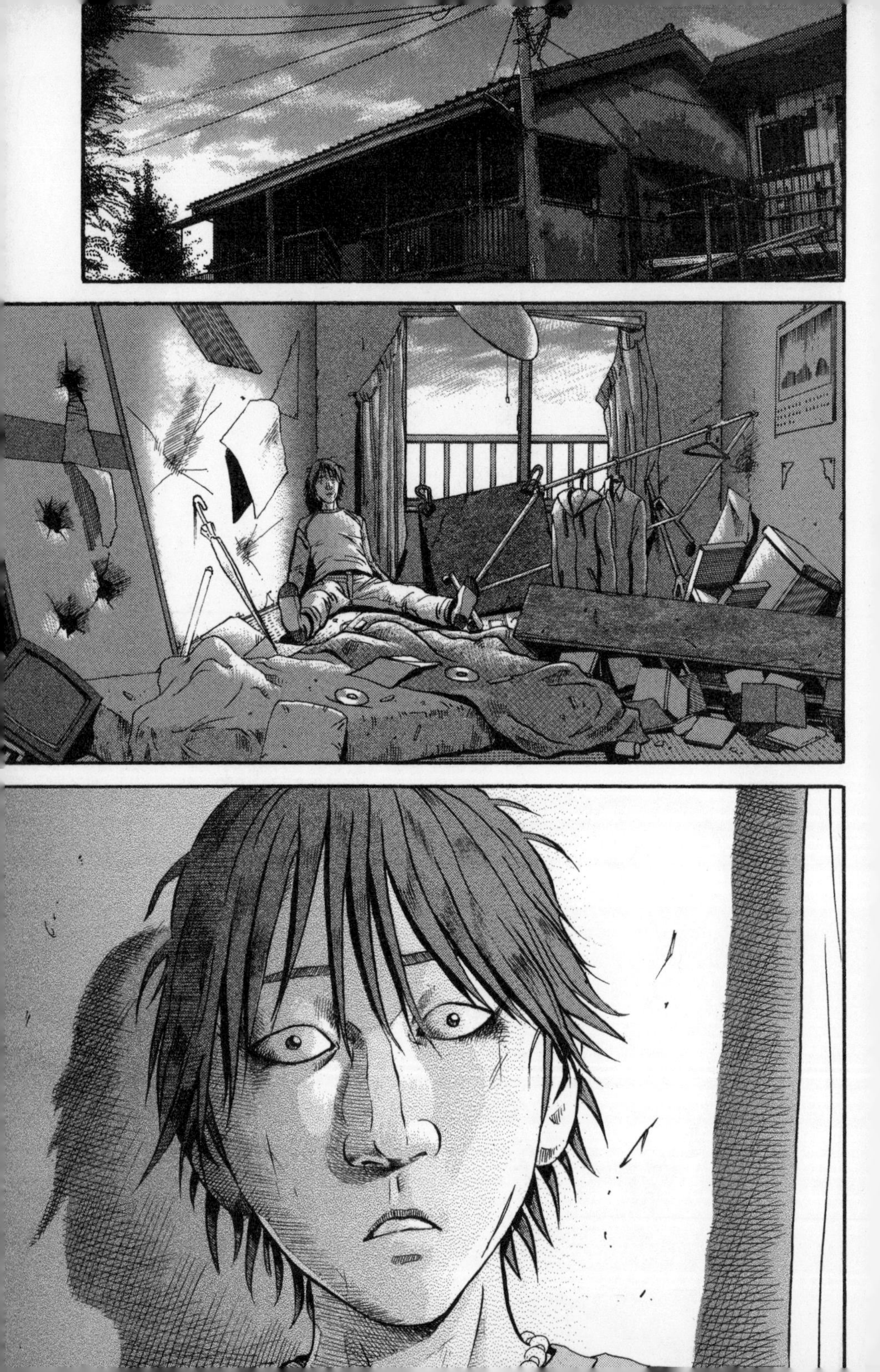

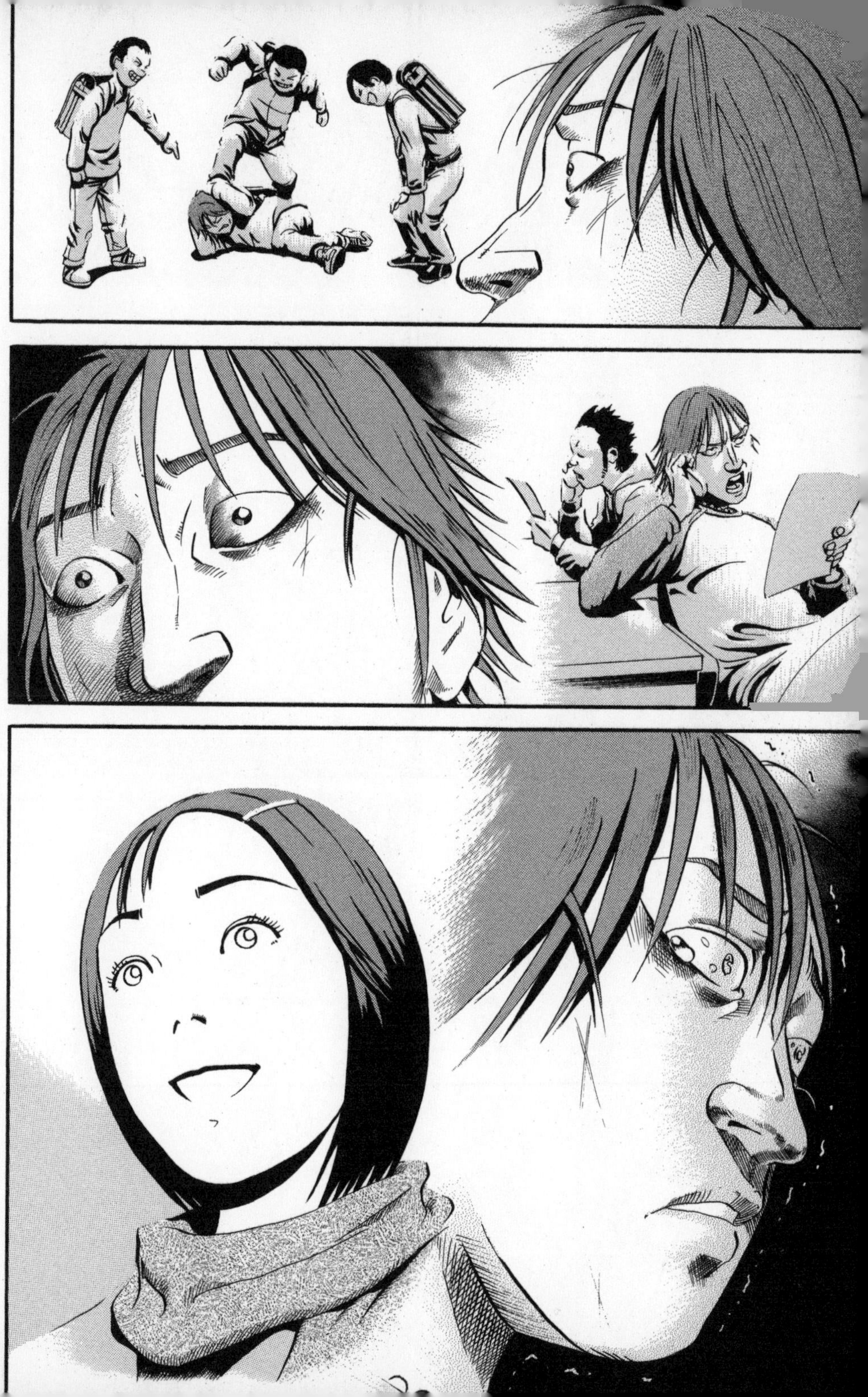

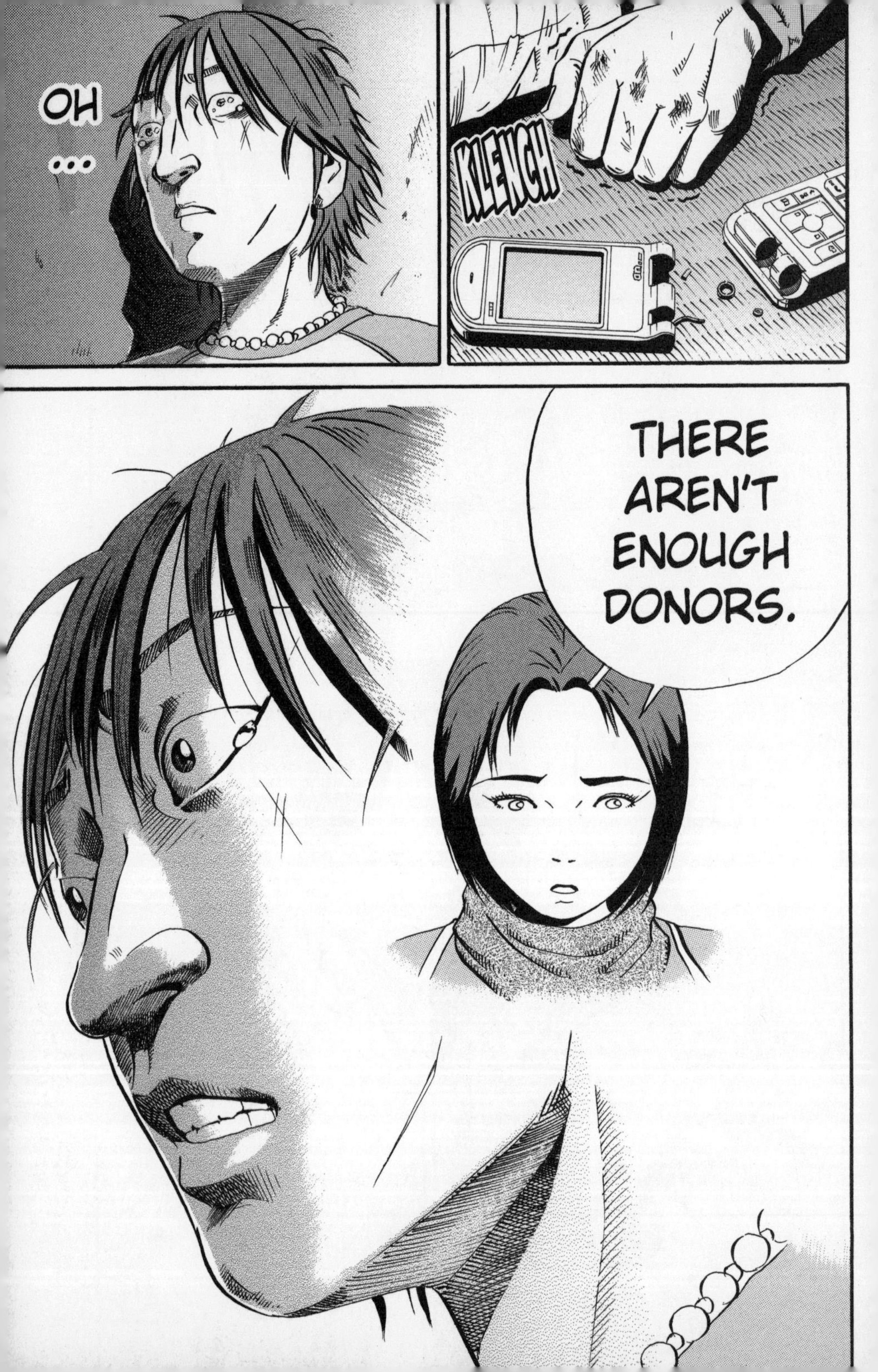
KLENCH
OH ...
THERE AREN'T ENOUGH DONORS.

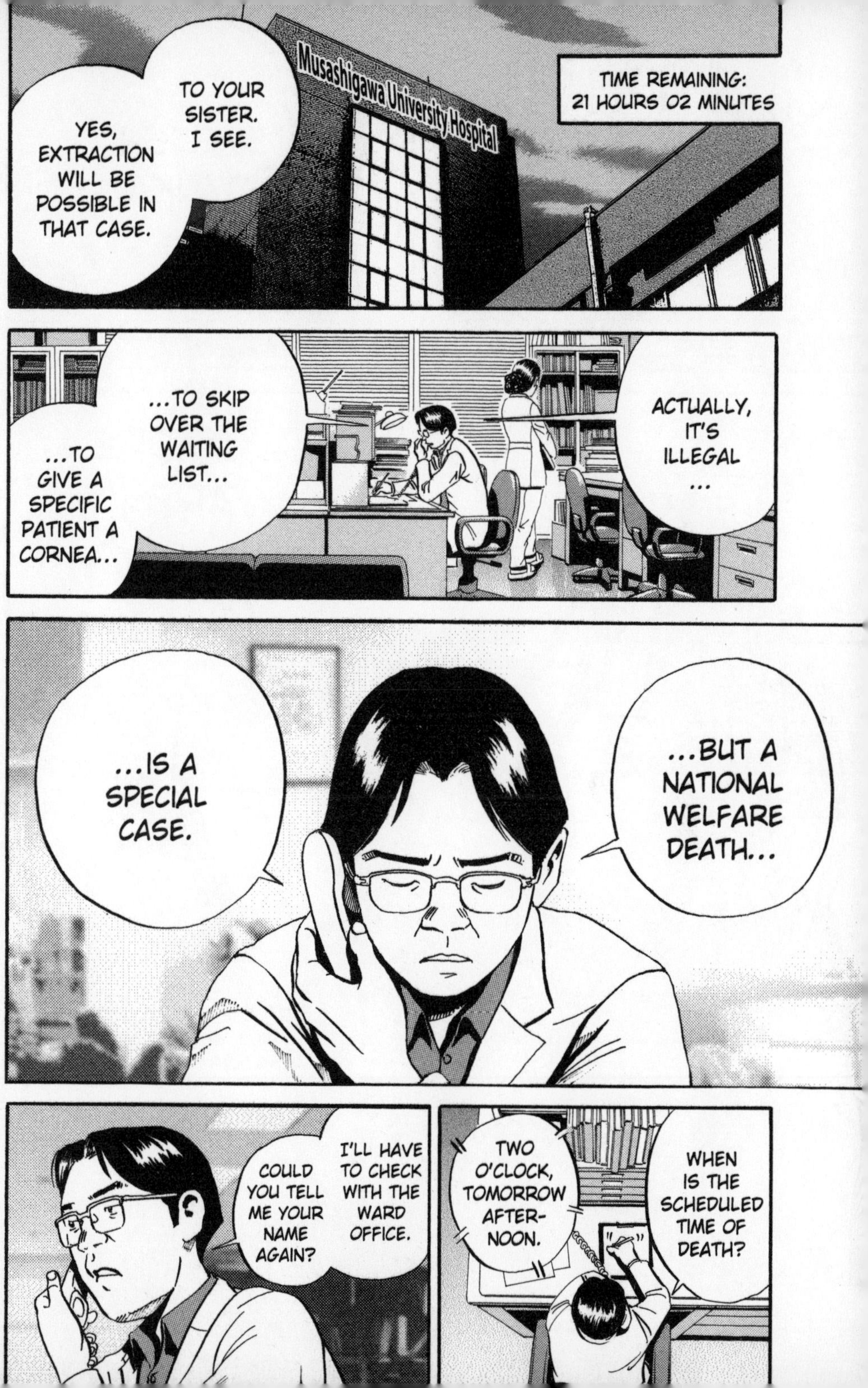
TIME REMAINING: 21 HOURS 02 MINUTES
Musashigawa University Hospital
TO YOUR SISTER. I SEE.
YES, EXTRACTION WILL BE POSSIBLE IN THAT CASE.
ACTUALLY, IT'S ILLEGAL ...
...TO SKIP OVER THE WAITING LIST...
...TO GIVE A SPECIFIC PATIENT A CORNEA...
...BUT A NATIONAL WELFARE DEATH...
...IS A SPECIAL CASE.
WHEN IS THE SCHEDULED TIME OF DEATH?
TWO O'CLOCK, TOMORROW AFTER-NOON.
I'LL HAVE TO CHECK WITH THE WARD OFFICE.
COULD YOU TELL ME YOUR NAME AGAIN?

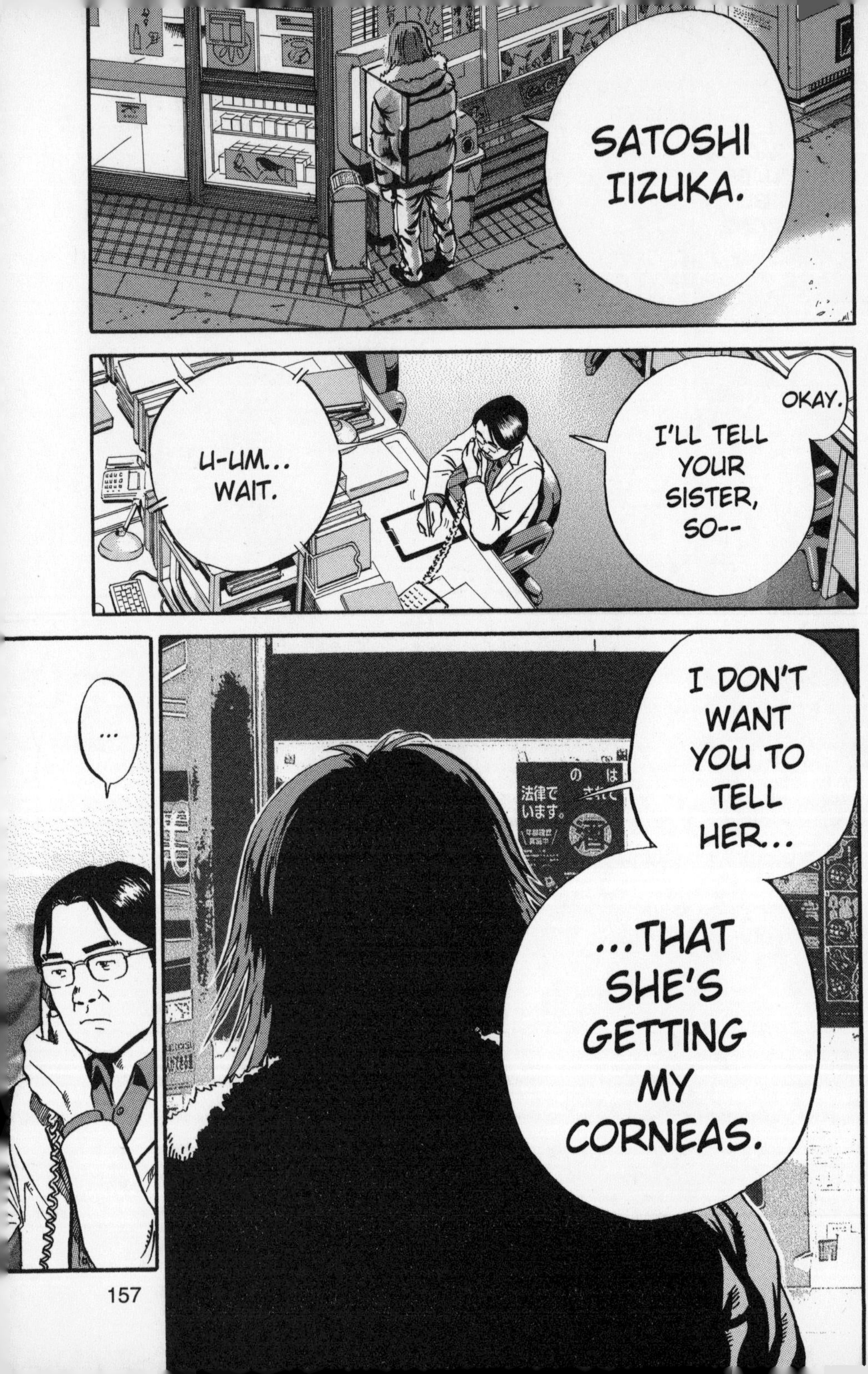
SATOSHI IIZUKA.
OKAY.
I'LL TELL YOUR SISTER, SO--
U-UM... WAIT.
I DON'T WANT YOU TO TELL HER...
...THAT SHE'S GETTING MY CORNEAS.
...

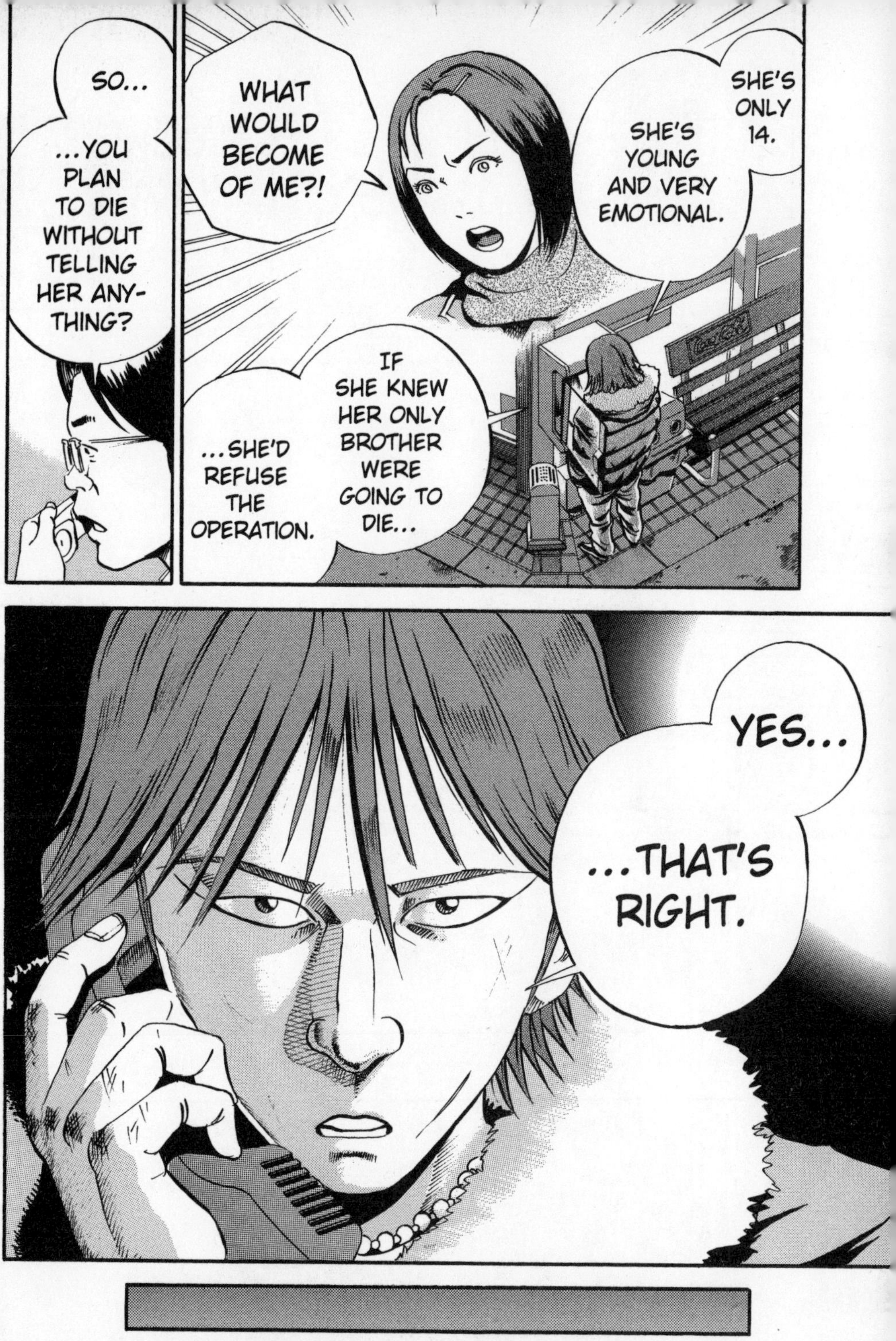
SHE'S ONLY 14.
SHE'S YOUNG AND VERY EMOTIONAL.
WHAT WOULD BECOME OF ME?!
IF SHE KNEW HER ONLY BROTHER WERE GOING TO DIE...
...SHE'D REFUSE THE OPERATION.
SO...
...YOU PLAN TO DIE WITHOUT TELLING HER ANYTHING?
YES...
...THAT'S RIGHT.

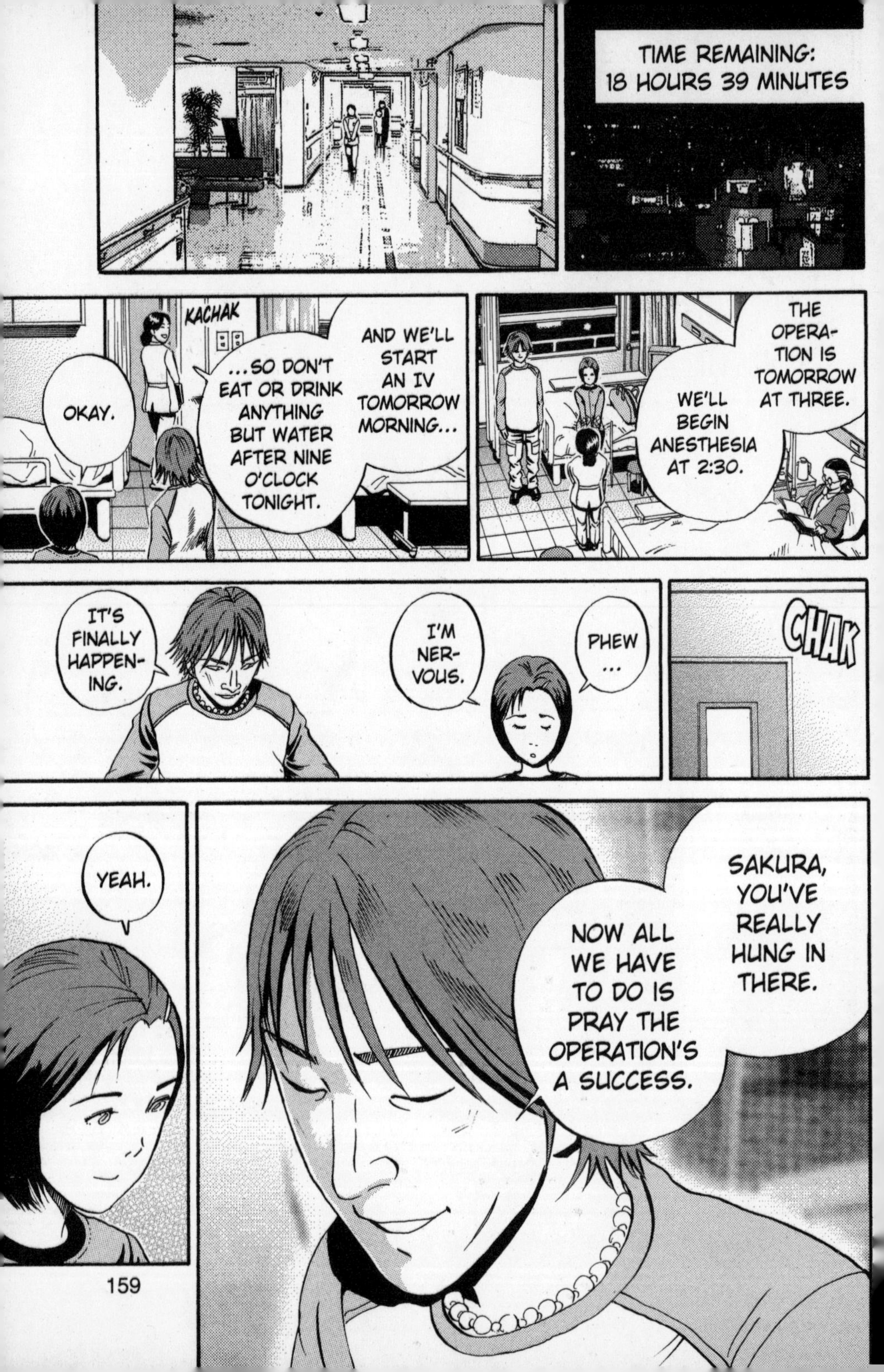
TIME REMAINING: 18 HOURS 39 MINUTES
THE OPERATION IS TOMORROW AT THREE.
WE'LL BEGIN ANESTHESIA AT 2:30.
AND WE'LL START AN IV TOMORROW MORNING...
...SO DON'T EAT OR DRINK ANYTHING BUT WATER AFTER NINE O'CLOCK TONIGHT.
KACHAK
OKAY.
CHAK
PHEW...
I'M NERVOUS.
IT'S FINALLY HAPPENING.
SAKURA, YOU'VE REALLY HUNG IN THERE.
NOW ALL WE HAVE TO DO IS PRAY THE OPERATION'S A SUCCESS.
YEAH.

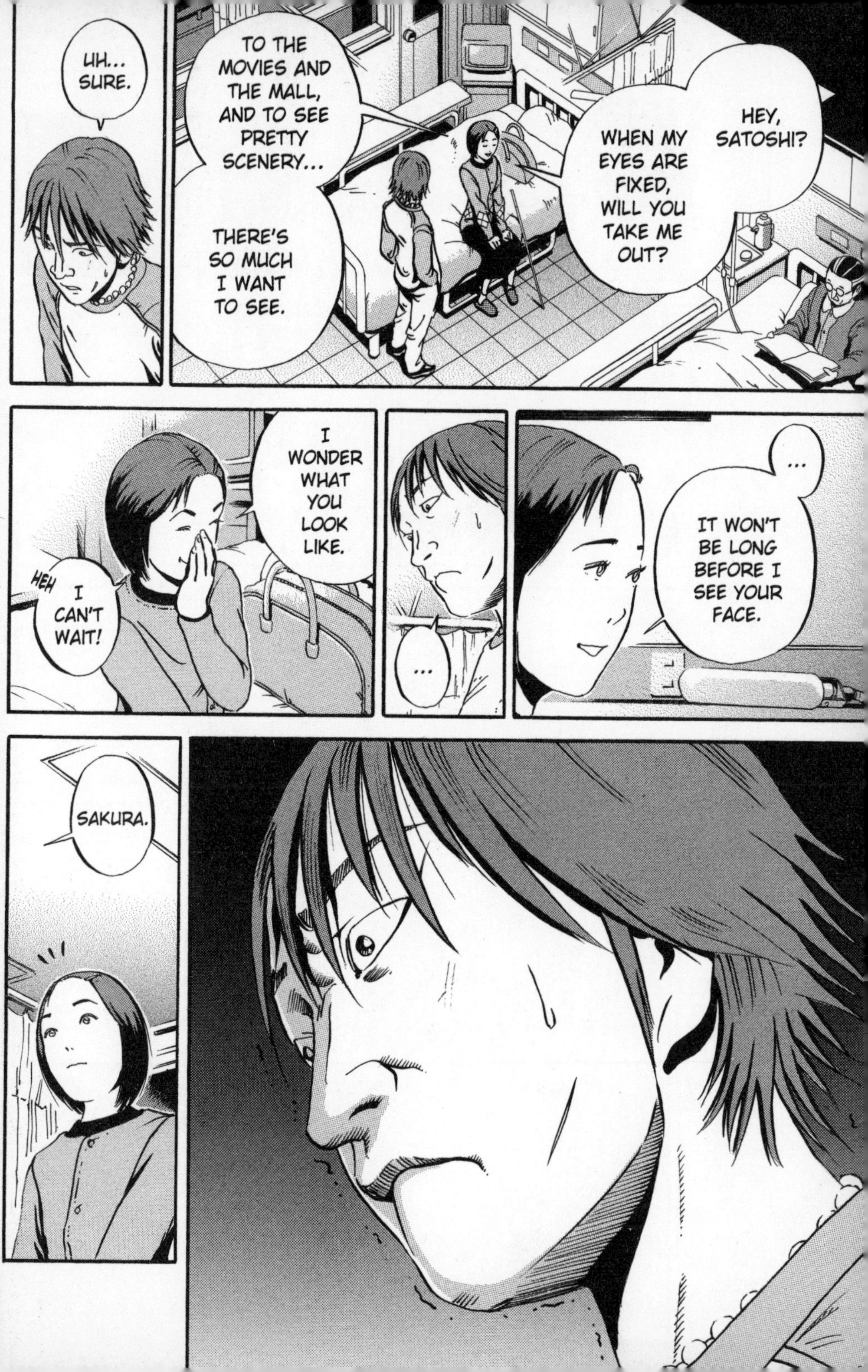
HEY, SATOSHI?
WHEN MY EYES ARE FIXED, WILL YOU TAKE ME OUT?
TO THE MOVIES AND THE MALL, AND TO SEE PRETTY SCENERY...
THERE'S SO MUCH I WANT TO SEE.
UH... SURE.
...
IT WON'T BE LONG BEFORE I SEE YOUR FACE.
...
I WONDER WHAT YOU LOOK LIKE.
HEH
I CAN'T WAIT!
SAKURA.

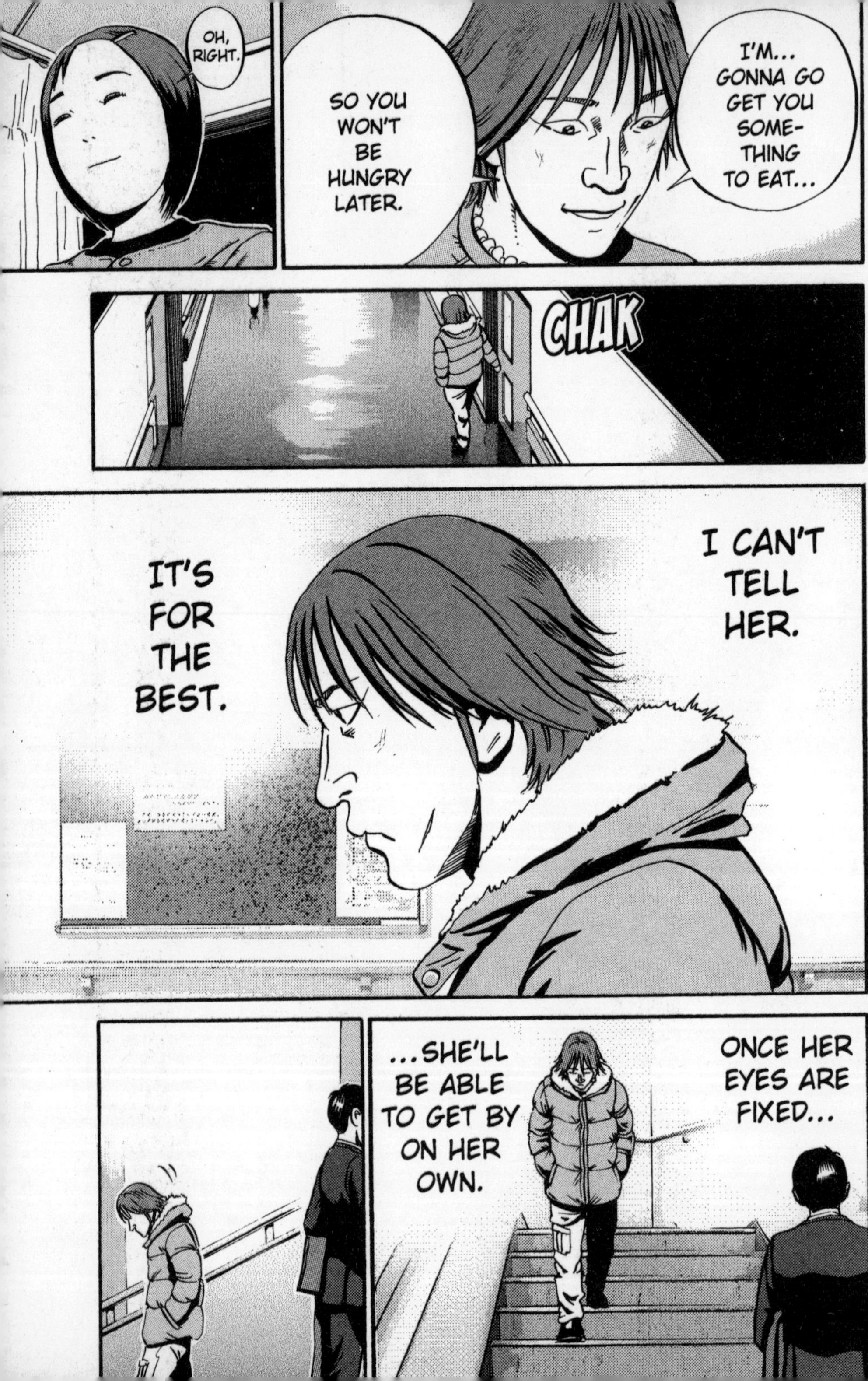
I'M... GONNA GO GET YOU SOME-THING TO EAT...
SO YOU WON'T BE HUNGRY LATER.
OH, RIGHT.
CHAK
I CAN'T TELL HER.
IT'S FOR THE BEST.
ONCE HER EYES ARE FIXED...
...SHE'LL BE ABLE TO GET BY ON HER OWN.

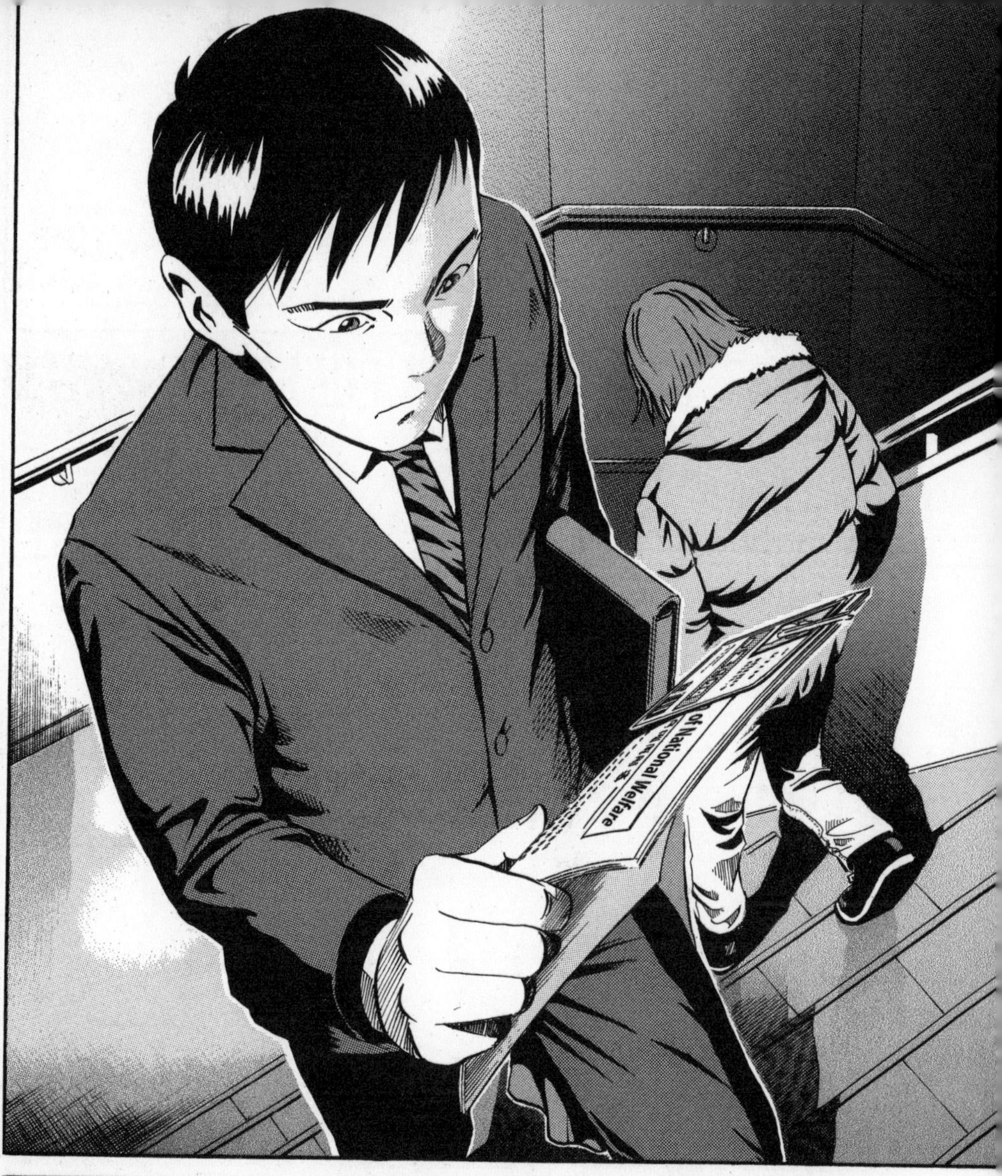
of National Welfare

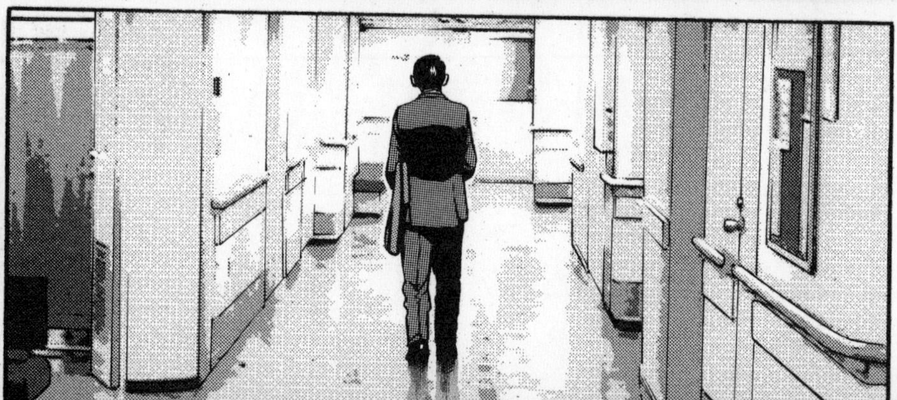

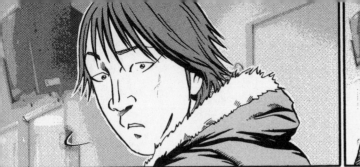
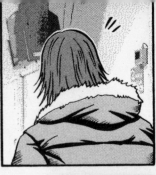

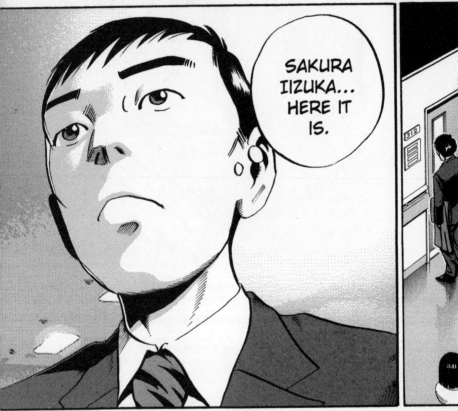

SAKURA IIZUKA... HERE IT IS.

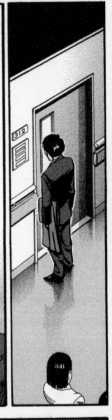

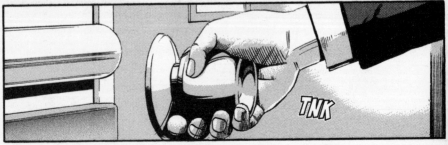

TNK

163

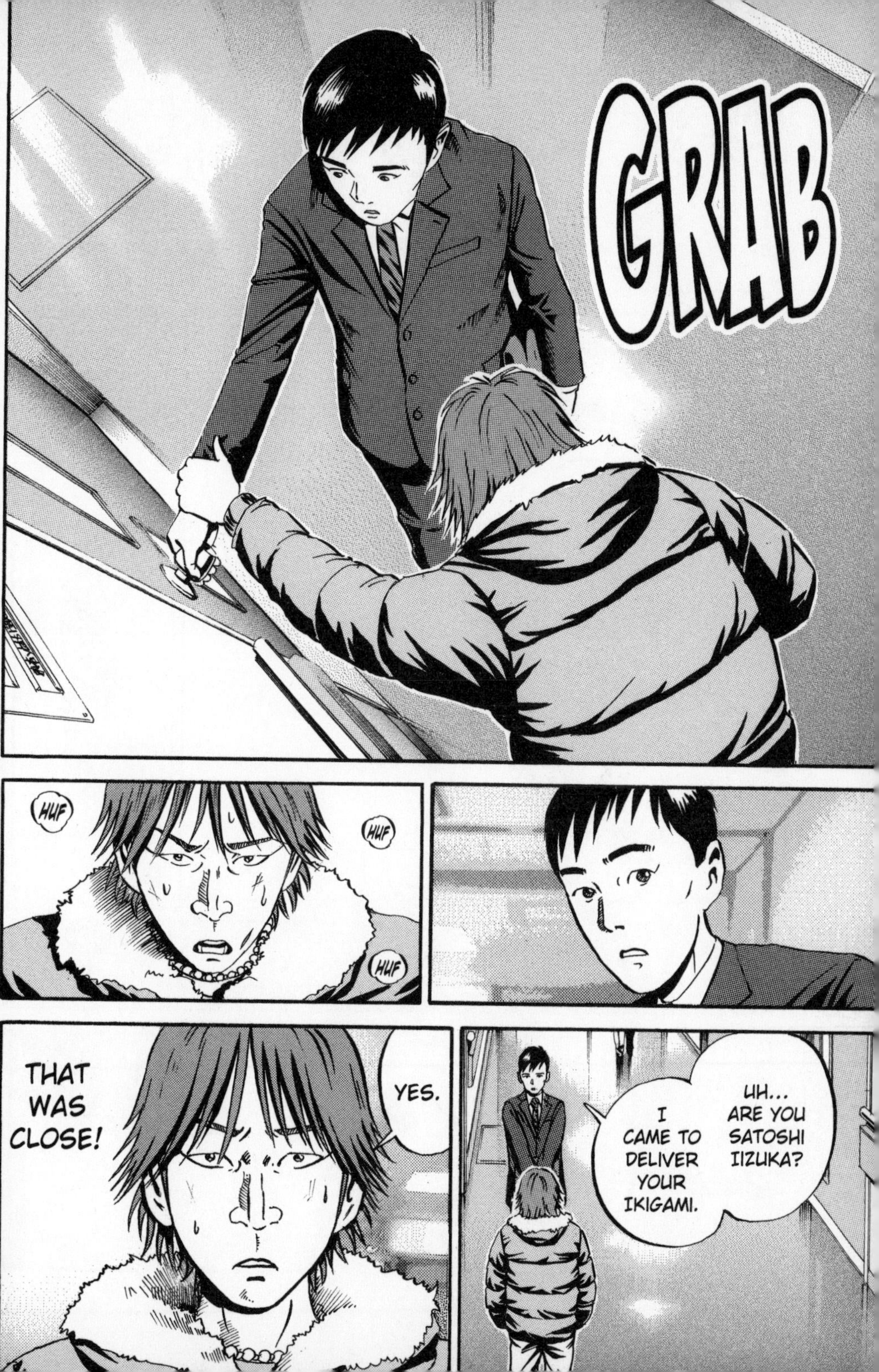
GRAB
HUF
HUF
HUF
UH... ARE YOU SATOSHI IIZUKA?
I CAME TO DELIVER YOUR IKIGAMI.
YES.
THAT WAS CLOSE!

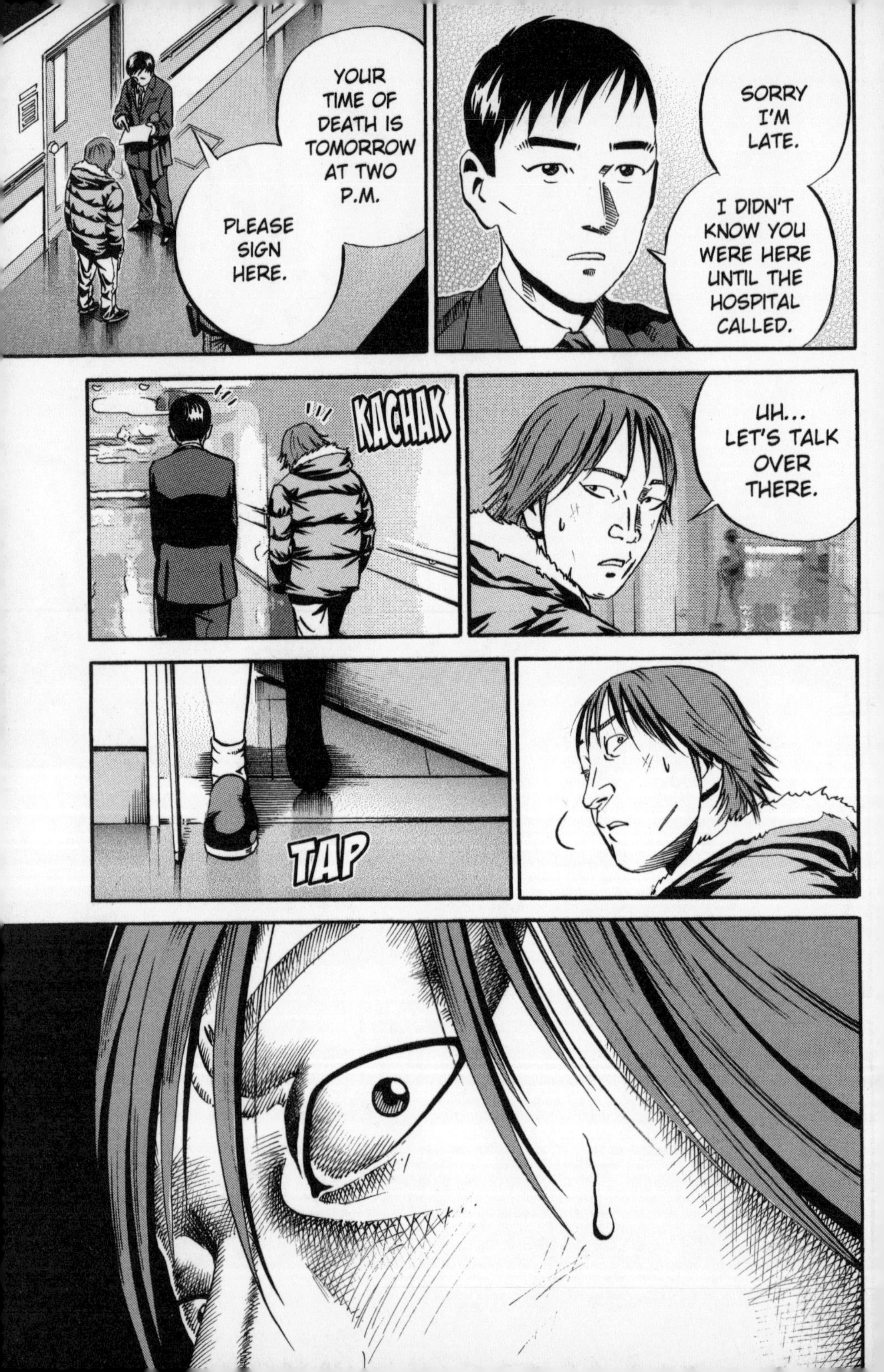
SORRY I'M LATE.
I DIDN'T KNOW YOU WERE HERE UNTIL THE HOSPITAL CALLED.
YOUR TIME OF DEATH IS TOMORROW AT TWO P.M.
PLEASE SIGN HERE.
UH... LET'S TALK OVER THERE.
KACHAK
TAP

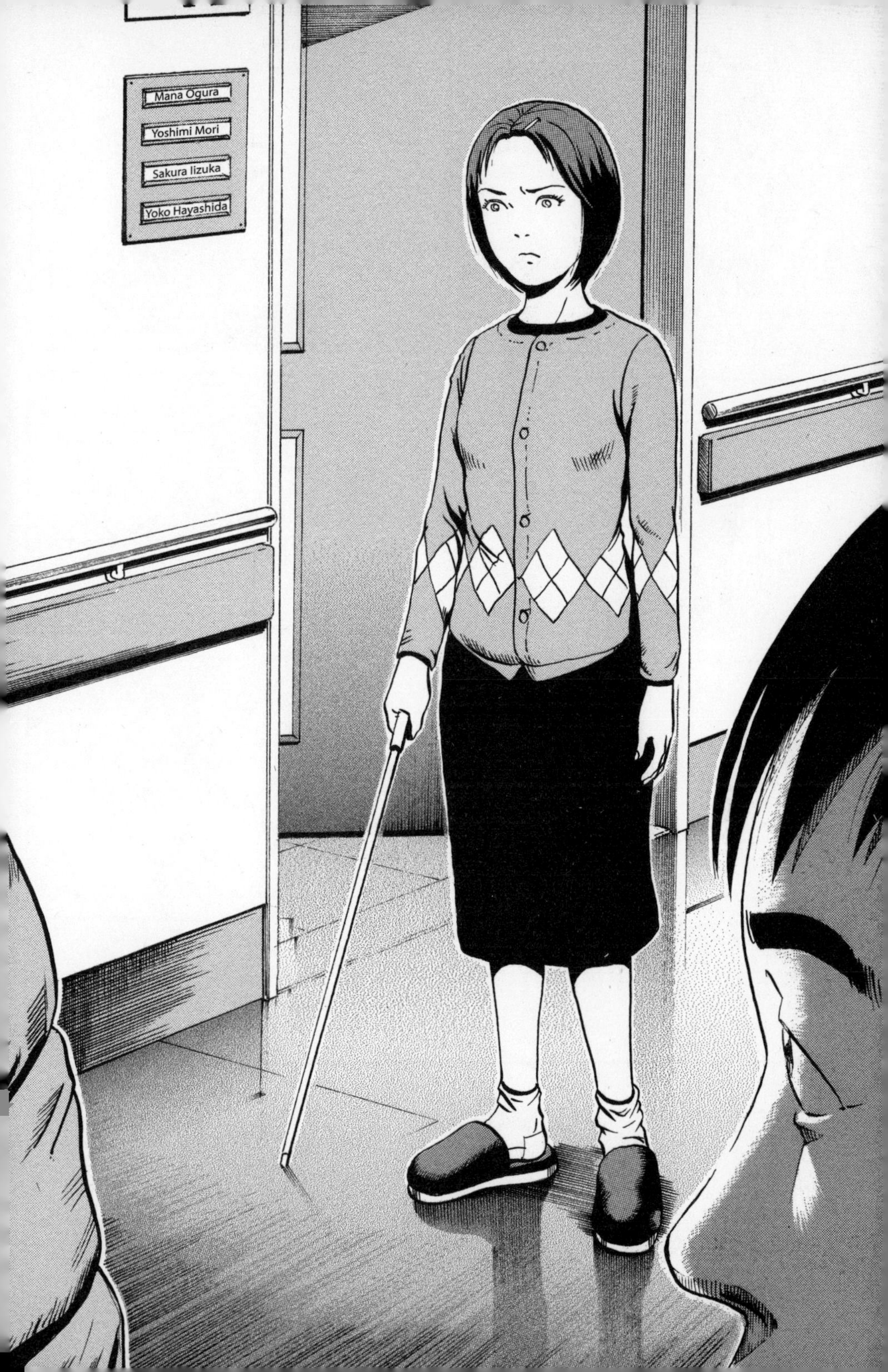
Mana Ogura
Yoshimi Mori
Sakura Iizuka
Yoko Hayashida

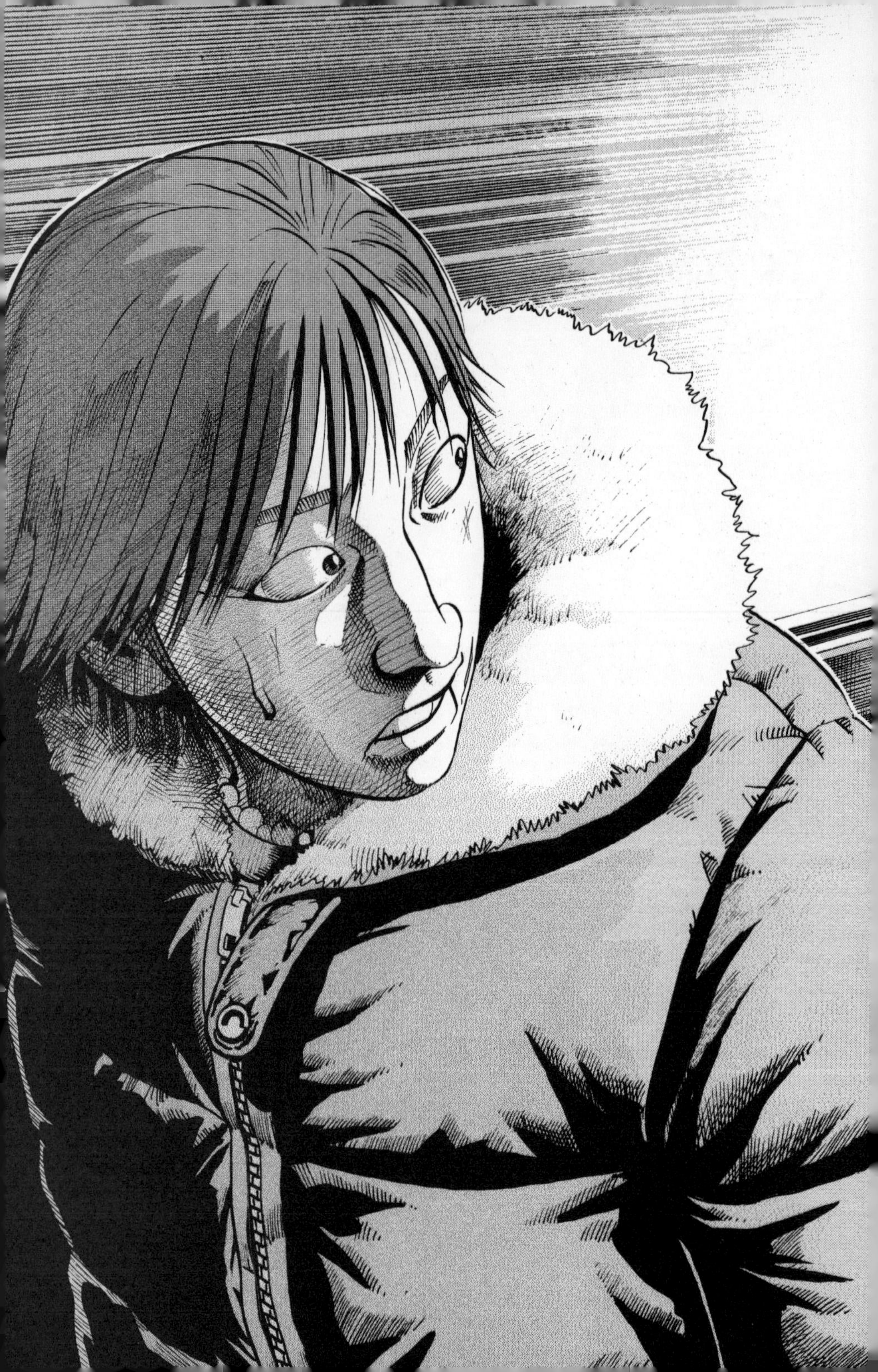

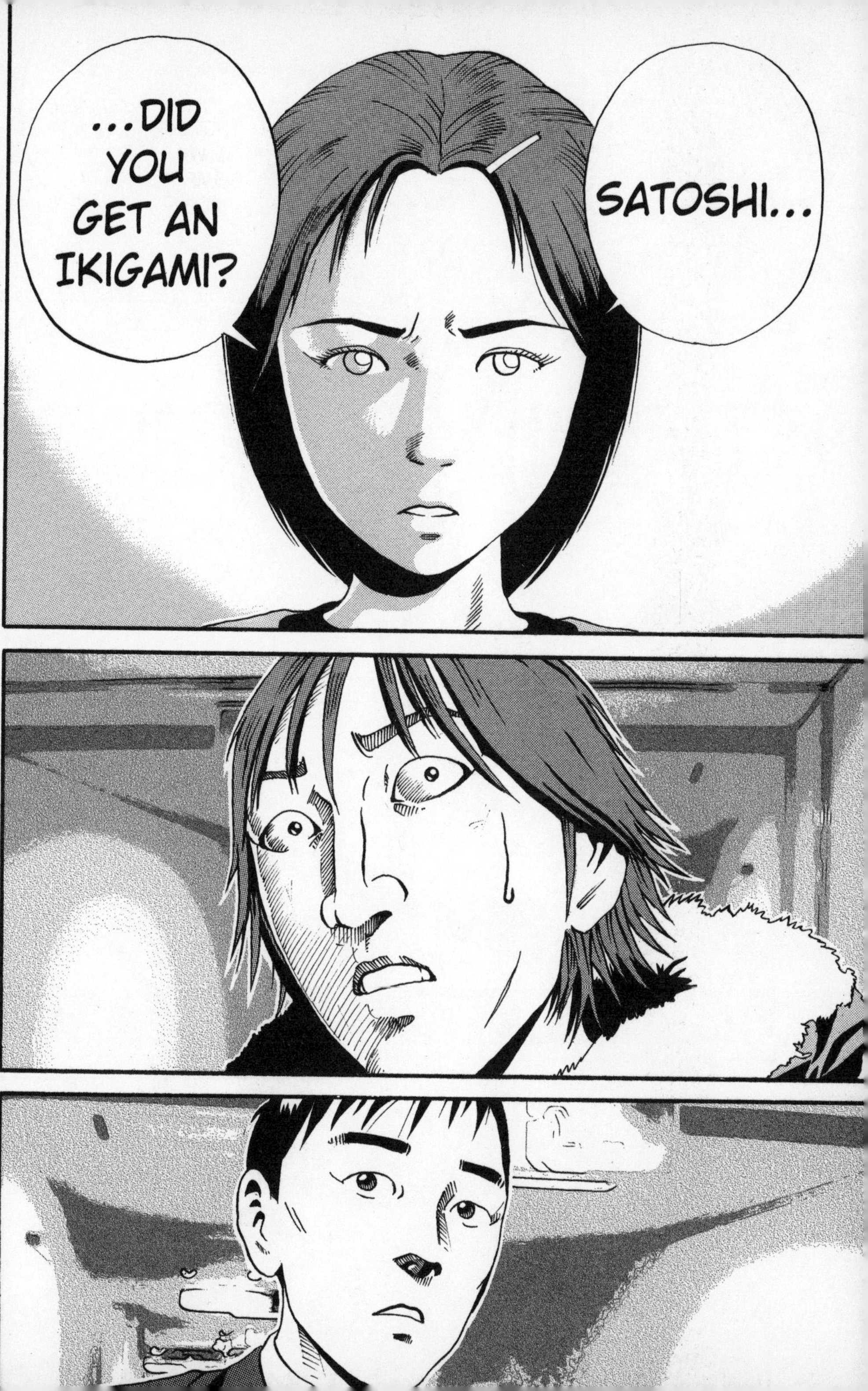
SATOSHI...
...DID YOU GET AN IKIGAMI?

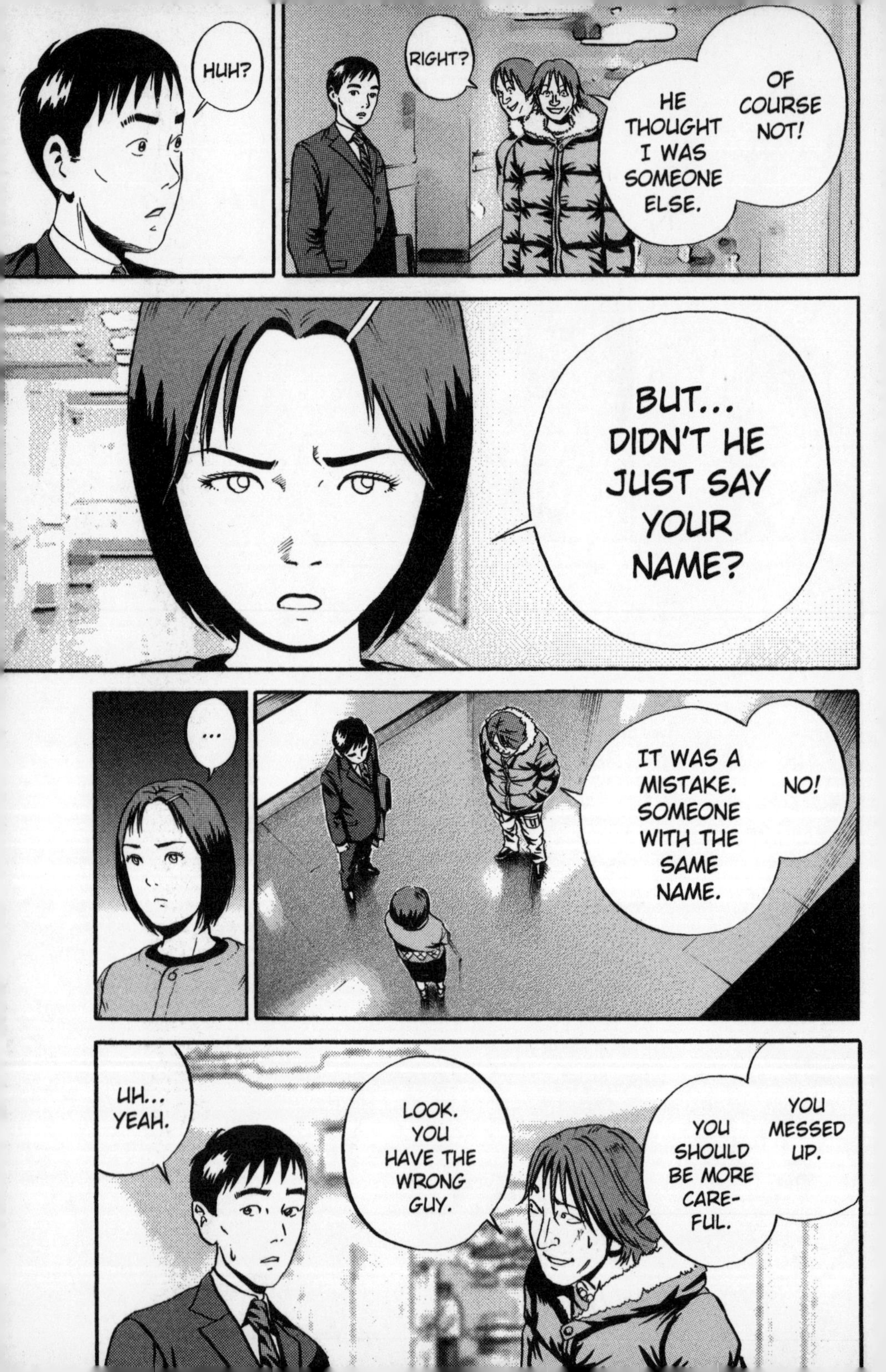
OF COURSE NOT! HE THOUGHT I WAS SOMEONE ELSE.
RIGHT?
HUH?
BUT... DIDN'T HE JUST SAY YOUR NAME?
NO! IT WAS A MISTAKE. SOMEONE WITH THE SAME NAME.
...
YOU MESSED UP. YOU SHOULD BE MORE CARE-FUL.
LOOK. YOU HAVE THE WRONG GUY.
UH... YEAH.

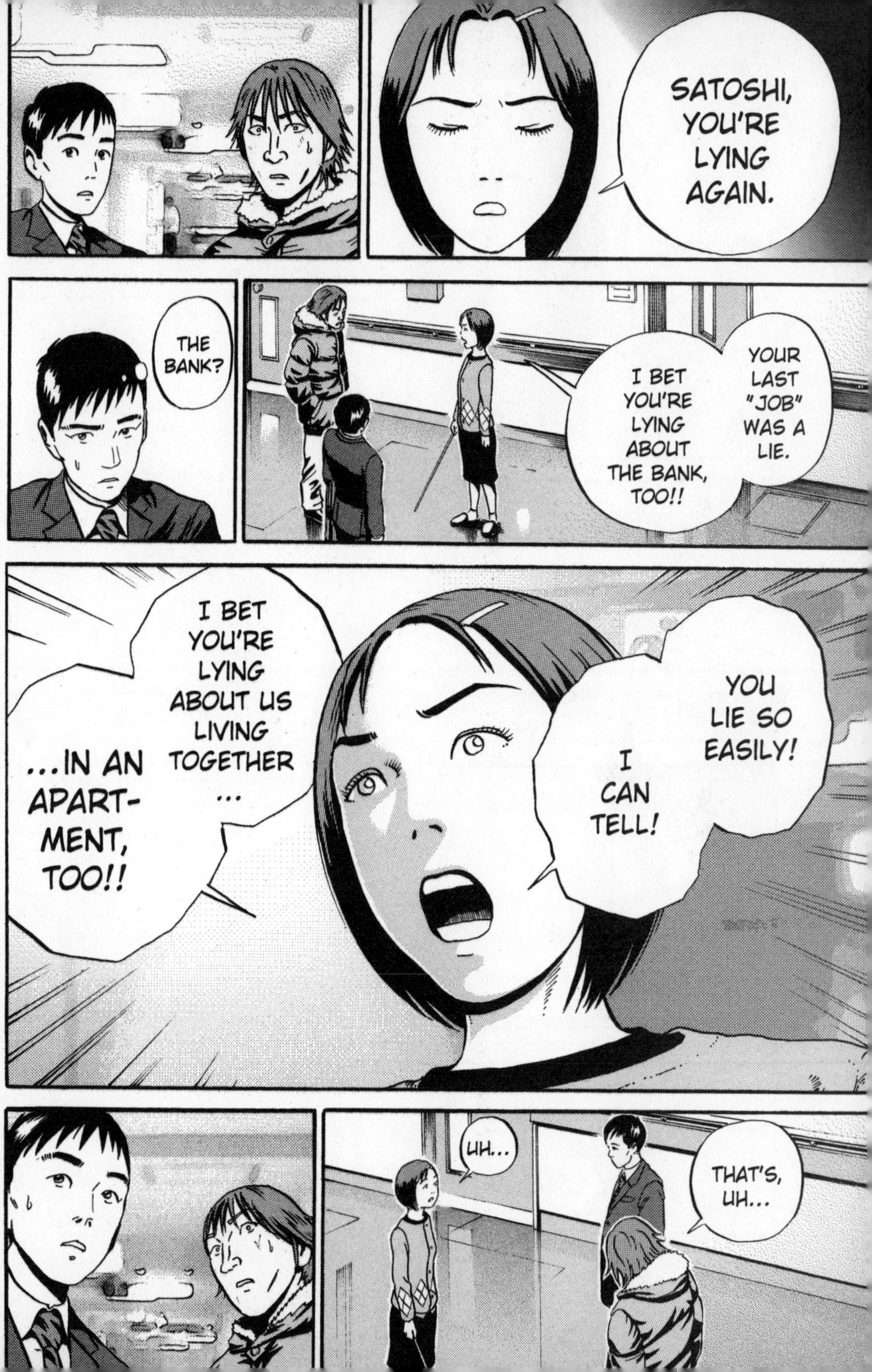
SATOSHI, YOU'RE LYING AGAIN.
YOUR LAST "JOB" WAS A LIE.
I BET YOU'RE LYING ABOUT THE BANK, TOO!!
THE BANK?
YOU LIE SO EASILY!
I CAN TELL!
I BET YOU'RE LYING ABOUT US LIVING TOGETHER...
...IN AN APART-MENT, TOO!!
THAT'S, UH...
UH...

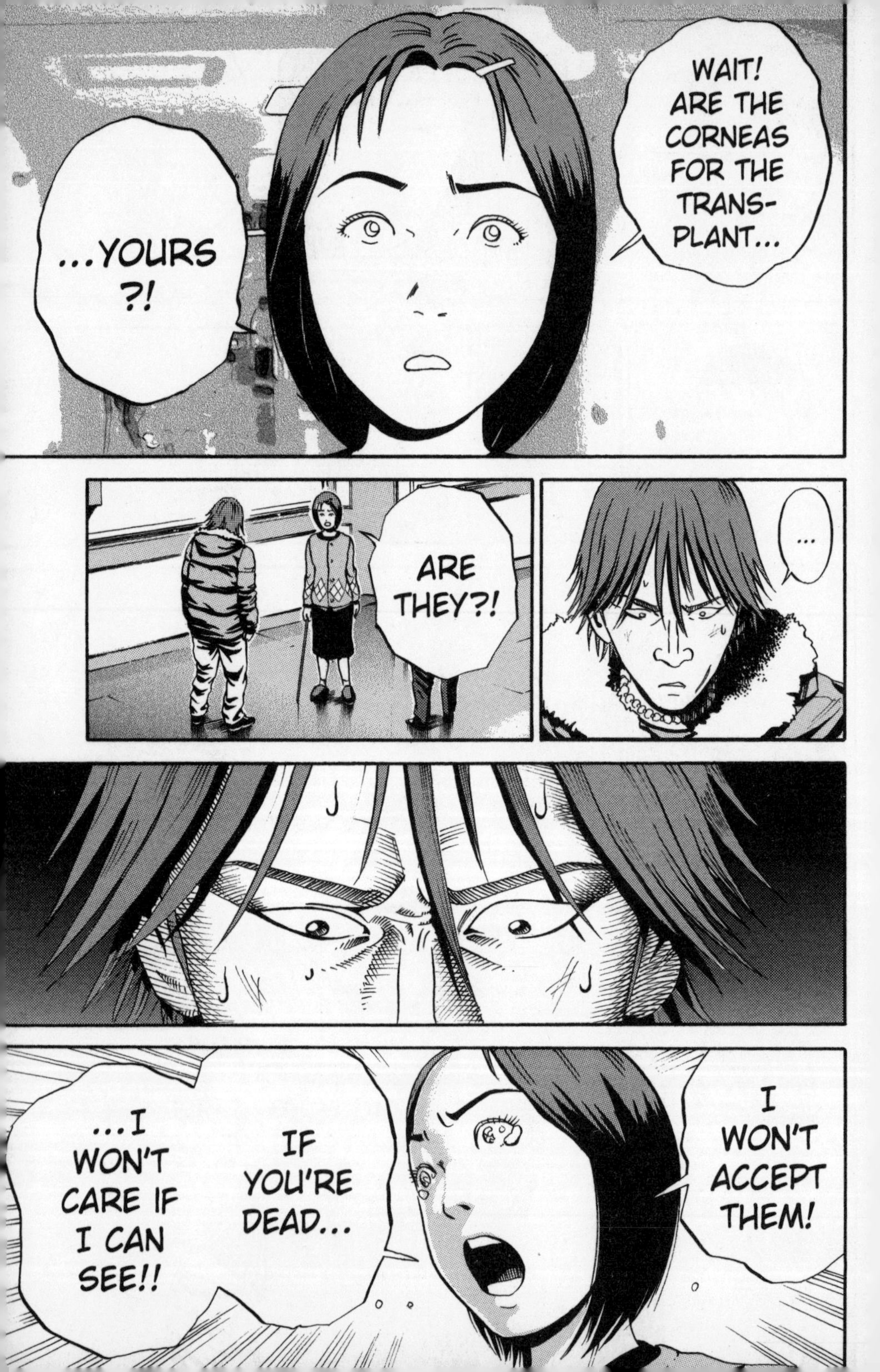
WAIT! ARE THE CORNEAS FOR THE TRANS-PLANT...
...YOURS ?!
...
ARE THEY?!
I WON'T ACCEPT THEM!
IF YOU'RE DEAD...
...I WON'T CARE IF I CAN SEE!!

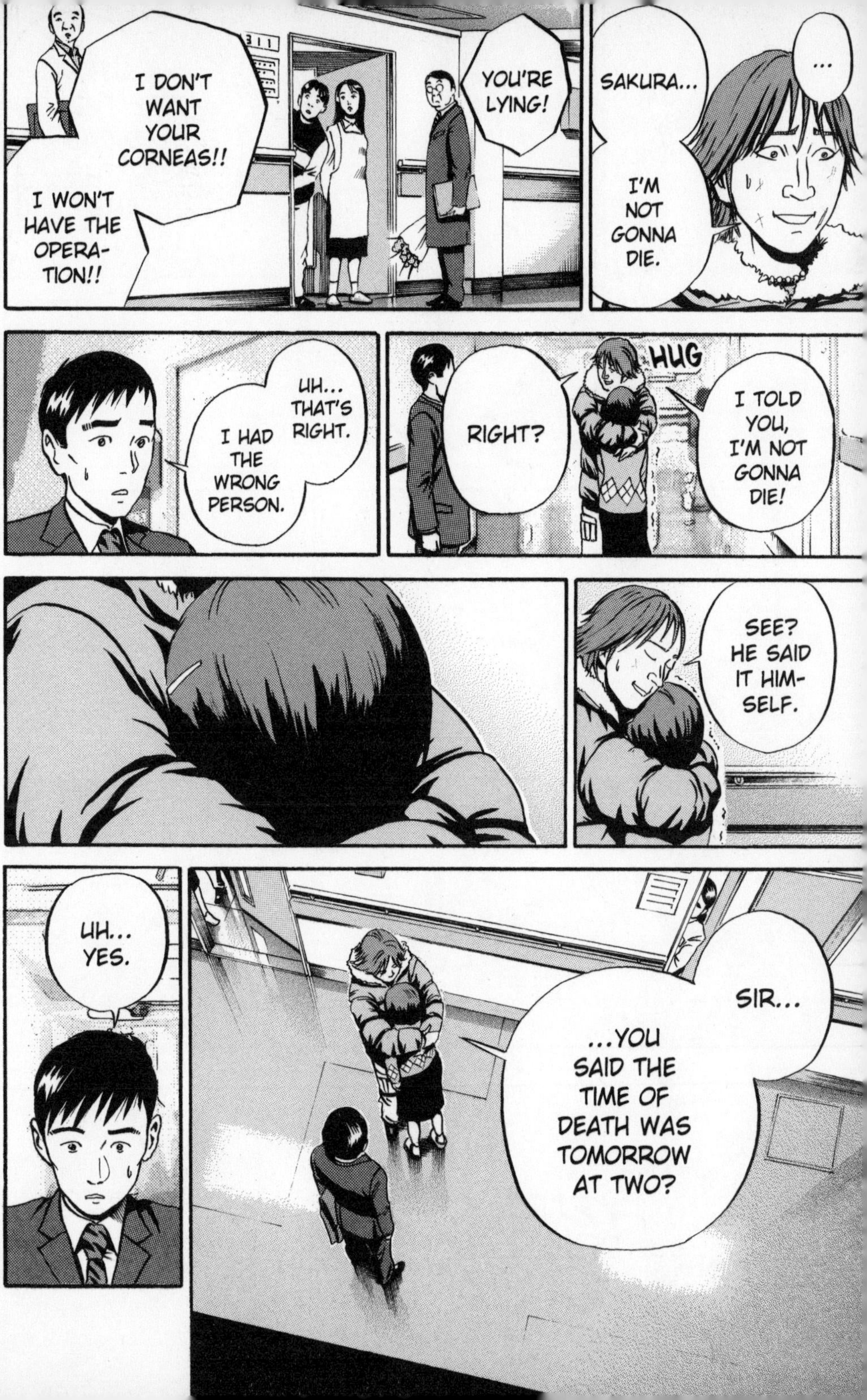
...
SAKURA...
I'M NOT GONNA DIE.
YOU'RE LYING!
I DON'T WANT YOUR CORNEAS!!
I WON'T HAVE THE OPERATION!!
HUG
I TOLD YOU, I'M NOT GONNA DIE!
RIGHT?
UH... THAT'S RIGHT.
I HAD THE WRONG PERSON.
SEE? HE SAID IT HIMSELF.
SIR...
...YOU SAID THE TIME OF DEATH WAS TOMORROW AT TWO?
UH... YES.

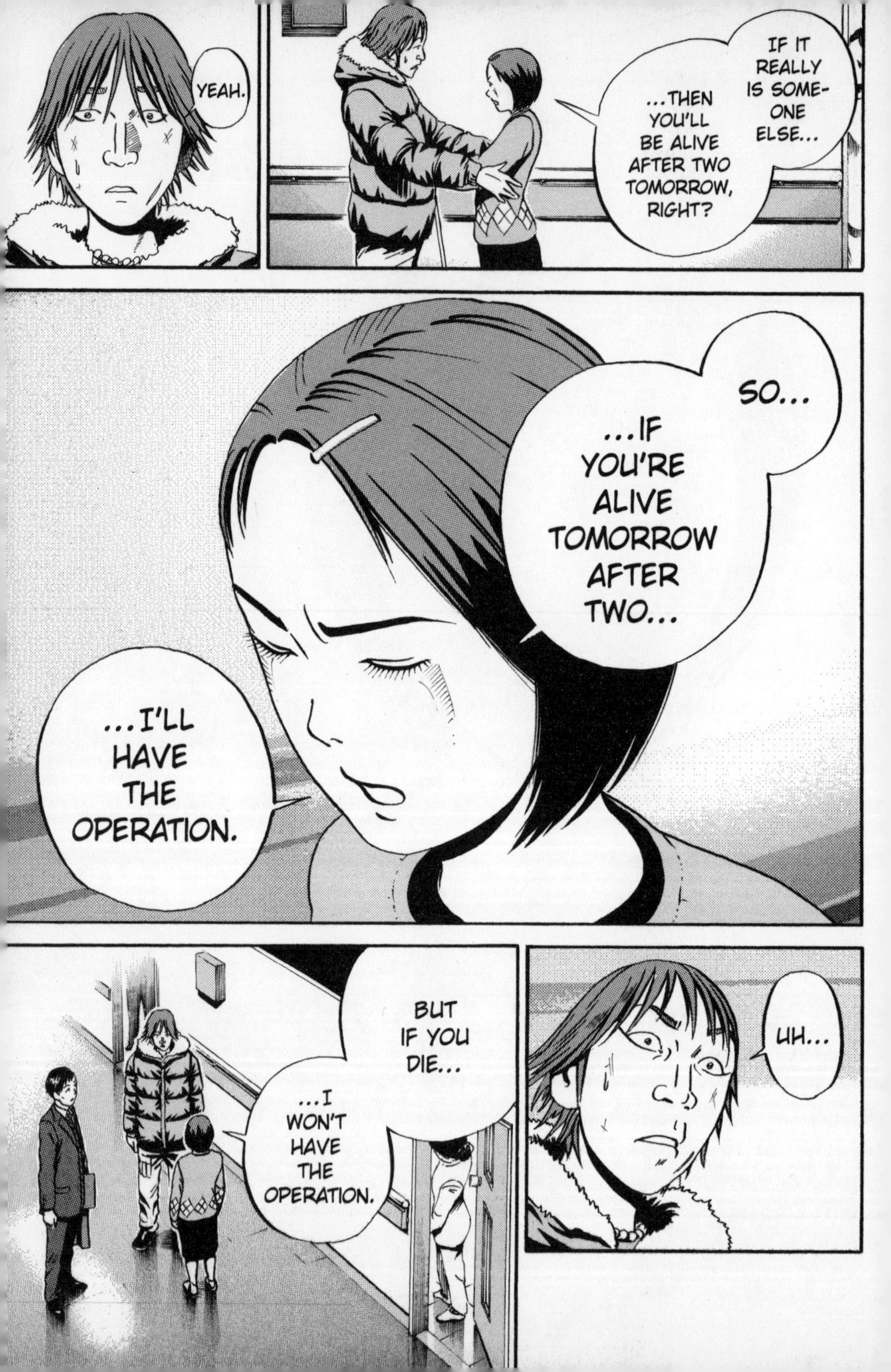
IF IT REALLY IS SOME-ONE ELSE...
...THEN YOU'LL BE ALIVE AFTER TWO TOMORROW, RIGHT?
YEAH.
SO...
...IF YOU'RE ALIVE TOMORROW AFTER TWO...
...I'LL HAVE THE OPERATION.
UH...
BUT IF YOU DIE...
...I WON'T HAVE THE OPERATION.

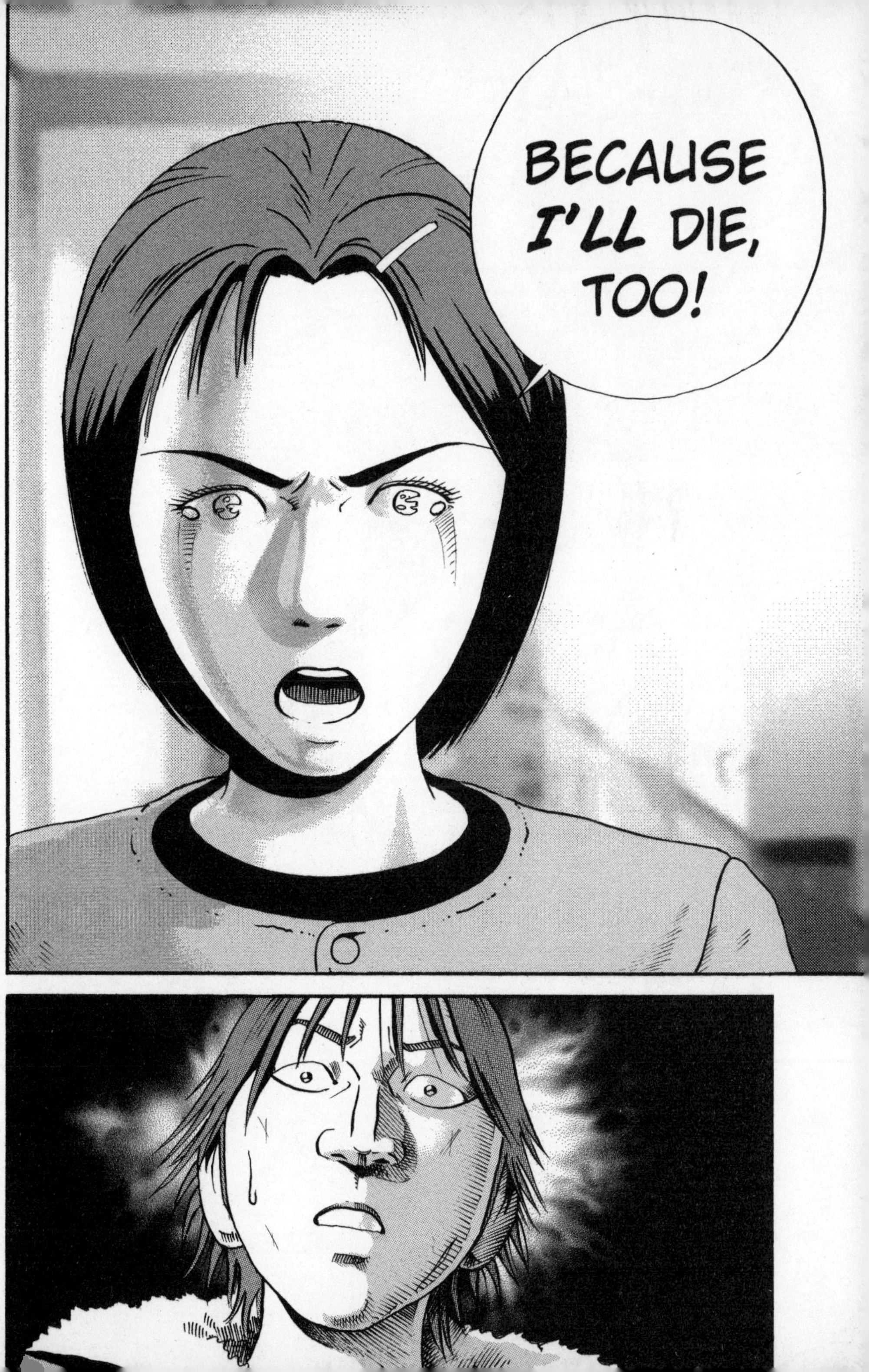
BECAUSE I'LL DIE, TOO!

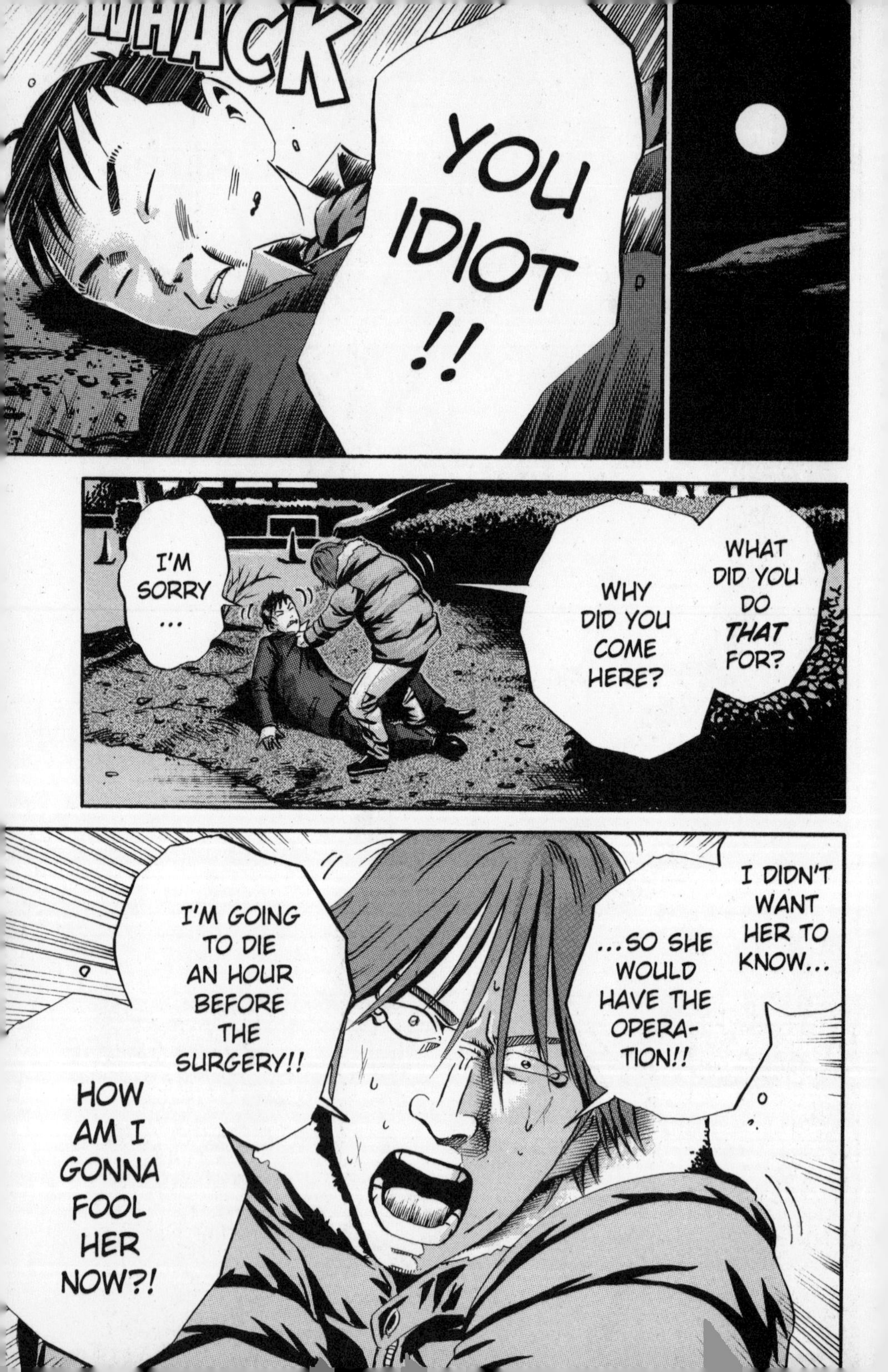
WHACK
YOU IDIOT!!
WHAT DID YOU DO THAT FOR?
WHY DID YOU COME HERE?
I'M SORRY...
I DIDN'T WANT HER TO KNOW...
...SO SHE WOULD HAVE THE OPERATION!!
I'M GOING TO DIE AN HOUR BEFORE THE SURGERY!!
HOW AM I GONNA FOOL HER NOW?!

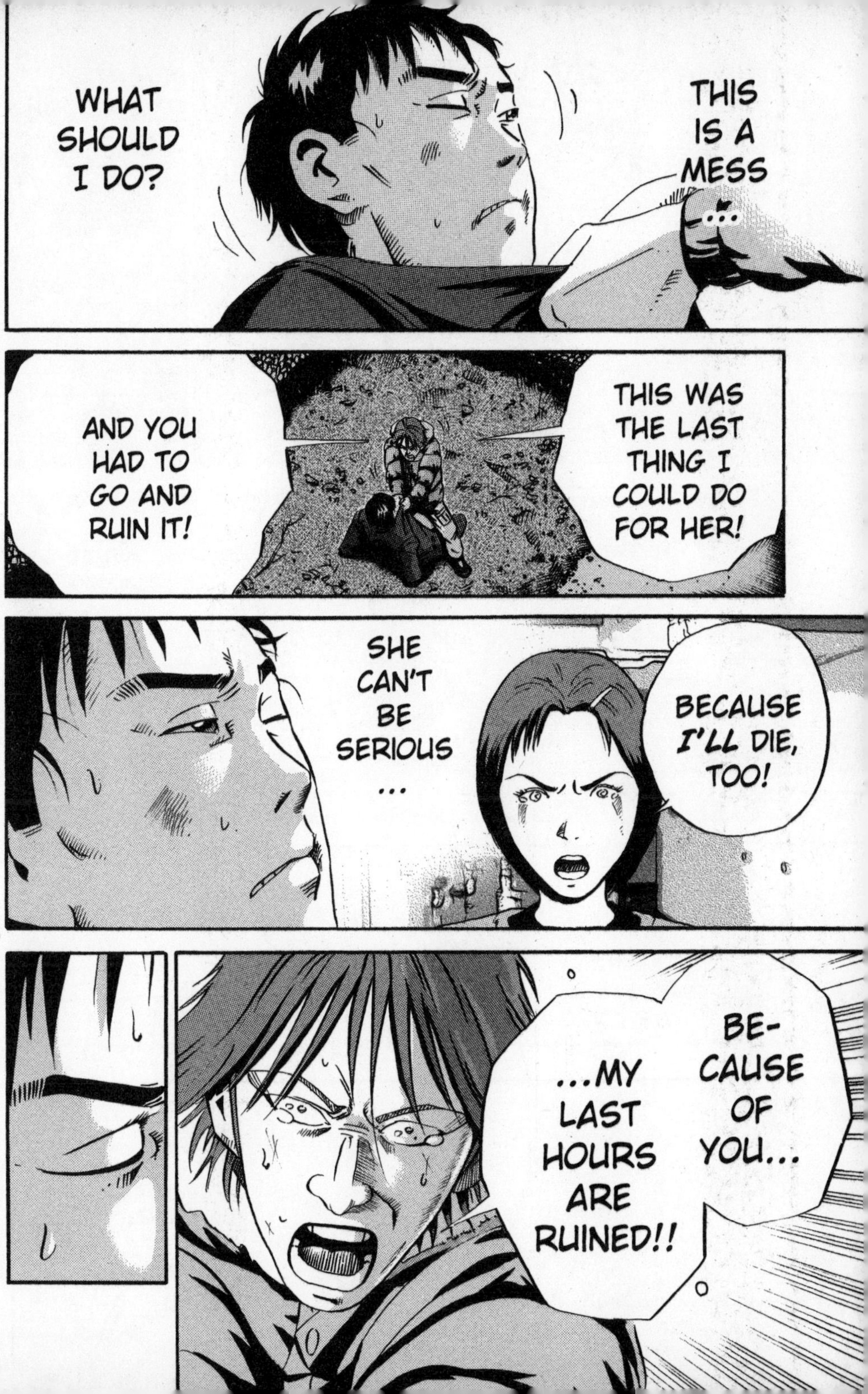
THIS IS A MESS...
WHAT SHOULD I DO?
THIS WAS THE LAST THING I COULD DO FOR HER!
AND YOU HAD TO GO AND RUIN IT!
BECAUSE *I'LL* DIE, TOO!
SHE CAN'T BE SERIOUS...
BE-CAUSE OF YOU...
...MY LAST HOURS ARE RUINED!!

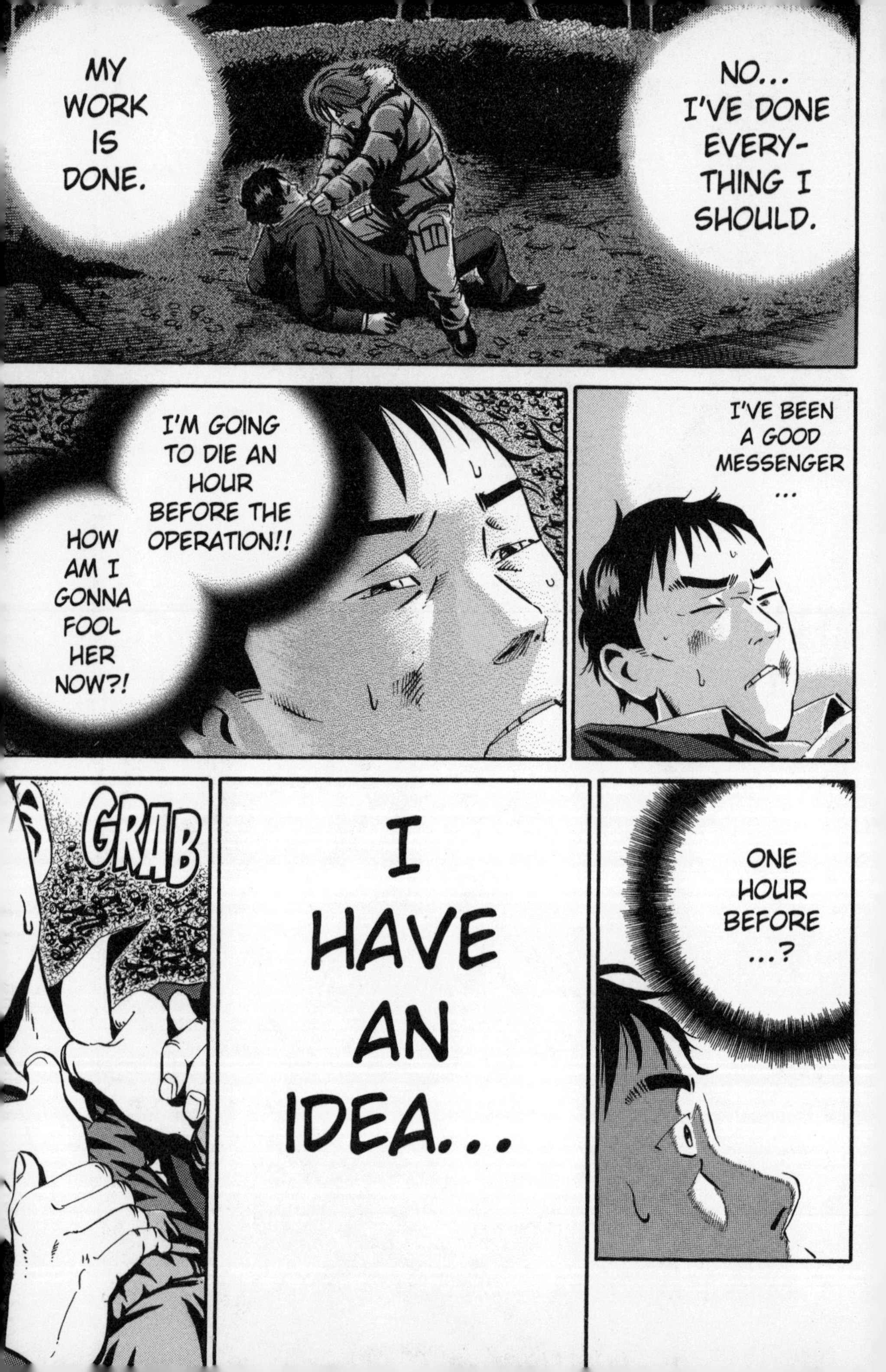
NO... I'VE DONE EVERYTHING I SHOULD.
MY WORK IS DONE.
I'VE BEEN A GOOD MESSENGER ...
I'M GOING TO DIE AN HOUR BEFORE THE OPERATION!!
HOW AM I GONNA FOOL HER NOW?!
ONE HOUR BEFORE ...?
I HAVE AN IDEA...
GRAB

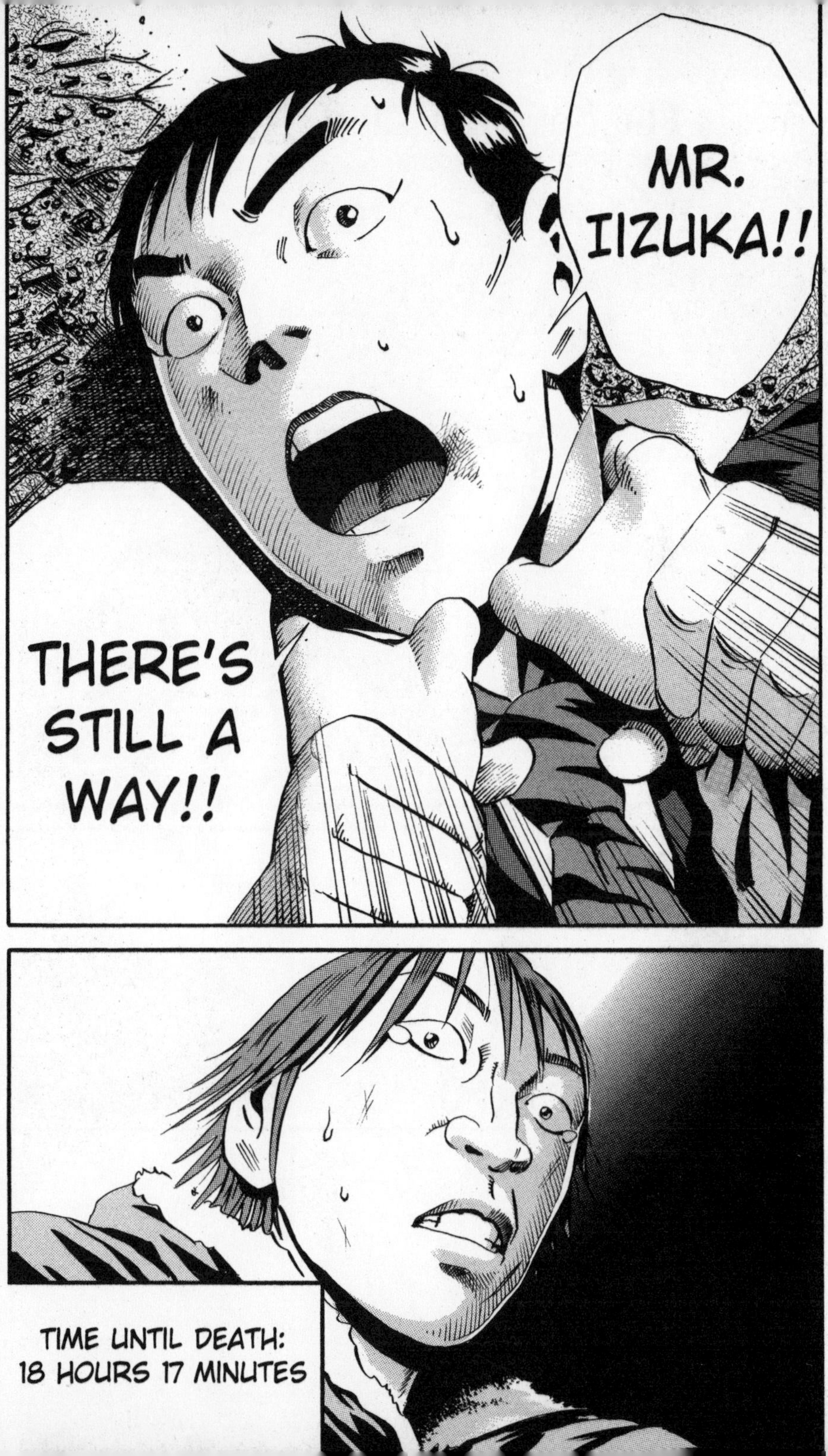
MR. IIZUKA!!
THERE'S STILL A WAY!!
TIME UNTIL DEATH: 18 HOURS 17 MINUTES

Episode 6 The Loveliest Lie Act 3

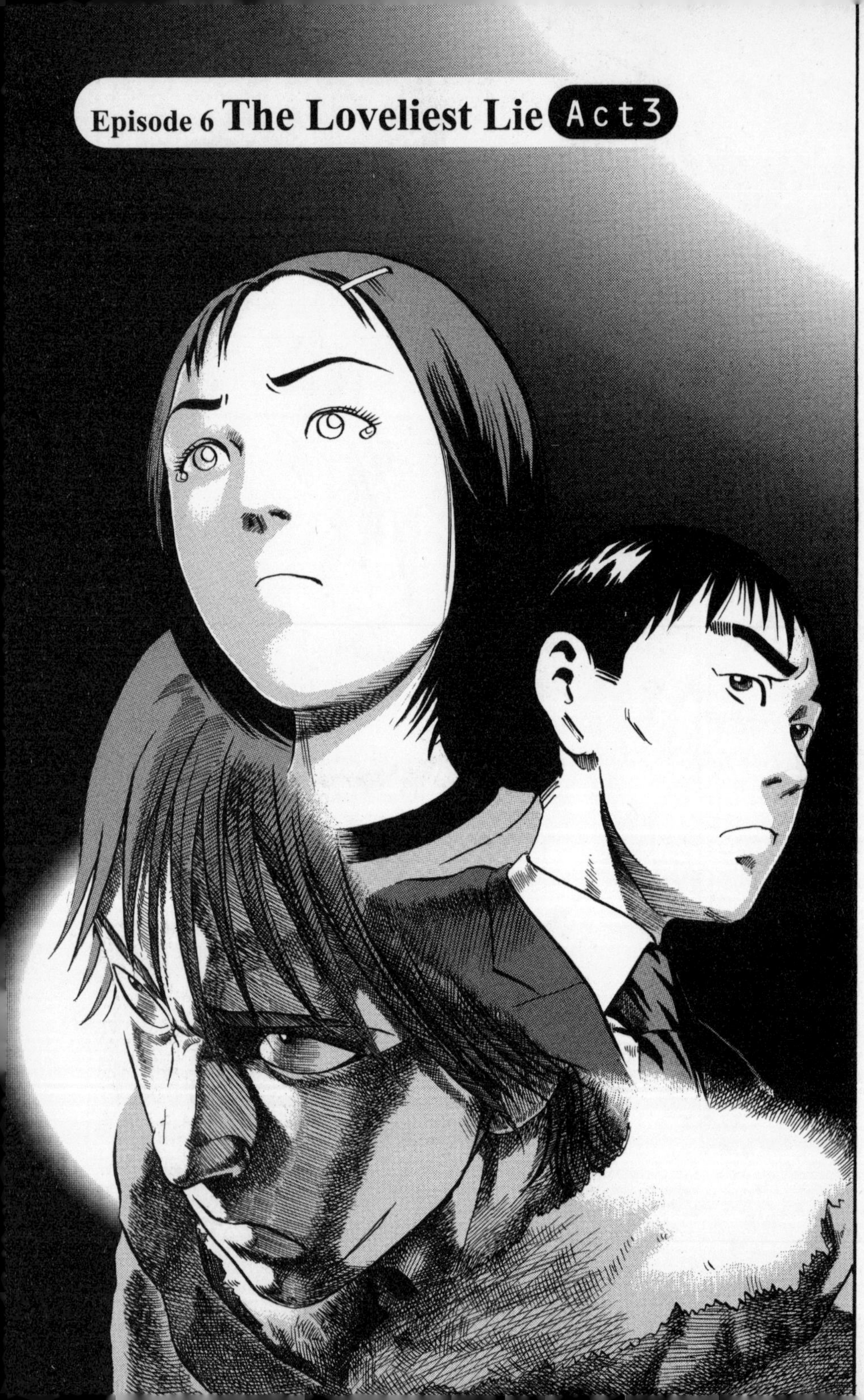

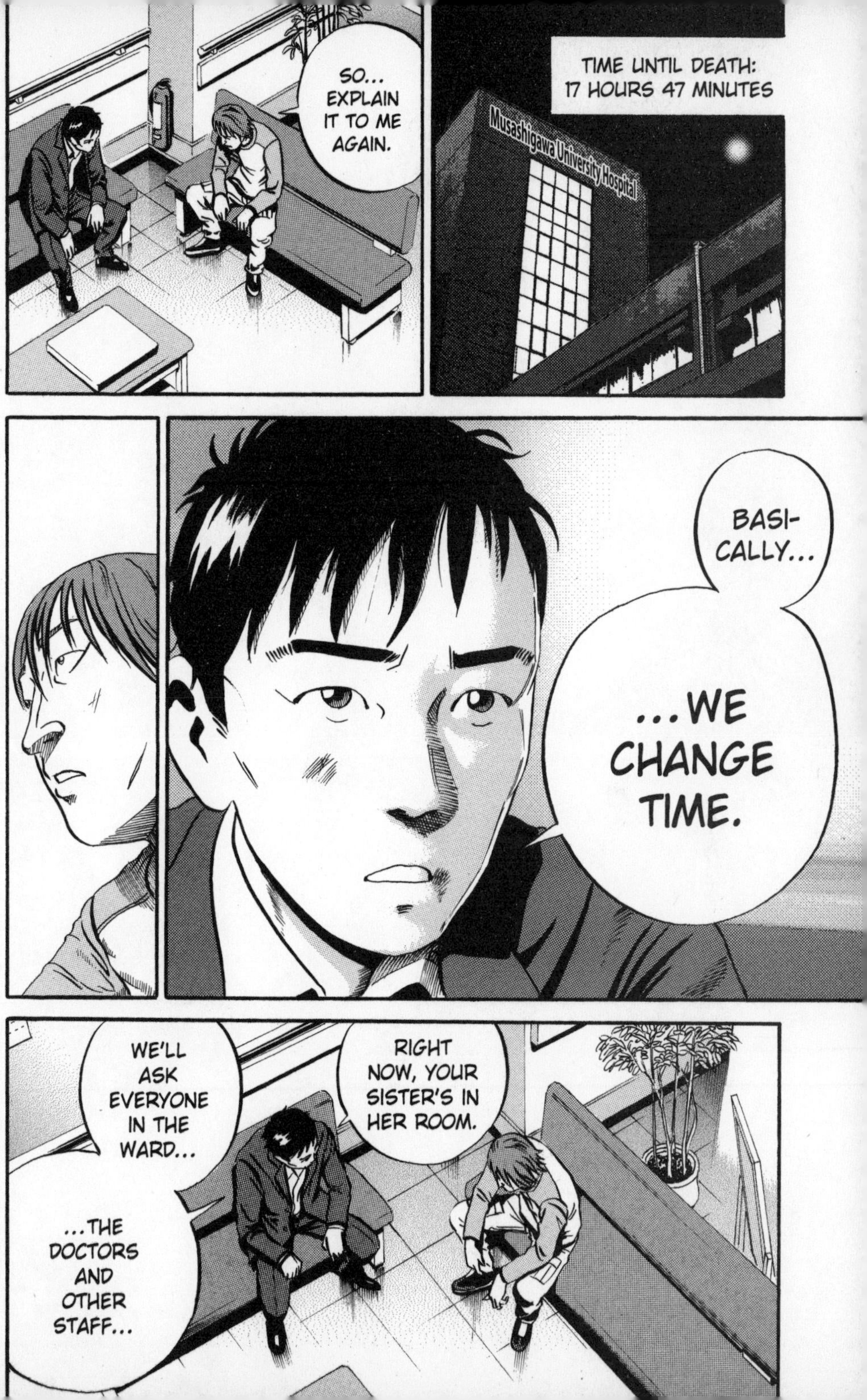
TIME UNTIL DEATH: 17 HOURS 47 MINUTES
Musashigawa University Hospital
SO... EXPLAIN IT TO ME AGAIN.
BASI-CALLY...
...WE CHANGE TIME.
RIGHT NOW, YOUR SISTER'S IN HER ROOM.
WE'LL ASK EVERYONE IN THE WARD...
...THE DOCTORS AND OTHER STAFF...

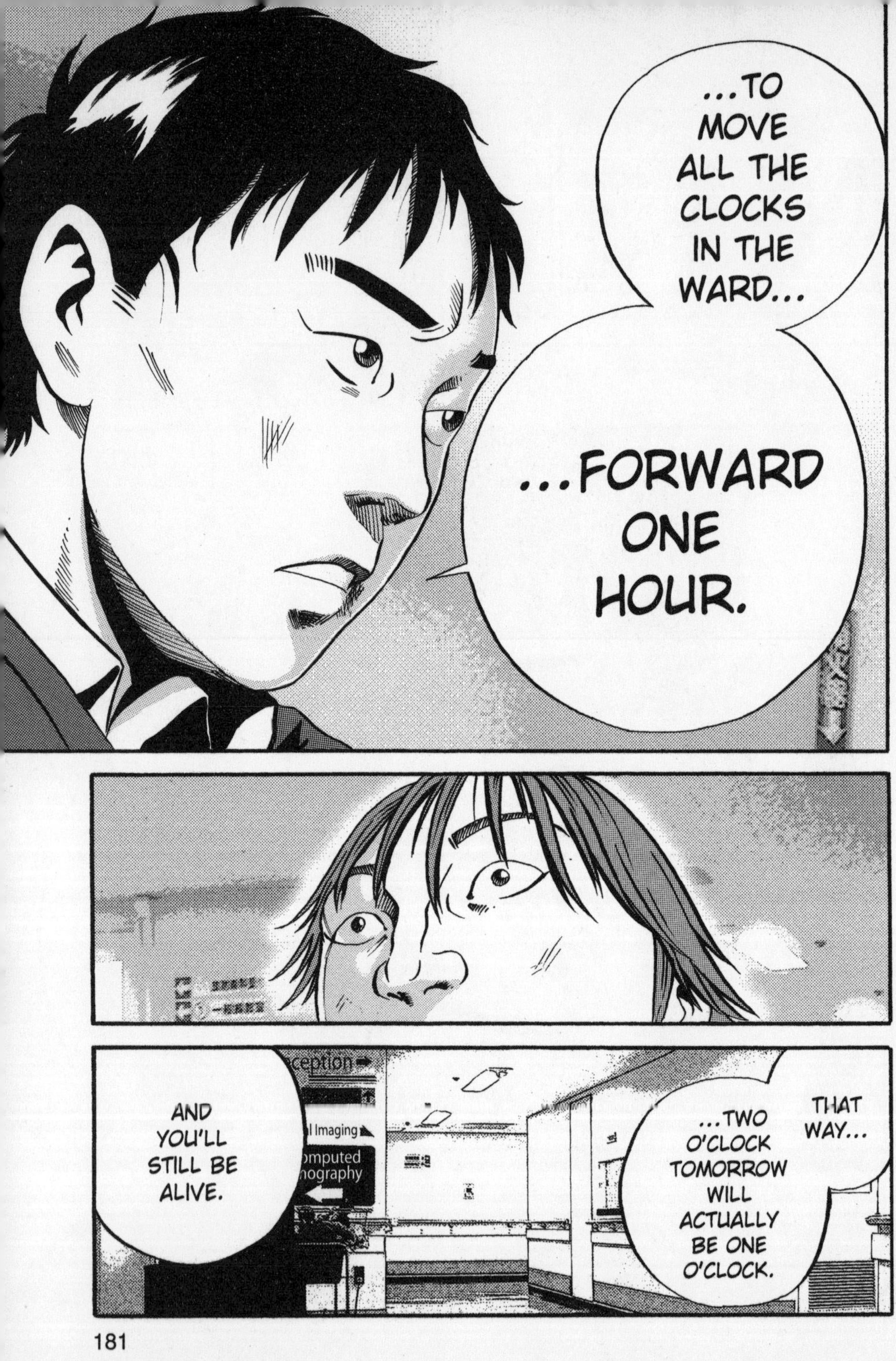
...TO MOVE ALL THE CLOCKS IN THE WARD...
...FORWARD ONE HOUR.
THAT WAY...
...TWO O'CLOCK TOMORROW WILL ACTUALLY BE ONE O'CLOCK.
AND YOU'LL STILL BE ALIVE.

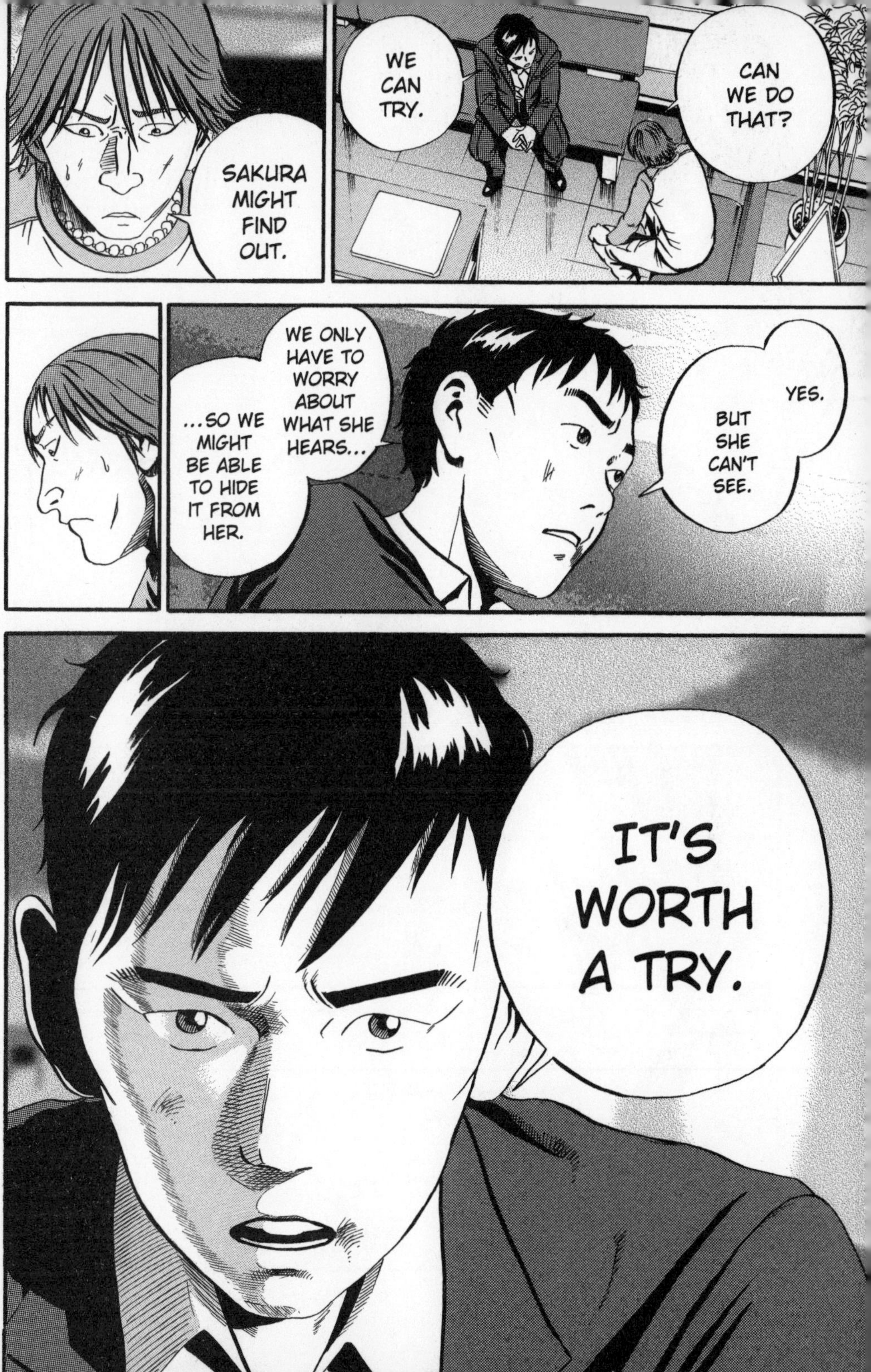
CAN WE DO THAT?
WE CAN TRY.
SAKURA MIGHT FIND OUT.
YES.
BUT SHE CAN'T SEE.
WE ONLY HAVE TO WORRY ABOUT WHAT SHE HEARS...
...SO WE MIGHT BE ABLE TO HIDE IT FROM HER.
IT'S WORTH A TRY.

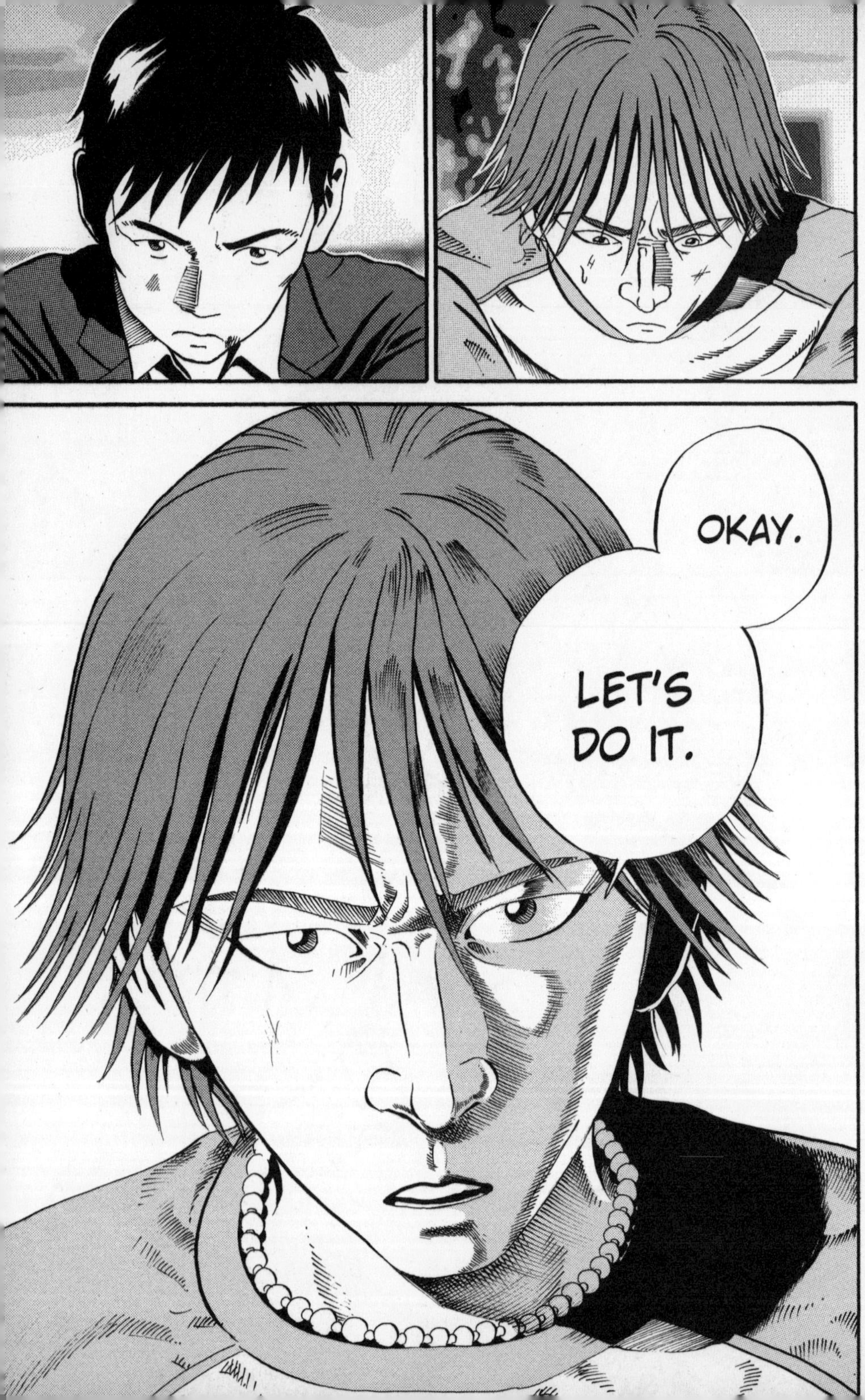
OKAY.
LET'S DO IT.

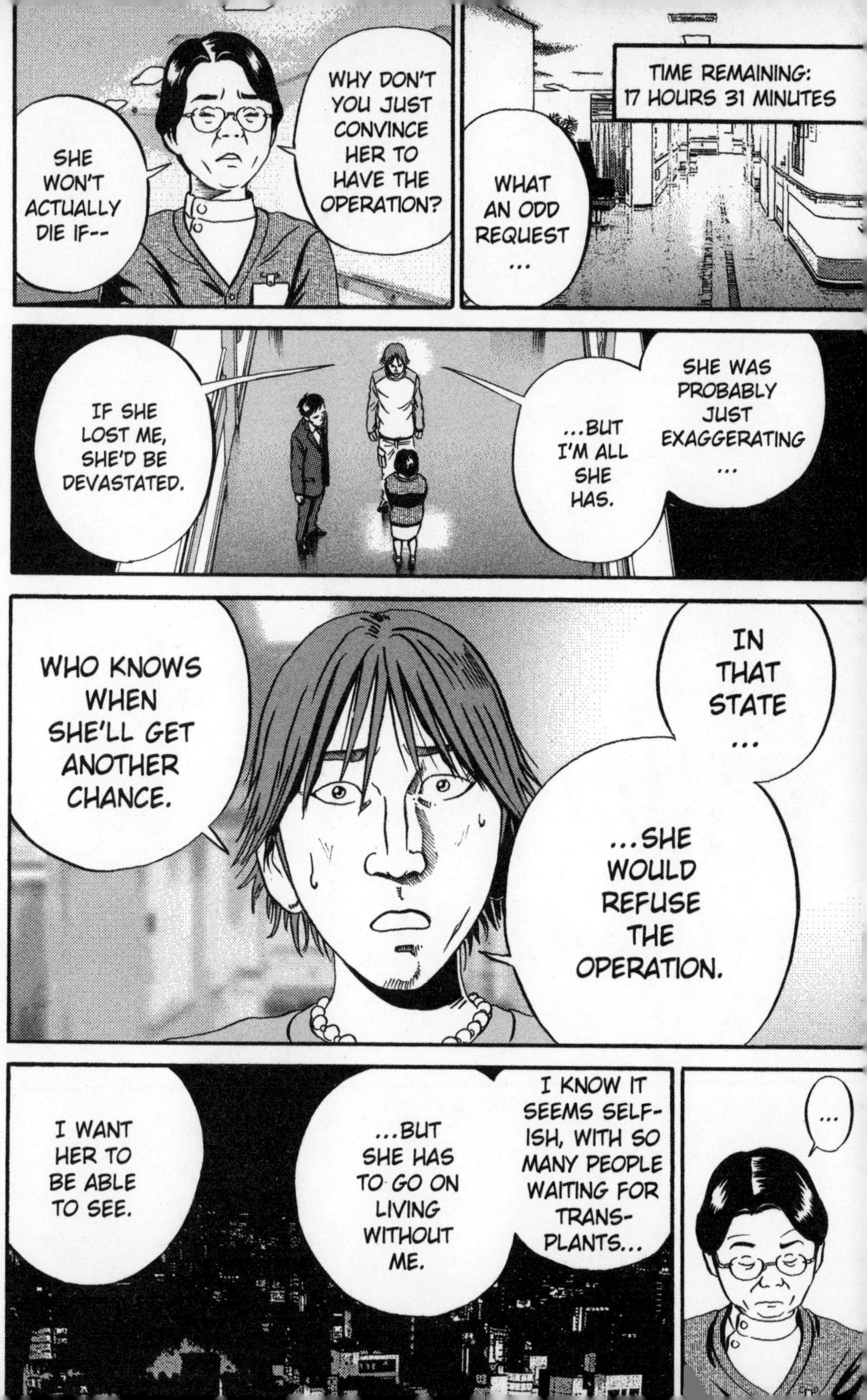
TIME REMAINING: 17 HOURS 31 MINUTES
WHAT AN ODD REQUEST ...
WHY DON'T YOU JUST CONVINCE HER TO HAVE THE OPERATION?
SHE WON'T ACTUALLY DIE IF--
SHE WAS PROBABLY JUST EXAGGERATING ...
...BUT I'M ALL SHE HAS.
IF SHE LOST ME, SHE'D BE DEVASTATED.
IN THAT STATE ...
...SHE WOULD REFUSE THE OPERATION.
WHO KNOWS WHEN SHE'LL GET ANOTHER CHANCE.
...
I KNOW IT SEEMS SELF-ISH, WITH SO MANY PEOPLE WAITING FOR TRANS-PLANTS...
...BUT SHE HAS TO GO ON LIVING WITHOUT ME.
I WANT HER TO BE ABLE TO SEE.

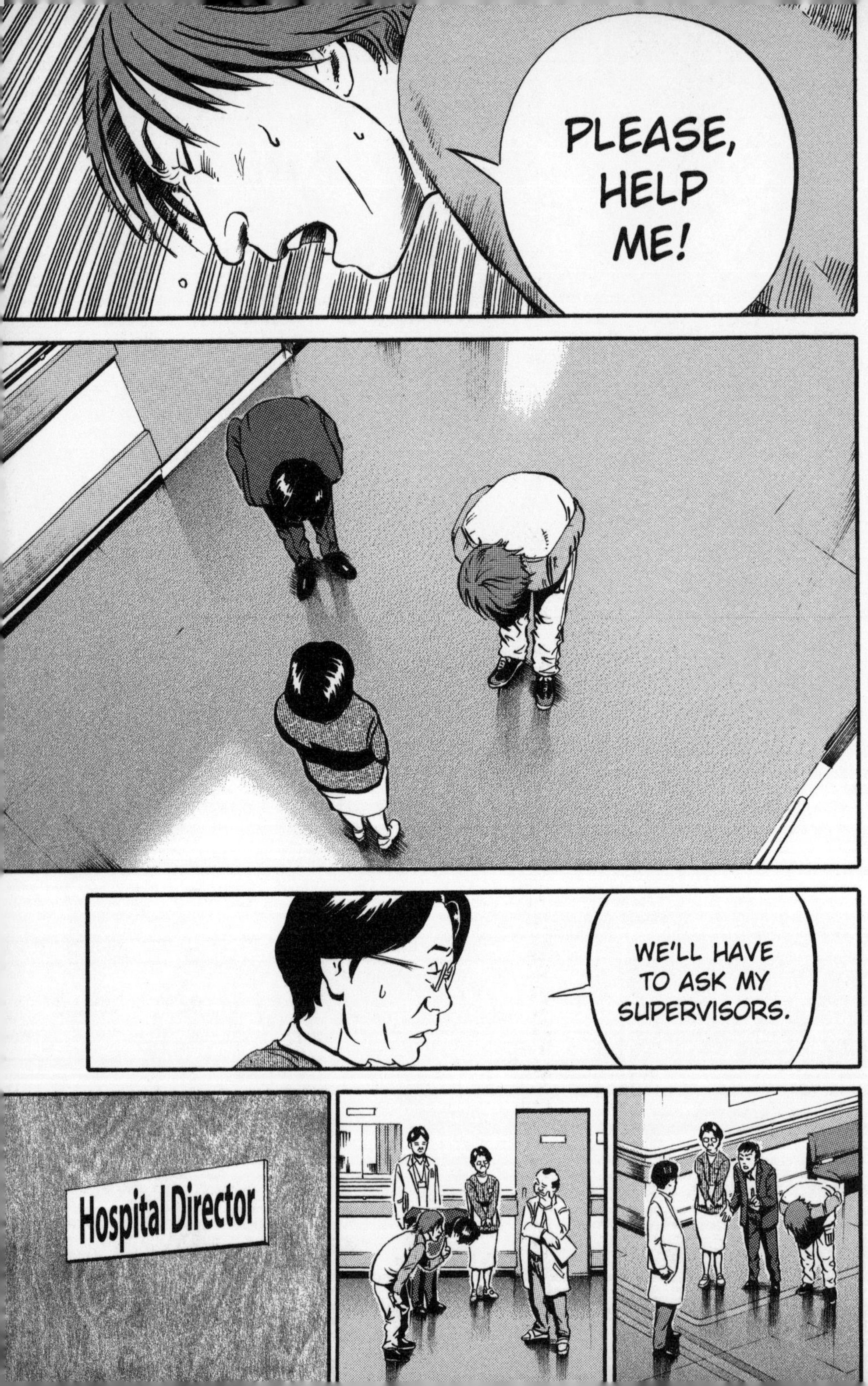
PLEASE, HELP ME!
WE'LL HAVE TO ASK MY SUPERVISORS.
Hospital Director

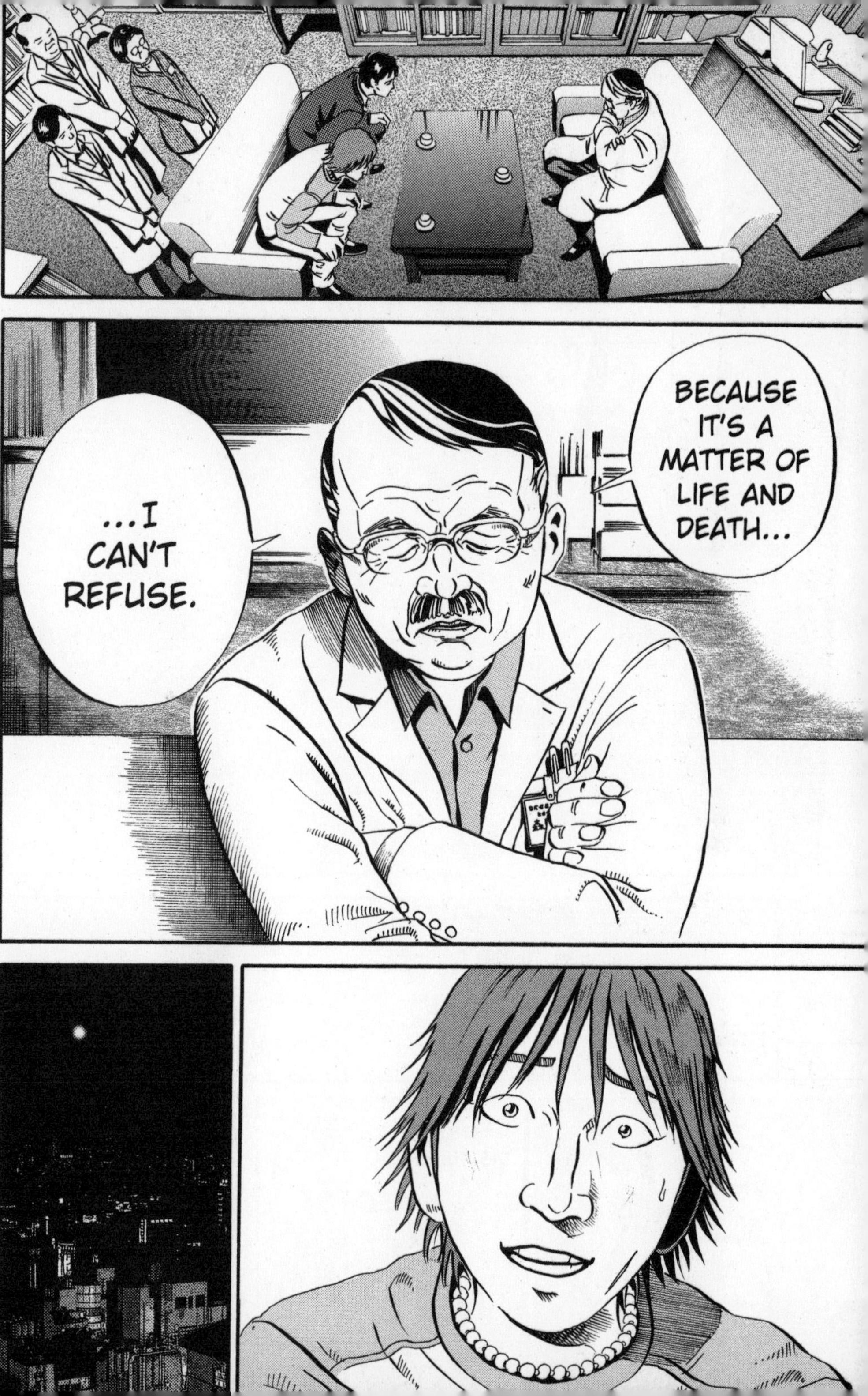
BECAUSE IT'S A MATTER OF LIFE AND DEATH...
...I CAN'T REFUSE.

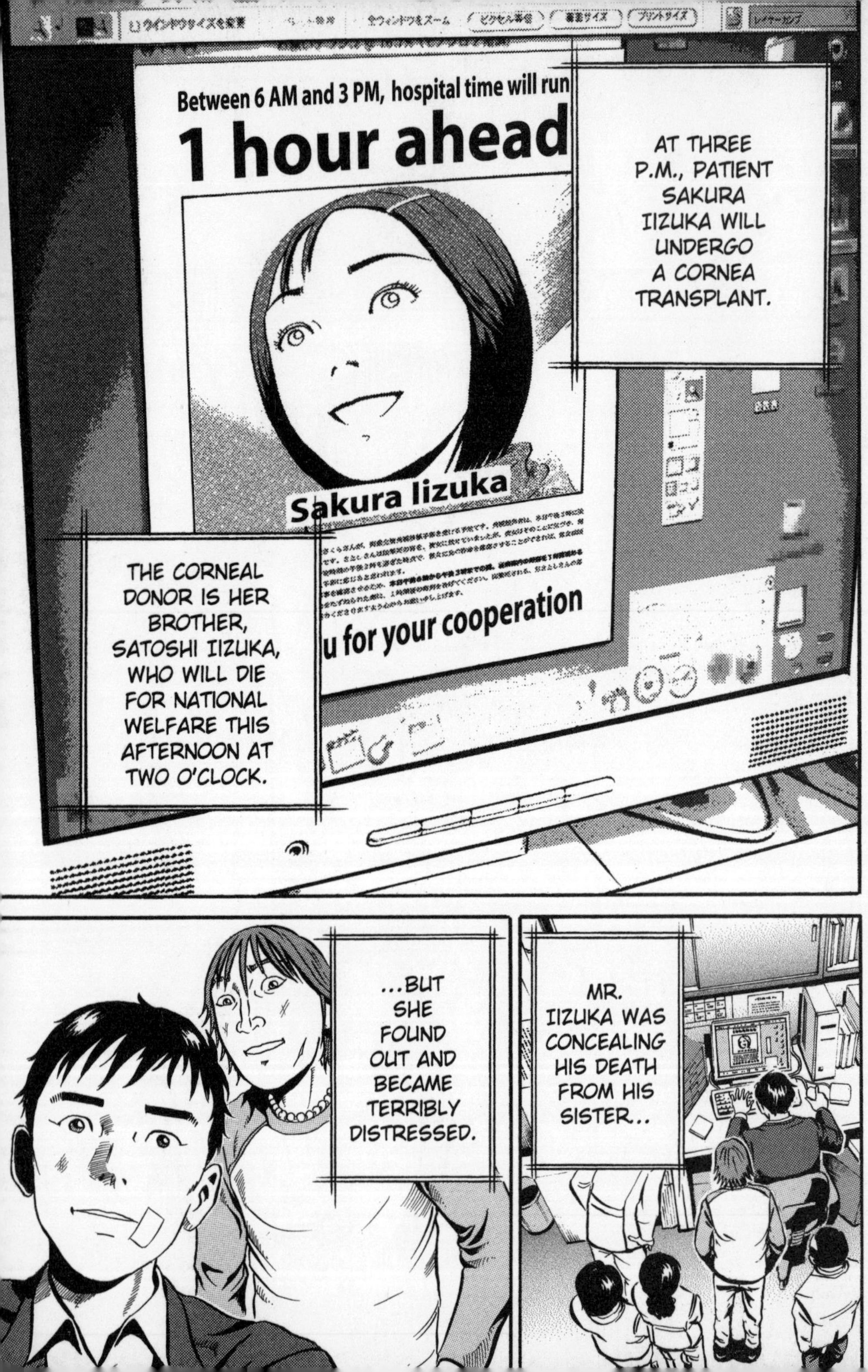
Between 6 AM and 3 PM, hospital time will run
1 hour ahead
Sakura Iizuka
u for your cooperation
AT THREE P.M., PATIENT SAKURA IIZUKA WILL UNDERGO A CORNEA TRANSPLANT.
THE CORNEAL DONOR IS HER BROTHER, SATOSHI IIZUKA, WHO WILL DIE FOR NATIONAL WELFARE THIS AFTERNOON AT TWO O'CLOCK.
MR. IIZUKA WAS CONCEALING HIS DEATH FROM HIS SISTER...
...BUT SHE FOUND OUT AND BECAME TERRIBLY DISTRESSED.

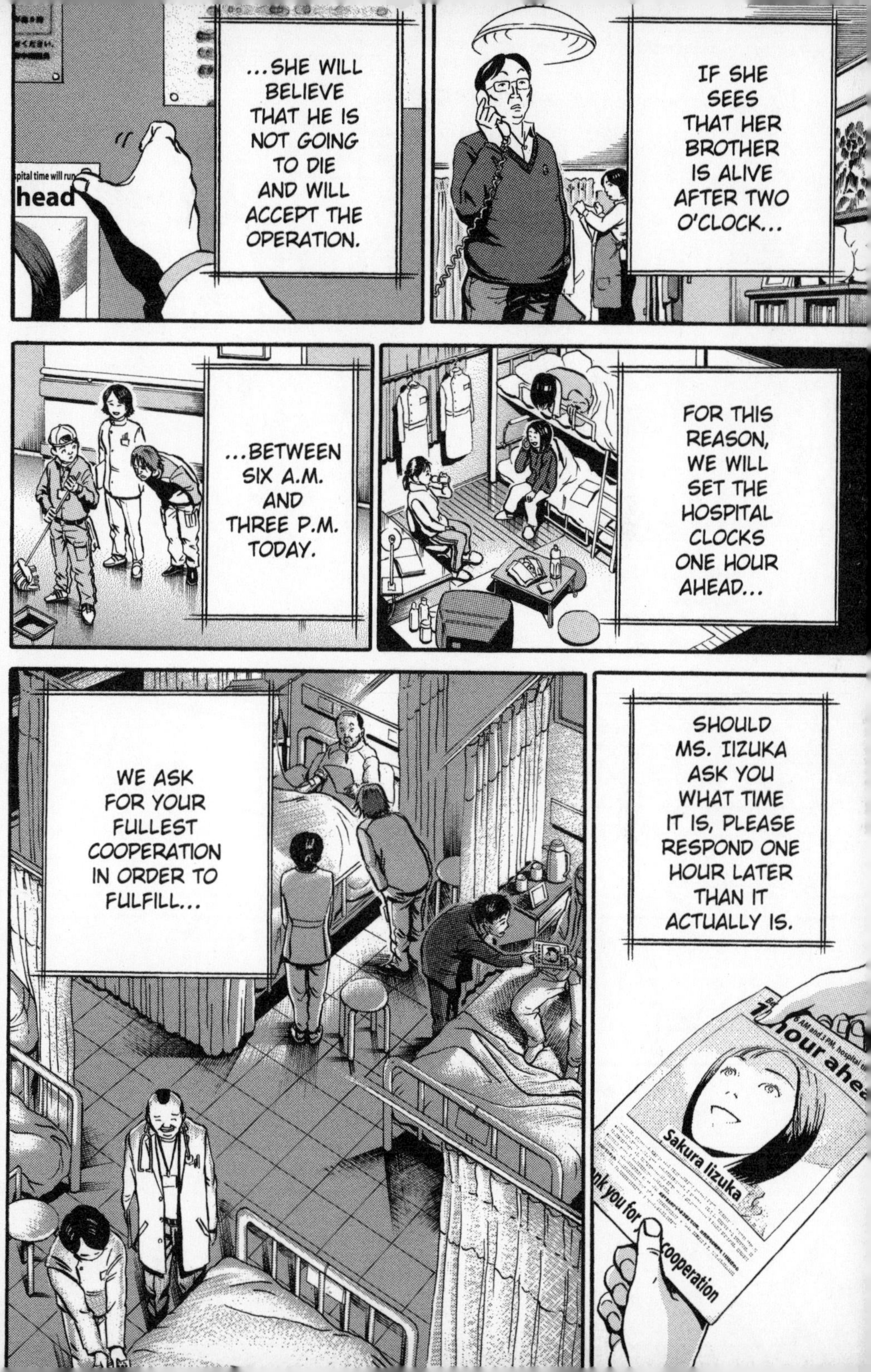
IF SHE SEES THAT HER BROTHER IS ALIVE AFTER TWO O'CLOCK...
...SHE WILL BELIEVE THAT HE IS NOT GOING TO DIE AND WILL ACCEPT THE OPERATION.
FOR THIS REASON, WE WILL SET THE HOSPITAL CLOCKS ONE HOUR AHEAD...
...BETWEEN SIX A.M. AND THREE P.M. TODAY.
SHOULD MS. IIZUKA ASK YOU WHAT TIME IT IS, PLEASE RESPOND ONE HOUR LATER THAN IT ACTUALLY IS.
Sakura Iizuka
WE ASK FOR YOUR FULLEST COOPERATION IN ORDER TO FULFILL...

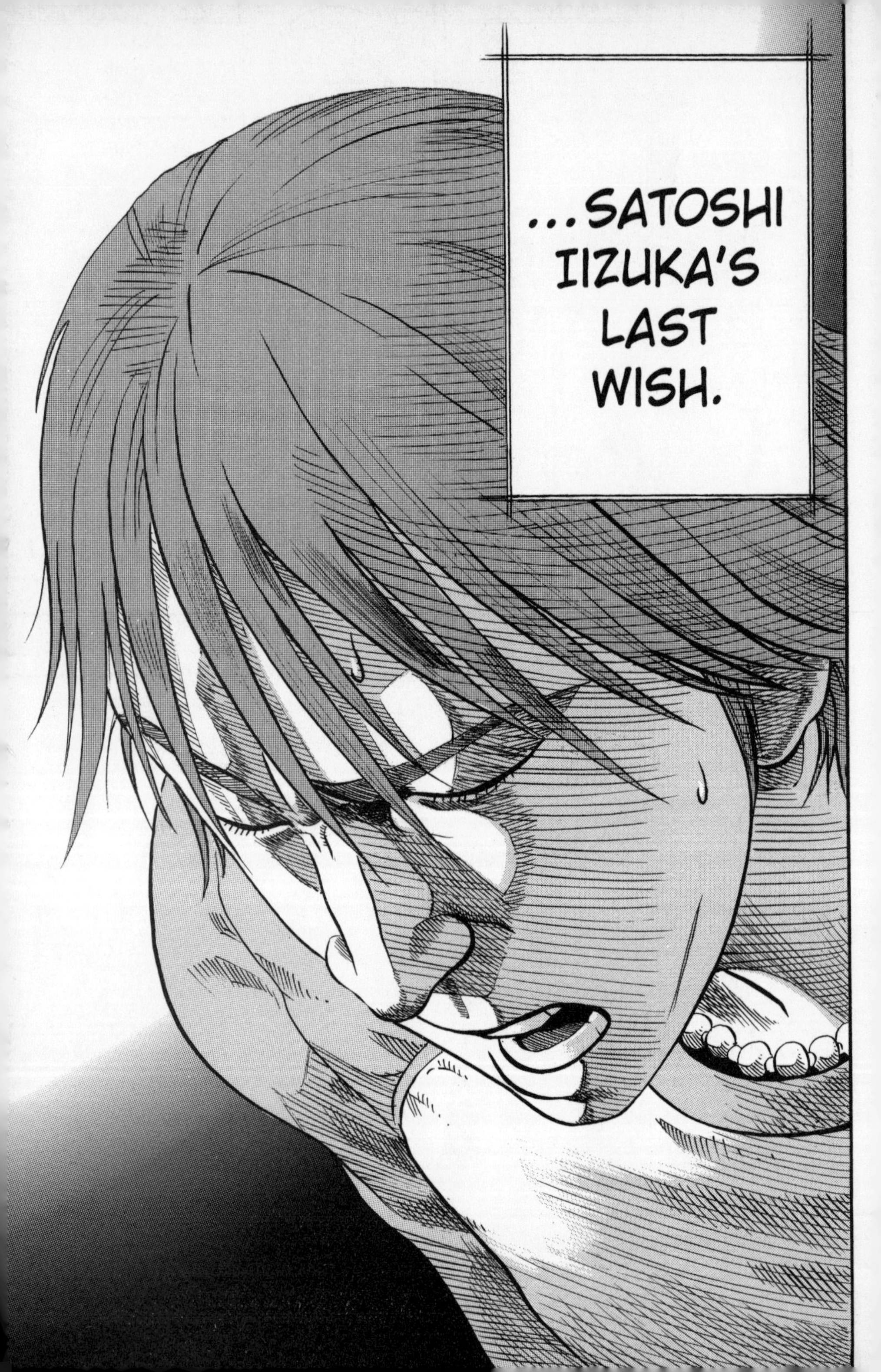
...SATOSHI IIZUKA'S LAST WISH.

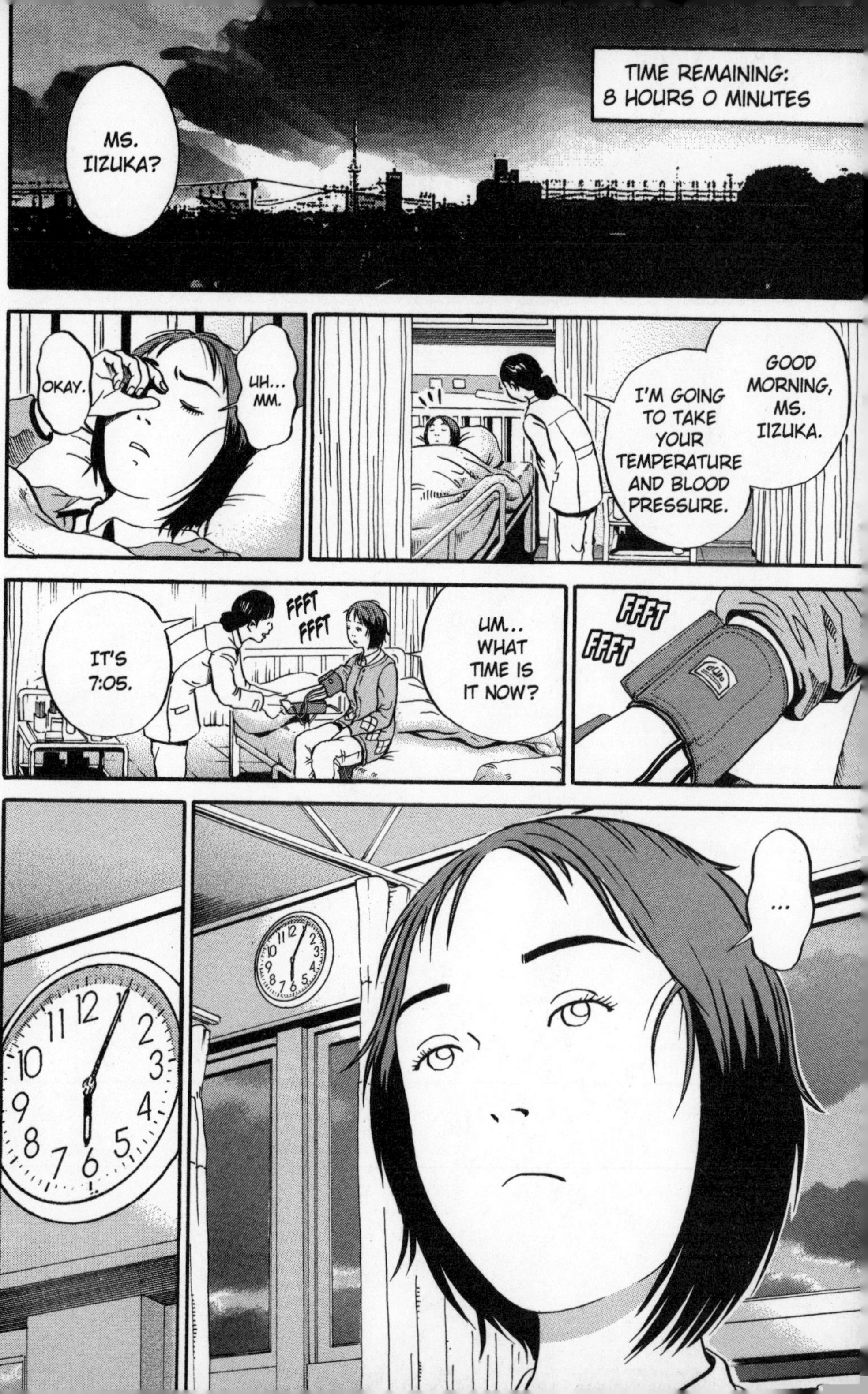
TIME REMAINING: 8 HOURS 0 MINUTES
MS. IIZUKA?
GOOD MORNING, MS. IIZUKA.
I'M GOING TO TAKE YOUR TEMPERATURE AND BLOOD PRESSURE.
UH... MM.
OKAY.
FFFT FFFT
UM... WHAT TIME IS IT NOW?
FFFT FFFT
IT'S 7:05.
...

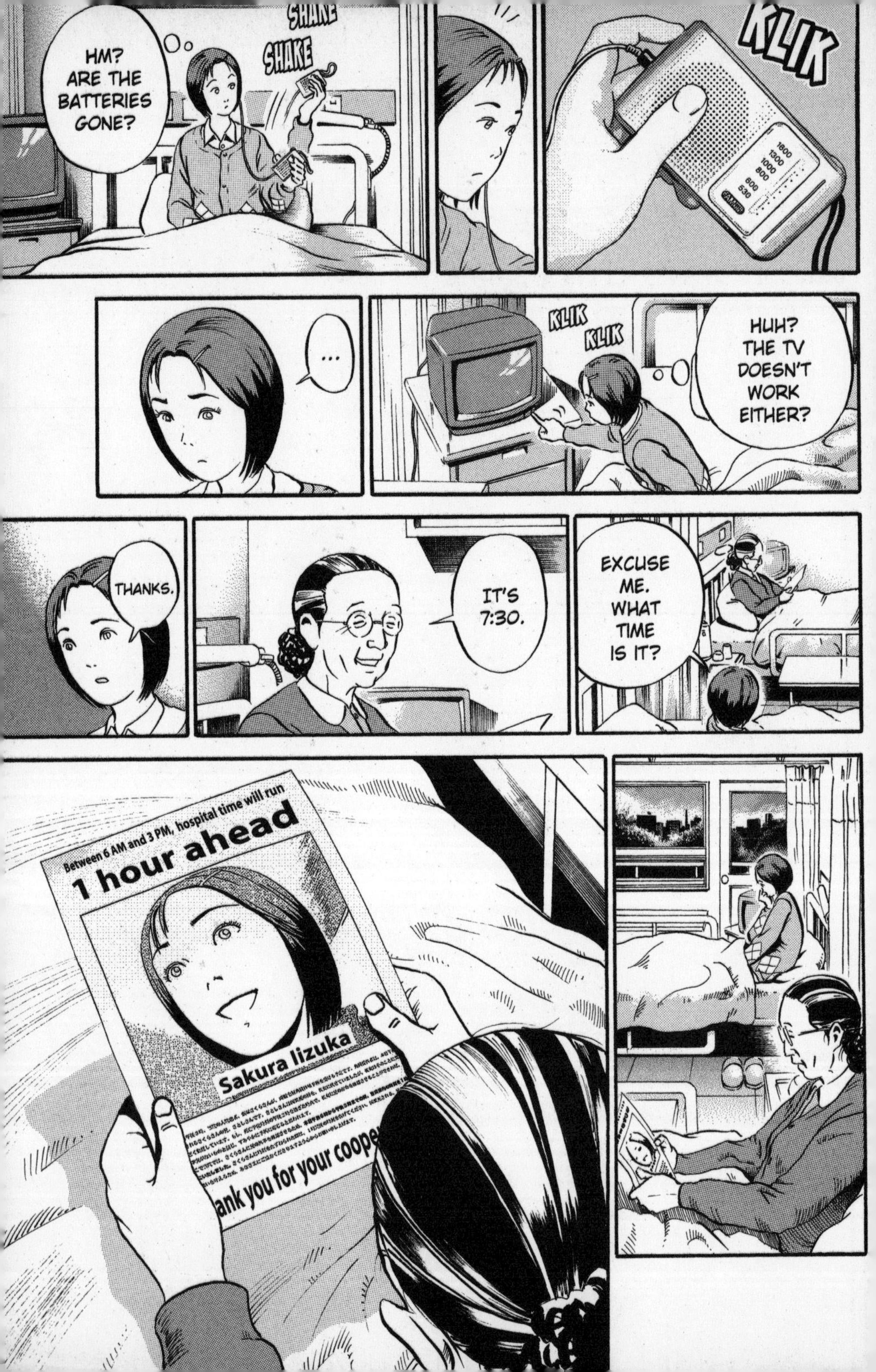
KLIK
1600
1300
1000
800
600
530
SHAKE
SHAKE
HM? ARE THE BATTERIES GONE?
HUH? THE TV DOESN'T WORK EITHER?
KLIK
KLIK
...
EXCUSE ME. WHAT TIME IS IT?
IT'S 7:30.
THANKS.
Between 6 AM and 3 PM, hospital time will run
1 hour ahead
Sakura Iizuka
ank you for your cooper

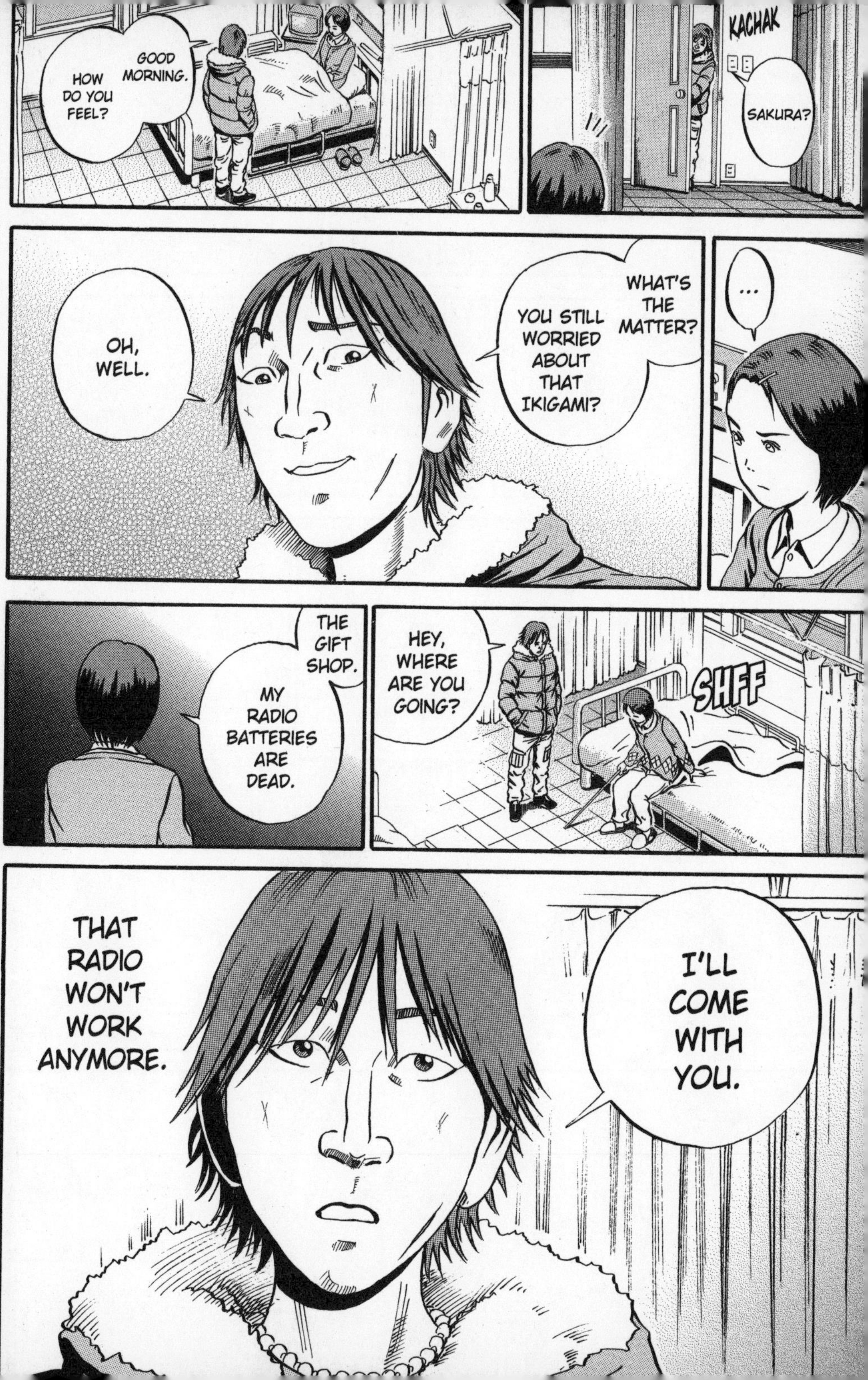
KACHAK
SAKURA?
GOOD MORNING.
HOW DO YOU FEEL?
...
WHAT'S THE MATTER?
YOU STILL WORRIED ABOUT THAT IKIGAMI?
OH, WELL.
SHFF
HEY, WHERE ARE YOU GOING?
THE GIFT SHOP.
MY RADIO BATTERIES ARE DEAD.
I'LL COME WITH YOU.
THAT RADIO WON'T WORK ANYMORE.

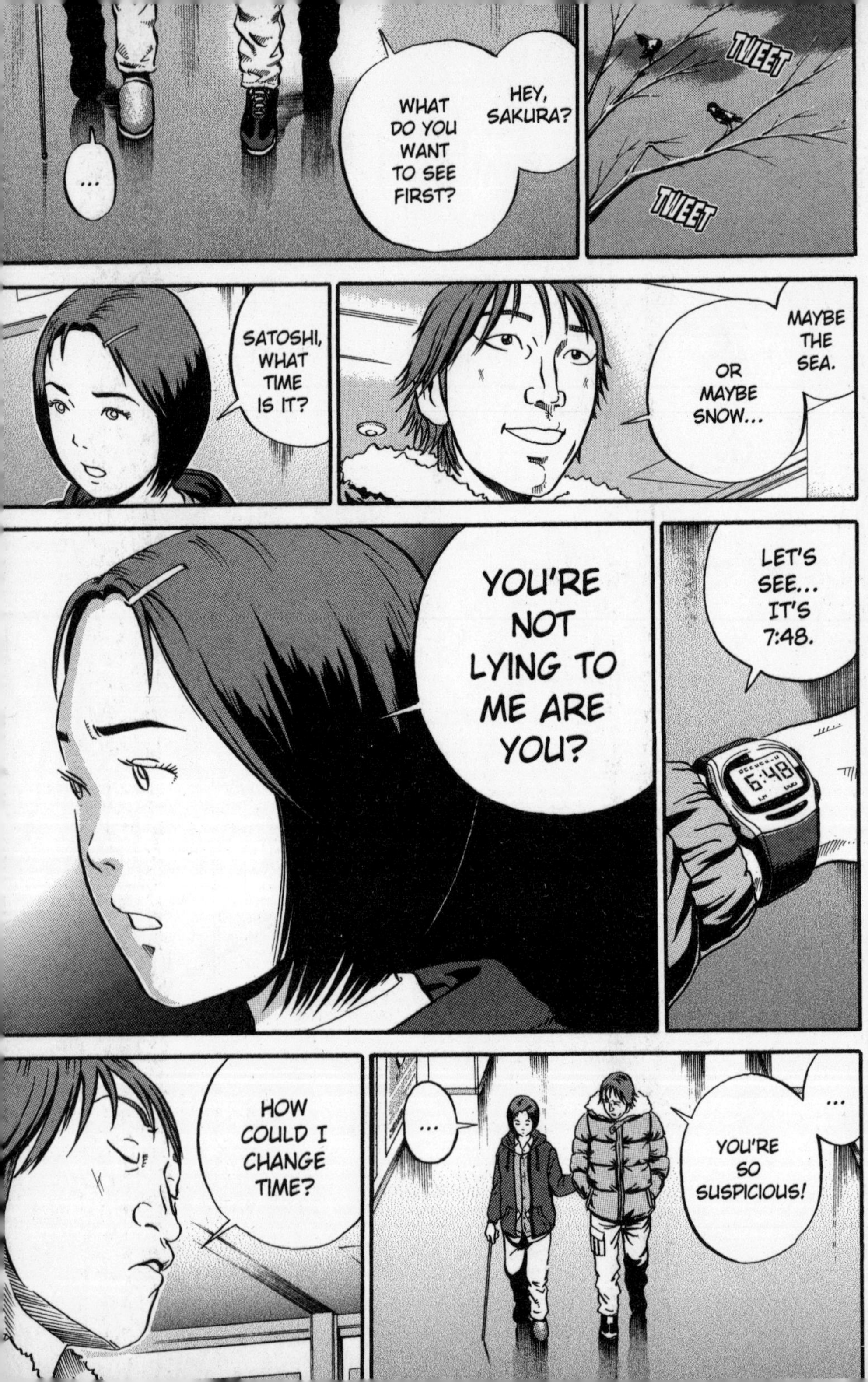
TWEET
TWEET
HEY, SAKURA? WHAT DO YOU WANT TO SEE FIRST?
...
MAYBE THE SEA. OR MAYBE SNOW...
SATOSHI, WHAT TIME IS IT?
LET'S SEE... IT'S 7:48.
6:48
YOU'RE NOT LYING TO ME ARE YOU?
... YOU'RE SO SUSPICIOUS!
...
HOW COULD I CHANGE TIME?

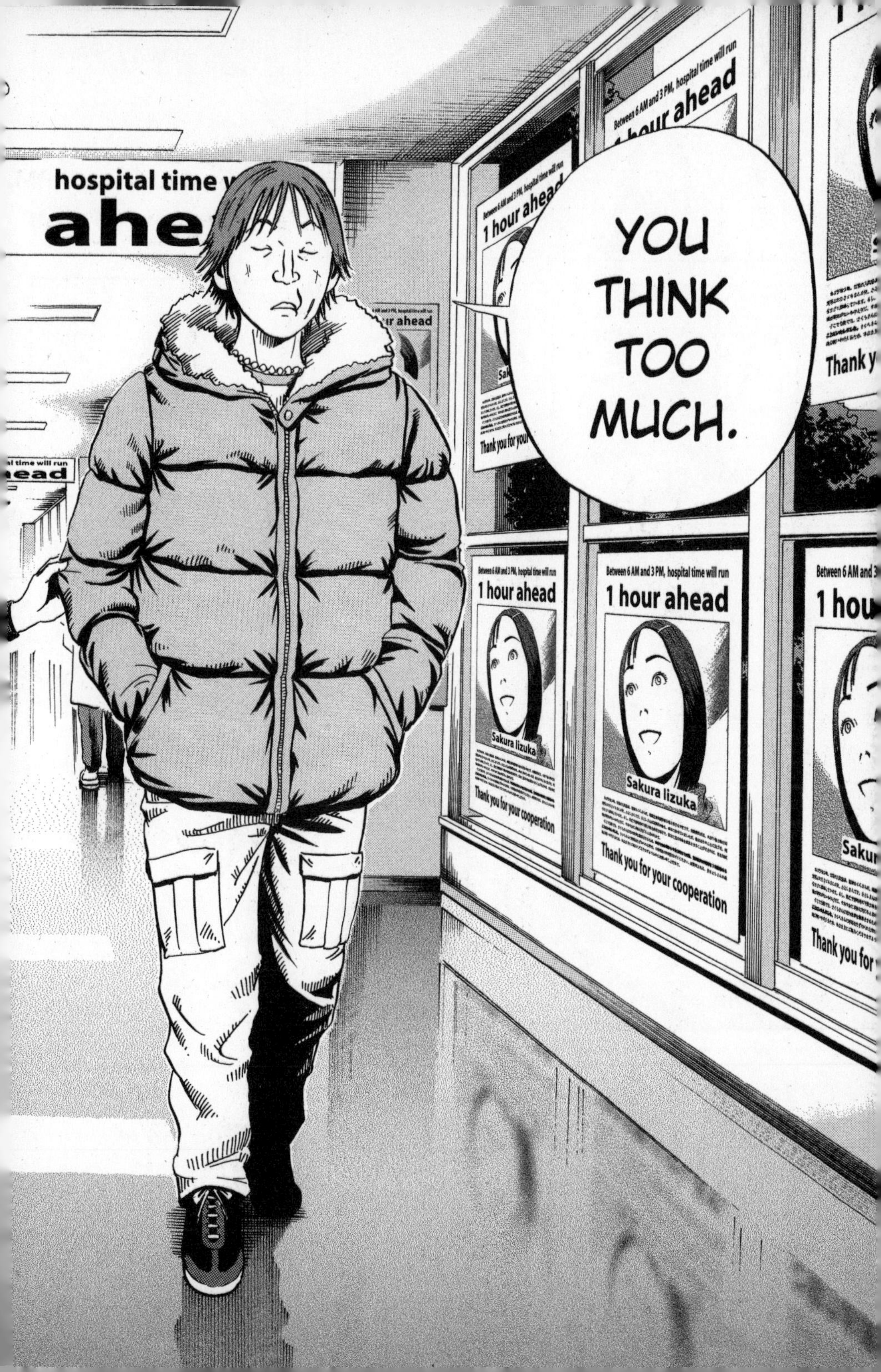
YOU THINK TOO MUCH.
Between 6 AM and 3 PM, hospital time will run
1 hour ahead
Sakura Iizuka
Thank you for your cooperation

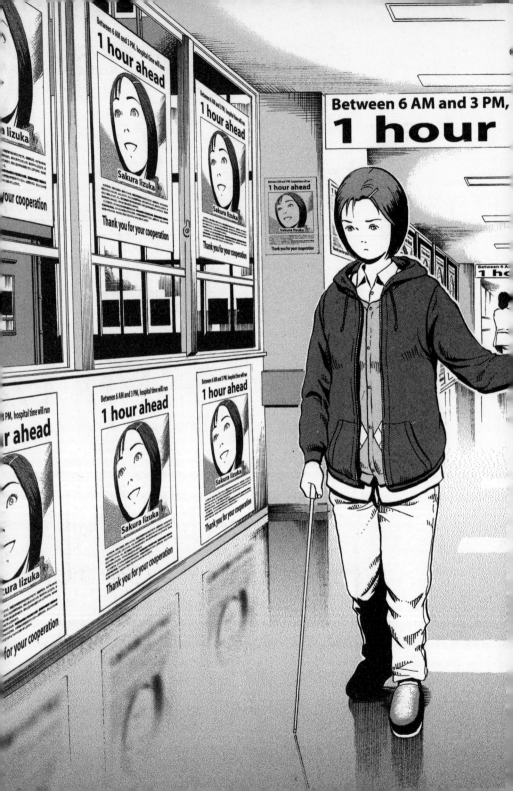

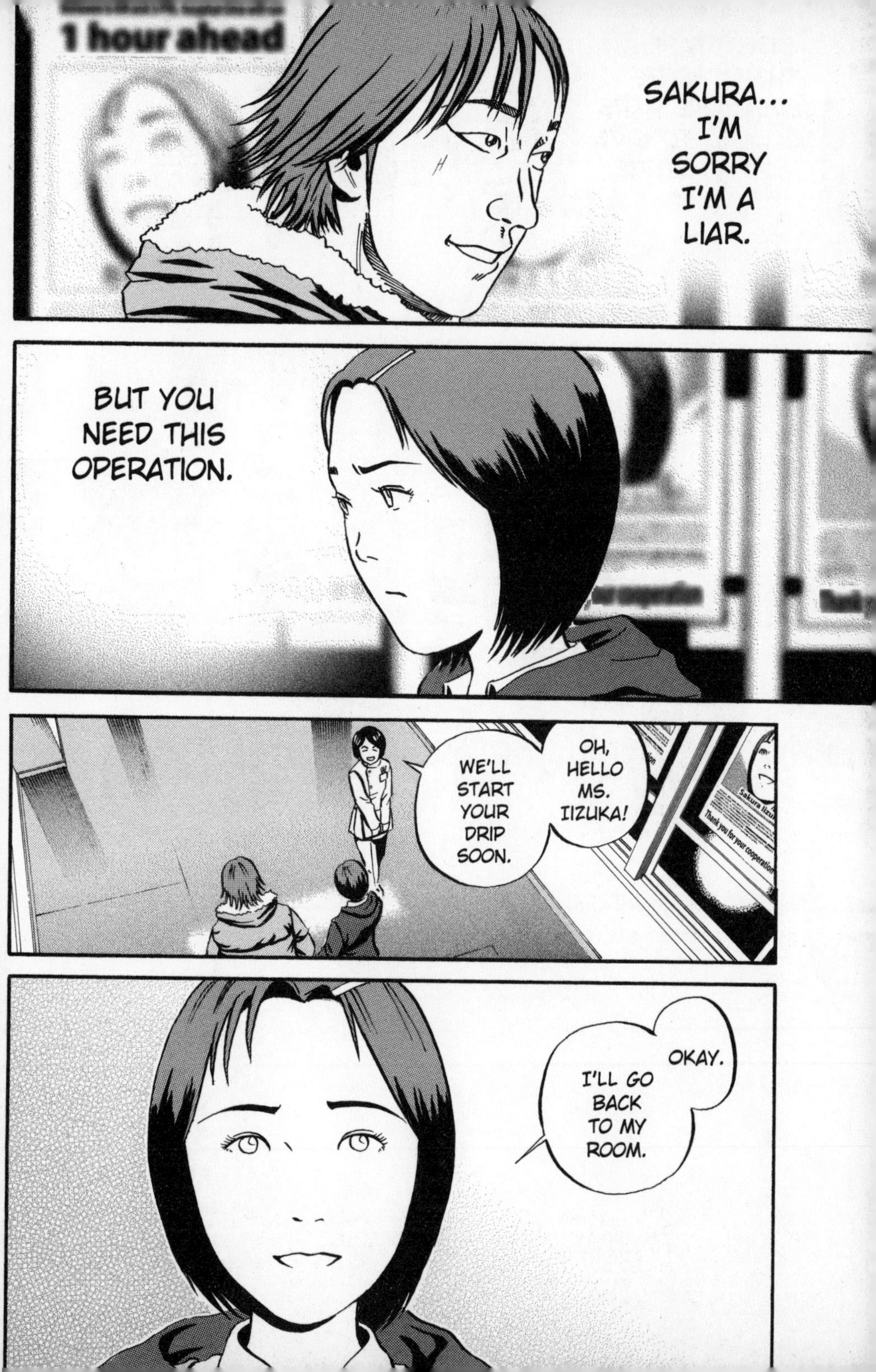
1 hour ahead
SAKURA... I'M SORRY I'M A LIAR.
BUT YOU NEED THIS OPERATION.
OH, HELLO MS. IIZUKA!
WE'LL START YOUR DRIP SOON.
Thank you for your cooperation
OKAY. I'LL GO BACK TO MY ROOM.

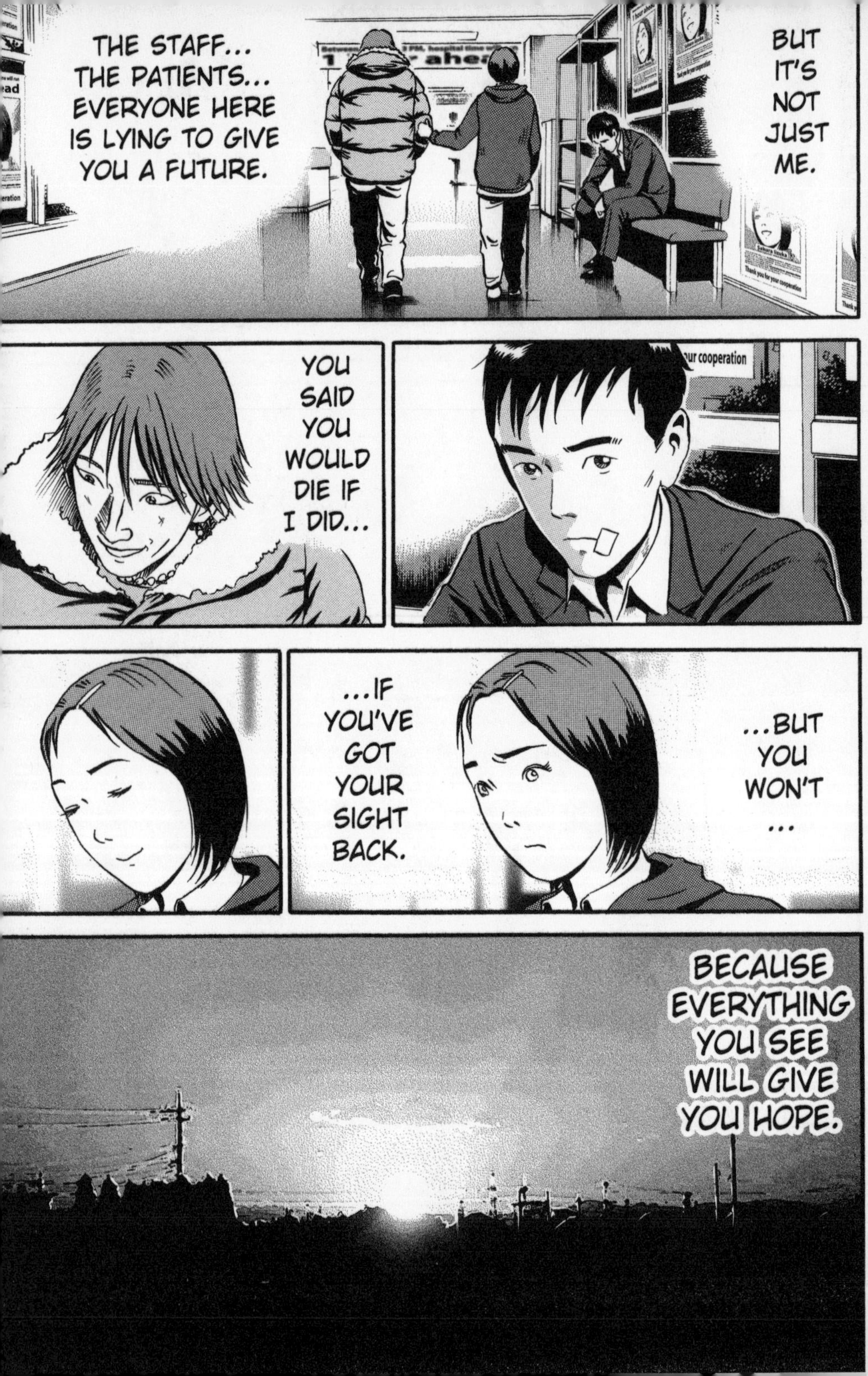
BUT IT'S NOT JUST ME.
THE STAFF... THE PATIENTS... EVERYONE HERE IS LYING TO GIVE YOU A FUTURE.
YOU SAID YOU WOULD DIE IF I DID...
...BUT YOU WON'T ...
...IF YOU'VE GOT YOUR SIGHT BACK.
BECAUSE EVERYTHING YOU SEE WILL GIVE YOU HOPE.

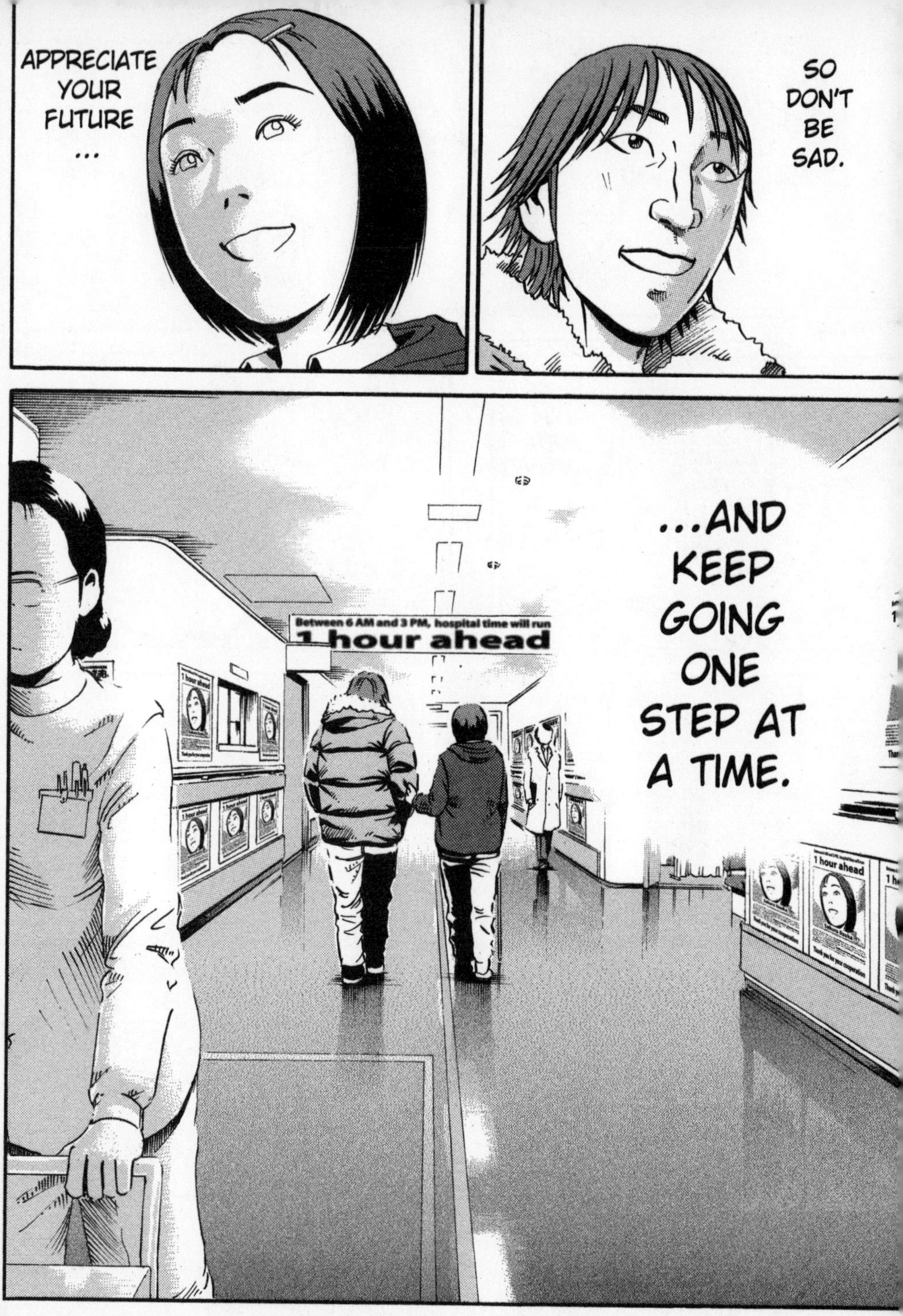
SO DON'T BE SAD.
APPRECIATE YOUR FUTURE ...
Between 6 AM and 3 PM, hospital time will run
1 hour ahead
...AND KEEP GOING ONE STEP AT A TIME.

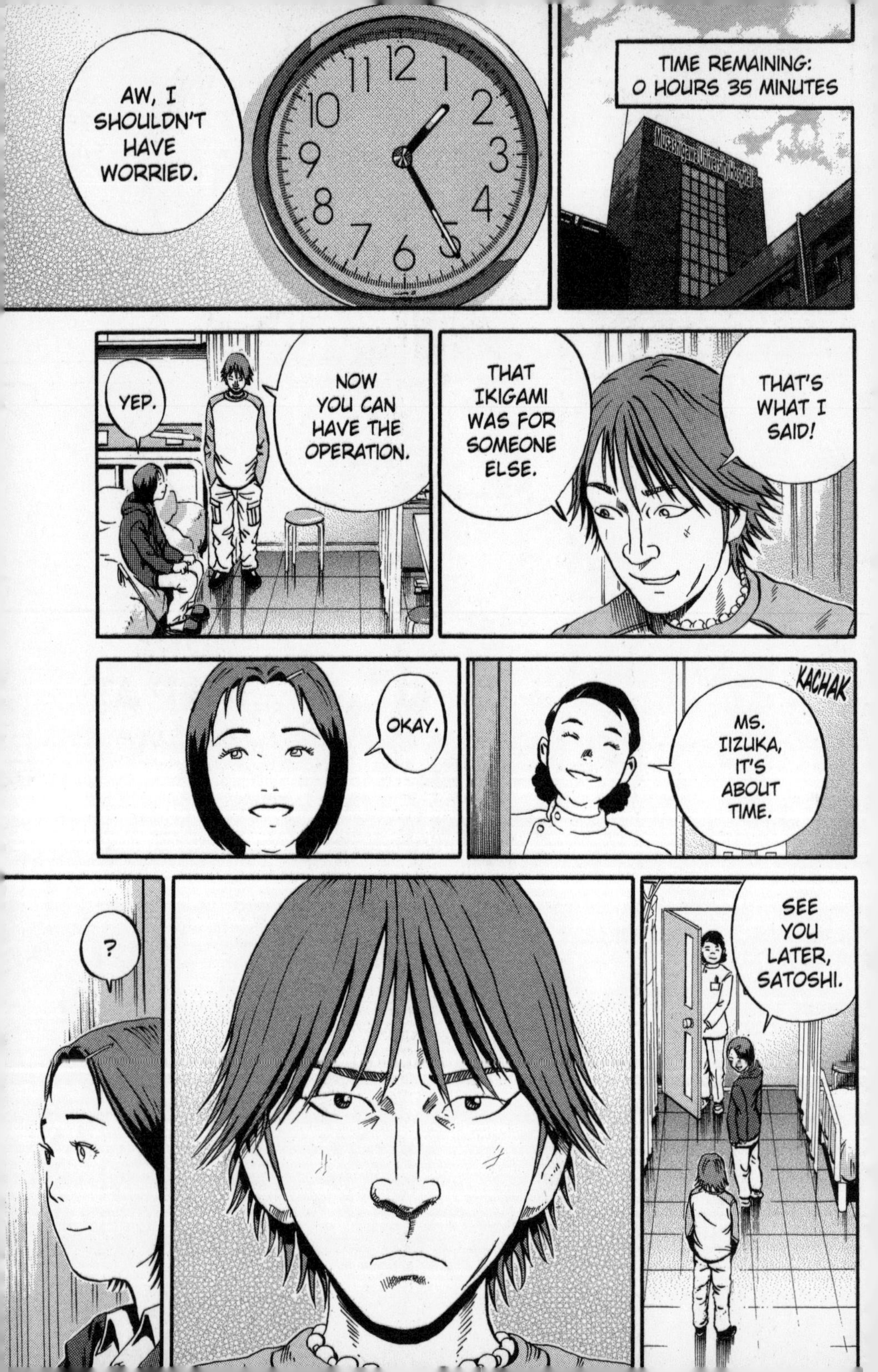
TIME REMAINING: 0 HOURS 35 MINUTES
Musashigawa University Hospital
AW, I SHOULDN'T HAVE WORRIED.
THAT'S WHAT I SAID!
THAT IKIGAMI WAS FOR SOMEONE ELSE.
NOW YOU CAN HAVE THE OPERATION.
YEP.
KACHAK
MS. IIZUKA, IT'S ABOUT TIME.
OKAY.
SEE YOU LATER, SATOSHI.
?

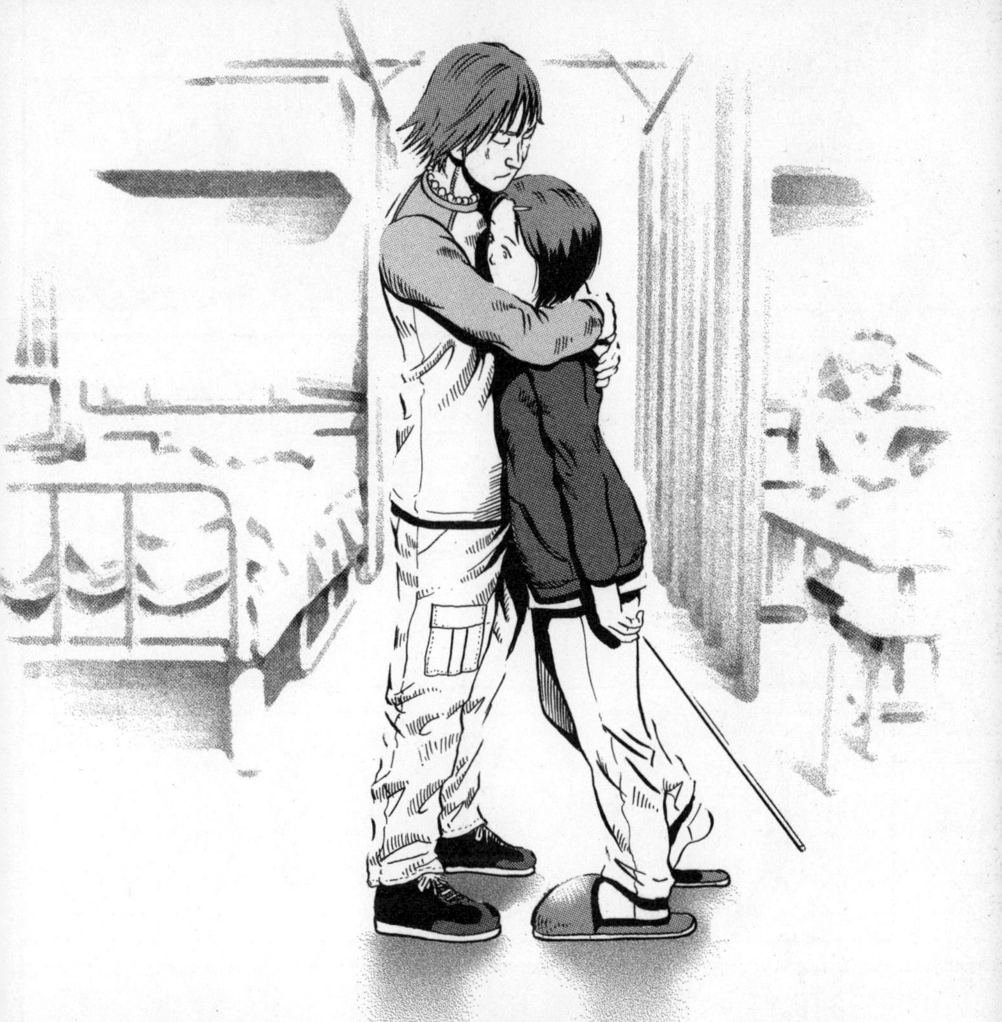

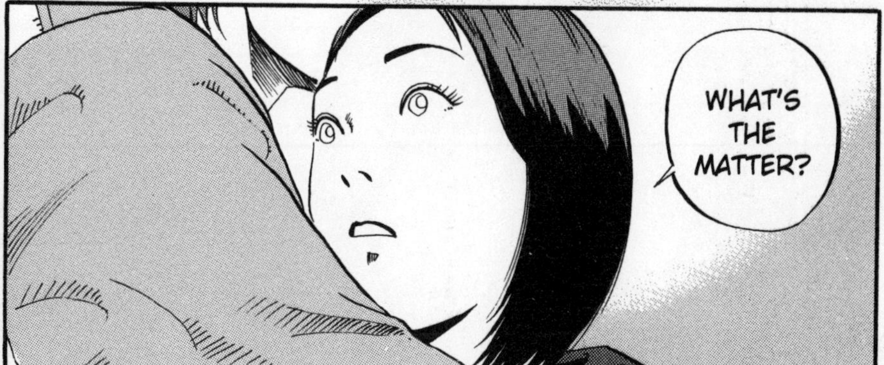
WHAT'S THE MATTER?

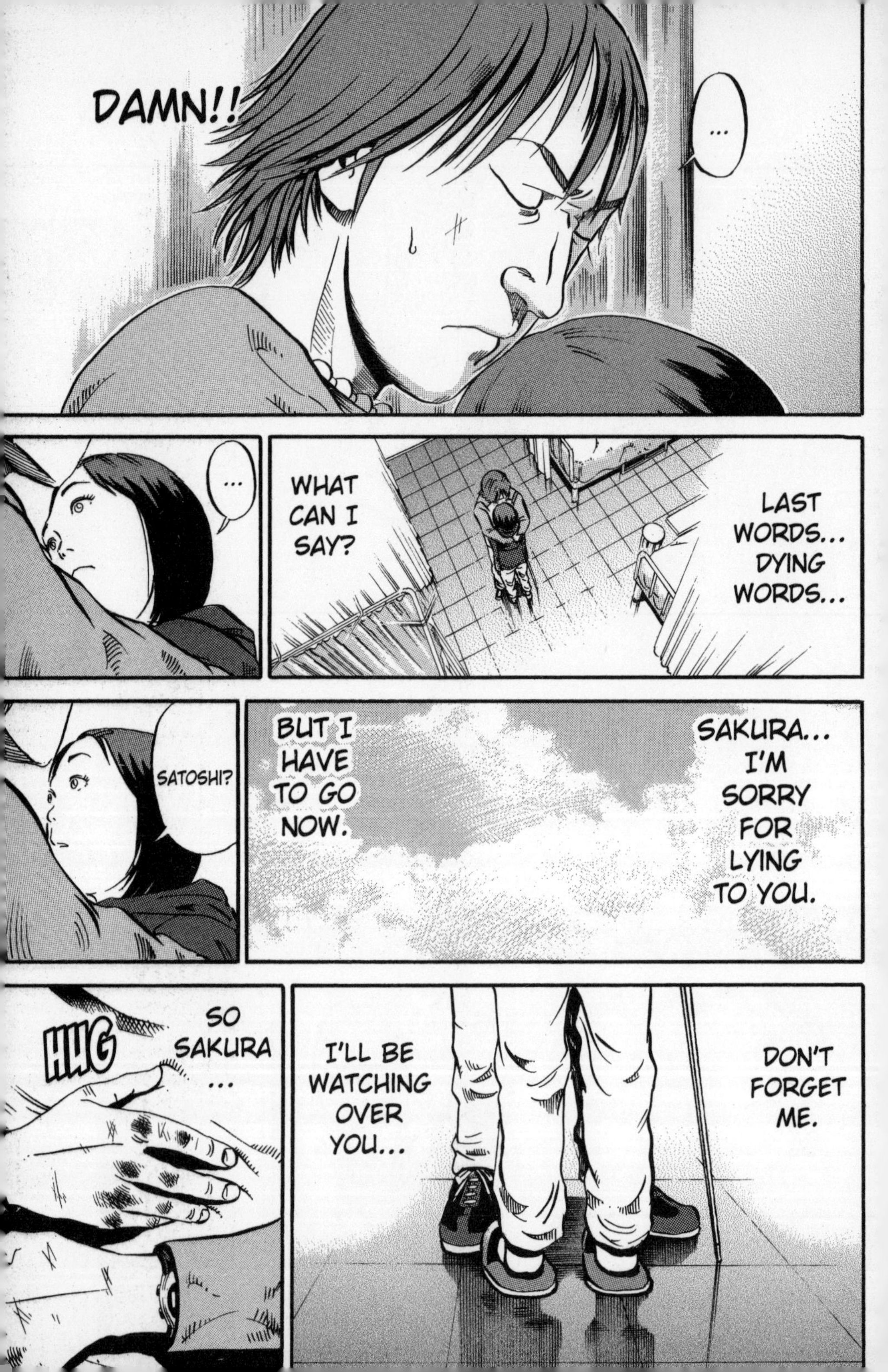
...
DAMN!!
LAST WORDS... DYING WORDS...
WHAT CAN I SAY?
...
SAKURA... I'M SORRY FOR LYING TO YOU.
BUT I HAVE TO GO NOW.
SATOSHI?
DON'T FORGET ME.
I'LL BE WATCHING OVER YOU...
SO SAKURA ...
HUG

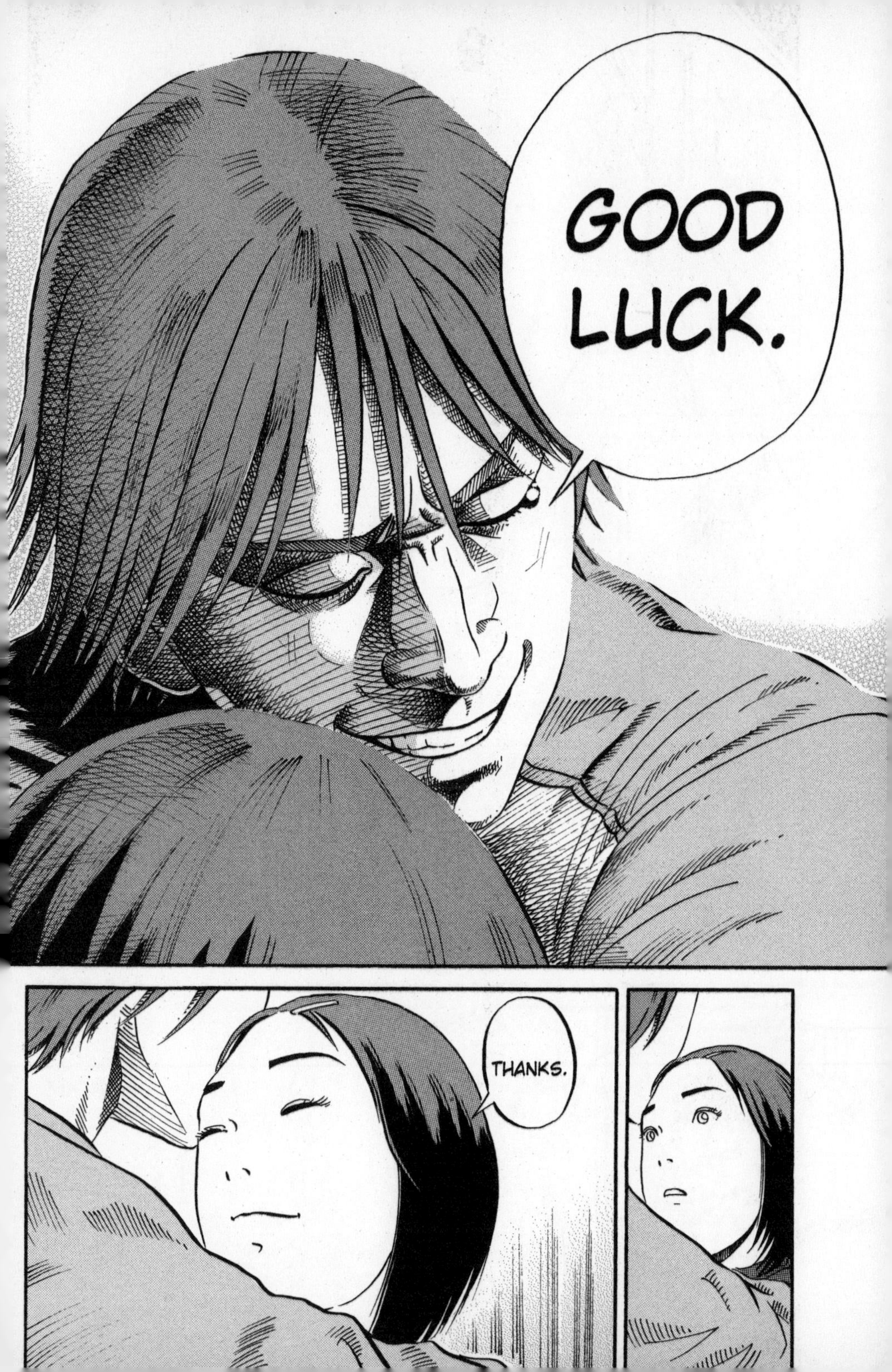
GOOD LUCK.
THANKS.

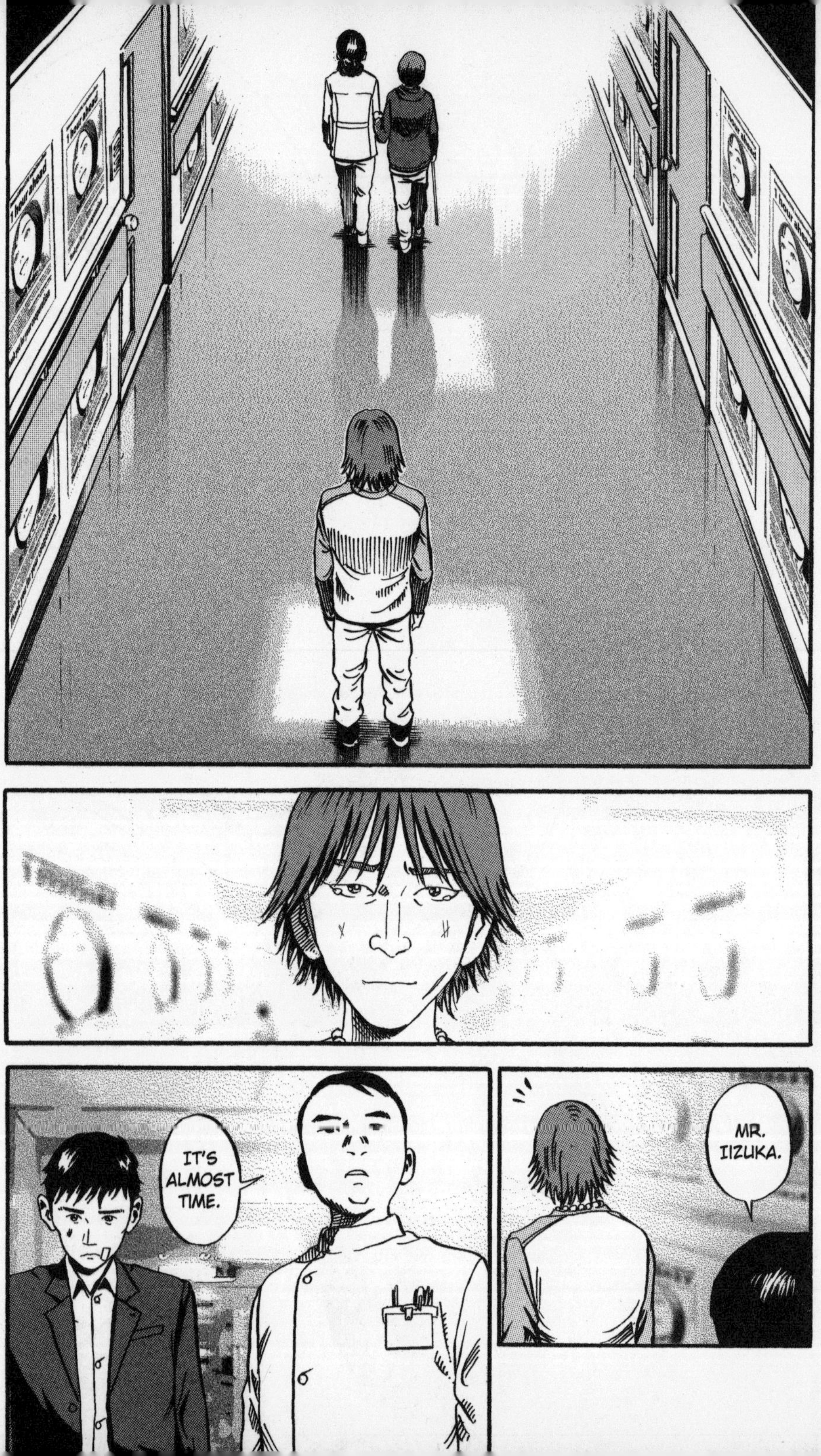
1 hour ahead
MR. IIZUKA.
IT'S ALMOST TIME.

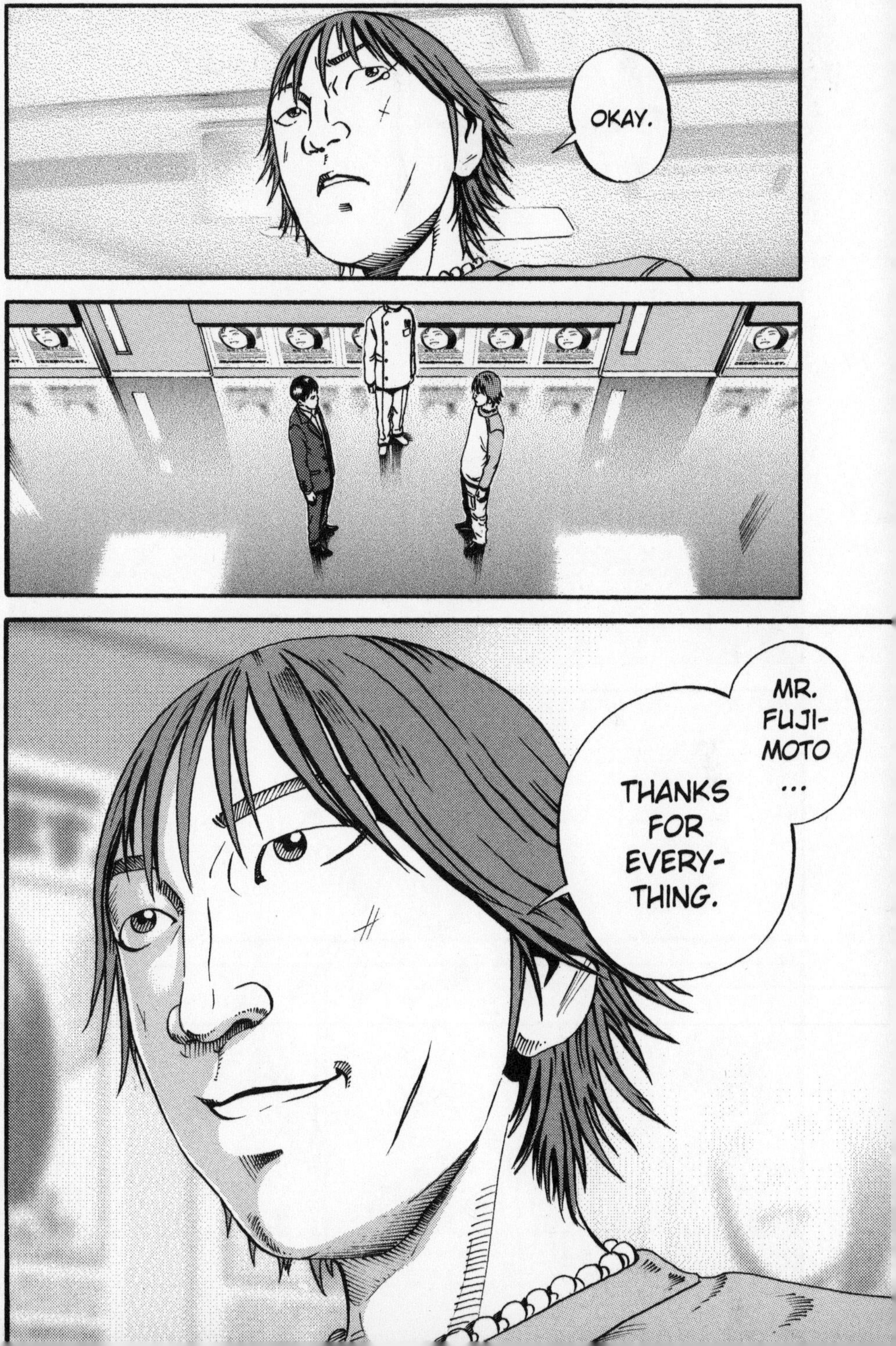
OKAY.
MR. FUJI-MOTO...
THANKS FOR EVERY-THING.

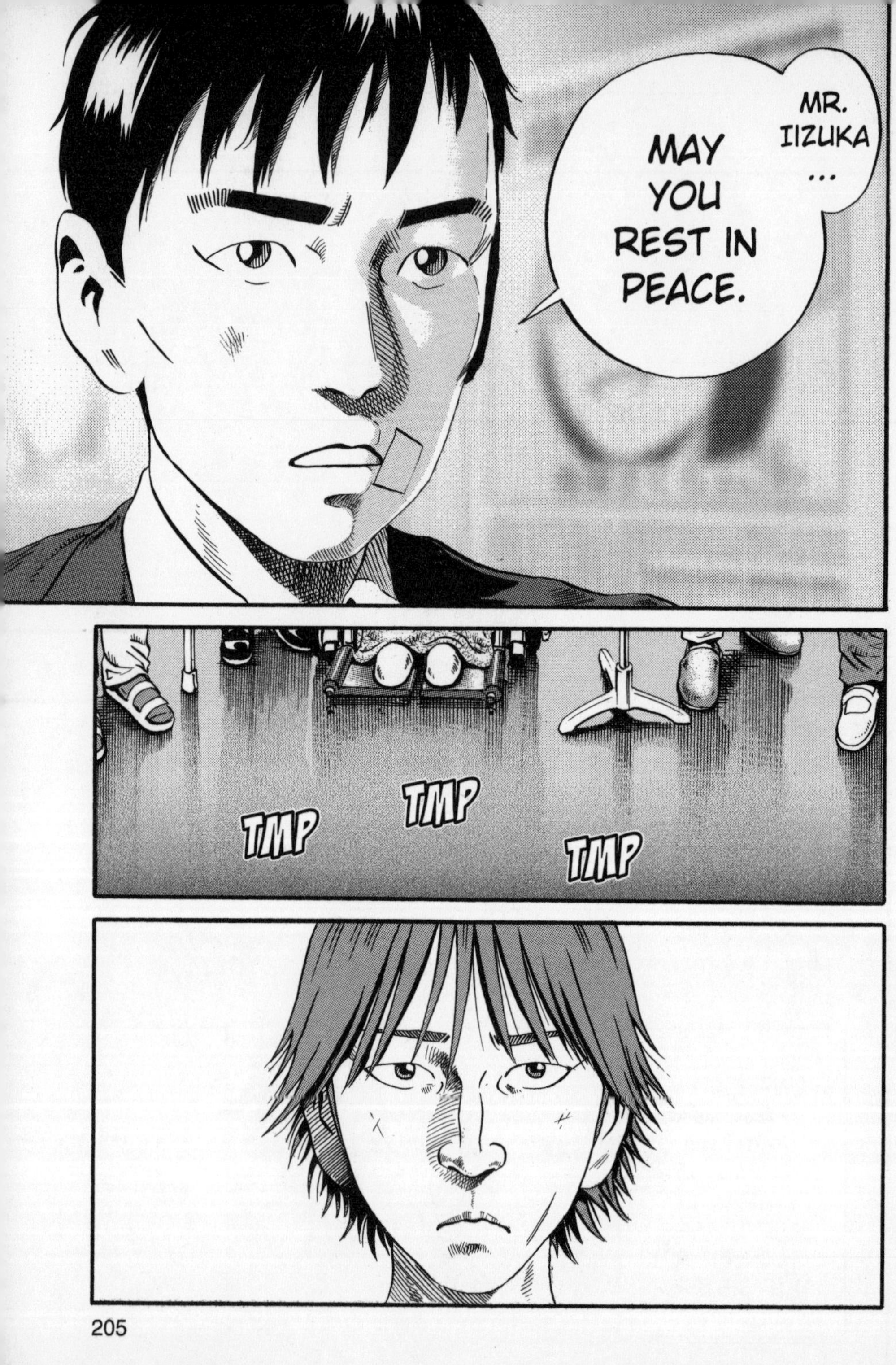
MR. IIZUKA ...
MAY YOU REST IN PEACE.
TMP
TMP
TMP

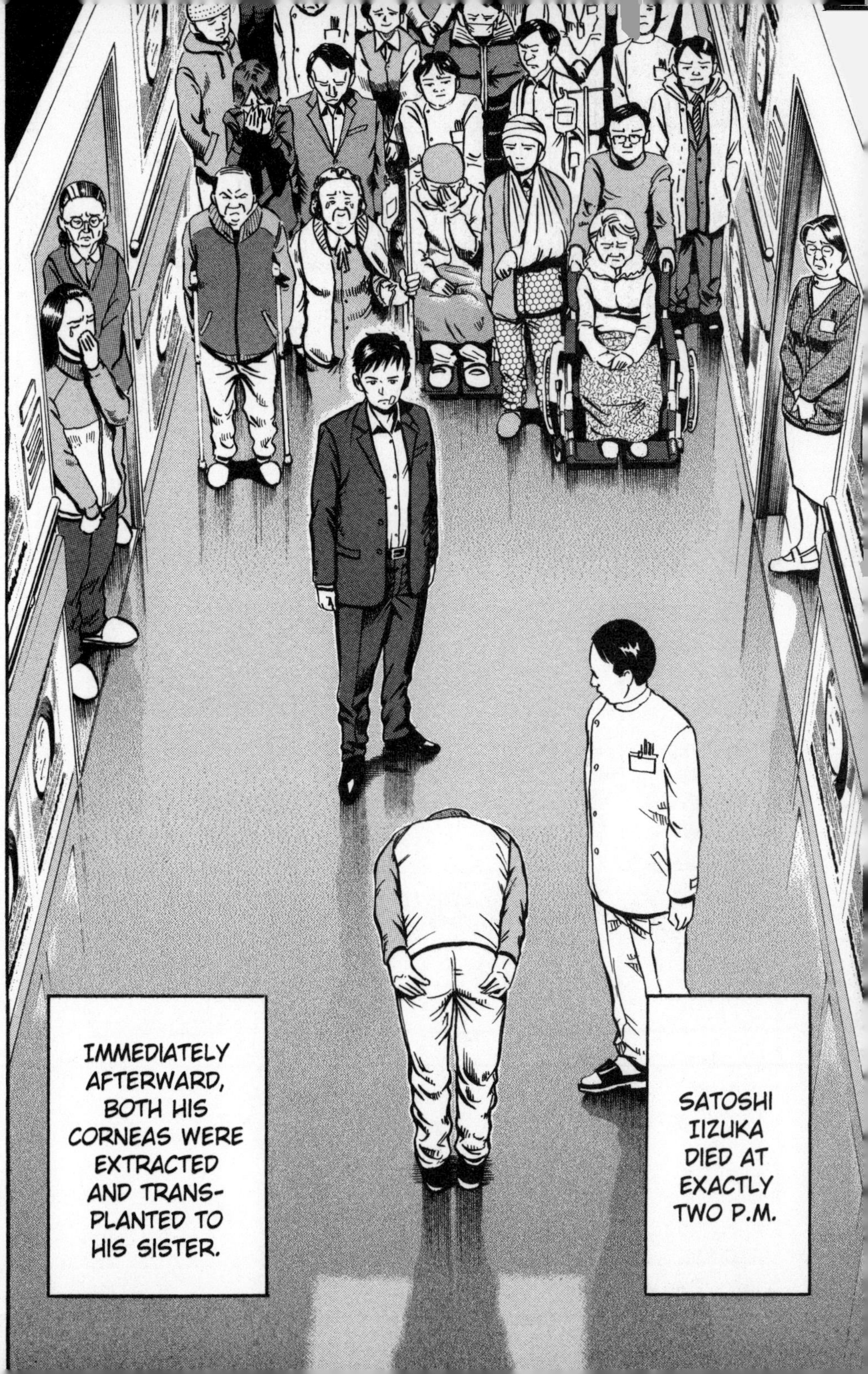
SATOSHI IIZUKA DIED AT EXACTLY TWO P.M.
IMMEDIATELY AFTERWARD, BOTH HIS CORNEAS WERE EXTRACTED AND TRANS-PLANTED TO HIS SISTER.

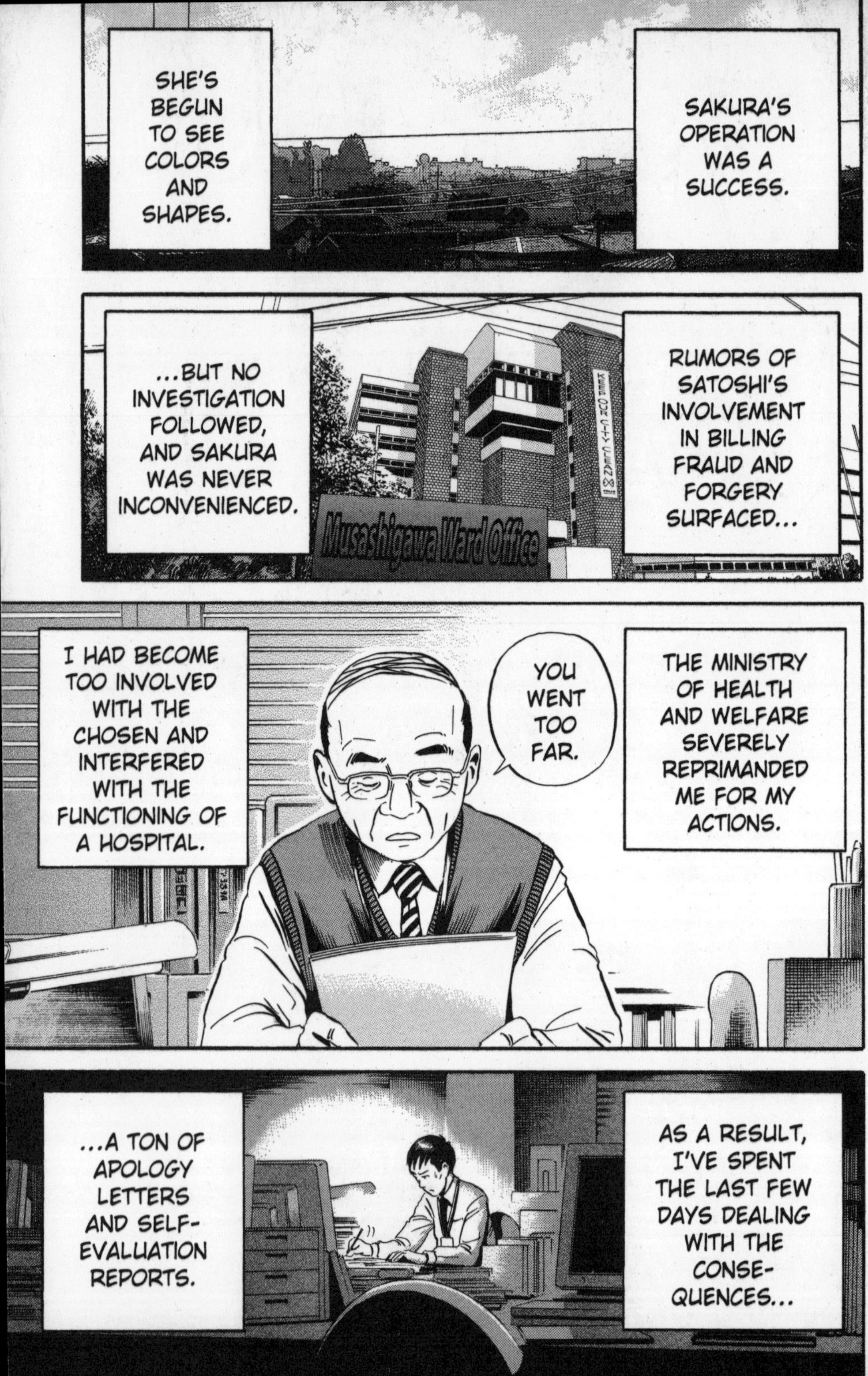
SAKURA'S OPERATION WAS A SUCCESS.
SHE'S BEGUN TO SEE COLORS AND SHAPES.
RUMORS OF SATOSHI'S INVOLVEMENT IN BILLING FRAUD AND FORGERY SURFACED...
KEEP OUR CITY CLEAN
Musashigawa Ward Office
...BUT NO INVESTIGATION FOLLOWED, AND SAKURA WAS NEVER INCONVENIENCED.
THE MINISTRY OF HEALTH AND WELFARE SEVERELY REPRIMANDED ME FOR MY ACTIONS.
YOU WENT TOO FAR.
I HAD BECOME TOO INVOLVED WITH THE CHOSEN AND INTERFERED WITH THE FUNCTIONING OF A HOSPITAL.
AS A RESULT, I'VE SPENT THE LAST FEW DAYS DEALING WITH THE CONSE-QUENCES...
...A TON OF APOLOGY LETTERS AND SELF-EVALUATION REPORTS.

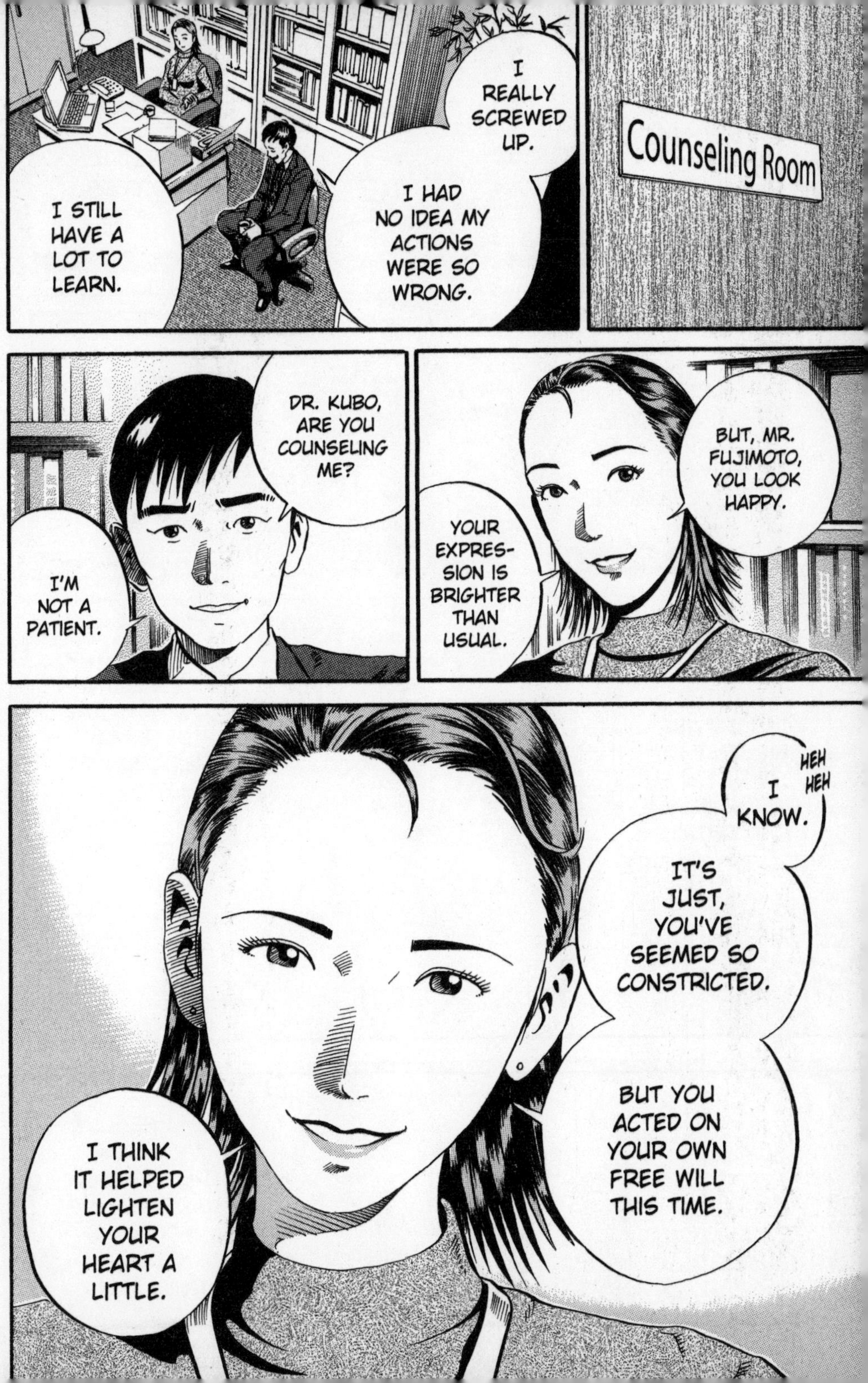
Counseling Room
I REALLY SCREWED UP.
I HAD NO IDEA MY ACTIONS WERE SO WRONG.
I STILL HAVE A LOT TO LEARN.
BUT, MR. FUJIMOTO, YOU LOOK HAPPY.
YOUR EXPRESSION IS BRIGHTER THAN USUAL.
DR. KUBO, ARE YOU COUNSELING ME?
I'M NOT A PATIENT.
HEH HEH
I KNOW.
IT'S JUST, YOU'VE SEEMED SO CONSTRICTED.
BUT YOU ACTED ON YOUR OWN FREE WILL THIS TIME.
I THINK IT HELPED LIGHTEN YOUR HEART A LITTLE.

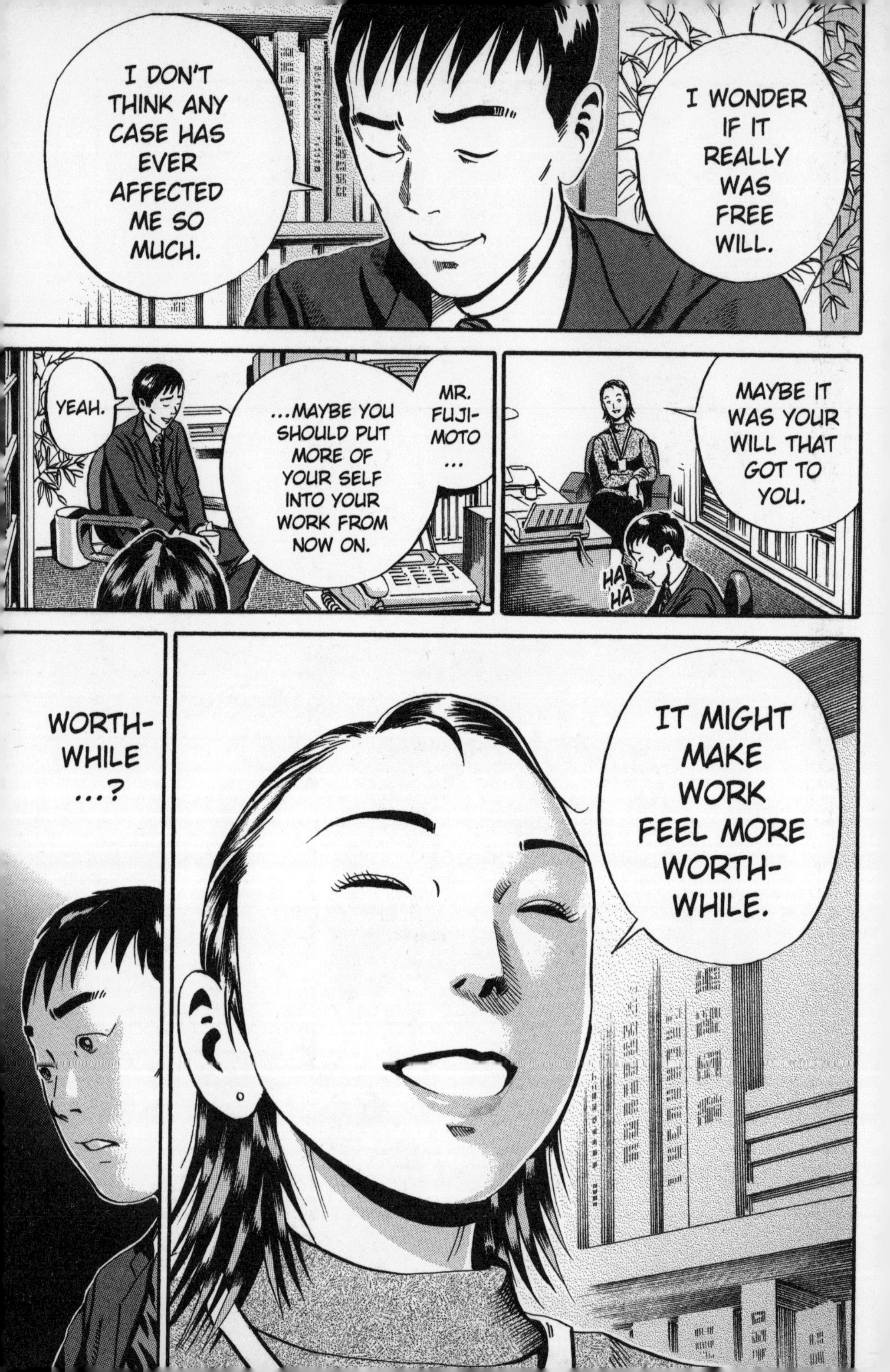
I WONDER IF IT REALLY WAS FREE WILL.
I DON'T THINK ANY CASE HAS EVER AFFECTED ME SO MUCH.
MAYBE IT WAS YOUR WILL THAT GOT TO YOU.
HA HA
MR. FUJI-MOTO ...
...MAYBE YOU SHOULD PUT MORE OF YOUR SELF INTO YOUR WORK FROM NOW ON.
YEAH.
IT MIGHT MAKE WORK FEEL MORE WORTH-WHILE.
WORTH-WHILE ...?

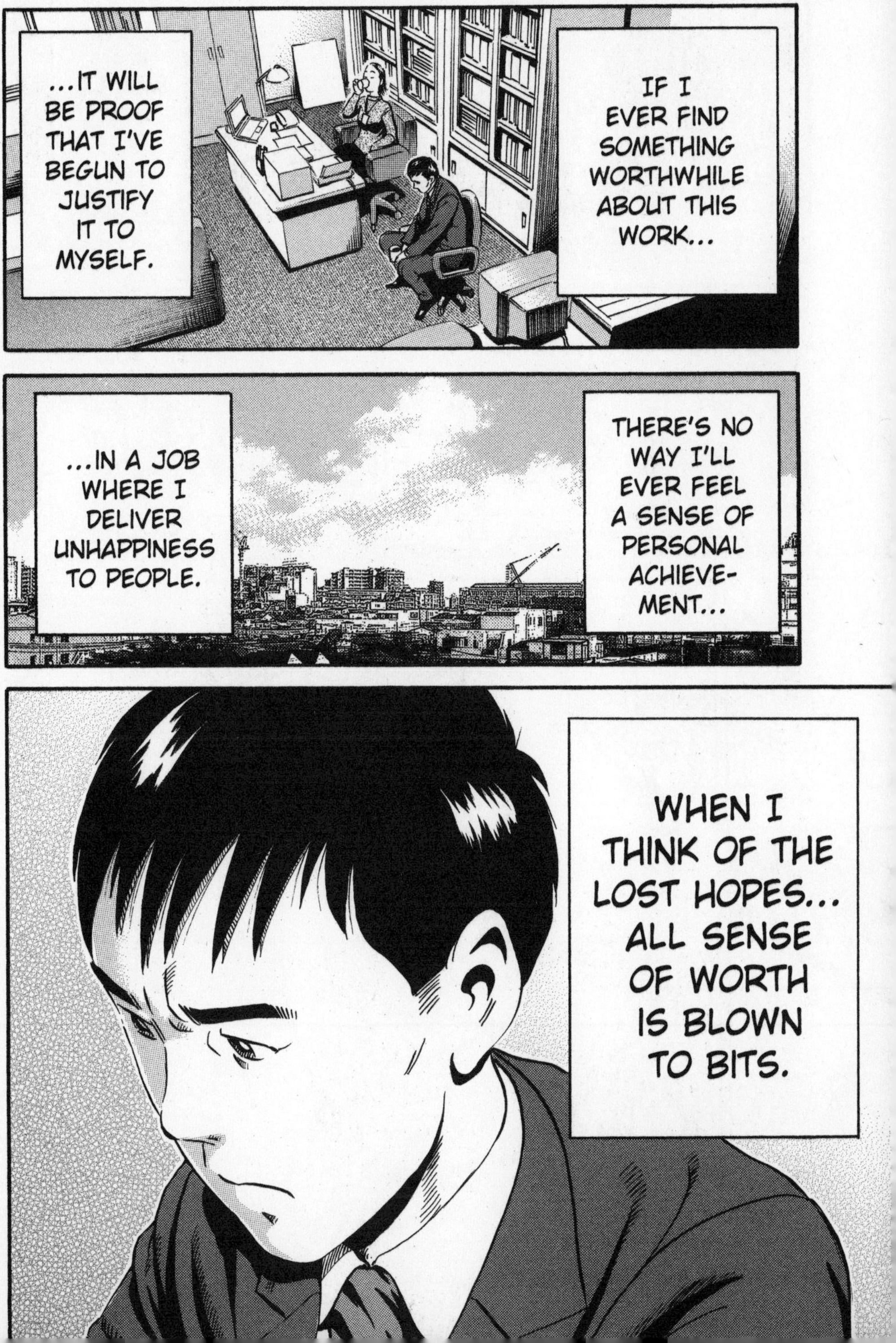
IF I EVER FIND SOMETHING WORTHWHILE ABOUT THIS WORK...
...IT WILL BE PROOF THAT I'VE BEGUN TO JUSTIFY IT TO MYSELF.
THERE'S NO WAY I'LL EVER FEEL A SENSE OF PERSONAL ACHIEVE-MENT...
...IN A JOB WHERE I DELIVER UNHAPPINESS TO PEOPLE.
WHEN I THINK OF THE LOST HOPES... ALL SENSE OF WORTH IS BLOWN TO BITS.

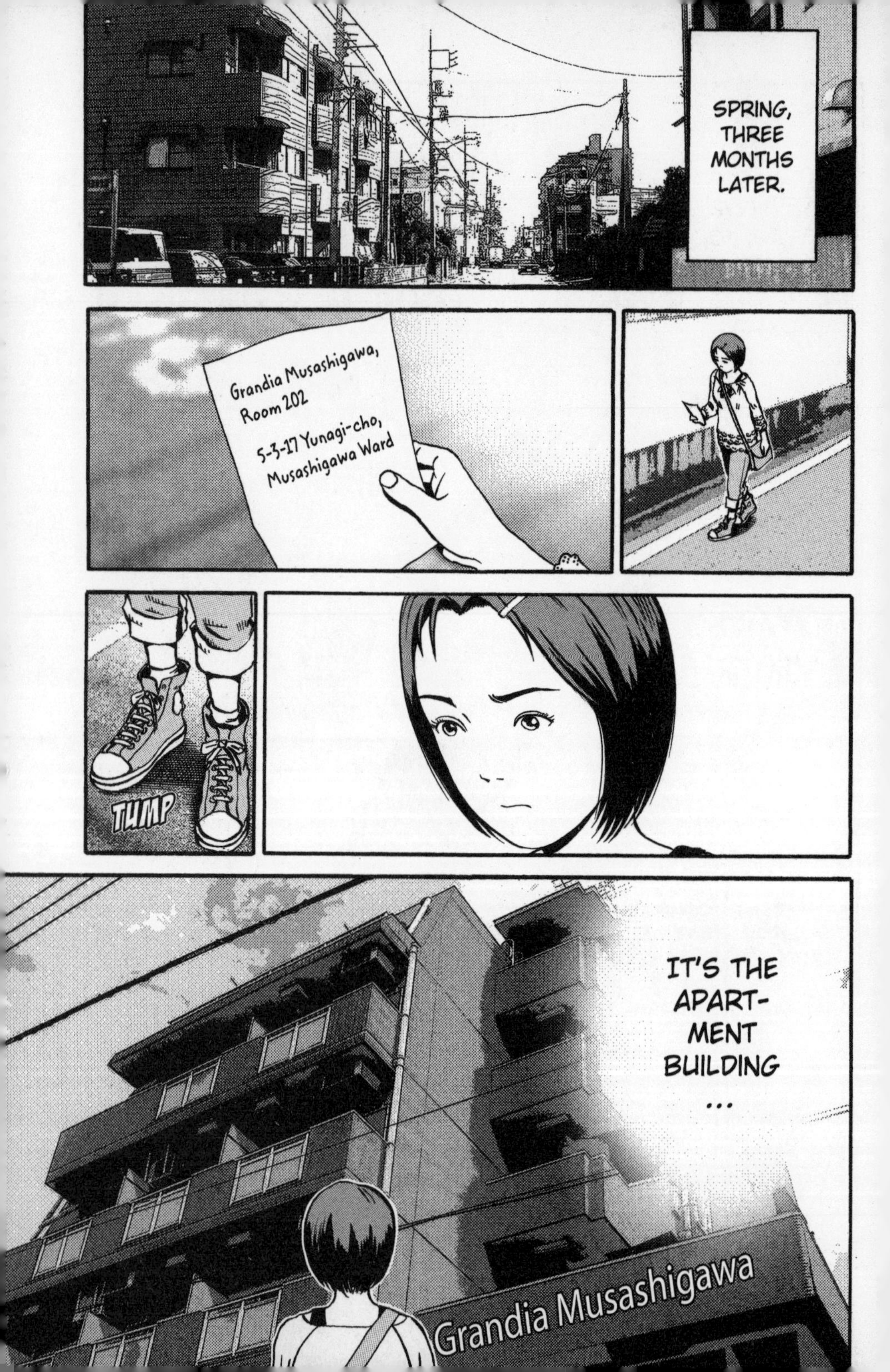
SPRING, THREE MONTHS LATER.
Grandia Musashigawa, Room 202
5-3-17 Yunagi-cho, Musashigawa Ward
TUMP
IT'S THE APART-MENT BUILDING ...
Grandia Musashigawa

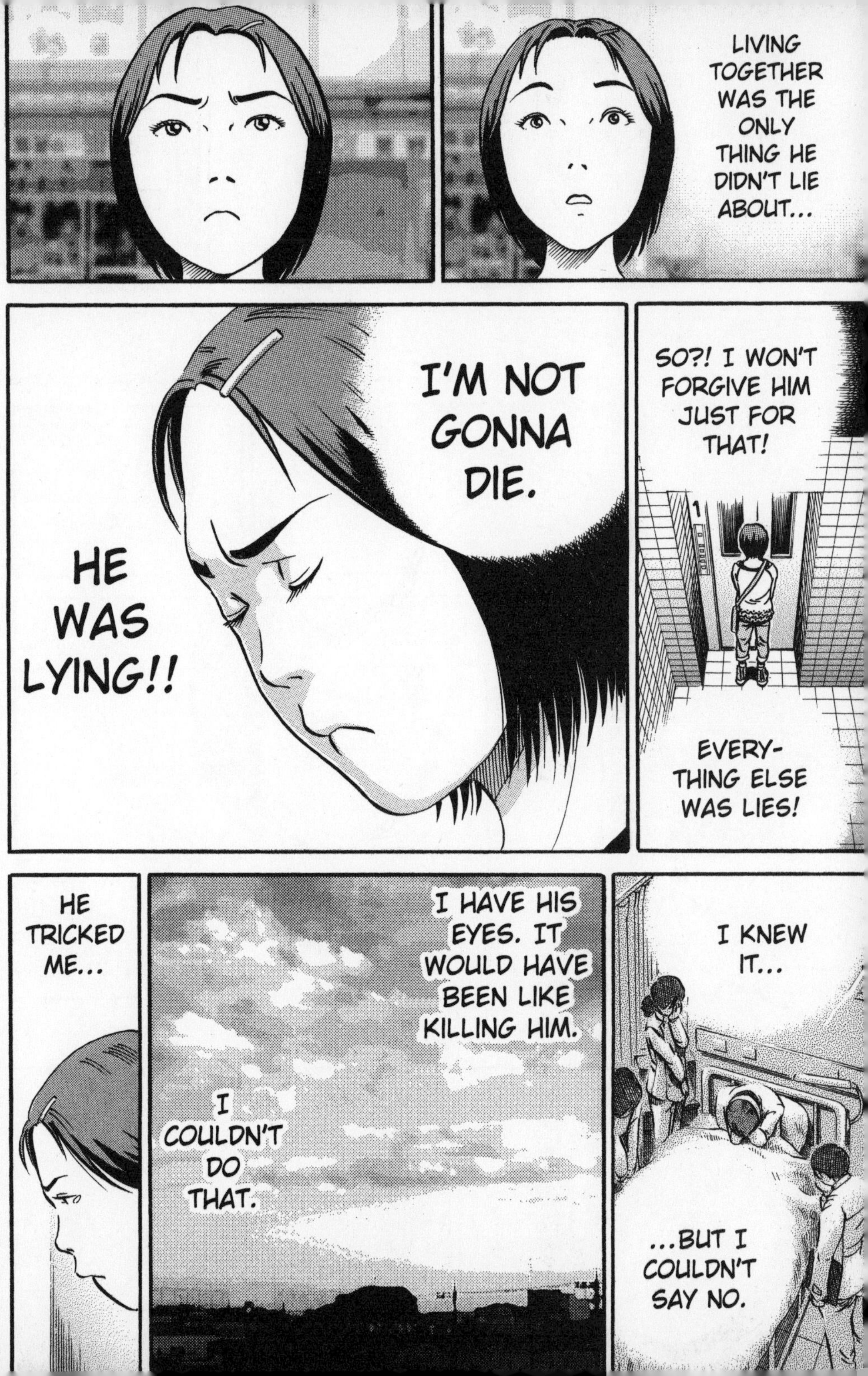
LIVING TOGETHER WAS THE ONLY THING HE DIDN'T LIE ABOUT...
SO?! I WON'T FORGIVE HIM JUST FOR THAT!
EVERY-THING ELSE WAS LIES!
I'M NOT GONNA DIE.
HE WAS LYING!!
I KNEW IT...
...BUT I COULDN'T SAY NO.
I HAVE HIS EYES. IT WOULD HAVE BEEN LIKE KILLING HIM.
I COULDN'T DO THAT.
HE TRICKED ME...

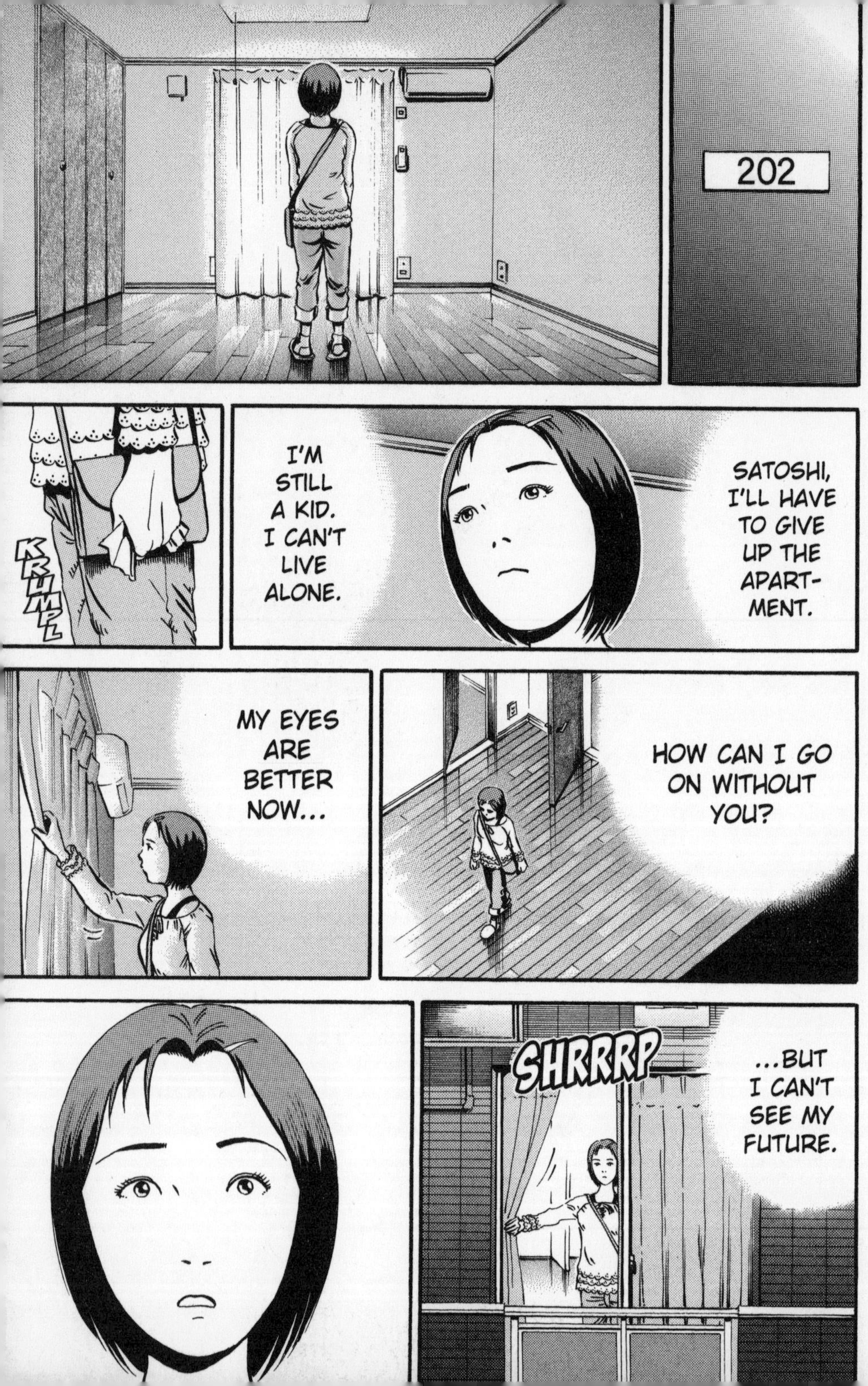
202
SATOSHI, I'LL HAVE TO GIVE UP THE APARTMENT.
I'M STILL A KID. I CAN'T LIVE ALONE.
KRUMPL
HOW CAN I GO ON WITHOUT YOU?
MY EYES ARE BETTER NOW...
SHRRRP
...BUT I CAN'T SEE MY FUTURE.

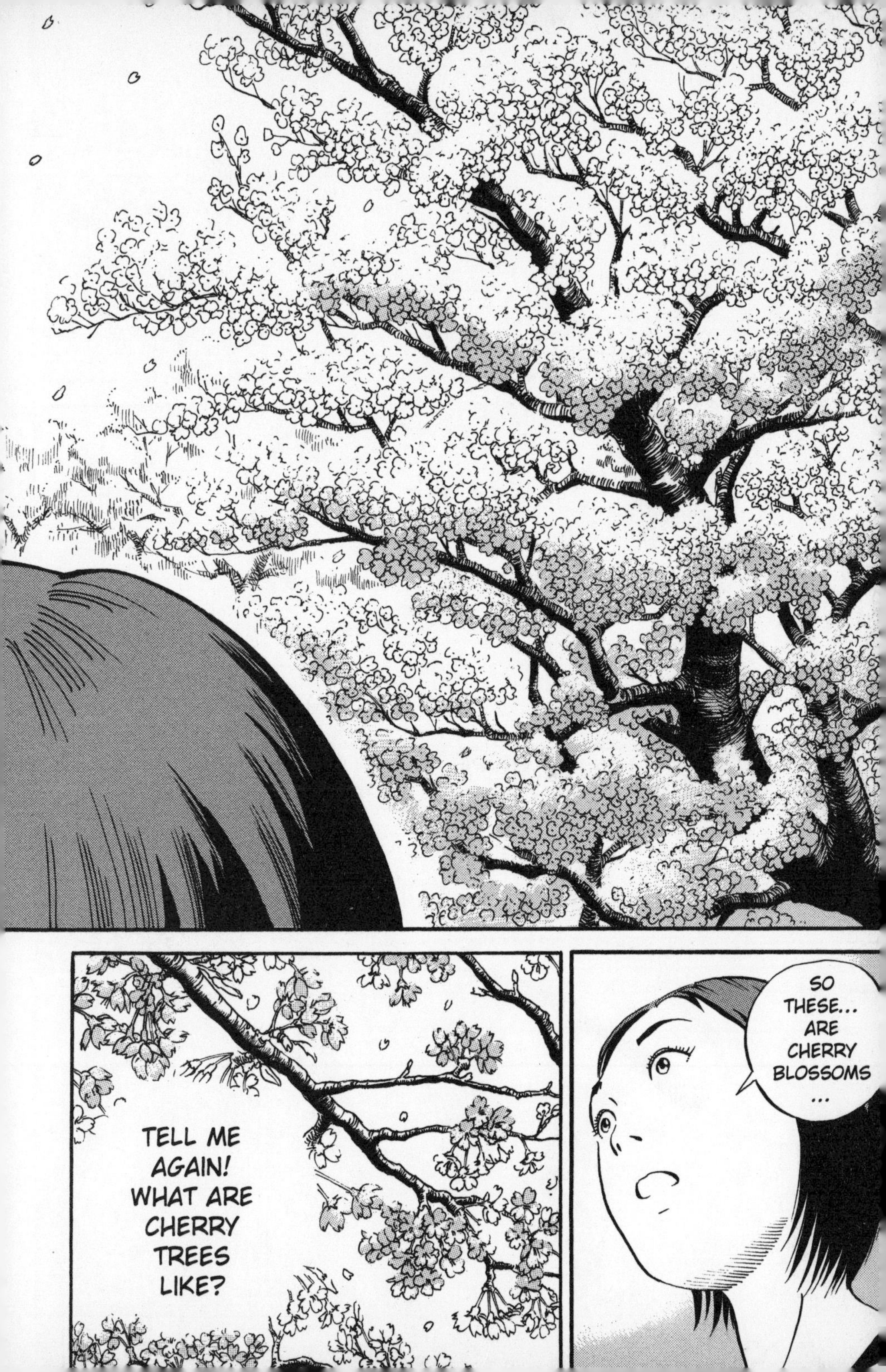
SO THESE... ARE CHERRY BLOSSOMS ...
TELL ME AGAIN! WHAT ARE CHERRY TREES LIKE?

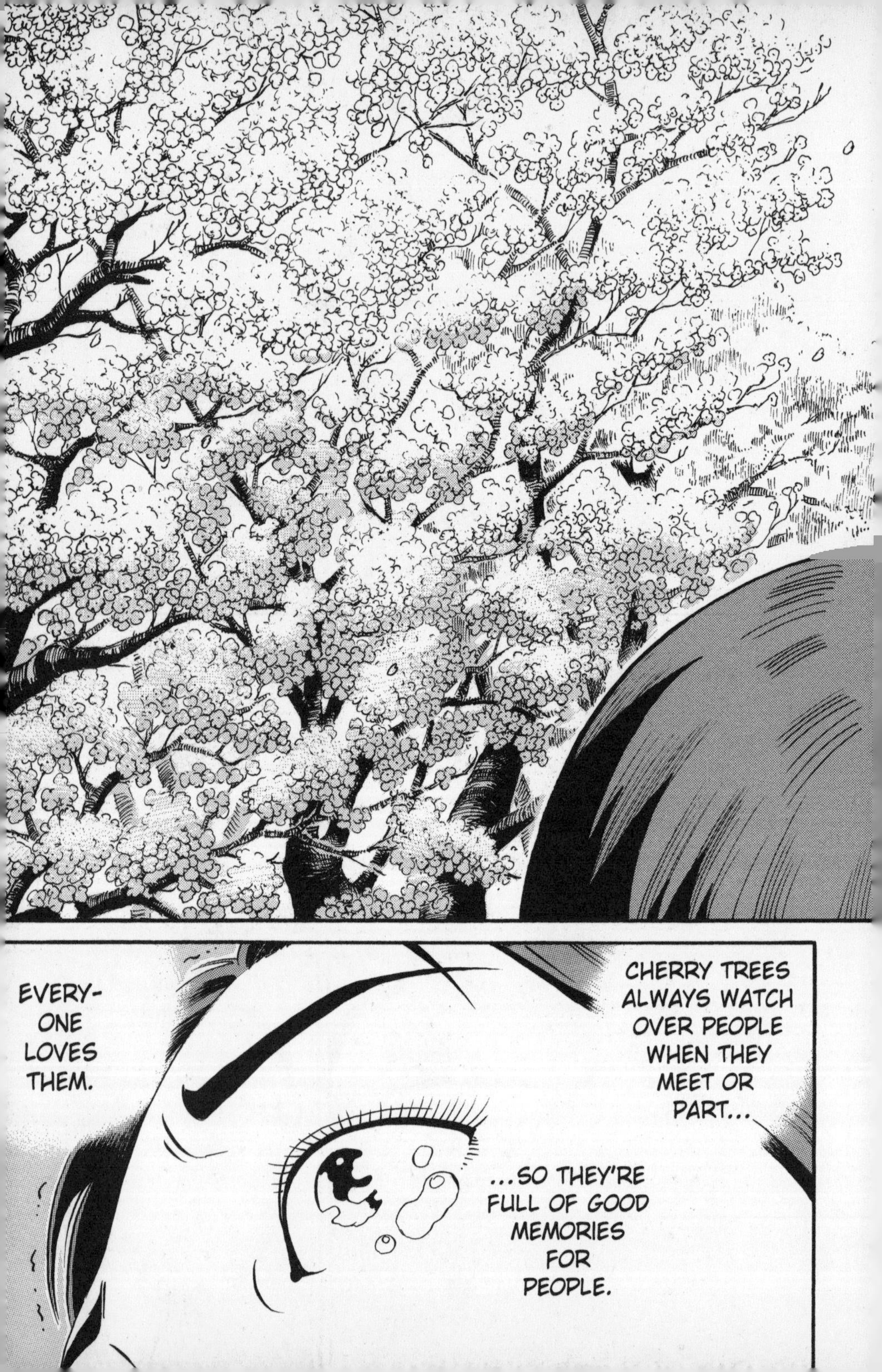
CHERRY TREES ALWAYS WATCH OVER PEOPLE WHEN THEY MEET OR PART...
...SO THEY'RE FULL OF GOOD MEMORIES FOR PEOPLE.
EVERY-ONE LOVES THEM.

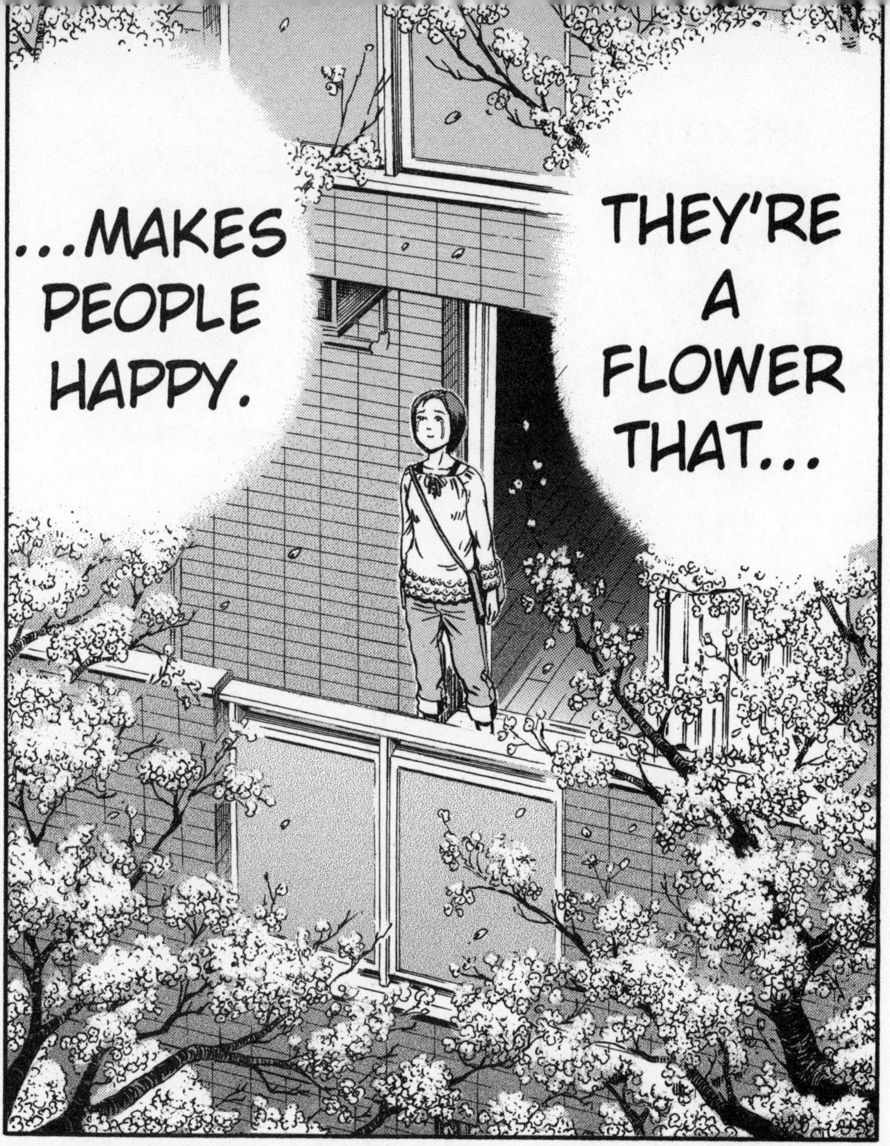
THEY'RE A FLOWER THAT...
...MAKES PEOPLE HAPPY.

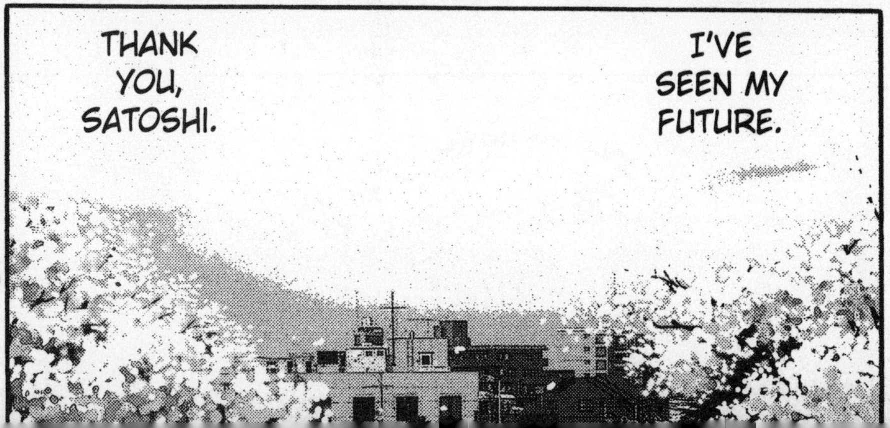
I'VE SEEN MY FUTURE.
THANK YOU, SATOSHI.

ARE *YOU* NEXT?

IKIGAMI

THE ULTIMATE LIMIT

VOL. 4

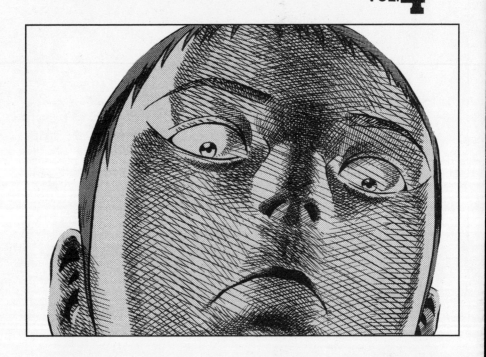

Featuring Episodes 7 *The Last Lesson* **& 8** *A Peaceful Place*!

Motoro Mase was born in Aichi in Japan in 1969 and is also the artist of *Kyoichi* and, with Keigo Higashino, *HE∀DS*, which, like *Ikigami*, was serialized in *Young Sunday*. In 1998, Mase's *AREA* was nominated for Shogakukan's 43rd grand prize for a comic by a new artist.

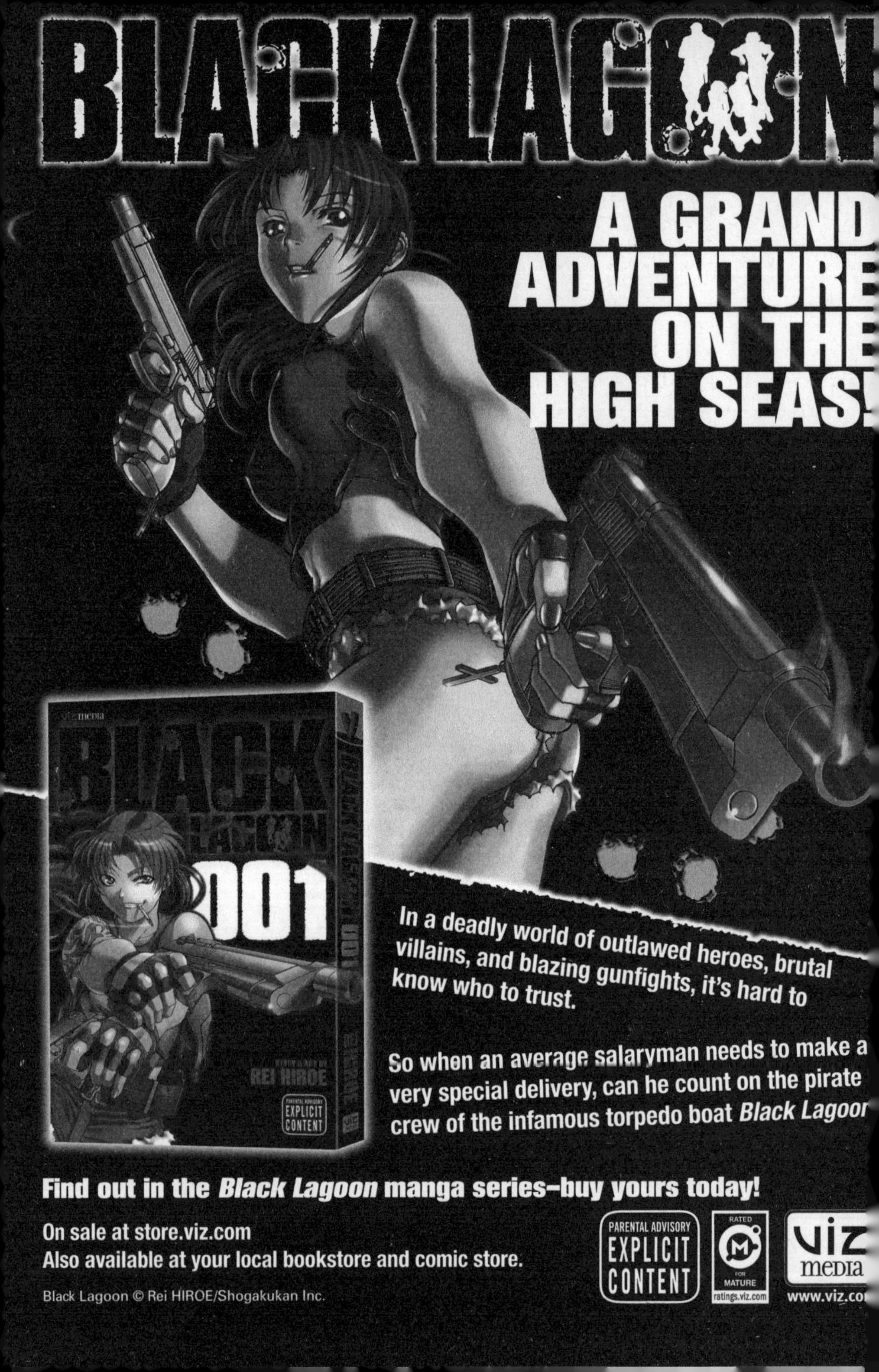
BLACK LAGOON
A GRAND ADVENTURE ON THE HIGH SEAS!
BLACK LAGOON 001
REI HIROE
PARENTAL ADVISORY EXPLICIT CONTENT
In a deadly world of outlawed heroes, brutal villains, and blazing gunfights, it's hard to know who to trust.
So when an average salaryman needs to make a very special delivery, can he count on the pirate crew of the infamous torpedo boat Black Lagoon
Find out in the Black Lagoon manga series–buy yours today!
On sale at store.viz.com
Also available at your local bookstore and comic store.
Black Lagoon © Rei HIROE/Shogakukan Inc.
PARENTAL ADVISORY EXPLICIT CONTENT
RATED M FOR MATURE ratings.viz.com
VIZ media
www.viz.co

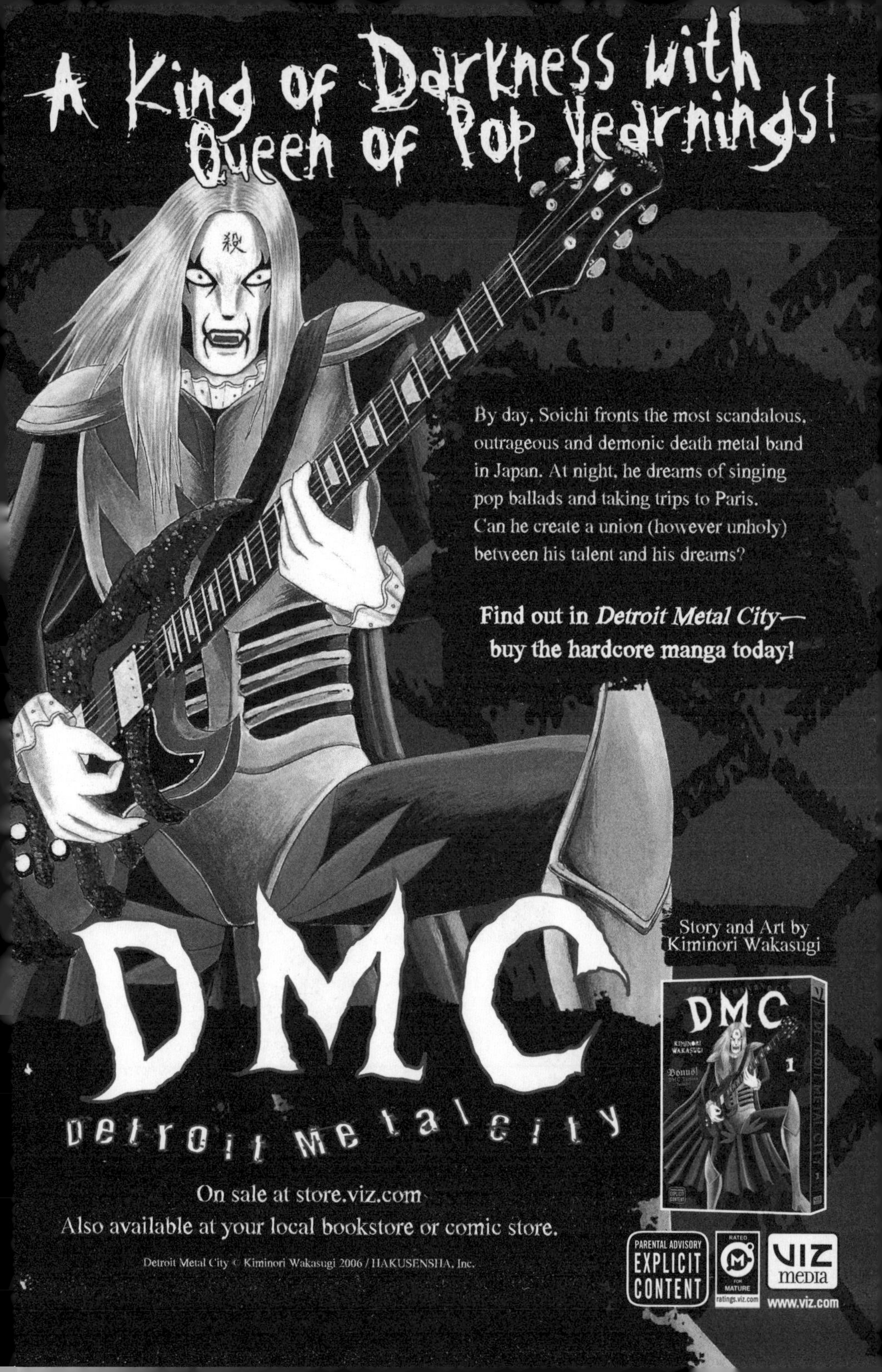
A King of Darkness with Queen of Pop Yearnings!
殺
By day, Soichi fronts the most scandalous, outrageous and demonic death metal band in Japan. At night, he dreams of singing pop ballads and taking trips to Paris. Can he create a union (however unholy) between his talent and his dreams?
Find out in Detroit Metal City—buy the hardcore manga today!
Story and Art by Kiminori Wakasugi
DMC
Detroit Metal City
On sale at store.viz.com
Also available at your local bookstore or comic store.
Detroit Metal City © Kiminori Wakasugi 2006 / HAKUSENSHA, Inc.
PARENTAL ADVISORY EXPLICIT CONTENT
RATED M FOR MATURE
ratings.viz.com
VIZ media
www.viz.com

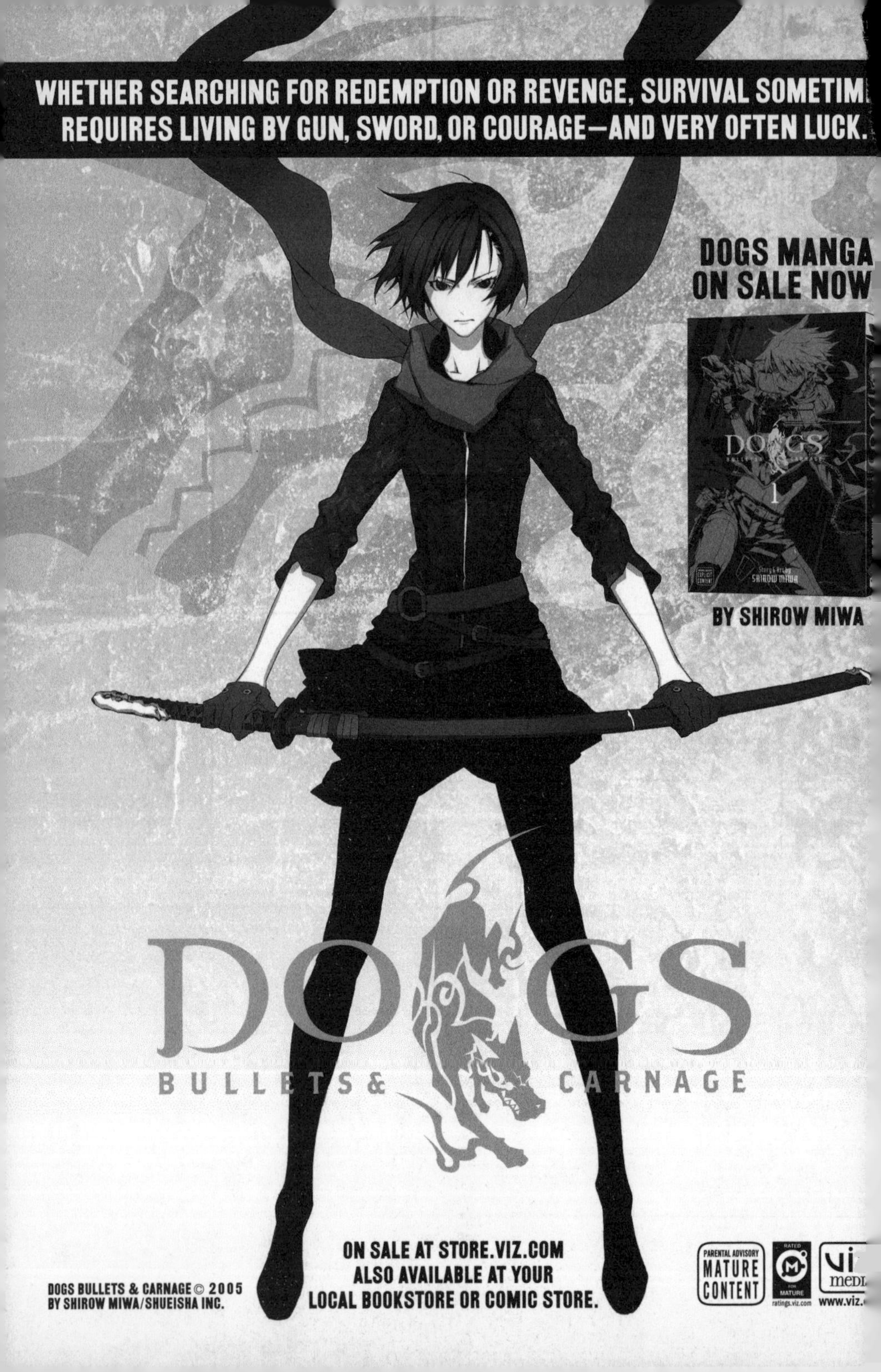
WHETHER SEARCHING FOR REDEMPTION OR REVENGE, SURVIVAL SOMETIM
REQUIRES LIVING BY GUN, SWORD, OR COURAGE—AND VERY OFTEN LUCK.
DOGS MANGA
ON SALE NOW
DOGS
BULLETS & CARNAGE
1
Story & Art by
SHIROW MIWA
BY SHIROW MIWA
DOGS
BULLETS & CARNAGE
ON SALE AT STORE.VIZ.COM
ALSO AVAILABLE AT YOUR
LOCAL BOOKSTORE OR COMIC STORE.
DOGS BULLETS & CARNAGE © 2005
BY SHIROW MIWA/SHUEISHA INC.
PARENTAL ADVISORY
MATURE
CONTENT
RATED
FOR
MATURE
ratings.viz.com

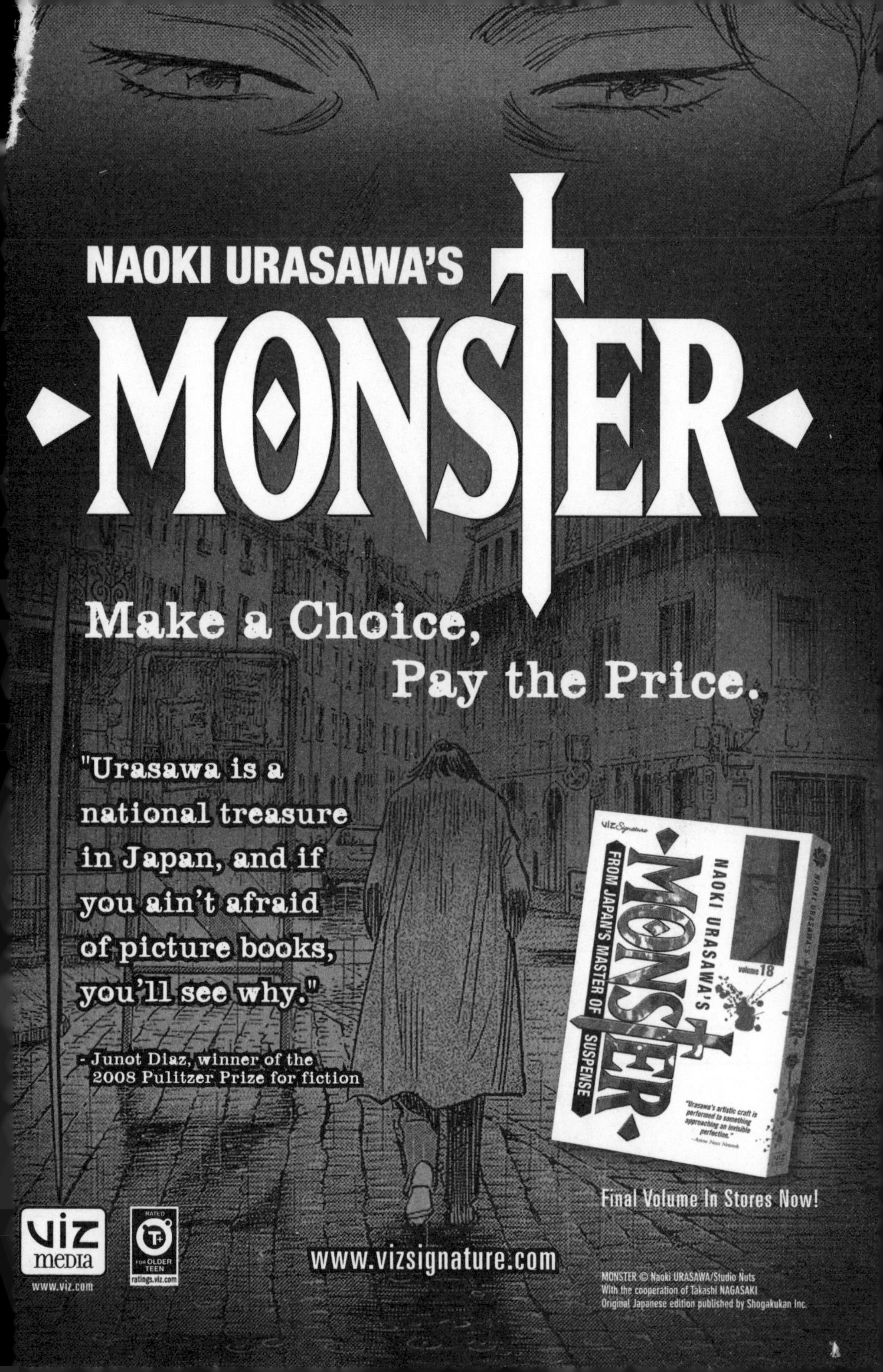
NAOKI URASAWA'S
MONSTER
Make a Choice,
Pay the Price.
"Urasawa is a national treasure in Japan, and if you ain't afraid of picture books, you'll see why."
- Junot Diaz, winner of the 2008 Pulitzer Prize for fiction
VIZ Signature
NAOKI URASAWA'S
MONSTER
FROM JAPAN'S MASTER OF SUSPENSE
volume 18
"Urasawa's artistic craft is performed to something approaching an invisible perfection."
—Anime News Network
Final Volume In Stores Now!
VIZ MEDIA
www.viz.com
RATED T+ FOR OLDER TEEN
ratings.viz.com
www.vizsignature.com
MONSTER © Naoki URASAWA/Studio Nuts
With the cooperation of Takashi NAGASAKI
Original Japanese edition published by Shogakukan Inc.

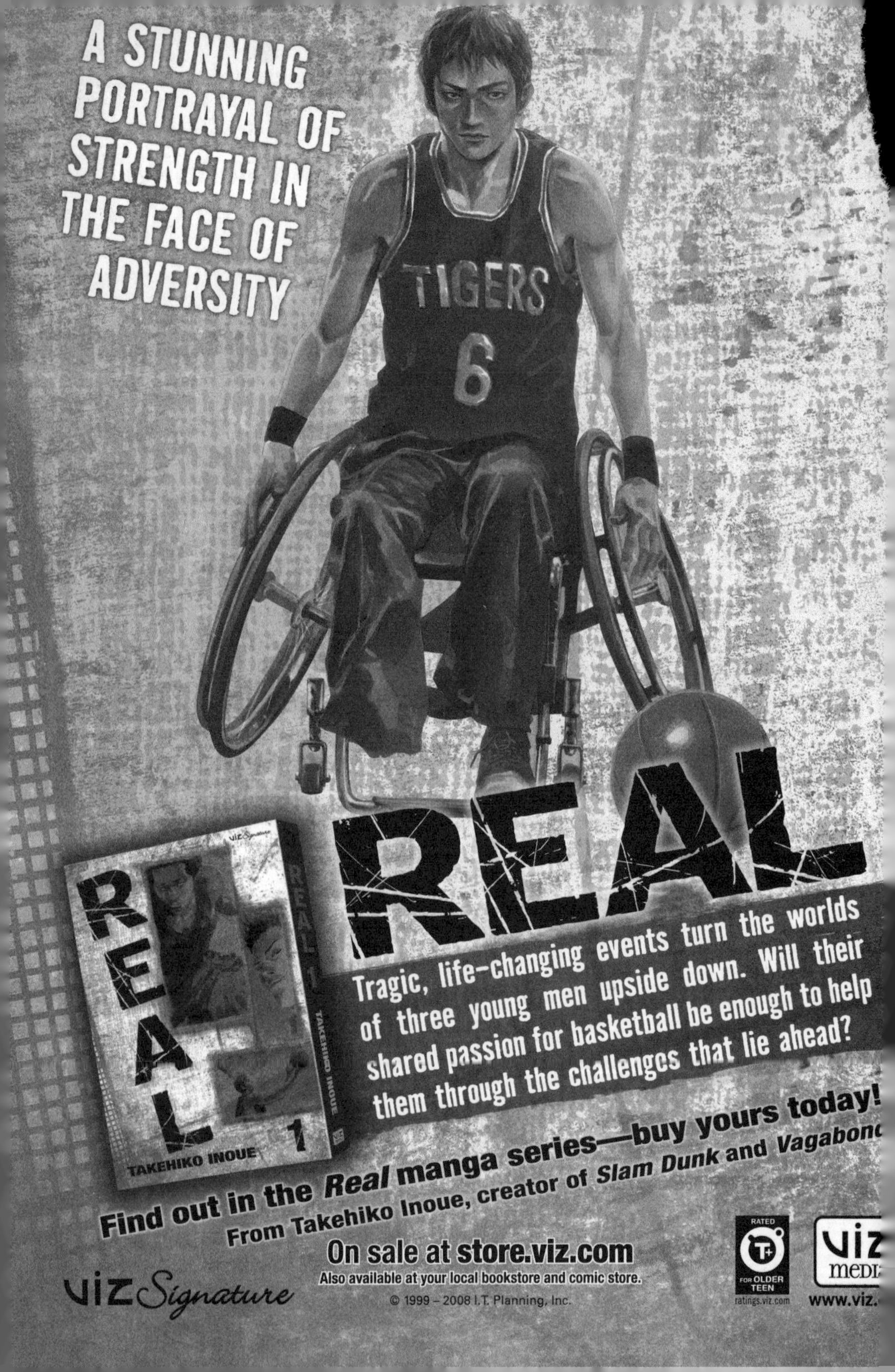
A STUNNING PORTRAYAL OF STRENGTH IN THE FACE OF ADVERSITY
TIGERS
6
REAL
TAKEHIKO INOUE
1
REAL
Tragic, life-changing events turn the worlds of three young men upside down. Will their shared passion for basketball be enough to help them through the challenges that lie ahead?
Find out in the Real manga series—buy yours today!
From Takehiko Inoue, creator of Slam Dunk and Vagabond
On sale at store.viz.com
Also available at your local bookstore and comic store.
© 1999 – 2008 I.T. Planning, Inc.
viz Signature
RATED T+ FOR OLDER TEEN
ratings.viz.com
viz media
www.viz.

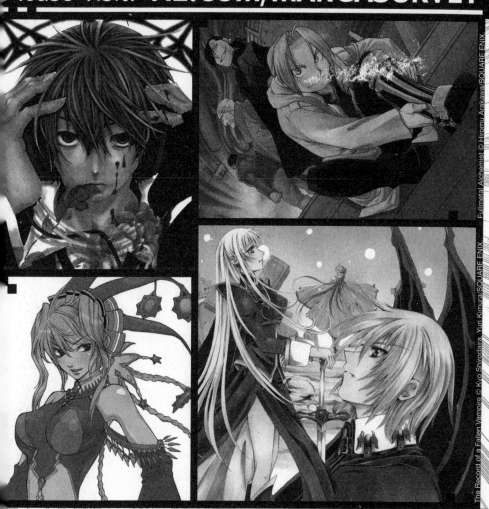